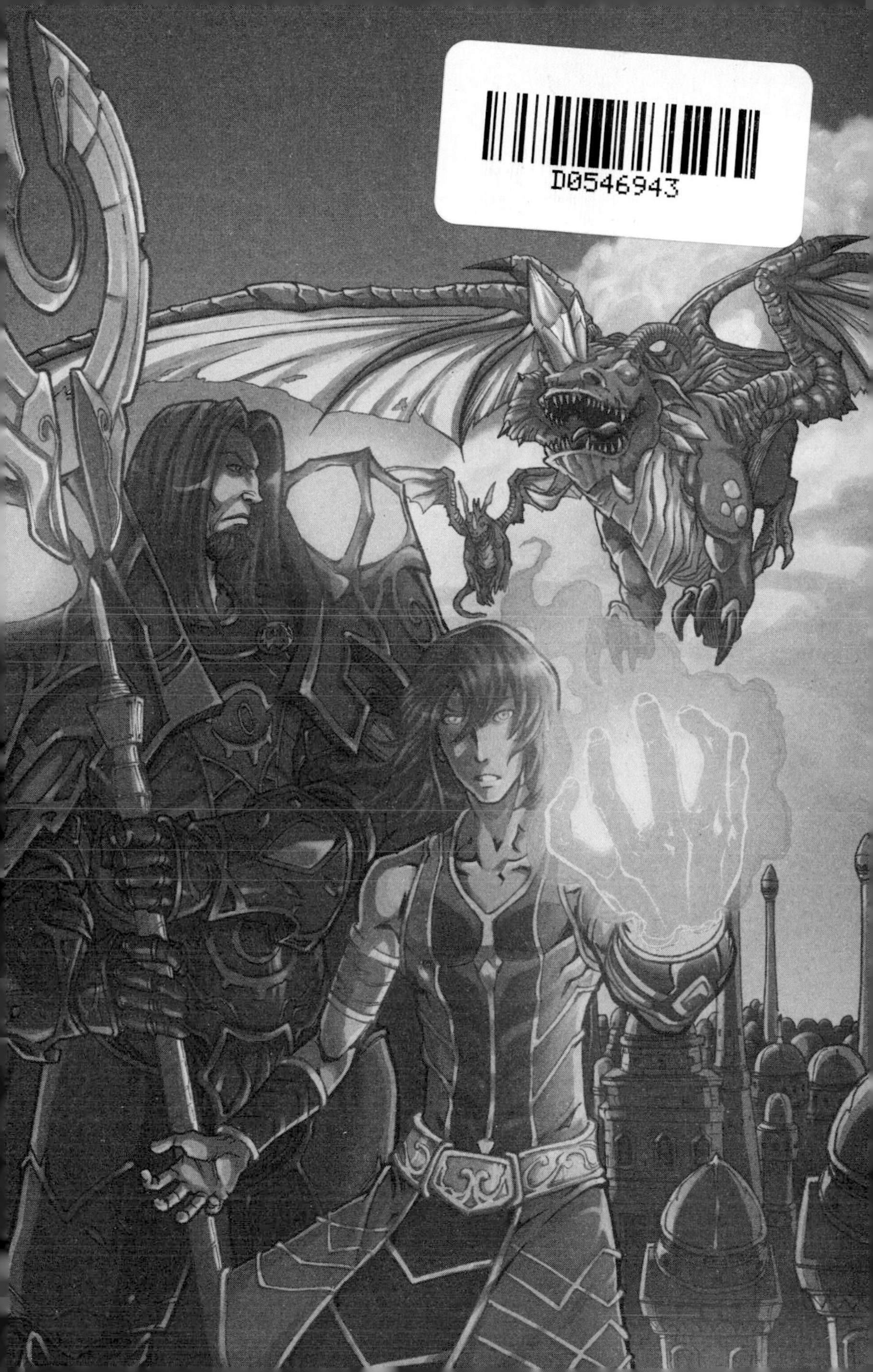

# *World Of Warcraft: Mage*

### Story by: Richard A. Knaak
### Art by: Ryo Kawakami

Retouch Artist, Layout & Lettering - Michael Paolilli
Creative Consultant - Michael Paolilli
Cover Designer - Louis Csontos
Cover Artist - Ryo Kawakami

Editors - Troy Lewter and Paul Morrissey
Print Production Manager - Lucas Rivera
Managing Editor - Vy Nguyen
Senior Designer - Louis Csontos
Art Director - Al-Insan Lashley
Director of Sales and Manufacturing - Allyson De Simone
Associate Publisher - Marco F. Pavia
President and C.O.O. - John Parker
C.E.O. and Chief Creative Officer - Stu Levy

## BLIZZARD ENTERTAINMENT
Senior Vice President, Creative Development - Chris Metzen
Director, Creative Development - Jeff Donais
Lead Developer, Licensed Products - Mike Hummel
Publishing Lead, Creative Development - Micky Neilson
Story Developer - James Waugh
Art Director - Glenn Rane
Director, Global Business
Development and Licensing - Cory Jones
Associate Licensing Manager - Jason Bischoff
Historian - Evelyn Fredericksen
Additional Development - Samwise Didier, Cameron Dayton and
Tommy Newcomer

A  Manga

TOKYOPOP and 🔊 are trademarks or registered trademarks of TOKYOPOP Inc.

TOKYOPOP Inc.
5900 Wilshire Blvd. Suite 2000
Los Angeles, CA 90036

E-mail: info@TOKYOPOP.com
Come visit us online at www.TOKYOPOP.com

ISBN: 978-1-4278-1497-5

First TOKYOPOP printing: June 2010
10  9  8  7  6  5  4  3  2  1
Printed in the USA

# WORLD OF WARCRAFT

## MAGE

STORY BY
# RICHARD A. KNAAK

ART BY
# RYO KAWAKAMI

 TOKYOPOP®

HAMBURG // LONDON // LOS ANGELES // TOKYO

# WORLD OF WARCRAFT
## MAGE

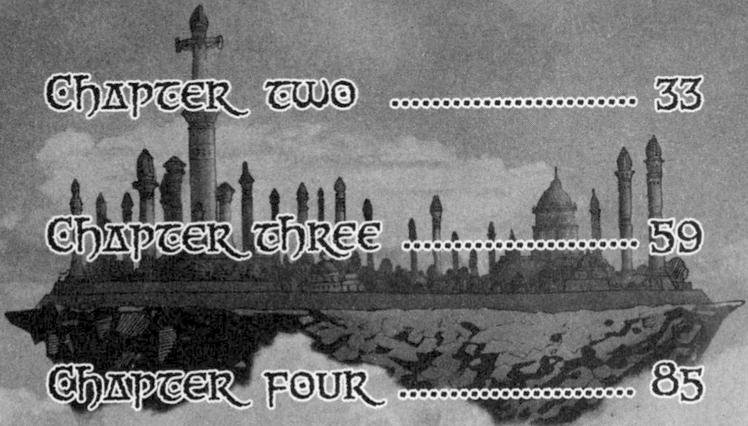

# CHAPTER ONE

# CITY IN THE SKY

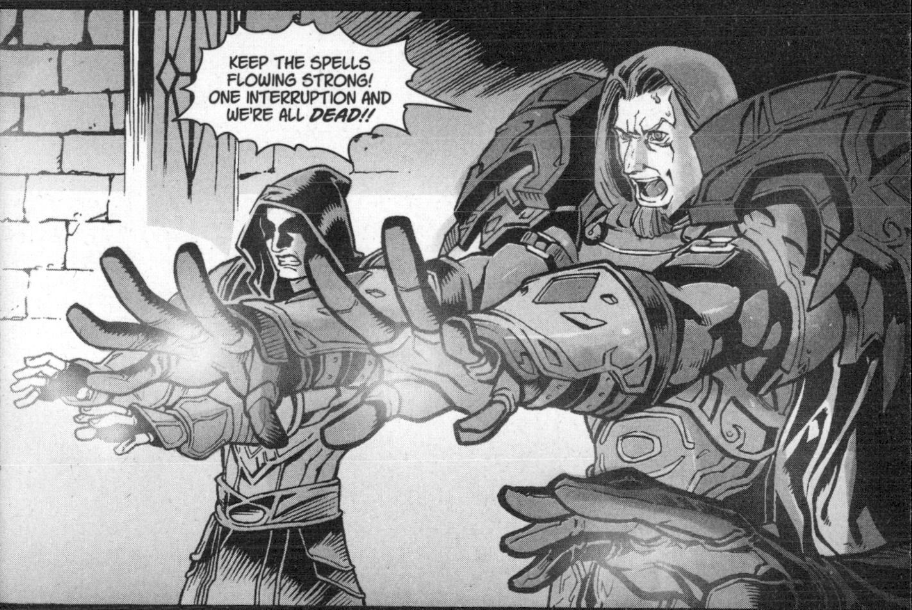
KEEP THE SPELLS FLOWING STRONG! ONE INTERRUPTION AND WE'RE ALL DEAD!!

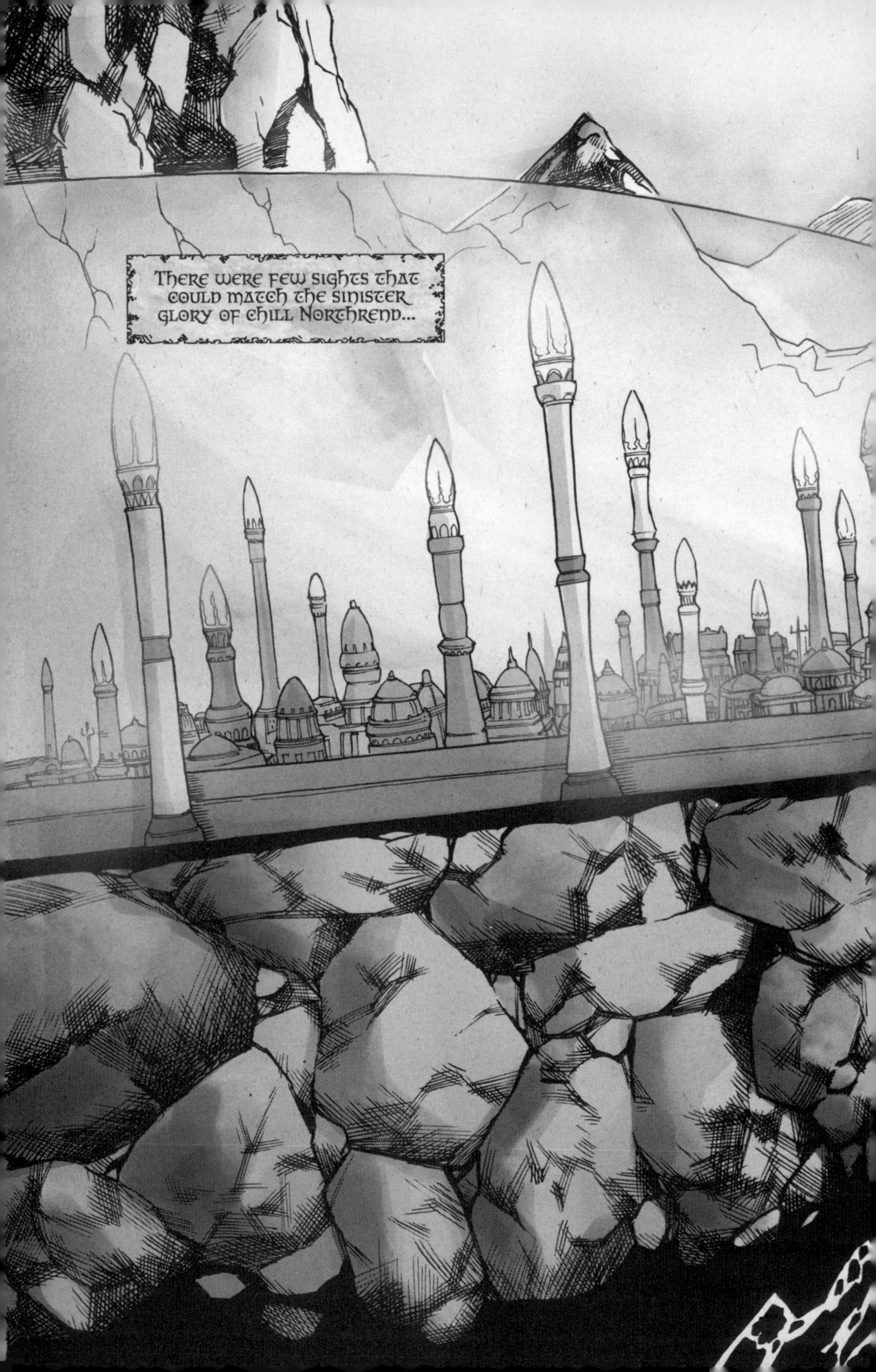
There were few sights that could match the sinister glory of chill Northrend...

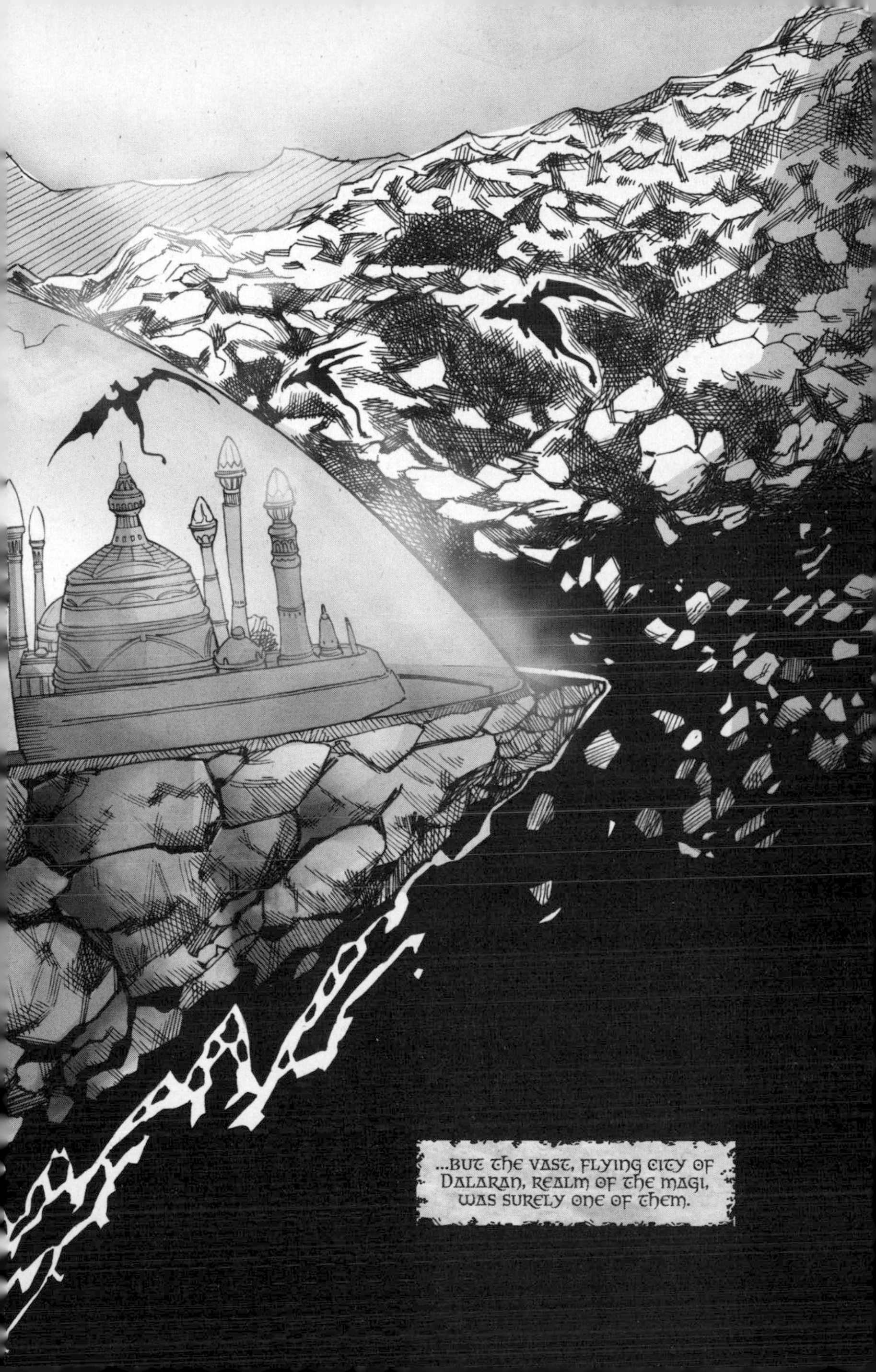
...BUT THE VAST, FLYING CITY OF DALARAN, REALM OF THE MAGI, WAS SURELY ONE OF THEM.

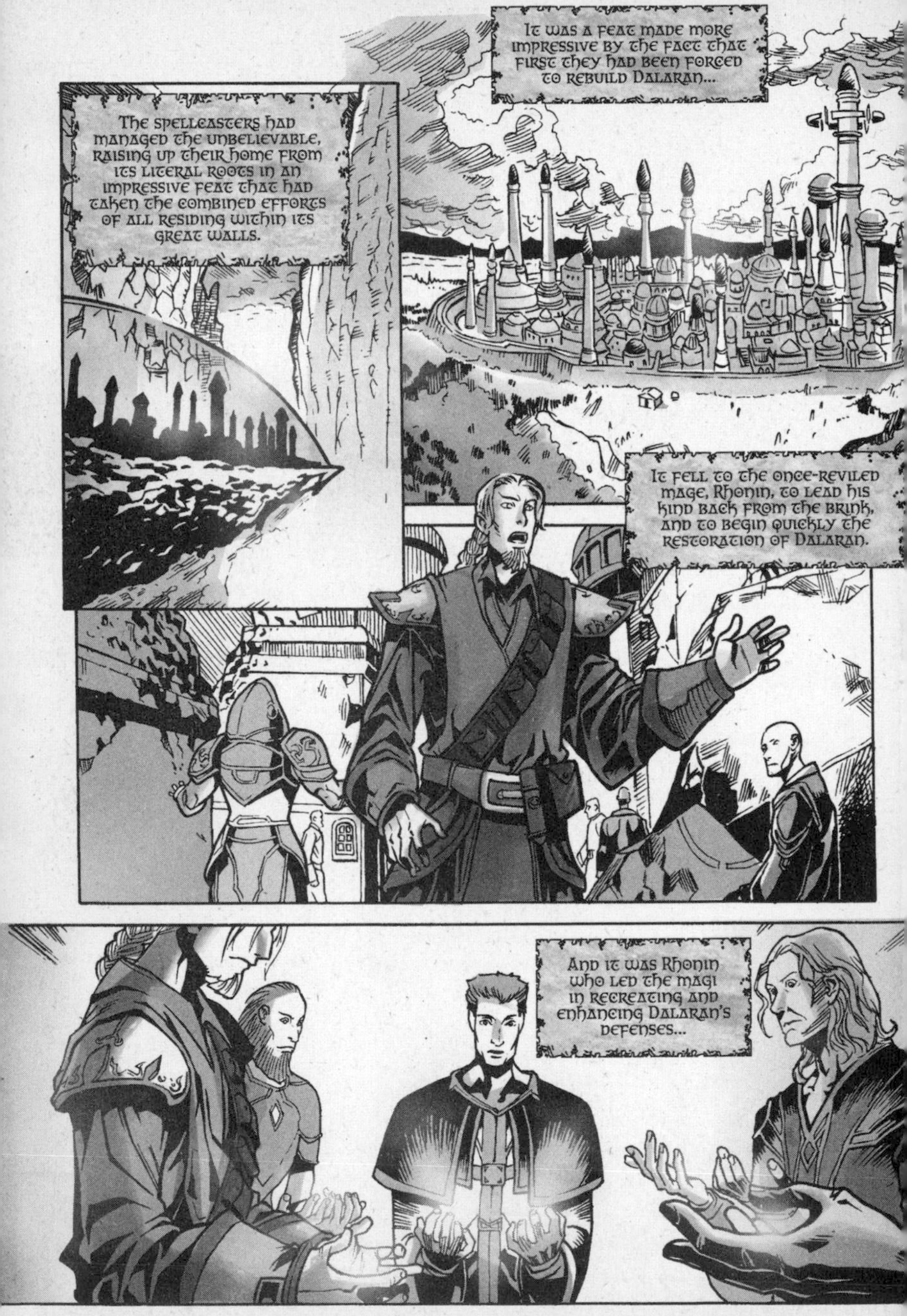

The spellcasters had managed the unbelievable, raising up their home from its literal roots in an impressive feat that had taken the combined efforts of all residing within its great walls.
It was a feat made more impressive by the fact that first they had been forced to rebuild Dalaran...
It fell to the once-reviled mage, Rhonin, to lead his kind back from the brink, and to begin quickly the restoration of Dalaran.
And it was Rhonin who led the magi in recreating and enhancing Dalaran's defenses...

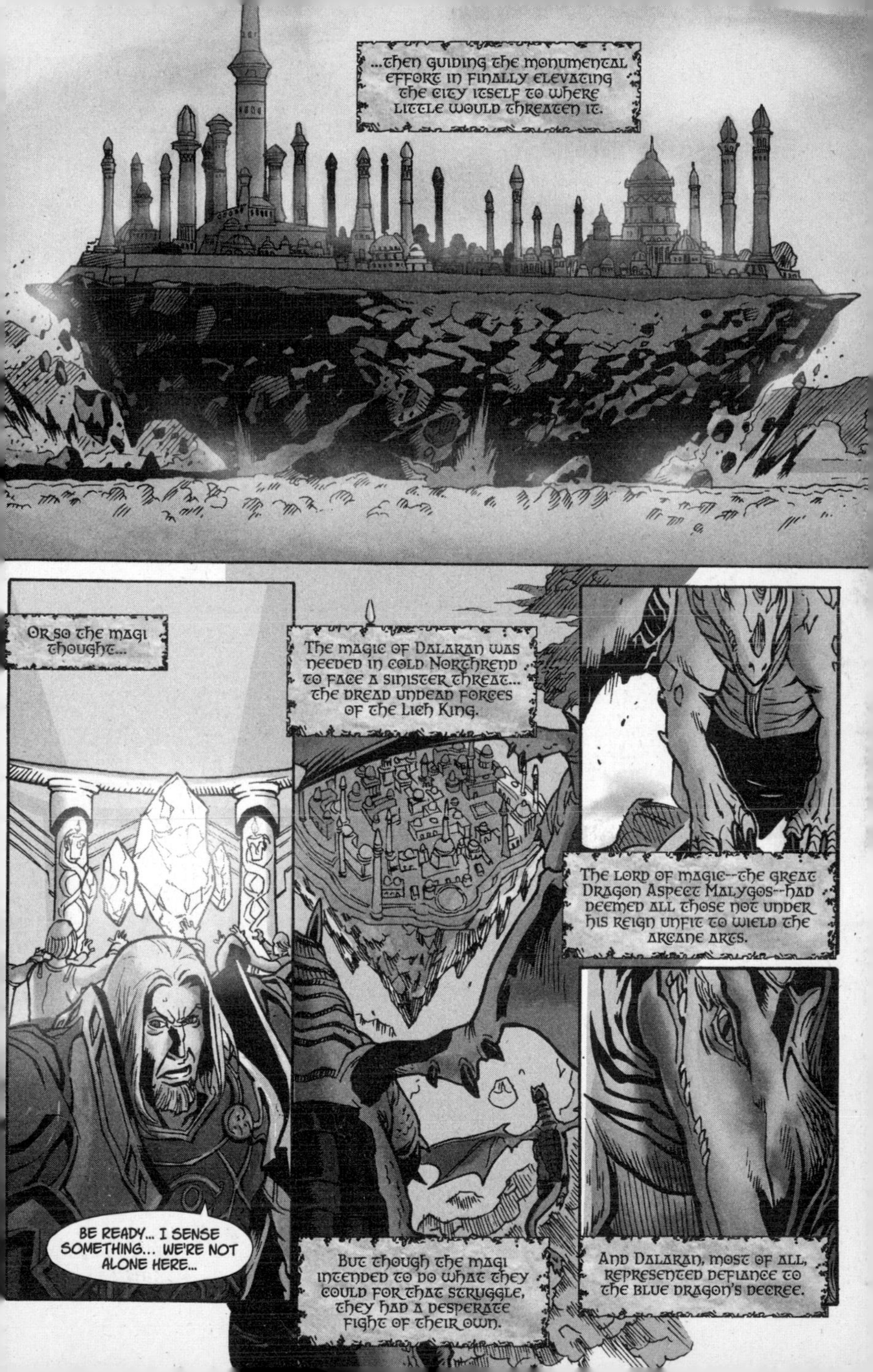

...THEN GUIDING THE MONUMENTAL EFFORT IN FINALLY ELEVATING THE CITY ITSELF TO WHERE LITTLE WOULD THREATEN IT.
OR SO THE MAGI THOUGHT...
BE READY... I SENSE SOMETHING... WE'RE NOT ALONE HERE...
THE MAGIC OF DALARAN WAS NEEDED IN COLD NORTHREND TO FACE A SINISTER THREAT... THE DREAD UNDEAD FORCES OF THE LICH KING.
BUT THOUGH THE MAGI INTENDED TO DO WHAT THEY COULD FOR THAT STRUGGLE, THEY HAD A DESPERATE FIGHT OF THEIR OWN.
THE LORD OF MAGIC--THE GREAT DRAGON ASPECT MALYGOS--HAD DEEMED ALL THOSE NOT UNDER HIS REIGN UNFIT TO WIELD THE ARCANE ARTS.
AND DALARAN, MOST OF ALL, REPRESENTED DEFIANCE TO THE BLUE DRAGON'S DECREE.

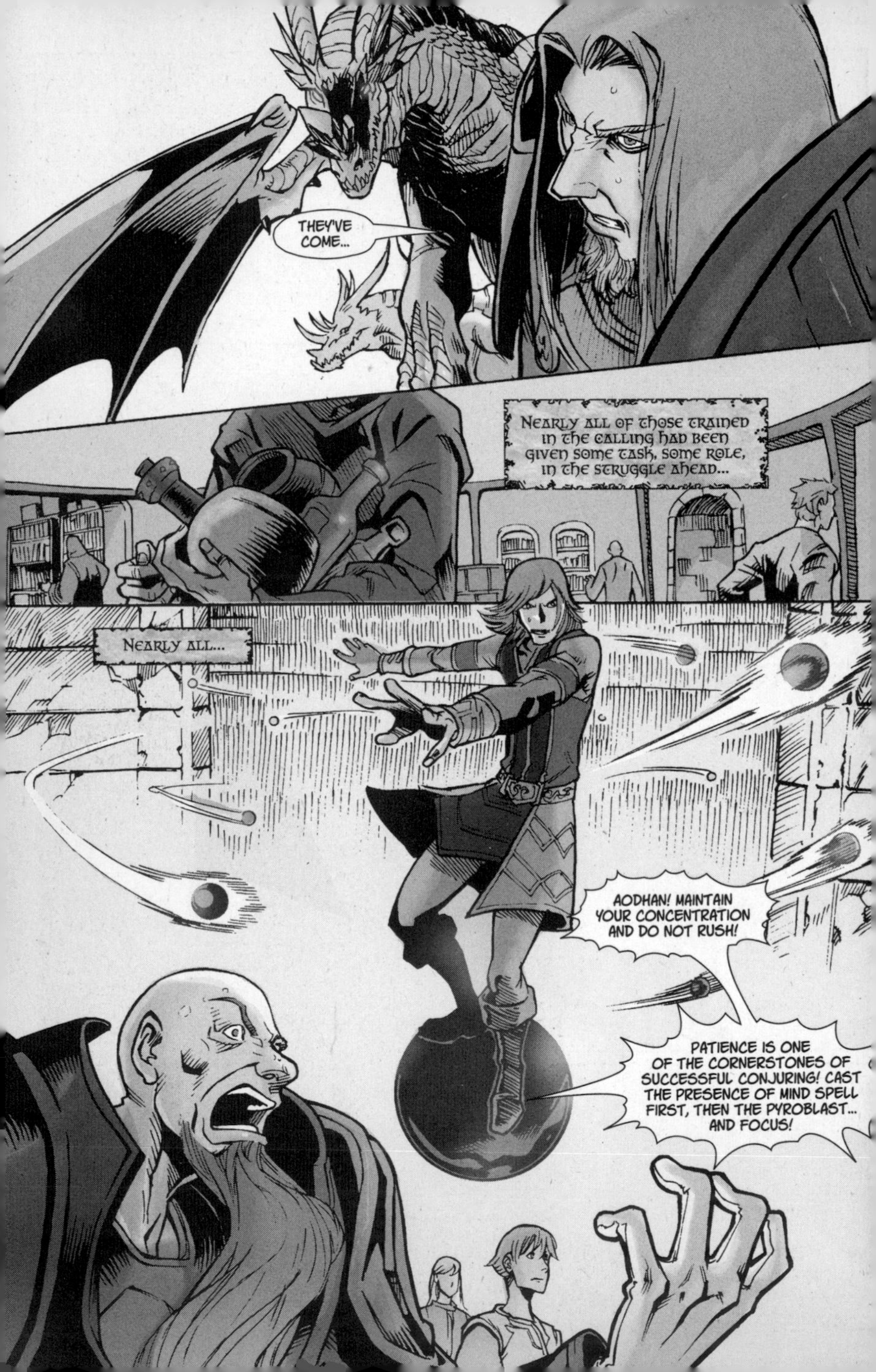
THEY'VE COME...
NEARLY ALL OF THOSE TRAINED IN THE CALLING HAD BEEN GIVEN SOME TASK, SOME ROLE, IN THE STRUGGLE AHEAD...
NEARLY ALL...
AODHAN! MAINTAIN YOUR CONCENTRATION AND DO NOT RUSH!
PATIENCE IS ONE OF THE CORNERSTONES OF SUCCESSFUL CONJURING! CAST THE PRESENCE OF MIND SPELL FIRST, THEN THE PYROBLAST... AND FOCUS!

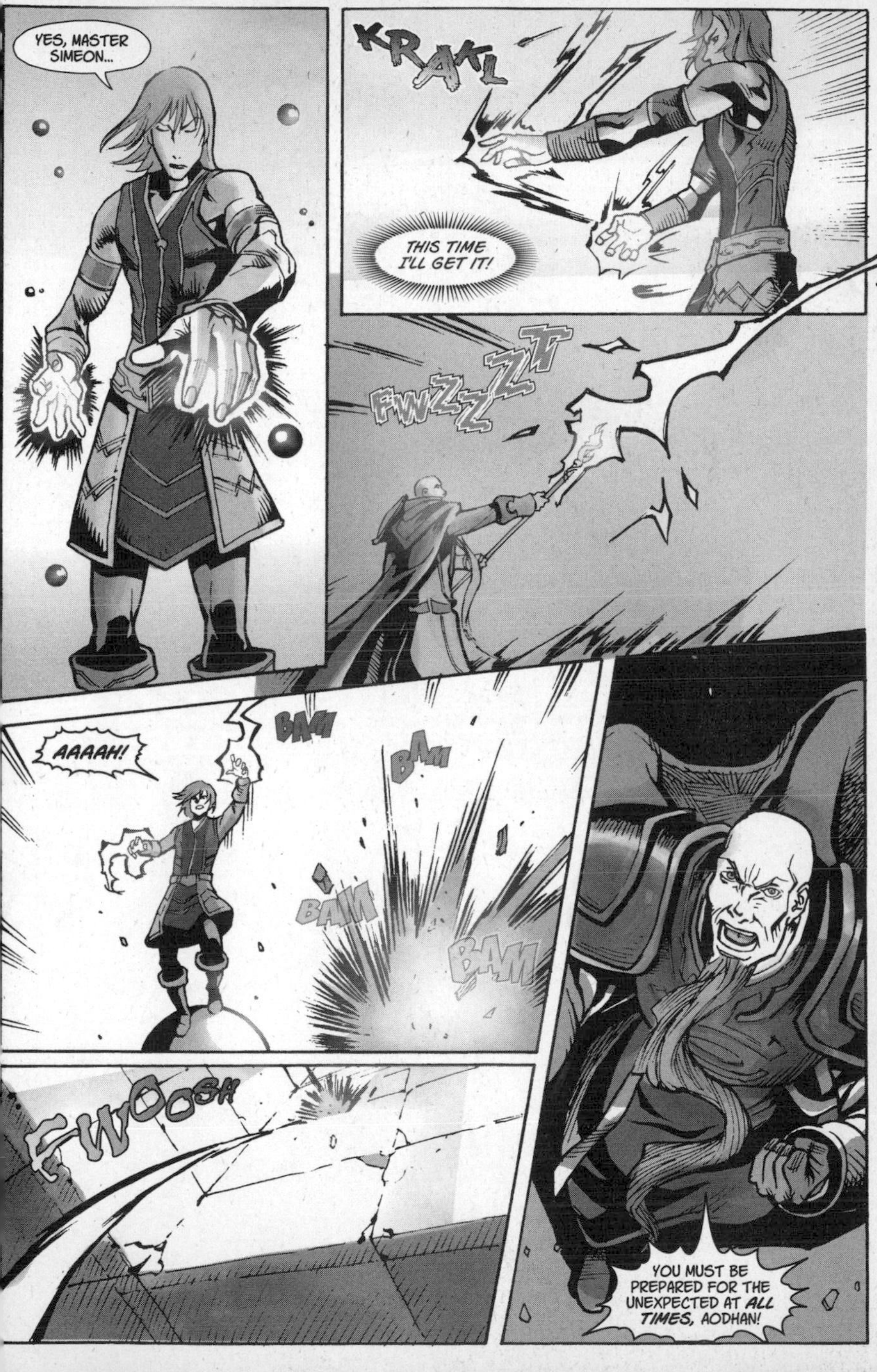
YES, MASTER SIMEON...
KRAKL
THIS TIME I'LL GET IT!
FWZZZZT
AAAAH!
BAM
BAM
BAM
BAM
FWOOSH
YOU MUST BE PREPARED FOR THE UNEXPECTED AT ALL TIMES, AODHAN!

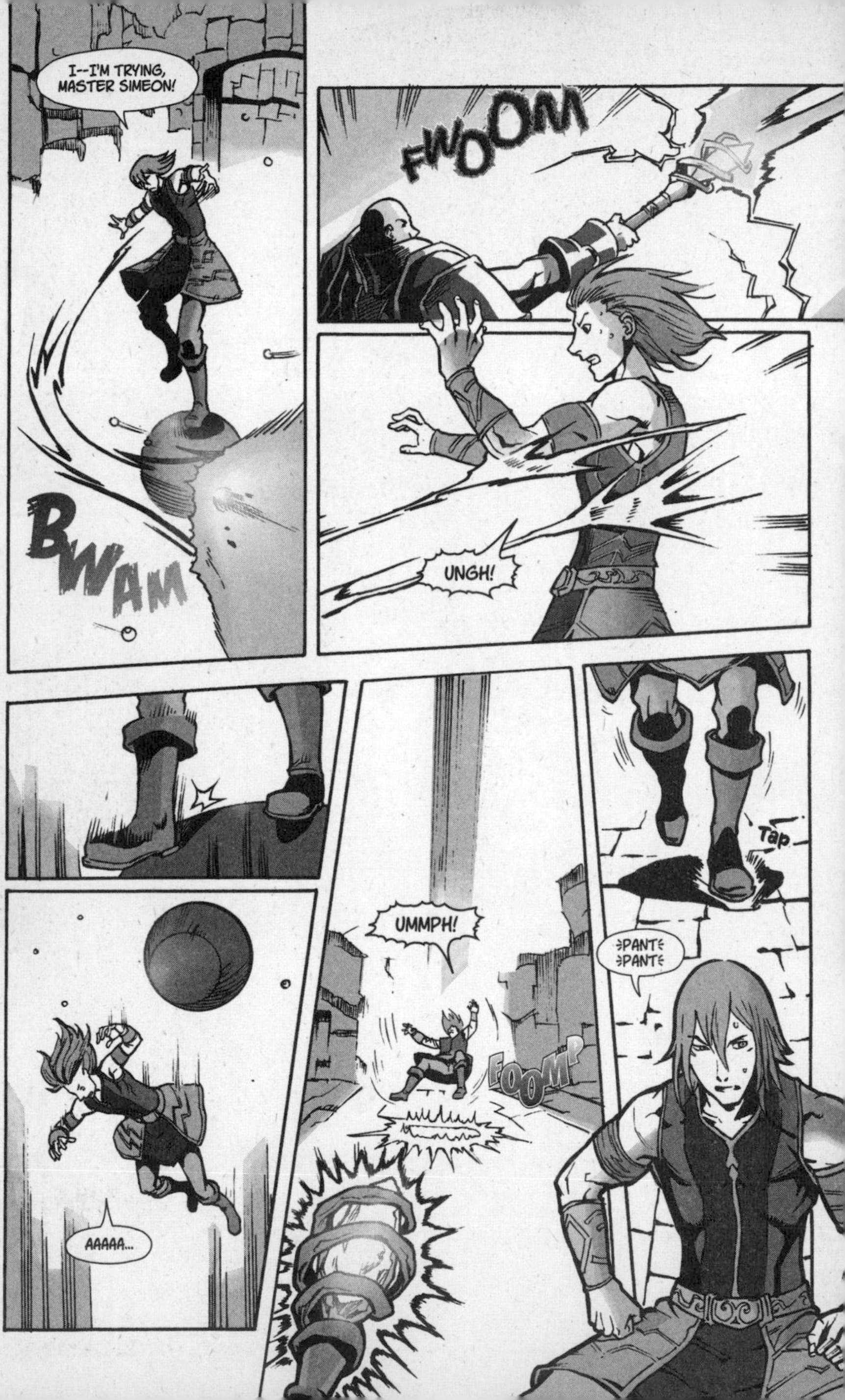
I--I'M TRYING, MASTER SIMEON!
BWAM
FWOOM
UNGH!
AAAAA...
UMMPH!
FOOMP
Tap
PANT
PANT

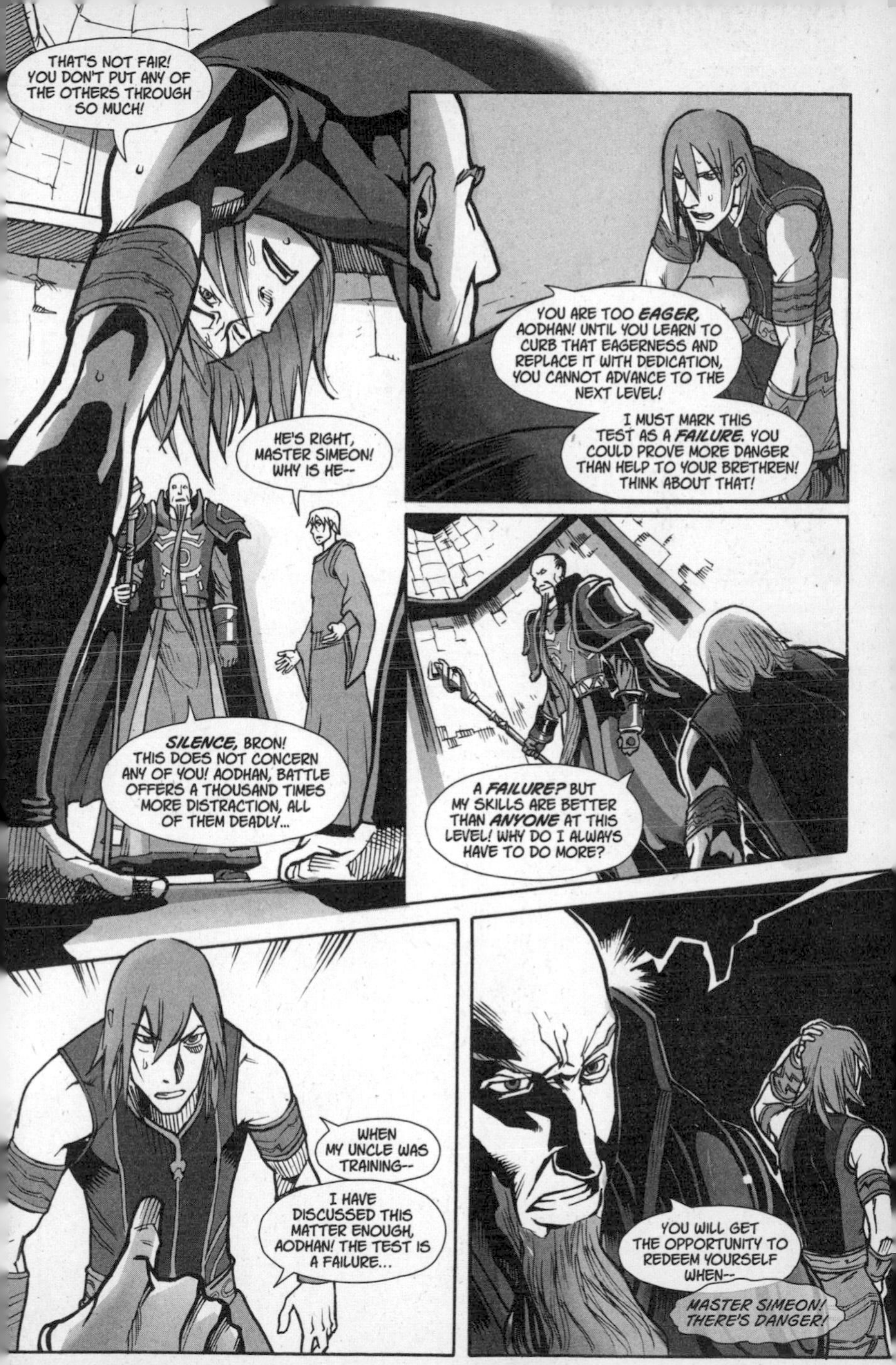
THAT'S NOT FAIR! YOU DON'T PUT ANY OF THE OTHERS THROUGH SO MUCH!
YOU ARE TOO EAGER, AODHAN! UNTIL YOU LEARN TO CURB THAT EAGERNESS AND REPLACE IT WITH DEDICATION, YOU CANNOT ADVANCE TO THE NEXT LEVEL!
I MUST MARK THIS TEST AS A FAILURE. YOU COULD PROVE MORE DANGER THAN HELP TO YOUR BRETHREN! THINK ABOUT THAT!
HE'S RIGHT, MASTER SIMEON! WHY IS HE--
SILENCE, BRON! THIS DOES NOT CONCERN ANY OF YOU! AODHAN, BATTLE OFFERS A THOUSAND TIMES MORE DISTRACTION, ALL OF THEM DEADLY...
A FAILURE? BUT MY SKILLS ARE BETTER THAN ANYONE AT THIS LEVEL! WHY DO I ALWAYS HAVE TO DO MORE?
WHEN MY UNCLE WAS TRAINING--
I HAVE DISCUSSED THIS MATTER ENOUGH, AODHAN! THE TEST IS A FAILURE...
YOU WILL GET THE OPPORTUNITY TO REDEEM YOURSELF WHEN--
MASTER SIMEON! THERE'S DANGER!

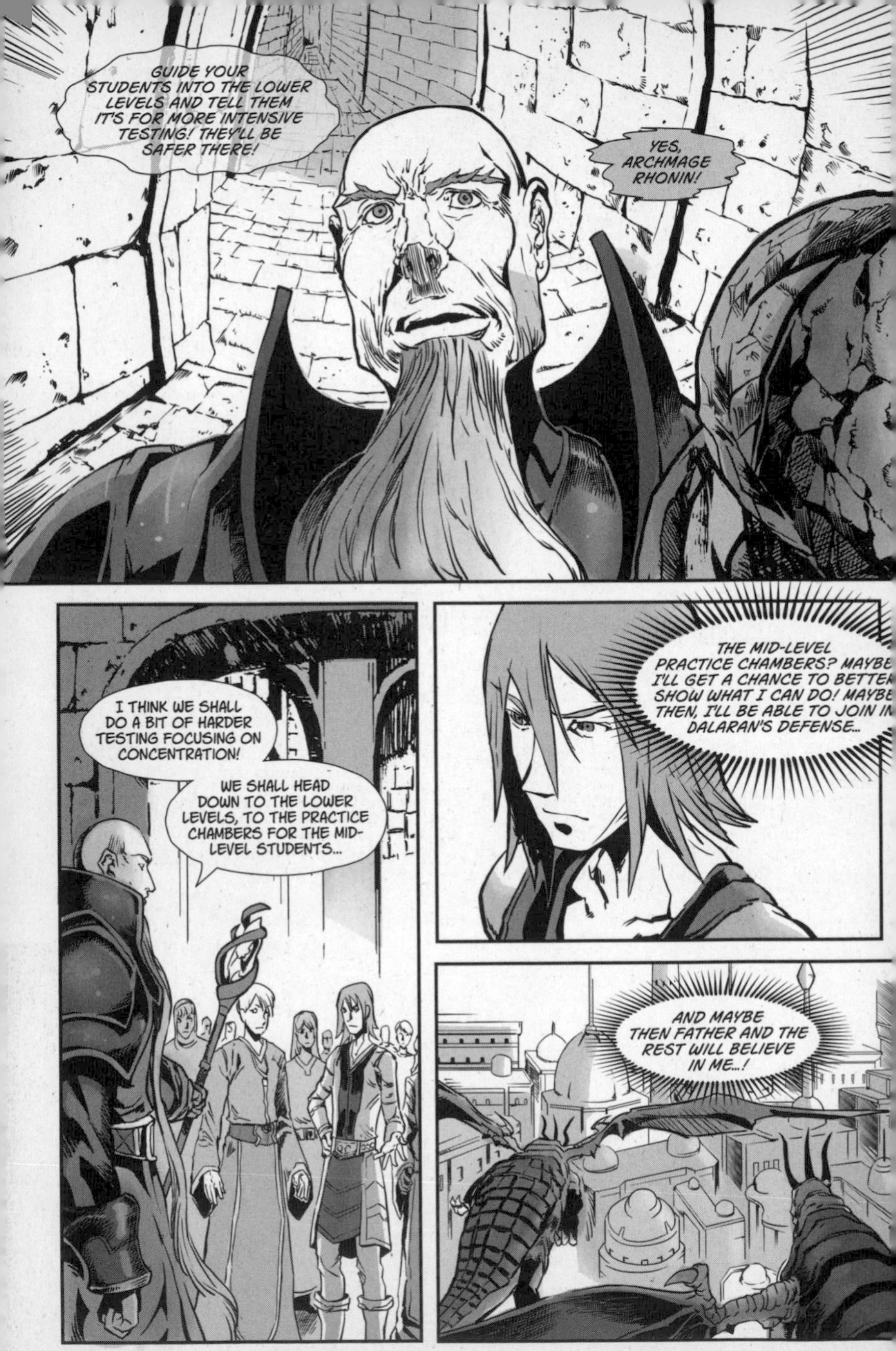
GUIDE YOUR STUDENTS INTO THE LOWER LEVELS AND TELL THEM IT'S FOR MORE INTENSIVE TESTING! THEY'LL BE SAFER THERE!
YES, ARCHMAGE RHONIN!
I THINK WE SHALL DO A BIT OF HARDER TESTING FOCUSING ON CONCENTRATION!
WE SHALL HEAD DOWN TO THE LOWER LEVELS, TO THE PRACTICE CHAMBERS FOR THE MID-LEVEL STUDENTS...
THE MID-LEVEL PRACTICE CHAMBERS? MAYBE I'LL GET A CHANCE TO BETTER SHOW WHAT I CAN DO! MAYBE THEN, I'LL BE ABLE TO JOIN IN DALARAN'S DEFENSE...
AND MAYBE THEN FATHER AND THE REST WILL BELIEVE IN ME...!

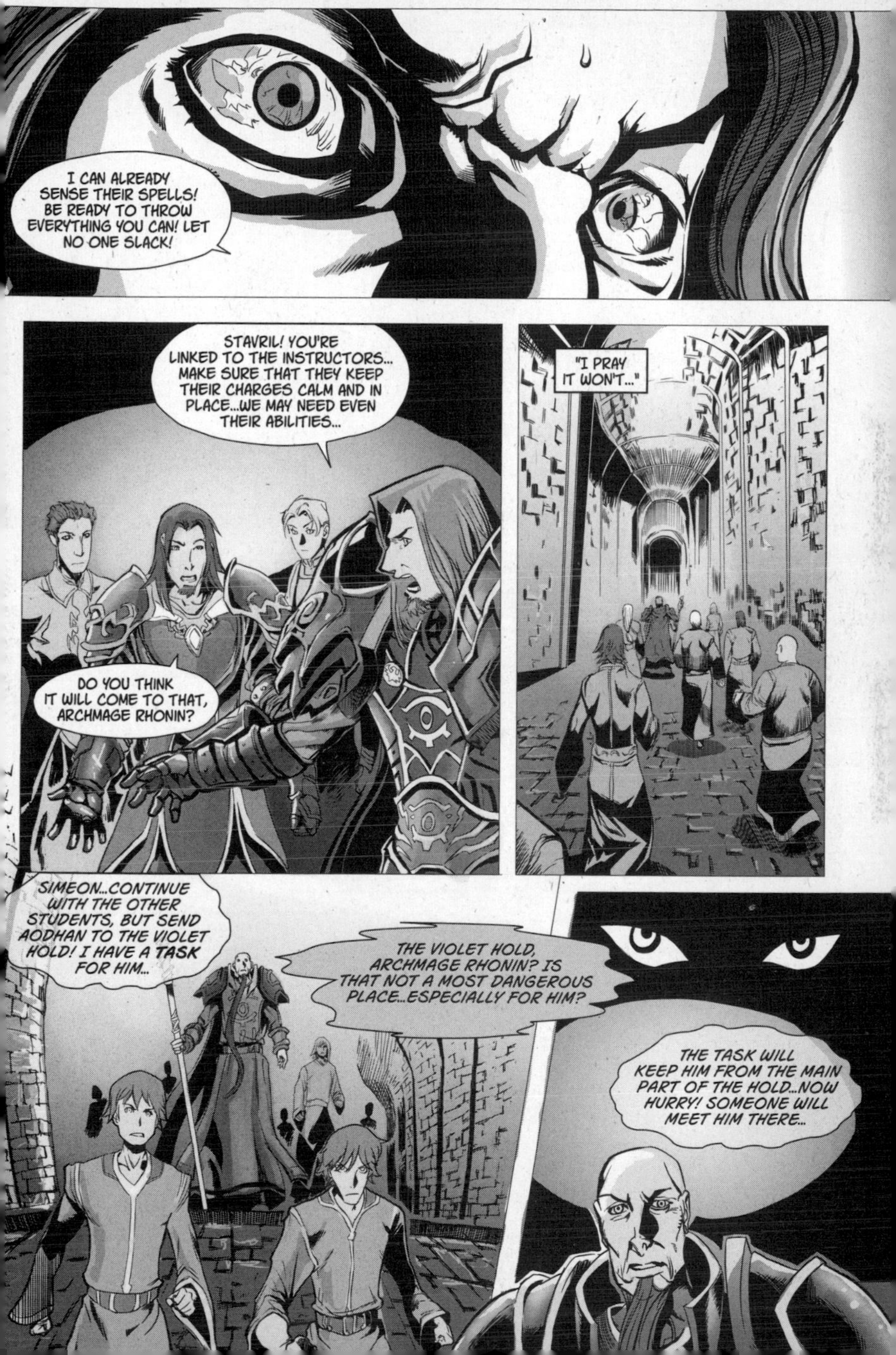
I CAN ALREADY SENSE THEIR SPELLS! BE READY TO THROW EVERYTHING YOU CAN! LET NO ONE SLACK!
STAVRIL! YOU'RE LINKED TO THE INSTRUCTORS... MAKE SURE THAT THEY KEEP THEIR CHARGES CALM AND IN PLACE...WE MAY NEED EVEN THEIR ABILITIES...
DO YOU THINK IT WILL COME TO THAT, ARCHMAGE RHONIN?
"I PRAY IT WON'T..."
SIMEON...CONTINUE WITH THE OTHER STUDENTS, BUT SEND AODHAN TO THE VIOLET HOLD! I HAVE A TASK FOR HIM...
THE VIOLET HOLD, ARCHMAGE RHONIN? IS THAT NOT A MOST DANGEROUS PLACE...ESPECIALLY FOR HIM?
THE TASK WILL KEEP HIM FROM THE MAIN PART OF THE HOLD...NOW HURRY! SOMEONE WILL MEET HIM THERE...

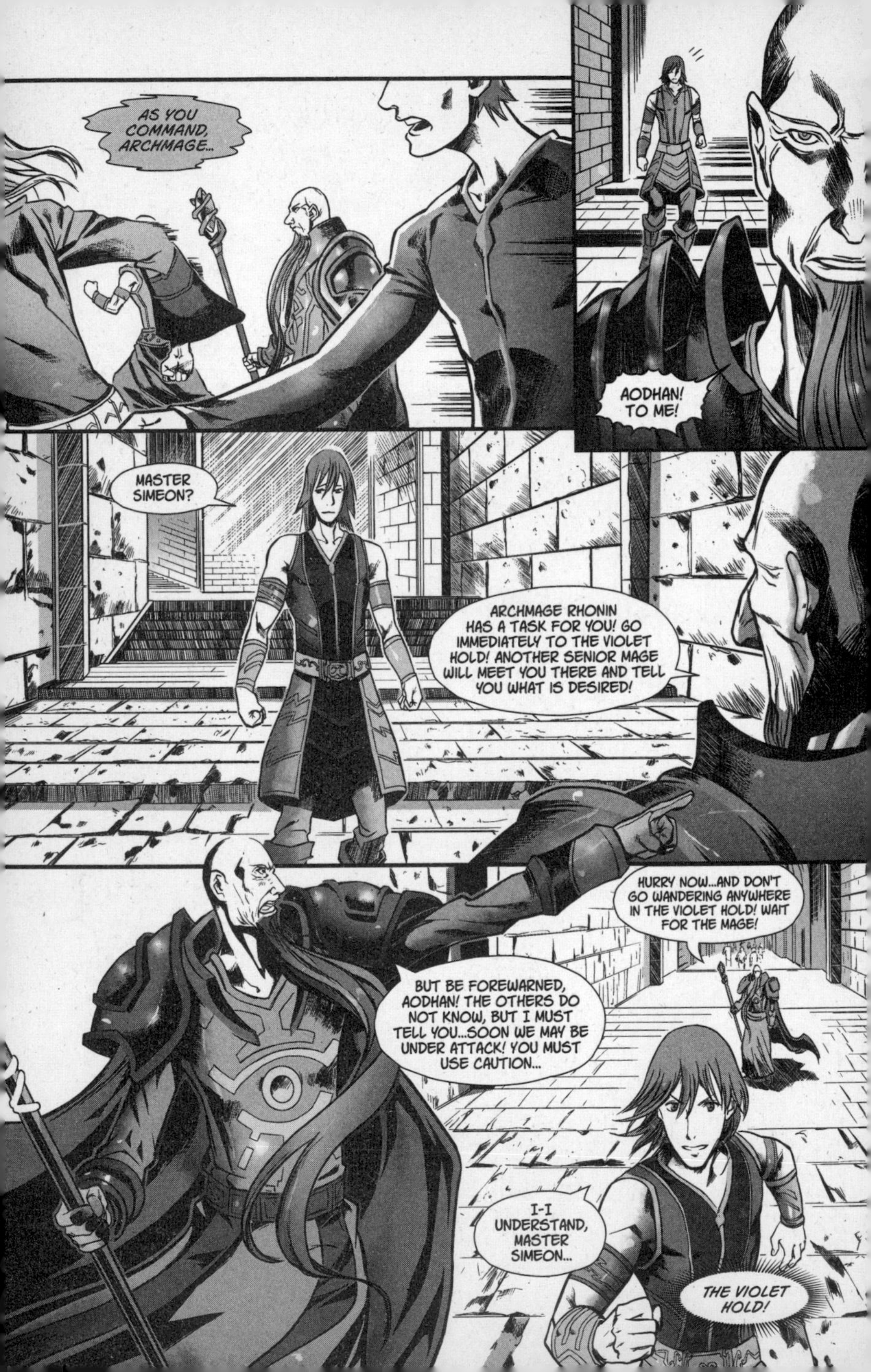
AS YOU COMMAND, ARCHMAGE...
AODHAN! TO ME!
MASTER SIMEON?
ARCHMAGE RHONIN HAS A TASK FOR YOU! GO IMMEDIATELY TO THE VIOLET HOLD! ANOTHER SENIOR MAGE WILL MEET YOU THERE AND TELL YOU WHAT IS DESIRED!
BUT BE FOREWARNED, AODHAN! THE OTHERS DO NOT KNOW, BUT I MUST TELL YOU...SOON WE MAY BE UNDER ATTACK! YOU MUST USE CAUTION...
I-I UNDERSTAND, MASTER SIMEON...
HURRY NOW...AND DON'T GO WANDERING ANYWHERE IN THE VIOLET HOLD! WAIT FOR THE MAGE!
THE VIOLET HOLD!

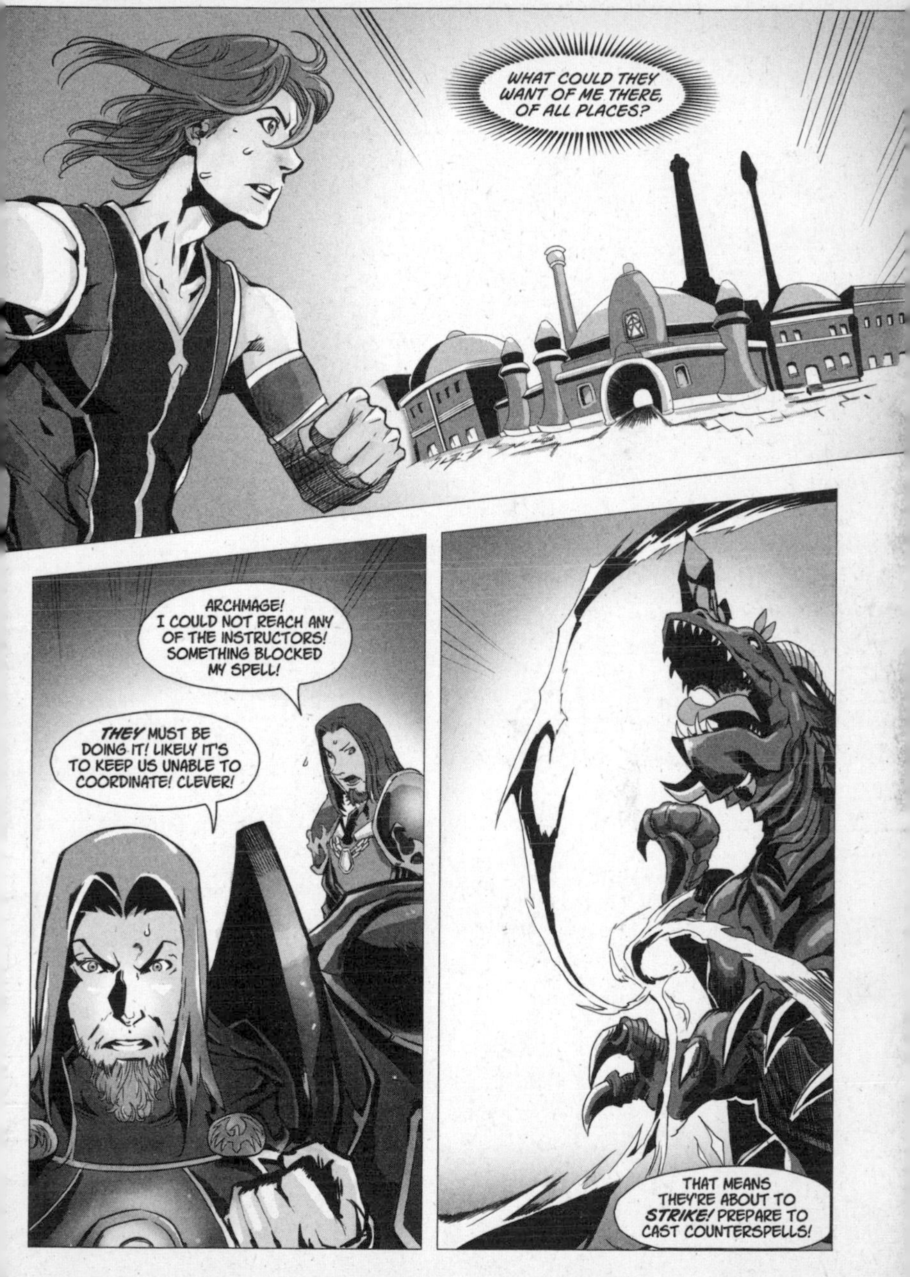
WHAT COULD THEY WANT OF ME THERE, OF ALL PLACES?
ARCHMAGE! I COULD NOT REACH ANY OF THE INSTRUCTORS! SOMETHING BLOCKED MY SPELL!
THEY MUST BE DOING IT! LIKELY IT'S TO KEEP US UNABLE TO COORDINATE! CLEVER!
THAT MEANS THEY'RE ABOUT TO STRIKE! PREPARE TO CAST COUNTERSPELLS!

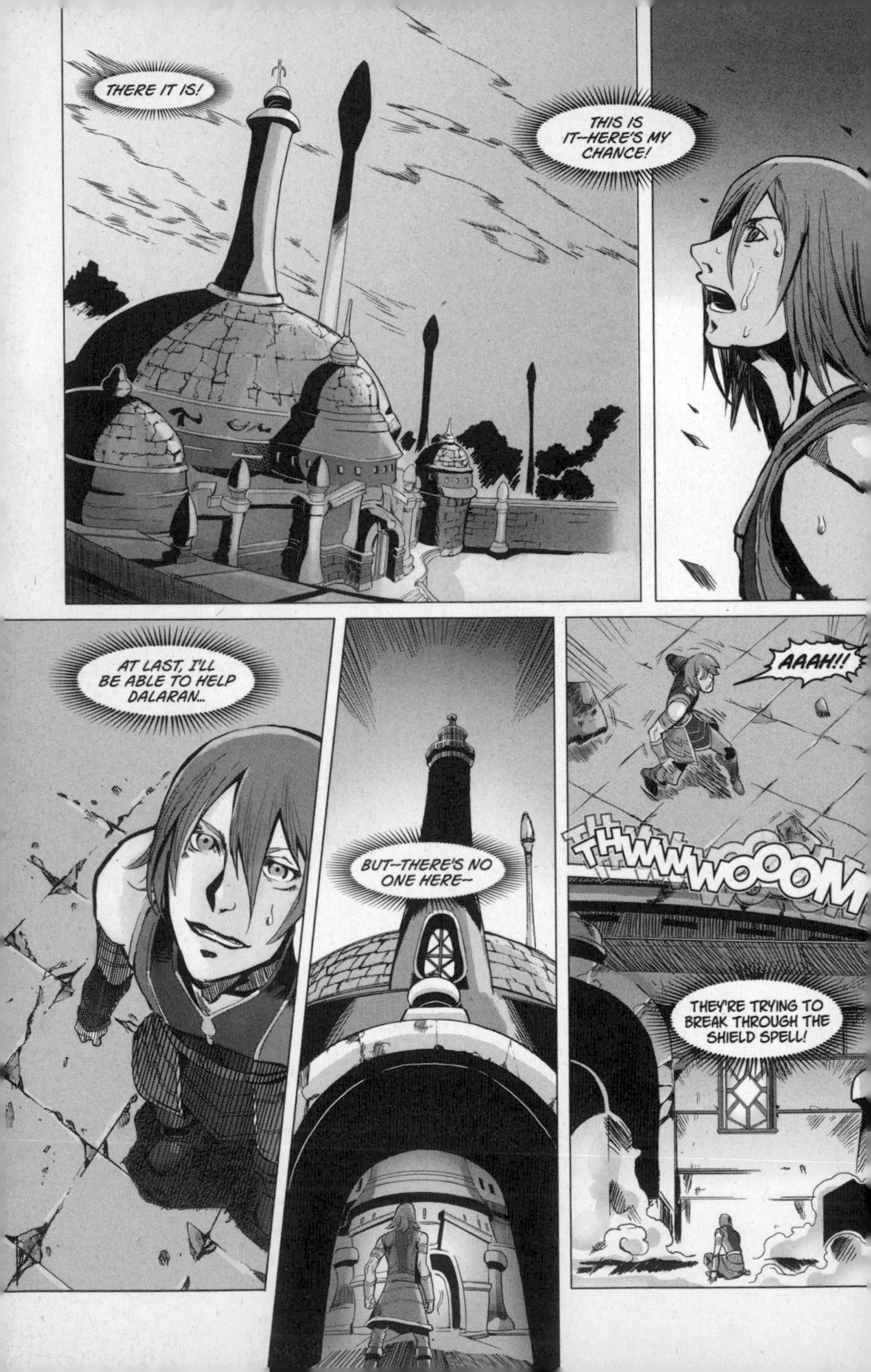
THERE IT IS!
THIS IS IT--HERE'S MY CHANCE!
AT LAST, I'LL BE ABLE TO HELP DALARAN...
BUT--THERE'S NO ONE HERE--
AAAH!!
THWWWWOOOOM
THEY'RE TRYING TO BREAK THROUGH THE SHIELD SPELL!

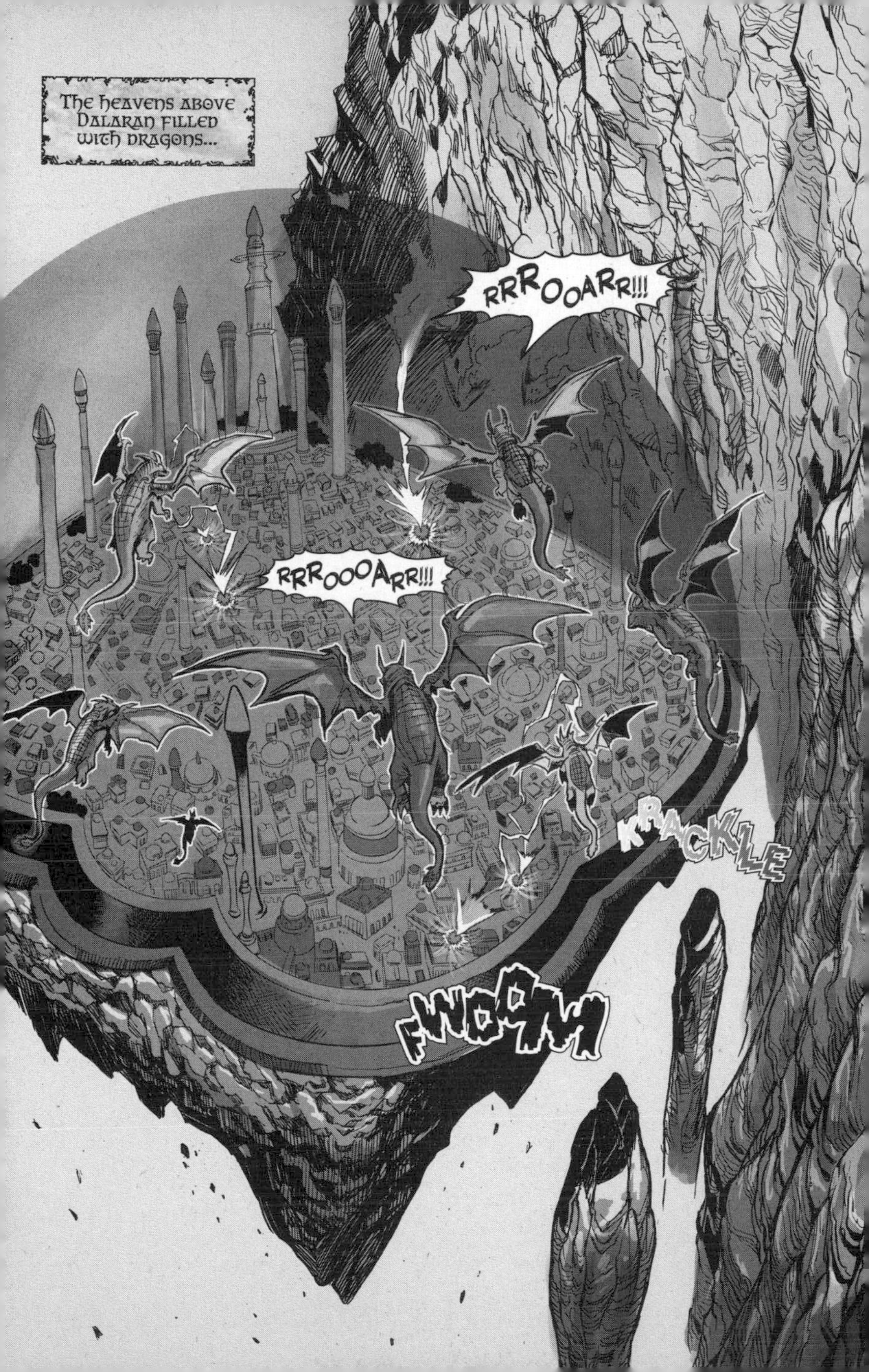
The heavens above Dalaran filled with dragons...
RRROOARR!!!
RRROOOARR!!!
KRACKLE
FWOOM

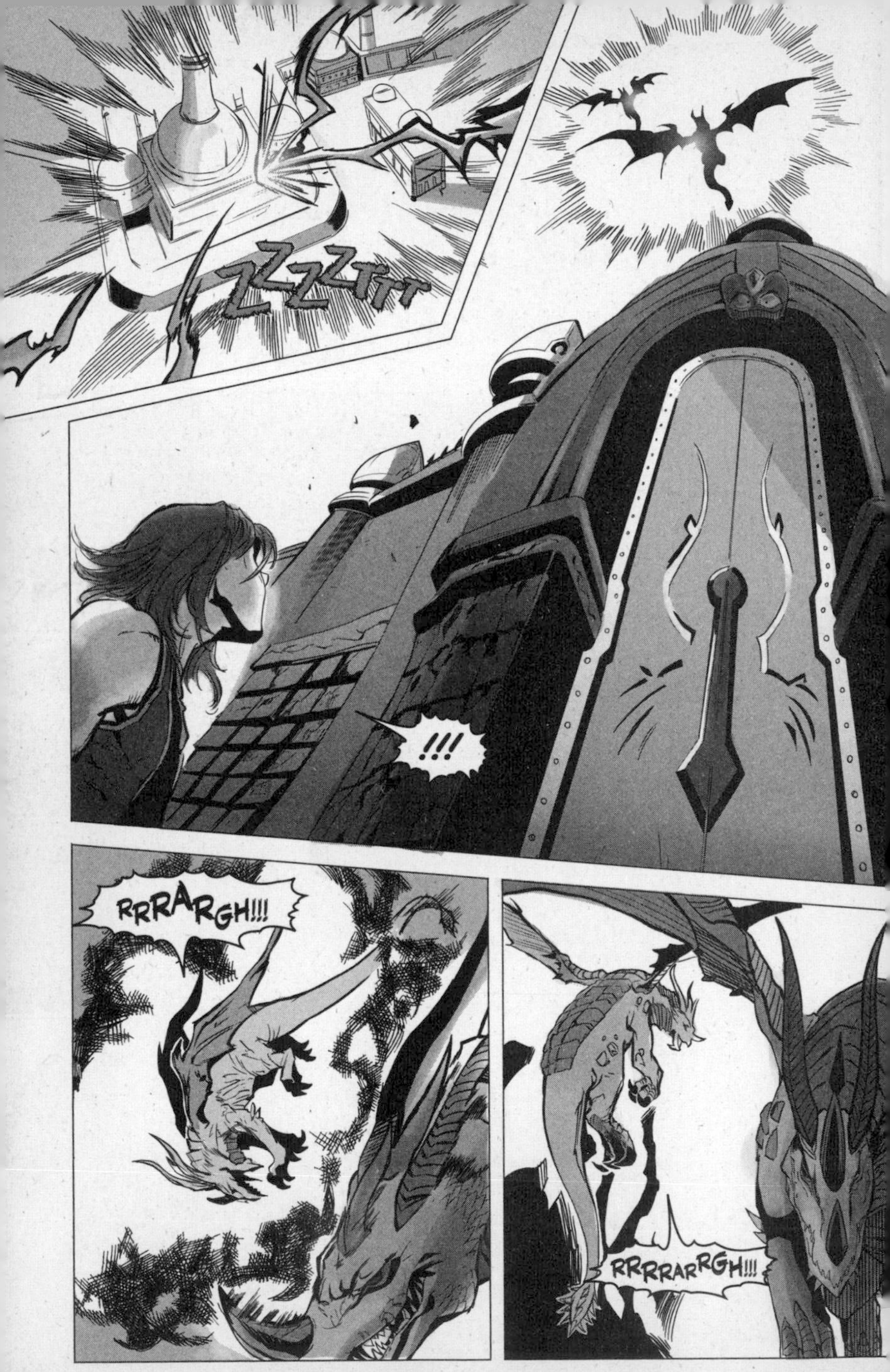
ZZZZTTT
!!!
RRRARGH!!!
RRRRARRGH!!!

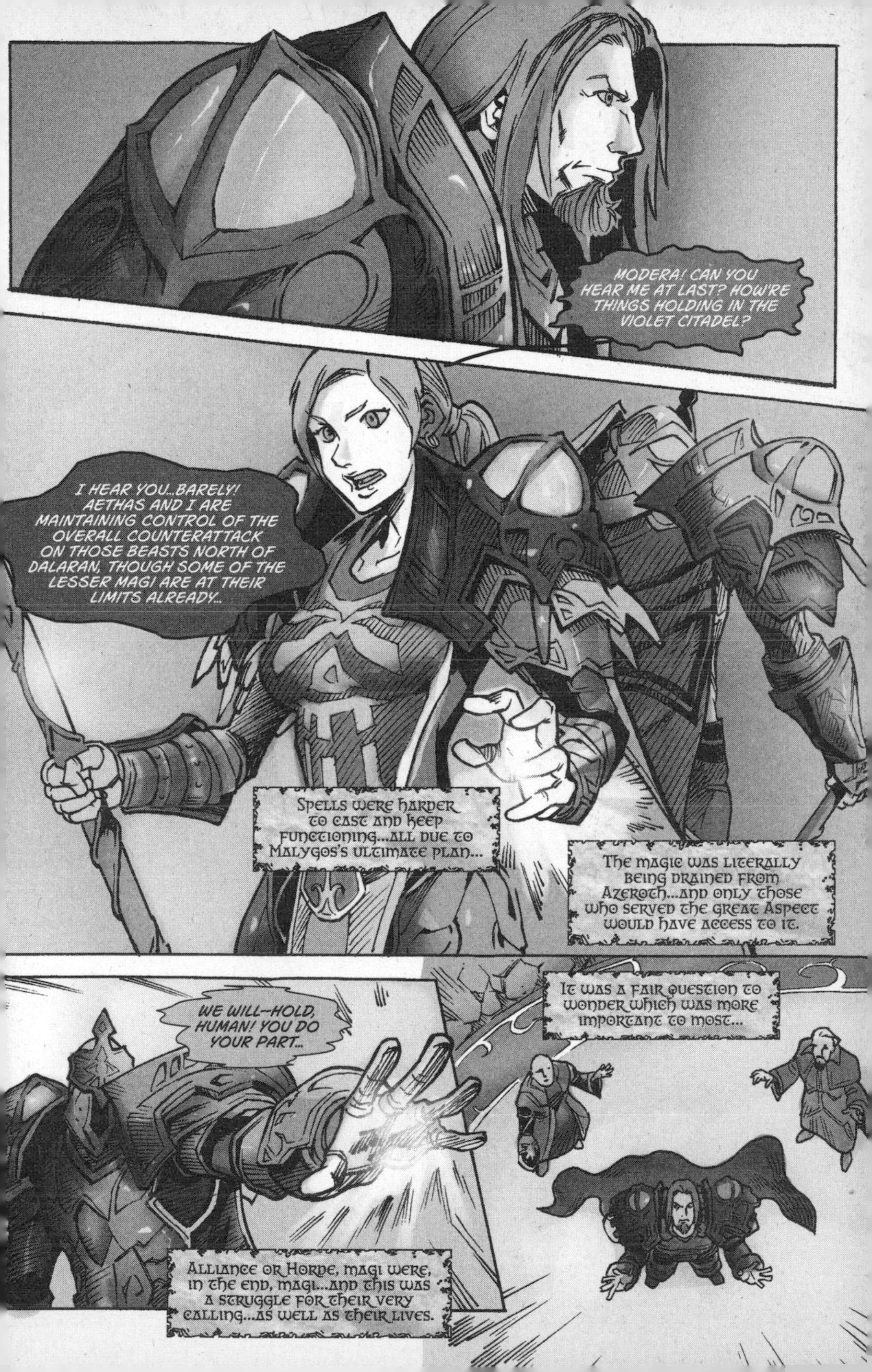
MODERA! CAN YOU HEAR ME AT LAST? HOW'RE THINGS HOLDING IN THE VIOLET CITADEL?
I HEAR YOU...BARELY! AETHAS AND I ARE MAINTAINING CONTROL OF THE OVERALL COUNTERATTACK ON THOSE BEASTS NORTH OF DALARAN, THOUGH SOME OF THE LESSER MAGI ARE AT THEIR LIMITS ALREADY...
Spells were harder to cast and keep functioning...all due to Malygos's ultimate plan...
The magic was literally being drained from Azeroth...and only those who served the great Aspect would have access to it.
WE WILL--HOLD, HUMAN! YOU DO YOUR PART...
It was a fair question to wonder which was more important to most...
Alliance or Horde, magi were, in the end, magi...and this was a struggle for their very calling...as well as their lives.

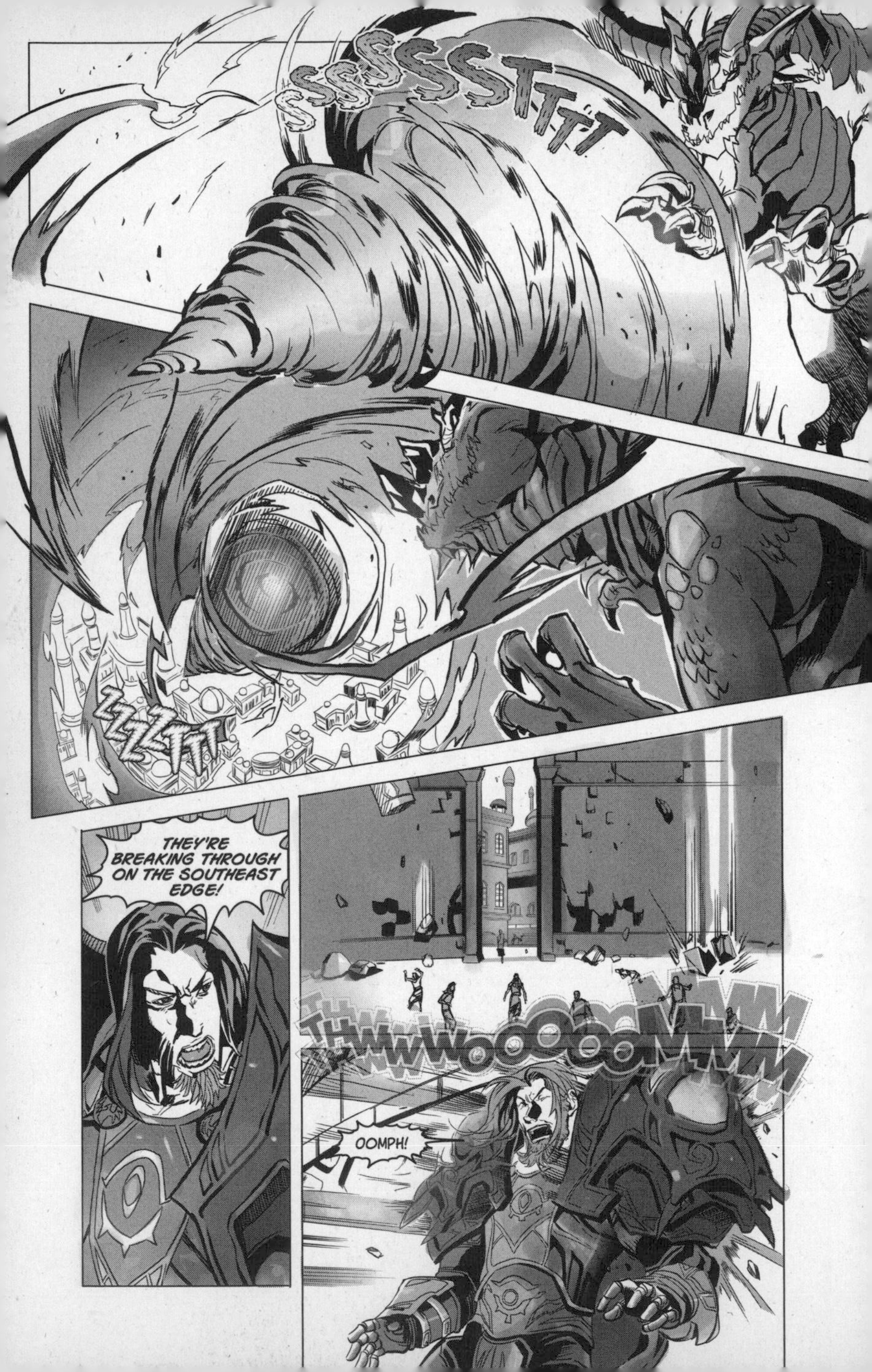
SSSSSTTT
ZZZTTT
THEY'RE BREAKING THROUGH ON THE SOUTHEAST EDGE!
THWWWOOOOOOMMMM!
OOMPH!

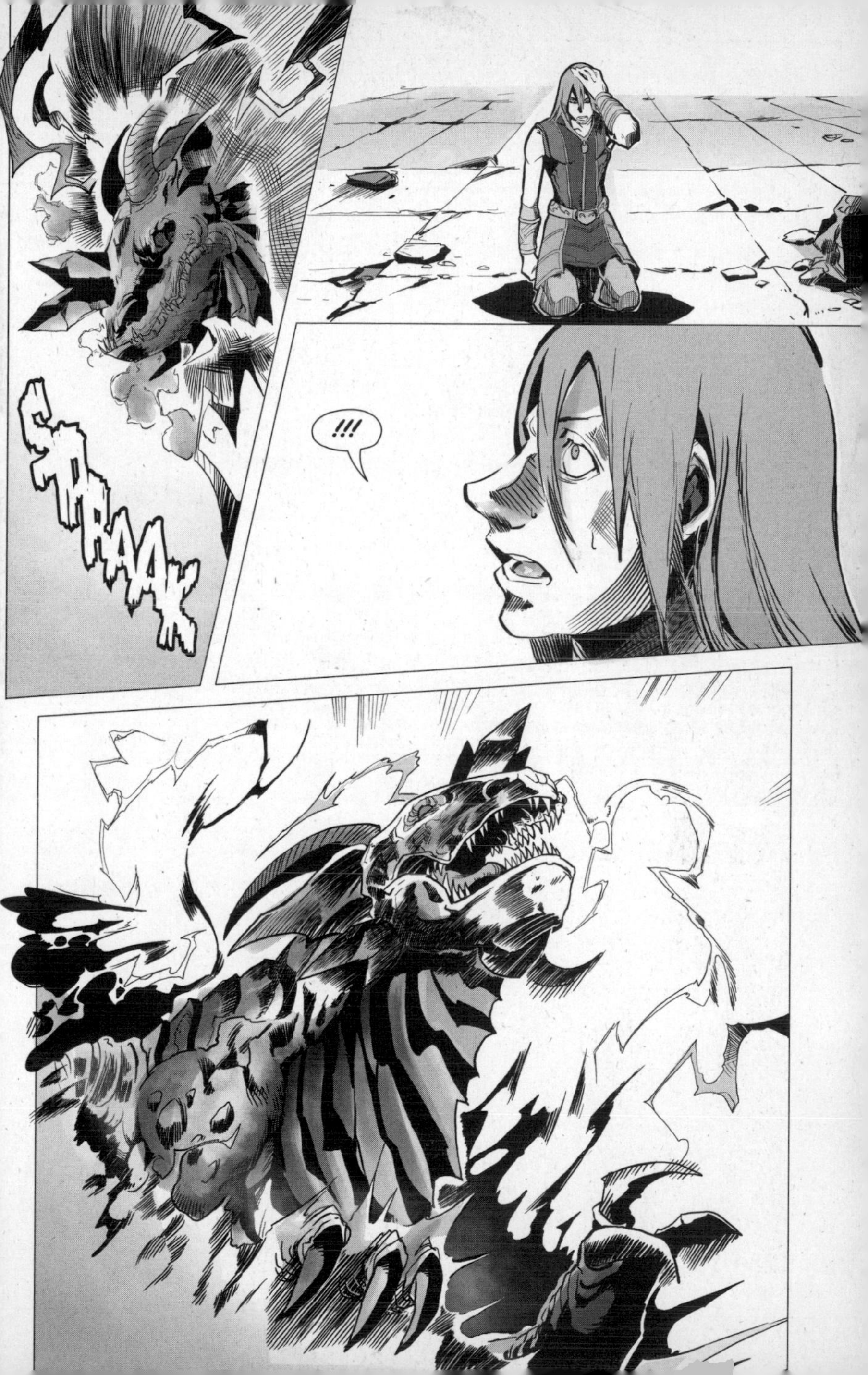
SPRAAK
!!!

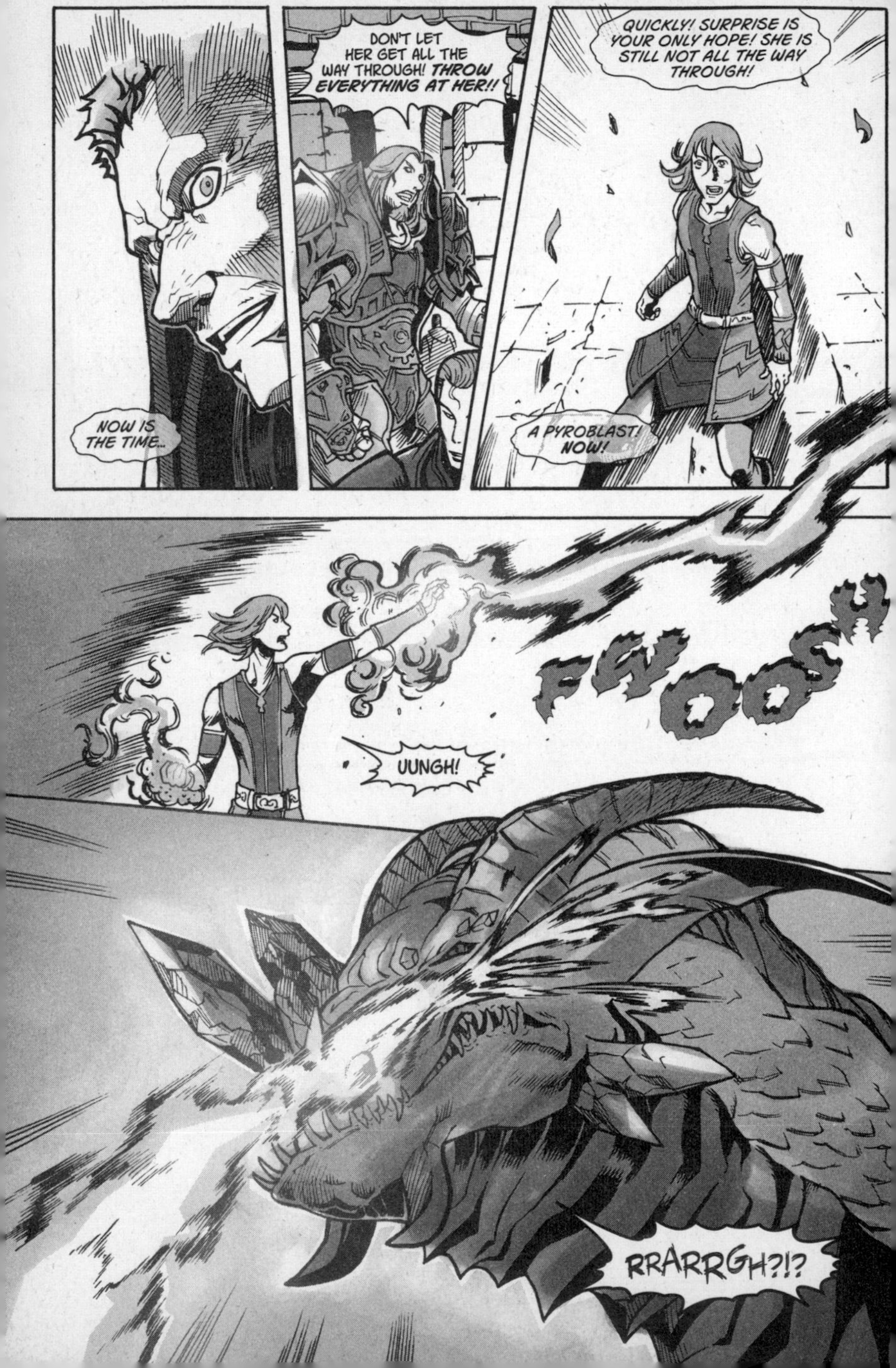
NOW IS THE TIME...
DON'T LET HER GET ALL THE WAY THROUGH! THROW EVERYTHING AT HER!!
QUICKLY! SURPRISE IS YOUR ONLY HOPE! SHE IS STILL NOT ALL THE WAY THROUGH!
A PYROBLAST! NOW!
FWOOSH
UUNGH!
RRARRGH?!?

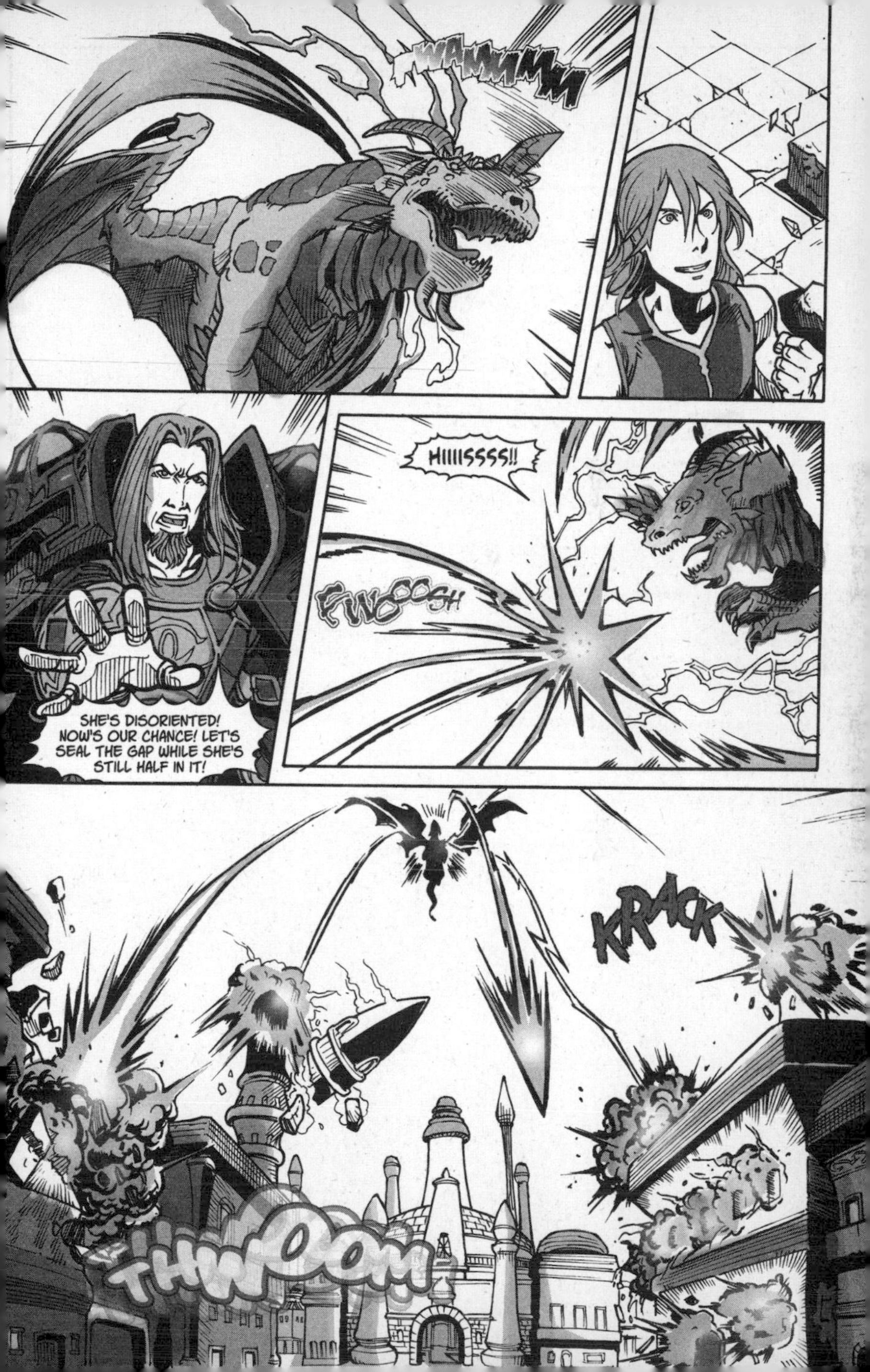
FWAMMMM
HIIIISSSS!!
FWOOOSH
SHE'S DISORIENTED! NOW'S OUR CHANCE! LET'S SEAL THE GAP WHILE SHE'S STILL HALF IN IT!
KRACK
THWOOM

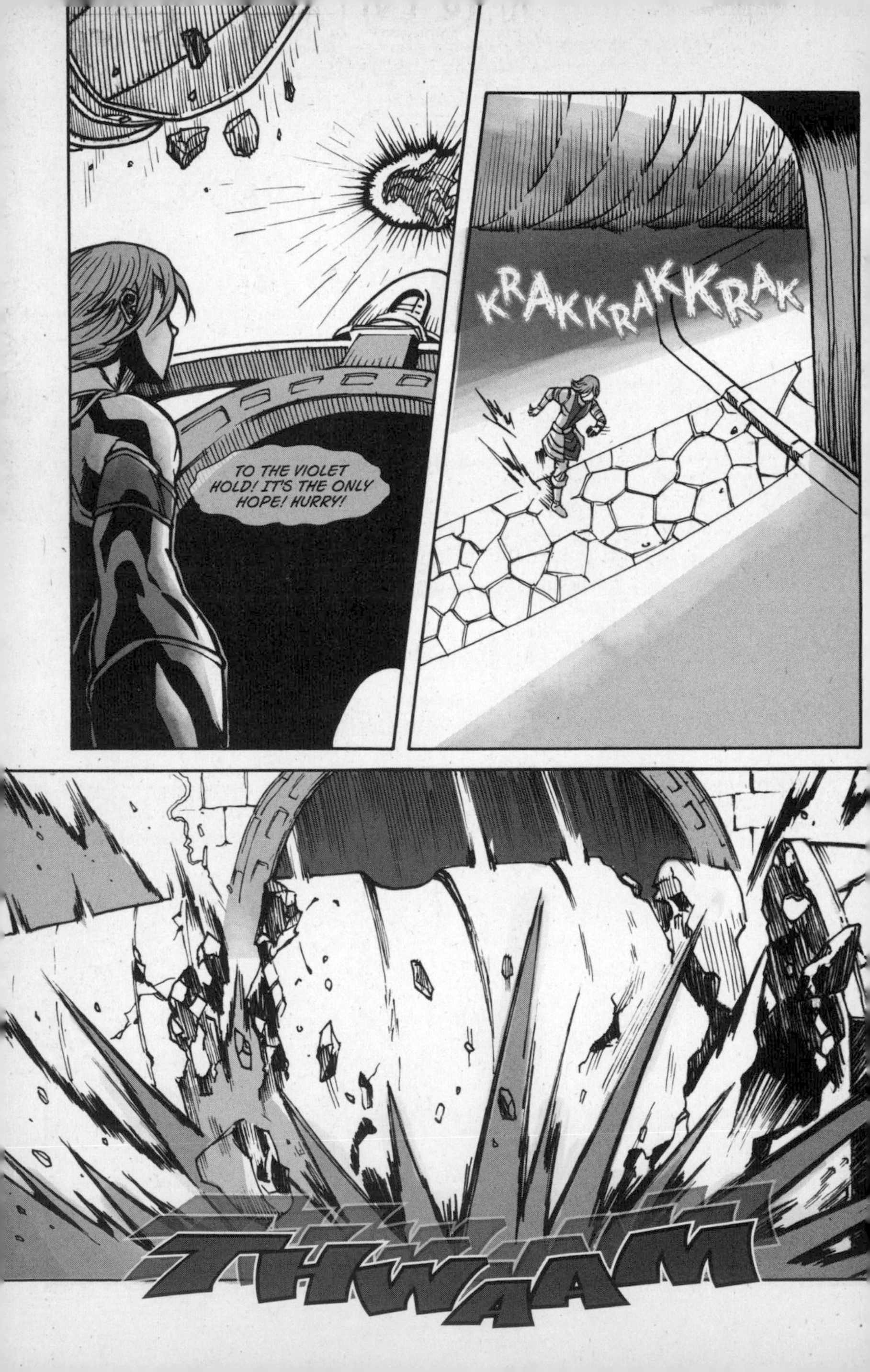
TO THE VIOLET HOLD! IT'S THE ONLY HOPE! HURRY!
KRAKKRAKKRAK
THWAAM

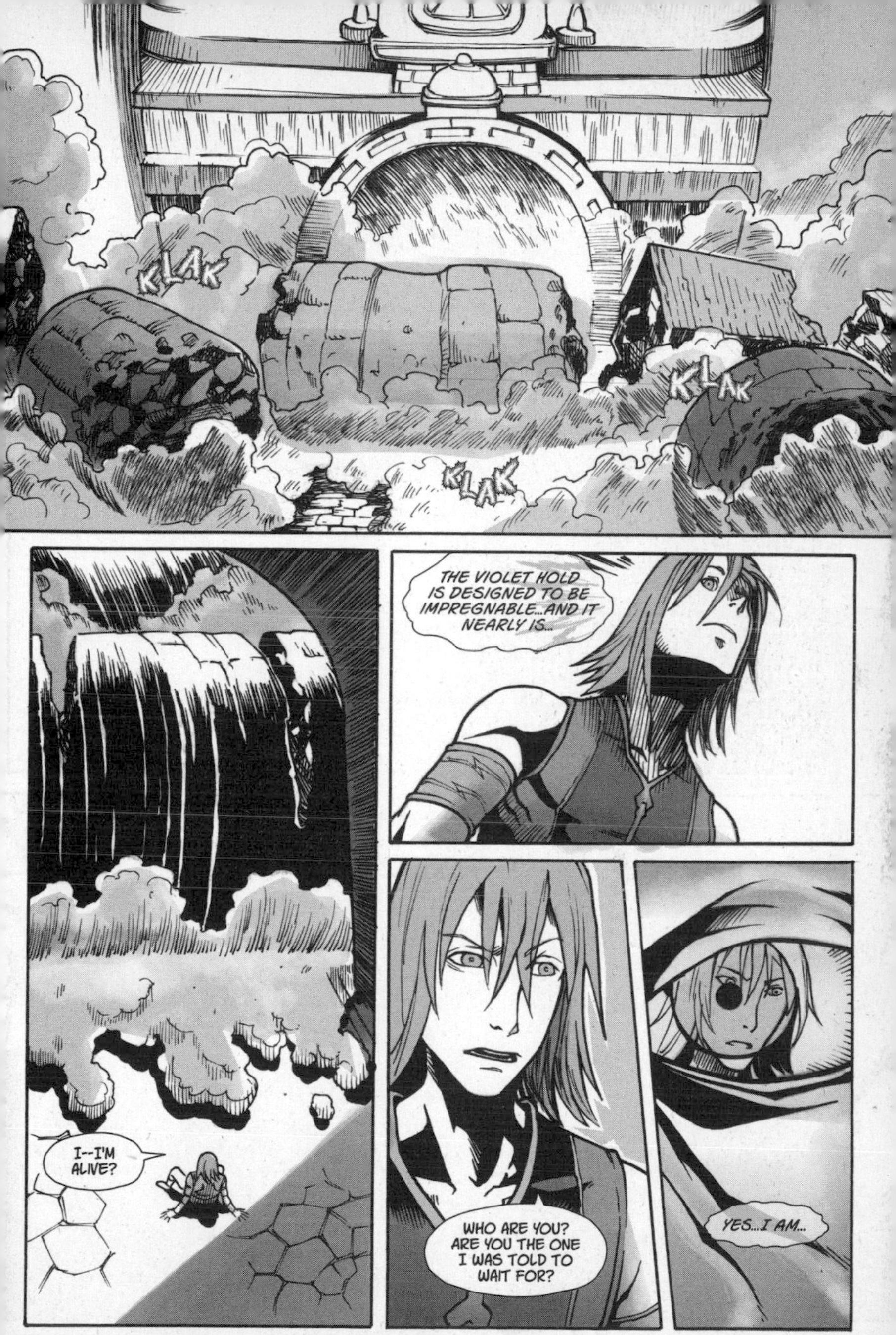
KLAK
KLAK
KLAK
I--I'M ALIVE?
THE VIOLET HOLD IS DESIGNED TO BE IMPREGNABLE...AND IT NEARLY IS...
WHO ARE YOU? ARE YOU THE ONE I WAS TOLD TO WAIT FOR?
YES...I AM...

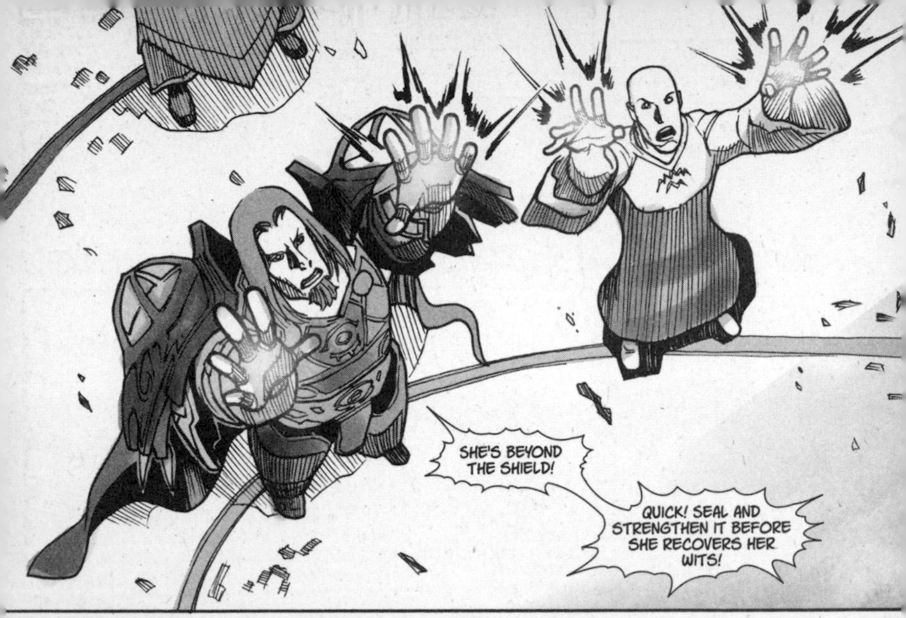
SHE'S BEYOND THE SHIELD!
QUICK! SEAL AND STRENGTHEN IT BEFORE SHE RECOVERS HER WITS!
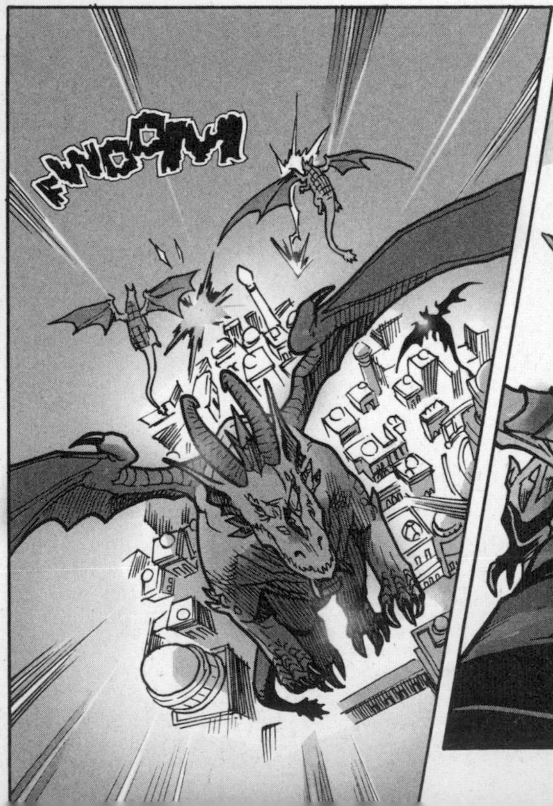
FWOOM
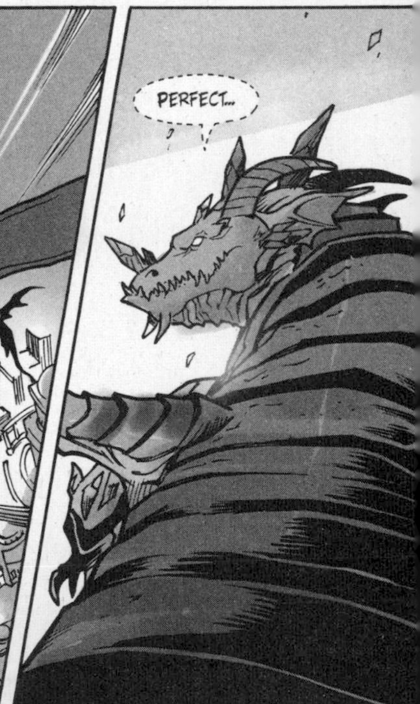
PERFECT...

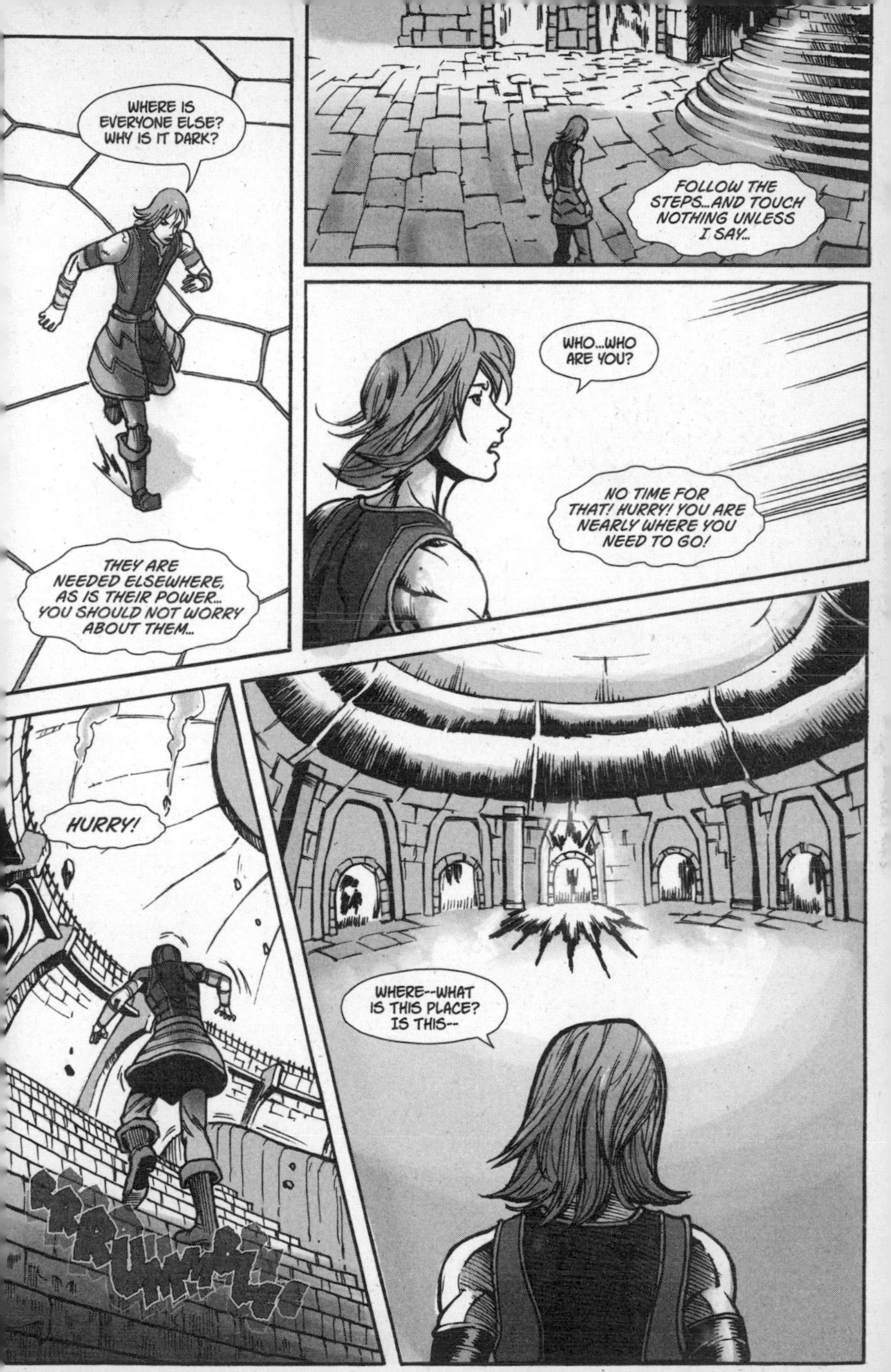
WHERE IS EVERYONE ELSE? WHY IS IT DARK?
THEY ARE NEEDED ELSEWHERE, AS IS THEIR POWER... YOU SHOULD NOT WORRY ABOUT THEM...
FOLLOW THE STEPS...AND TOUCH NOTHING UNLESS I SAY...
WHO...WHO ARE YOU?
NO TIME FOR THAT! HURRY! YOU ARE NEARLY WHERE YOU NEED TO GO!
HURRY!
WHERE--WHAT IS THIS PLACE? IS THIS--

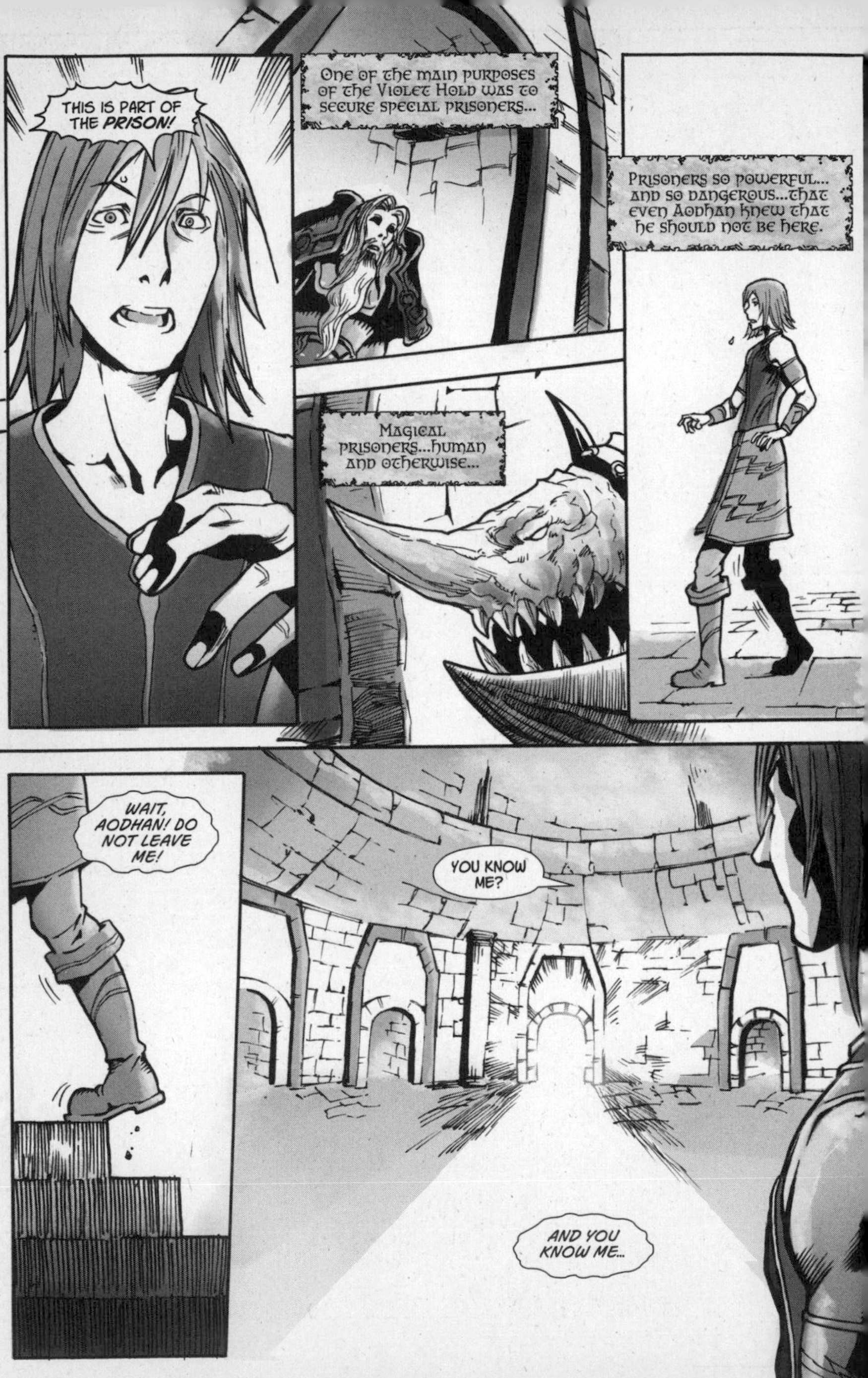
THIS IS PART OF THE PRISON!
One of the main purposes of the Violet Hold was to secure special prisoners...
Magical prisoners...human and otherwise...
Prisoners so powerful... and so dangerous...that even Aodhan knew that he should not be here.
WAIT, AODHAN! DO NOT LEAVE ME!
YOU KNOW ME?
AND YOU KNOW ME...

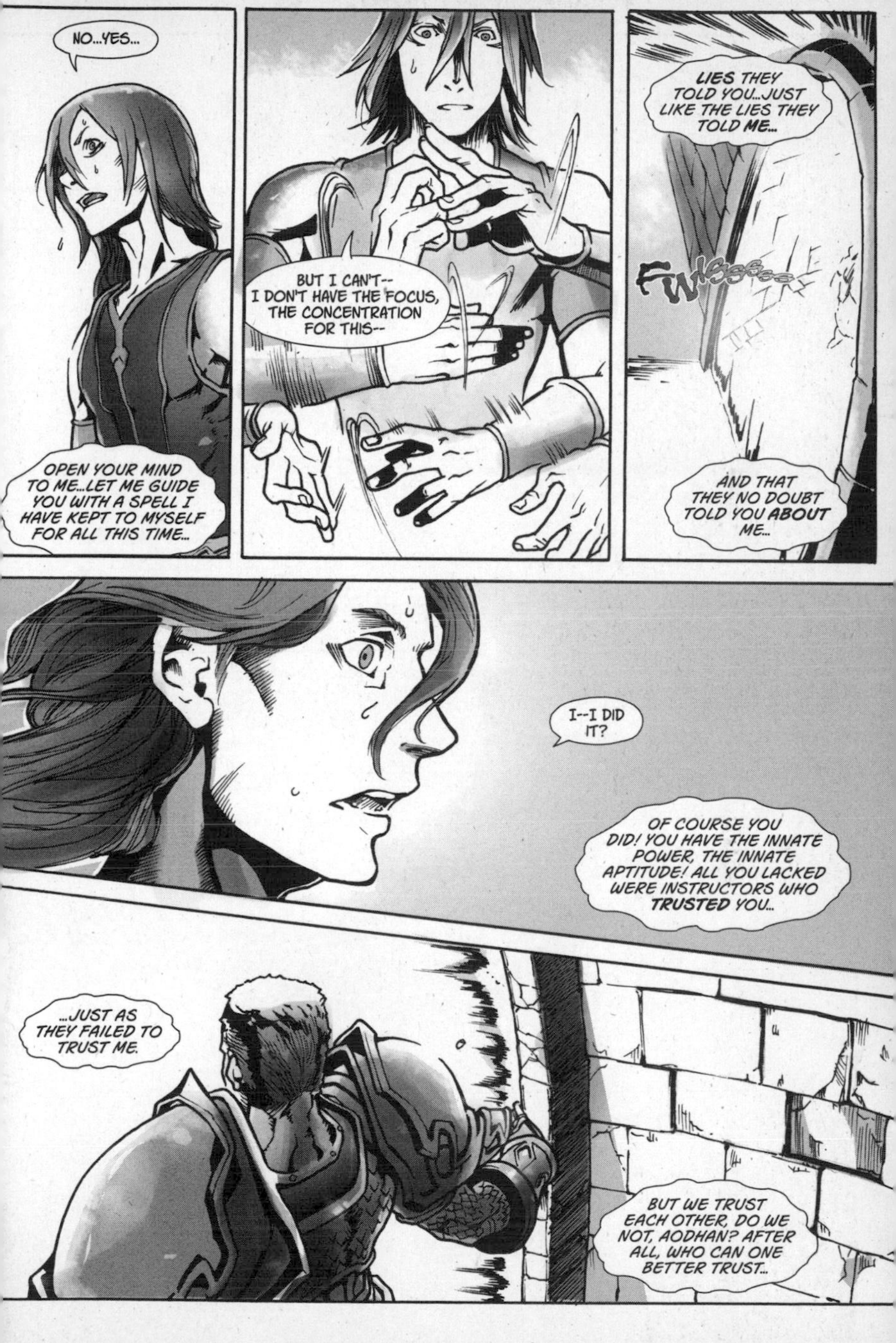
NO...YES...
OPEN YOUR MIND TO ME...LET ME GUIDE YOU WITH A SPELL I HAVE KEPT TO MYSELF FOR ALL THIS TIME...
BUT I CAN'T--
I DON'T HAVE THE FOCUS, THE CONCENTRATION FOR THIS--
LIES THEY TOLD YOU...JUST LIKE THE LIES THEY TOLD ME...
FWISSSSSS
AND THAT THEY NO DOUBT TOLD YOU ABOUT ME...
I--I DID IT?
OF COURSE YOU DID! YOU HAVE THE INNATE POWER, THE INNATE APTITUDE! ALL YOU LACKED WERE INSTRUCTORS WHO TRUSTED YOU...
...JUST AS THEY FAILED TO TRUST ME.
BUT WE TRUST EACH OTHER, DO WE NOT, AODHAN? AFTER ALL, WHO CAN ONE BETTER TRUST...

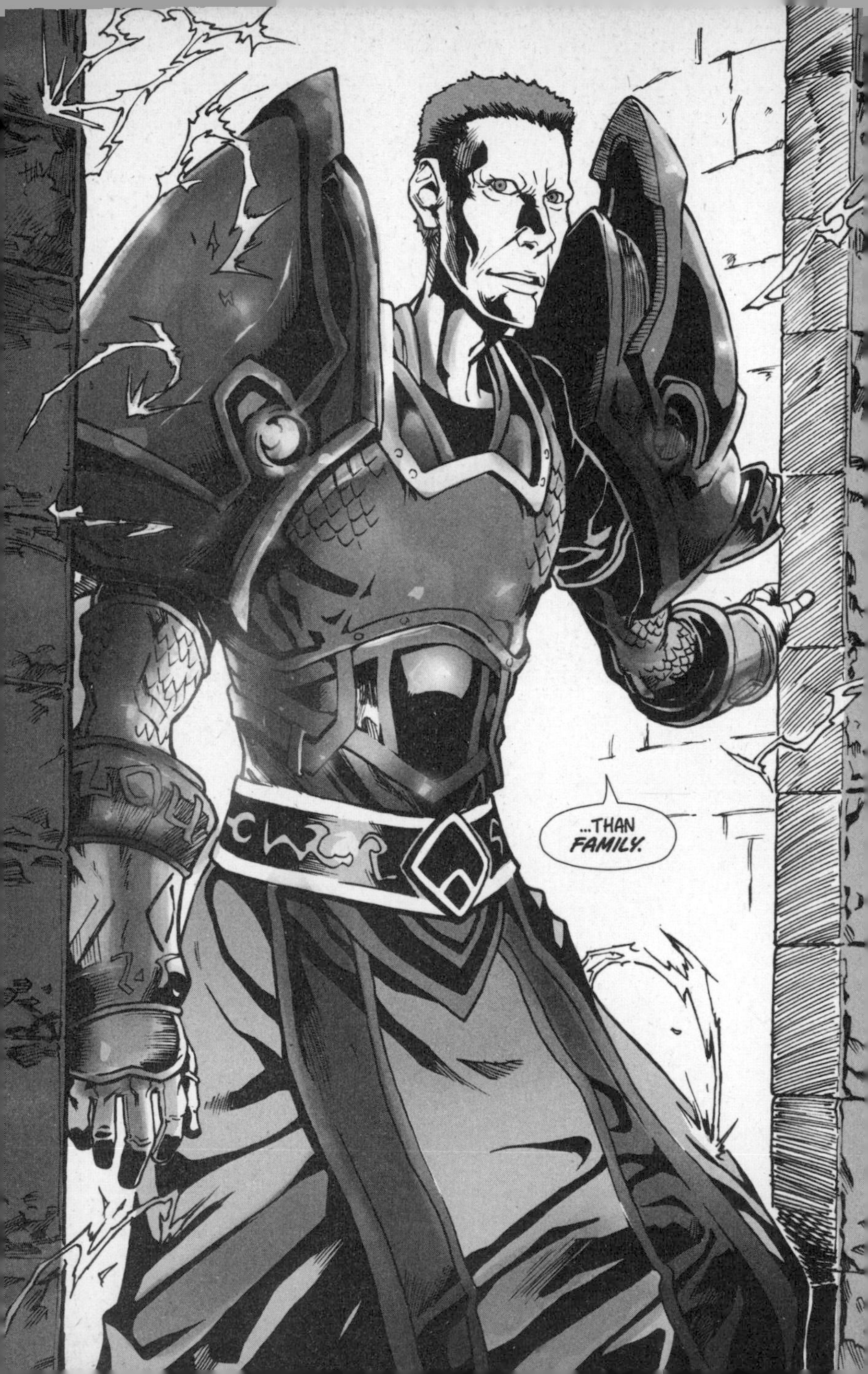
...THAN FAMILY.

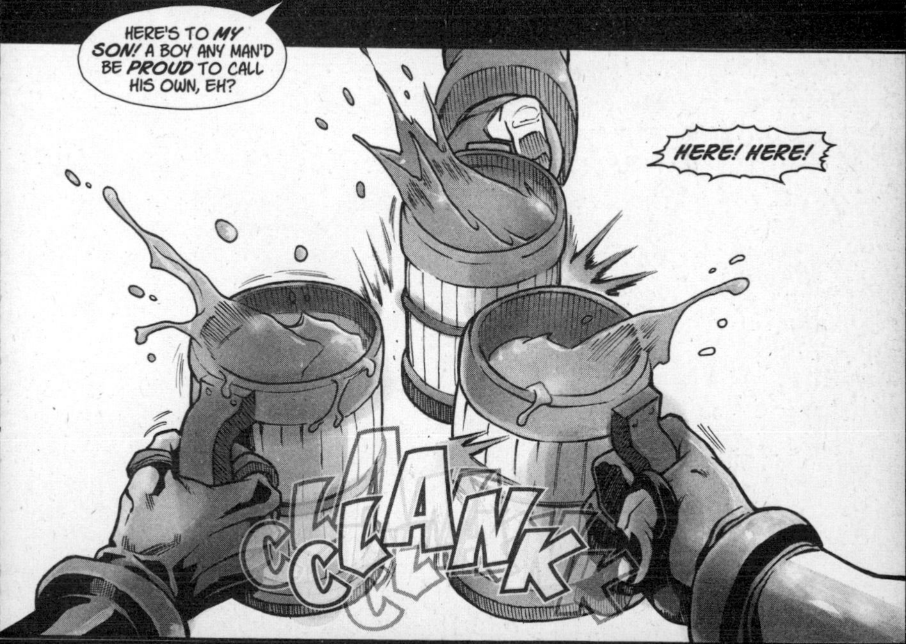
HERE'S TO MY SON! A BOY ANY MAN'D BE PROUD TO CALL HIS OWN, EH?
HERE! HERE!
CLANK

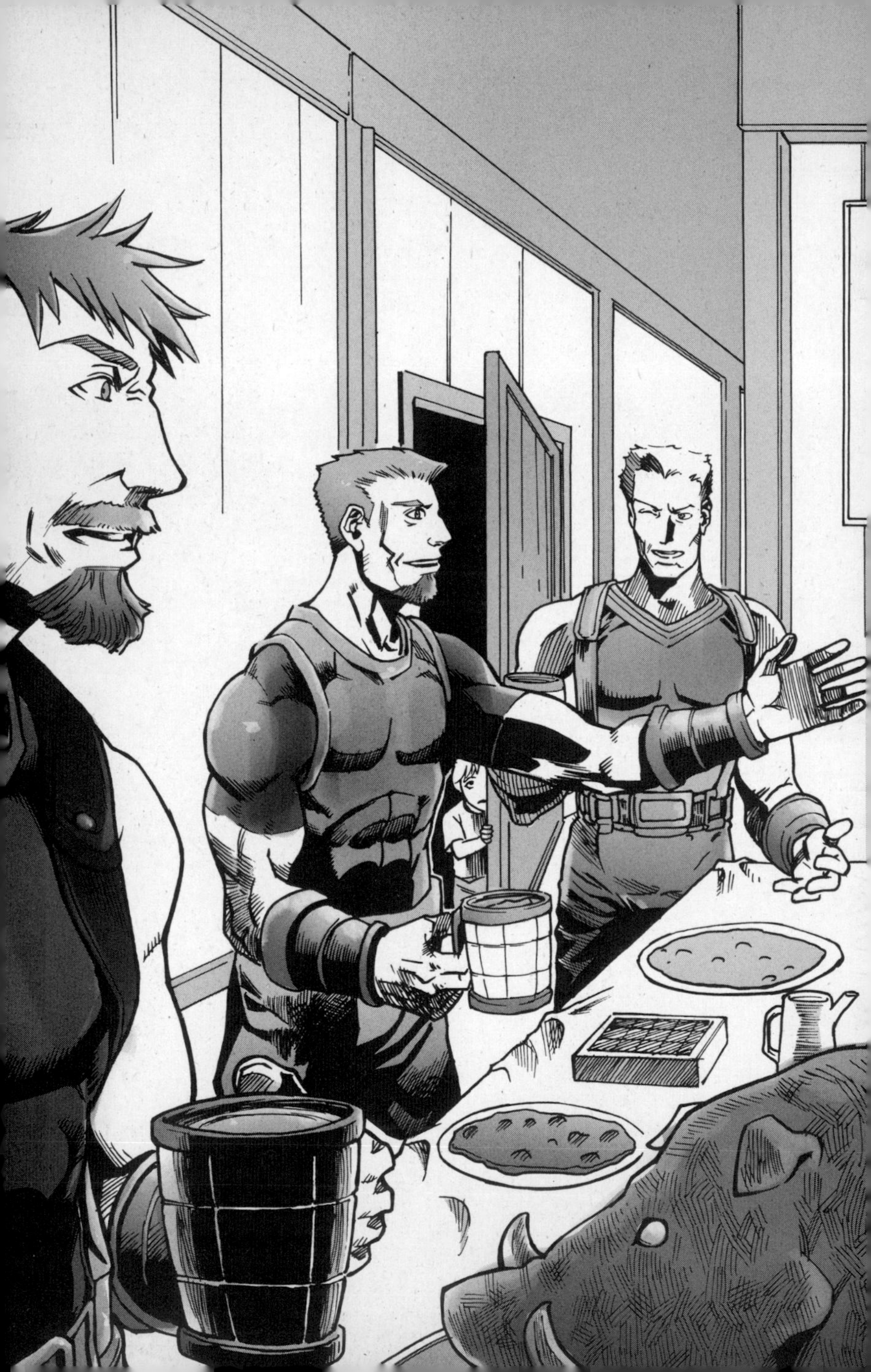

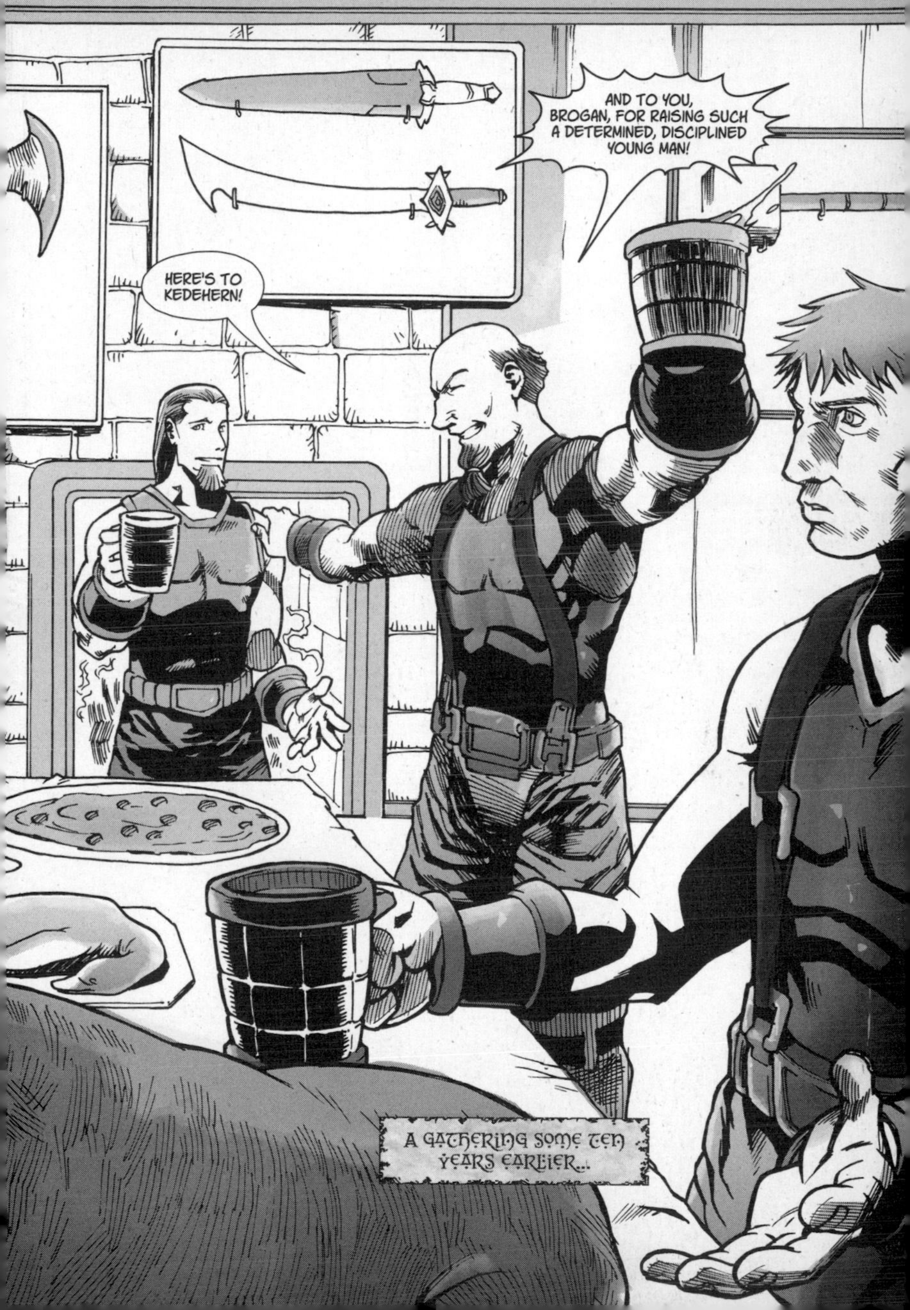
HERE'S TO KEDEHERN!
AND TO YOU, BROGAN, FOR RAISING SUCH A DETERMINED, DISCIPLINED YOUNG MAN!
A GATHERING SOME TEN YEARS EARLIER...

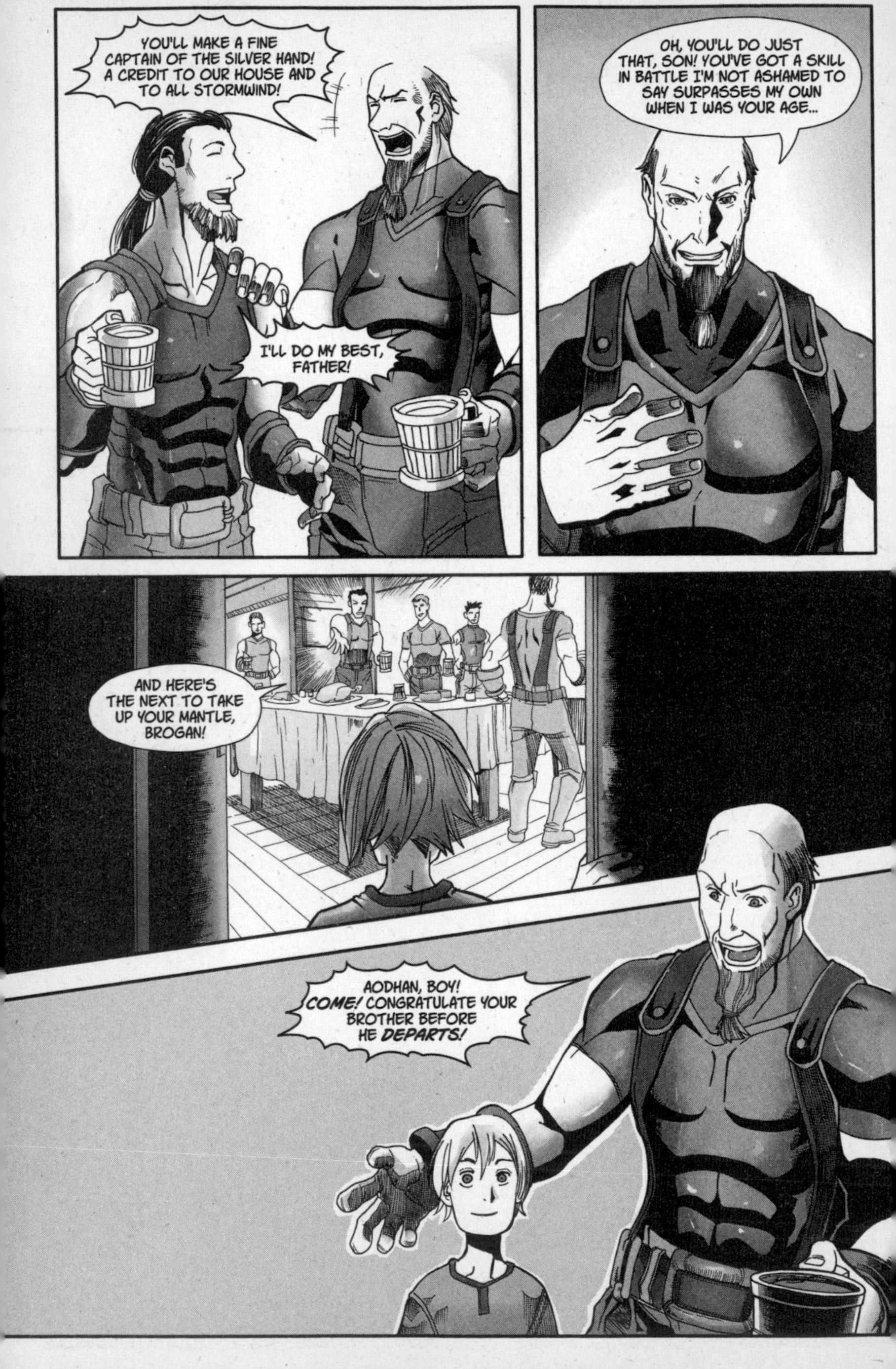
YOU'LL MAKE A FINE CAPTAIN OF THE SILVER HAND! A CREDIT TO OUR HOUSE AND TO ALL STORMWIND!
I'LL DO MY BEST, FATHER!
OH, YOU'LL DO JUST THAT, SON! YOU'VE GOT A SKILL IN BATTLE I'M NOT ASHAMED TO SAY SURPASSES MY OWN WHEN I WAS YOUR AGE...
AND HERE'S THE NEXT TO TAKE UP YOUR MANTLE, BROGAN!
AODHAN, BOY! COME! CONGRATULATE YOUR BROTHER BEFORE HE DEPARTS!

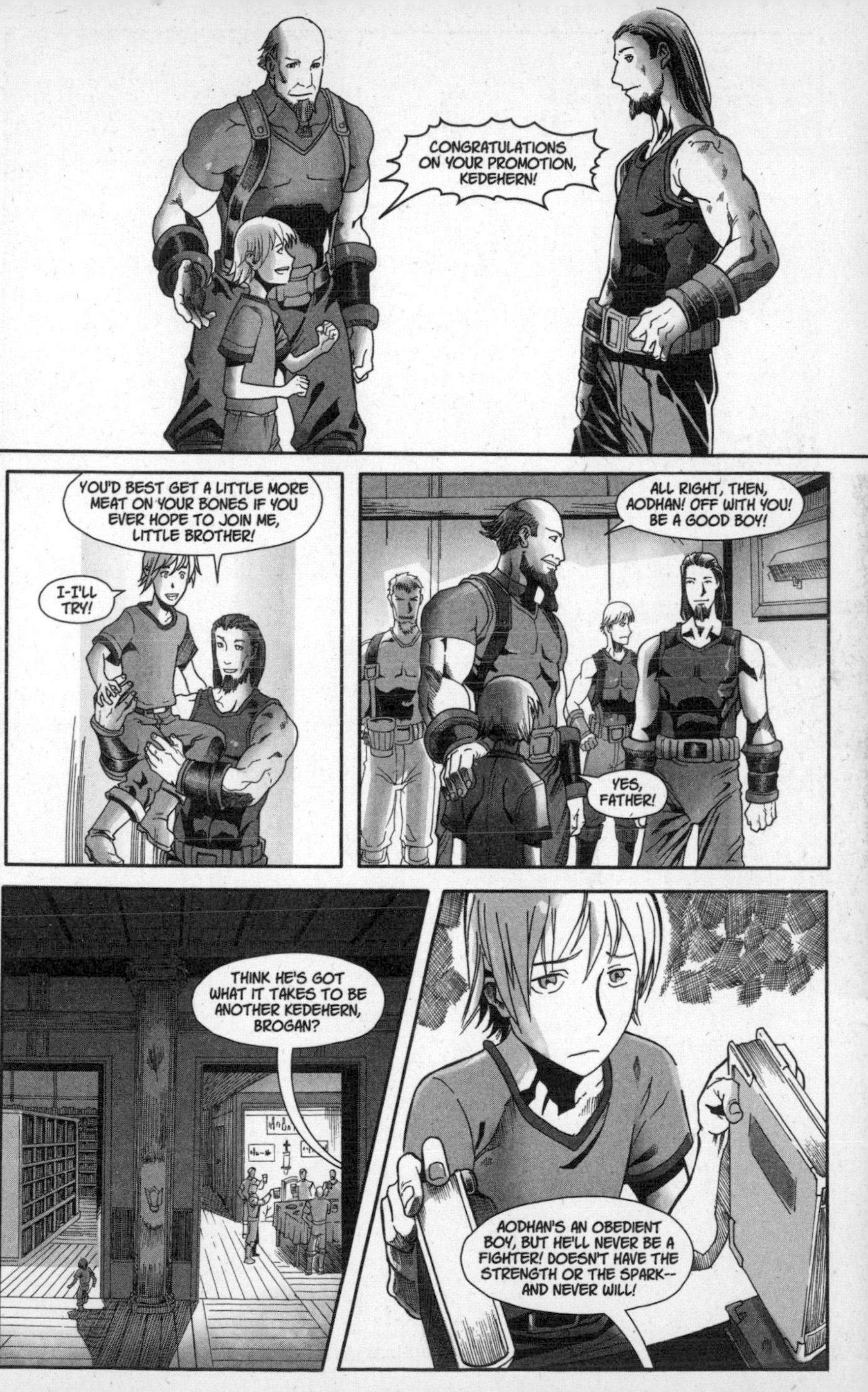
CONGRATULATIONS ON YOUR PROMOTION, KEDEHERN!
YOU'D BEST GET A LITTLE MORE MEAT ON YOUR BONES IF YOU EVER HOPE TO JOIN ME, LITTLE BROTHER!
I-I'LL TRY!
ALL RIGHT, THEN, AODHAN! OFF WITH YOU! BE A GOOD BOY!
YES, FATHER!
THINK HE'S GOT WHAT IT TAKES TO BE ANOTHER KEDEHERN, BROGAN?
AODHAN'S AN OBEDIENT BOY, BUT HE'LL NEVER BE A FIGHTER! DOESN'T HAVE THE STRENGTH OR THE SPARK--AND NEVER WILL!

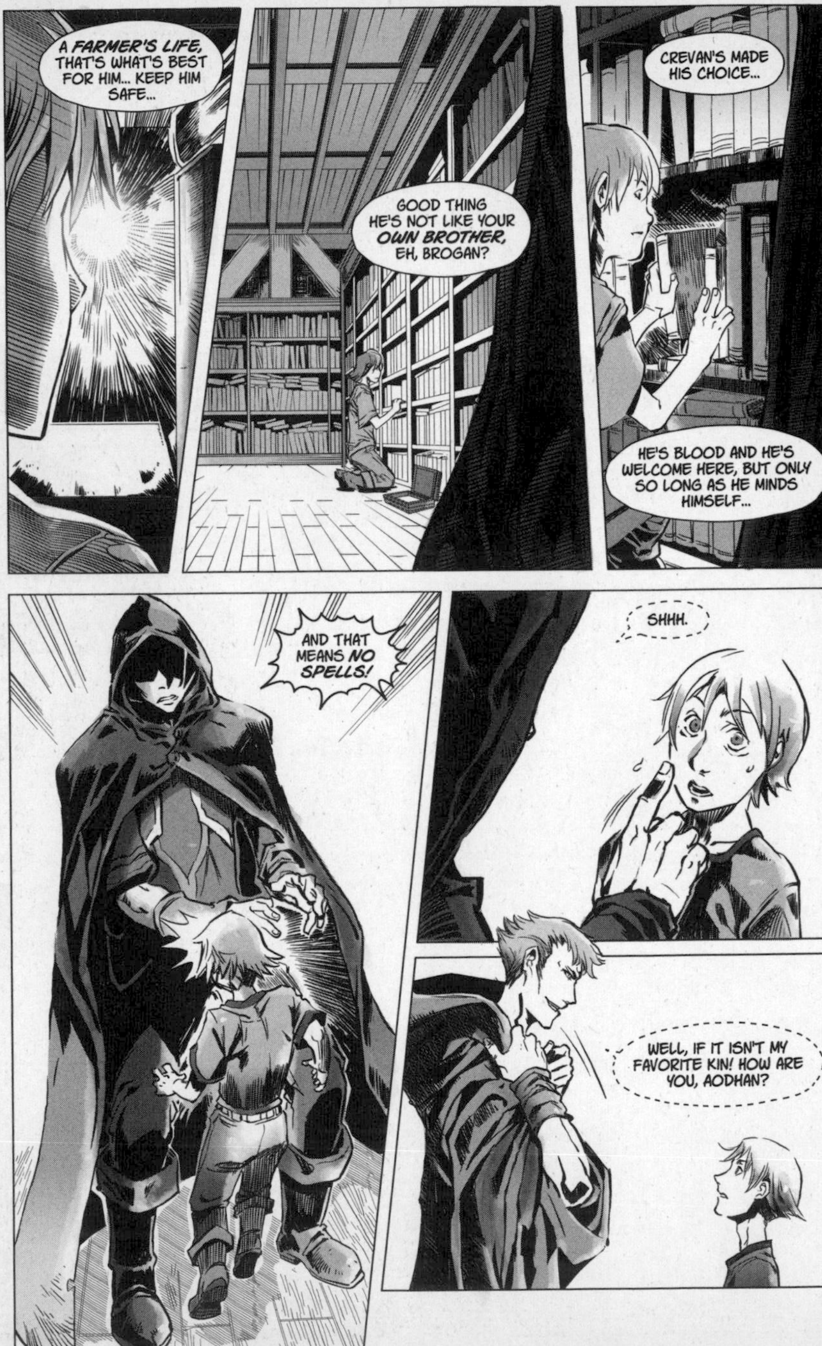
A FARMER'S LIFE, THAT'S WHAT'S BEST FOR HIM... KEEP HIM SAFE...
GOOD THING HE'S NOT LIKE YOUR OWN BROTHER, EH, BROGAN?
CREVAN'S MADE HIS CHOICE...
HE'S BLOOD AND HE'S WELCOME HERE, BUT ONLY SO LONG AS HE MINDS HIMSELF...
AND THAT MEANS NO SPELLS!
SHHH.
WELL, IF IT ISN'T MY FAVORITE KIN! HOW ARE YOU, AODHAN?

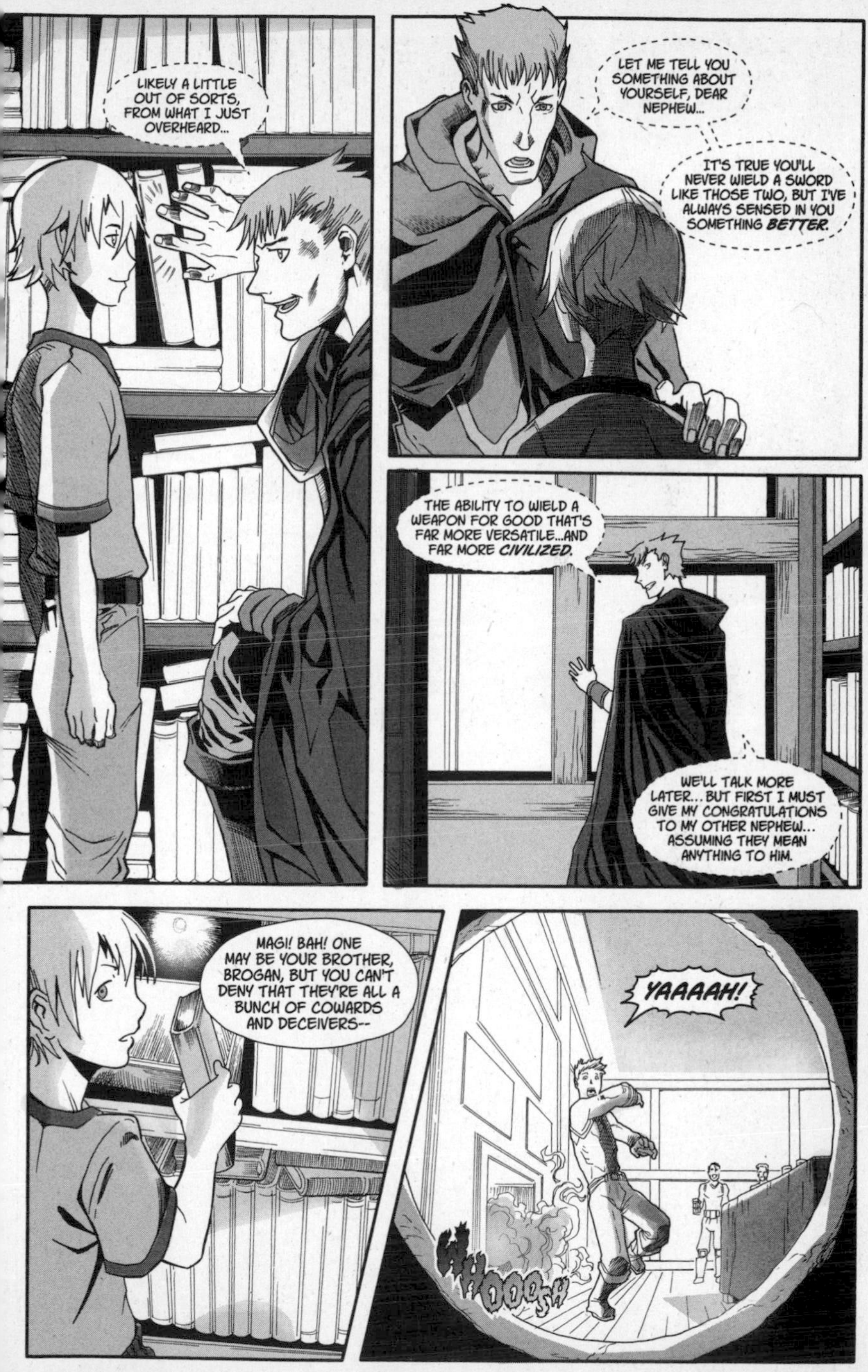
LIKELY A LITTLE OUT OF SORTS, FROM WHAT I JUST OVERHEARD...
LET ME TELL YOU SOMETHING ABOUT YOURSELF, DEAR NEPHEW...
IT'S TRUE YOU'LL NEVER WIELD A SWORD LIKE THOSE TWO, BUT I'VE ALWAYS SENSED IN YOU SOMETHING BETTER.
THE ABILITY TO WIELD A WEAPON FOR GOOD THAT'S FAR MORE VERSATILE...AND FAR MORE CIVILIZED.
WE'LL TALK MORE LATER... BUT FIRST I MUST GIVE MY CONGRATULATIONS TO MY OTHER NEPHEW... ASSUMING THEY MEAN ANYTHING TO HIM.
MAGI! BAH! ONE MAY BE YOUR BROTHER, BROGAN, BUT YOU CAN'T DENY THAT THEY'RE ALL A BUNCH OF COWARDS AND DECEIVERS--
YAAAAH!
WHOOOSH

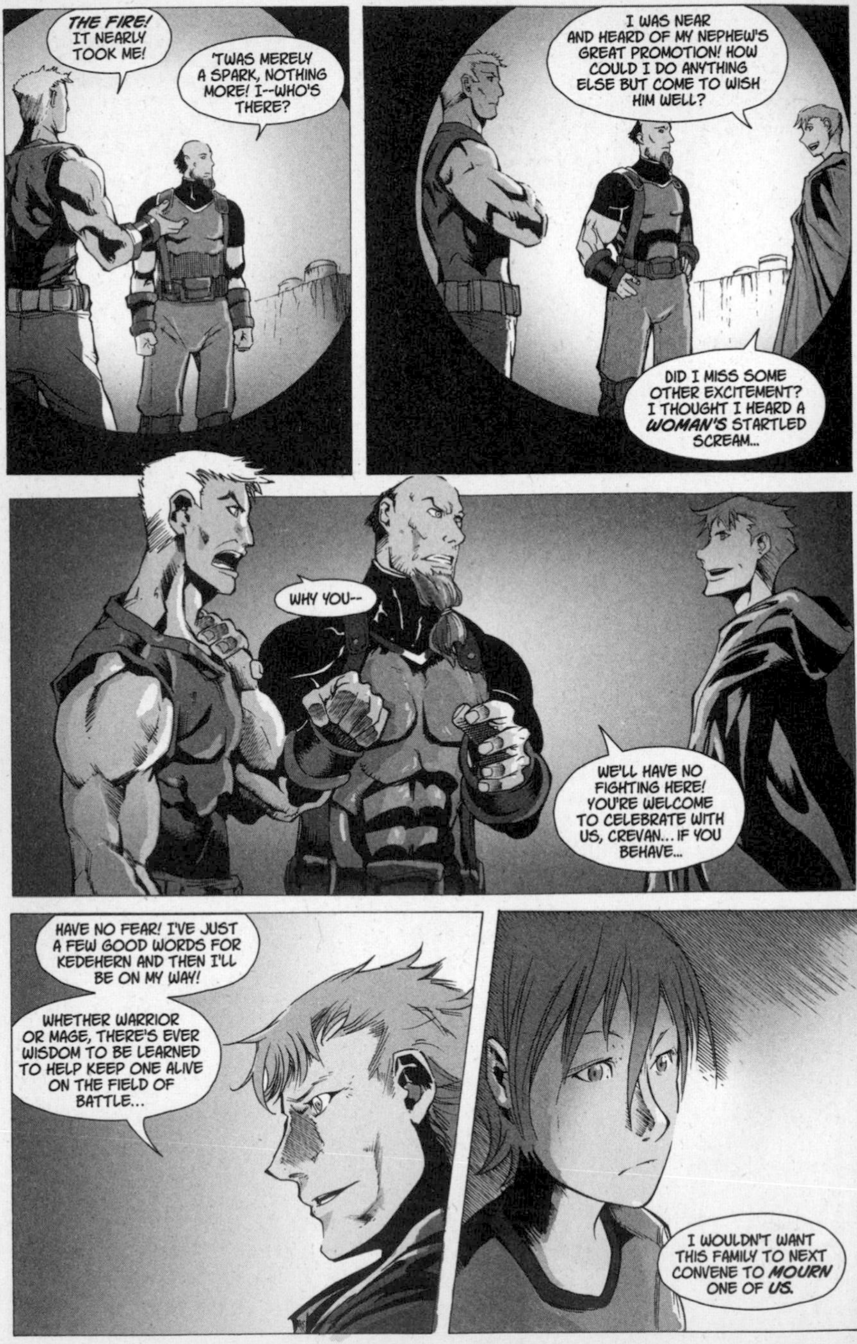
THE FIRE! IT NEARLY TOOK ME!
'TWAS MERELY A SPARK, NOTHING MORE! I--WHO'S THERE?
I WAS NEAR AND HEARD OF MY NEPHEW'S GREAT PROMOTION! HOW COULD I DO ANYTHING ELSE BUT COME TO WISH HIM WELL?
DID I MISS SOME OTHER EXCITEMENT? I THOUGHT I HEARD A WOMAN'S STARTLED SCREAM...
WHY YOU--
WE'LL HAVE NO FIGHTING HERE! YOU'RE WELCOME TO CELEBRATE WITH US, CREVAN... IF YOU BEHAVE...
HAVE NO FEAR! I'VE JUST A FEW GOOD WORDS FOR KEDEHERN AND THEN I'LL BE ON MY WAY!
WHETHER WARRIOR OR MAGE, THERE'S EVER WISDOM TO BE LEARNED TO HELP KEEP ONE ALIVE ON THE FIELD OF BATTLE...
I WOULDN'T WANT THIS FAMILY TO NEXT CONVENE TO MOURN ONE OF US.

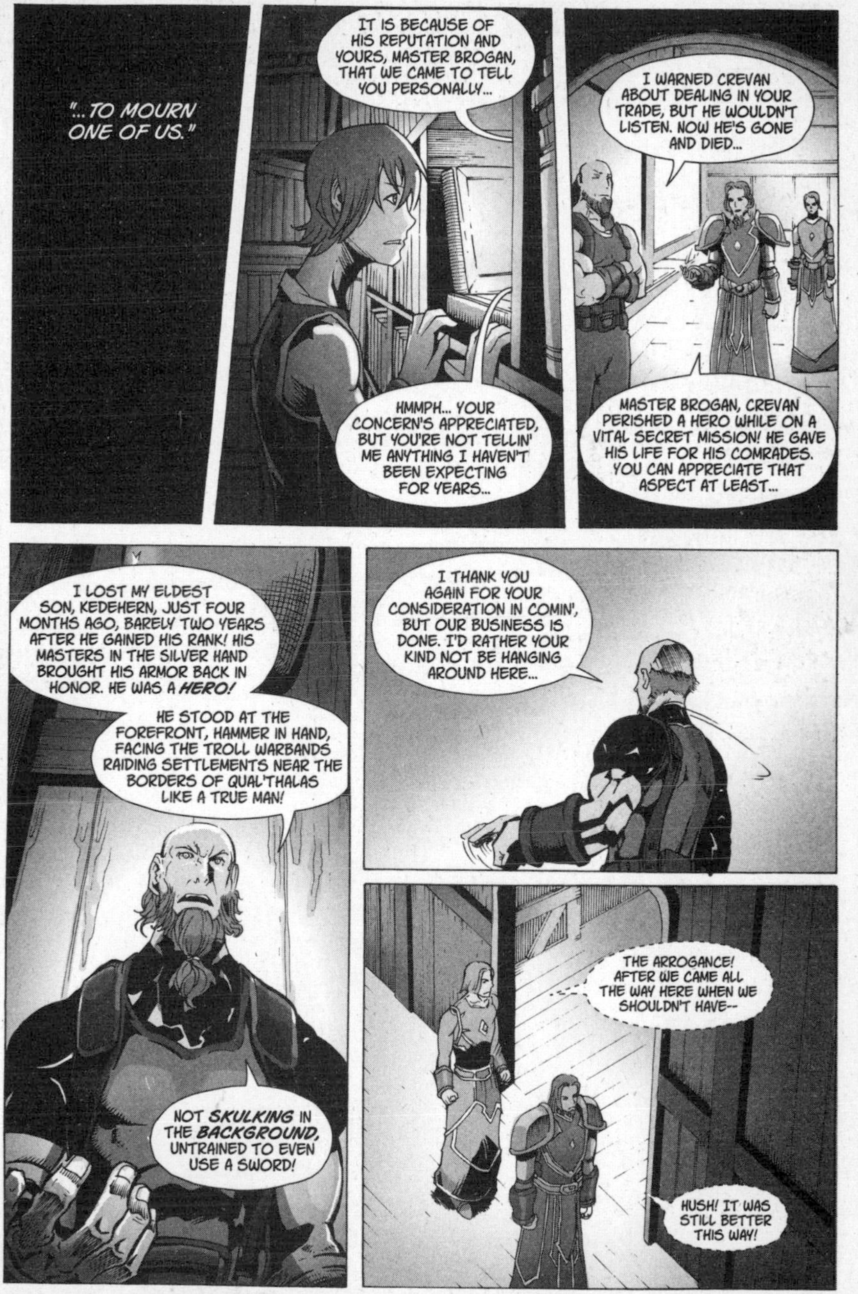
"...TO MOURN ONE OF US."
IT IS BECAUSE OF HIS REPUTATION AND YOURS, MASTER BROGAN, THAT WE CAME TO TELL YOU PERSONALLY...
HMMPH... YOUR CONCERN'S APPRECIATED, BUT YOU'RE NOT TELLIN' ME ANYTHING I HAVEN'T BEEN EXPECTING FOR YEARS...
I WARNED CREVAN ABOUT DEALING IN YOUR TRADE, BUT HE WOULDN'T LISTEN. NOW HE'S GONE AND DIED...
MASTER BROGAN, CREVAN PERISHED A HERO WHILE ON A VITAL SECRET MISSION! HE GAVE HIS LIFE FOR HIS COMRADES. YOU CAN APPRECIATE THAT ASPECT AT LEAST...
I LOST MY ELDEST SON, KEDEHERN, JUST FOUR MONTHS AGO, BARELY TWO YEARS AFTER HE GAINED HIS RANK! HIS MASTERS IN THE SILVER HAND BROUGHT HIS ARMOR BACK IN HONOR. HE WAS A ***HERO!***
HE STOOD AT THE FOREFRONT, HAMMER IN HAND, FACING THE TROLL WARBANDS RAIDING SETTLEMENTS NEAR THE BORDERS OF QUAL'THALAS LIKE A TRUE MAN!
NOT ***SKULKING*** IN THE ***BACKGROUND,*** UNTRAINED TO EVEN USE A SWORD!
I THANK YOU AGAIN FOR YOUR CONSIDERATION IN COMIN', BUT OUR BUSINESS IS DONE. I'D RATHER YOUR KIND NOT BE HANGING AROUND HERE...
THE ARROGANCE! AFTER WE CAME ALL THE WAY HERE WHEN WE SHOULDN'T HAVE--
HUSH! IT WAS STILL BETTER THIS WAY!

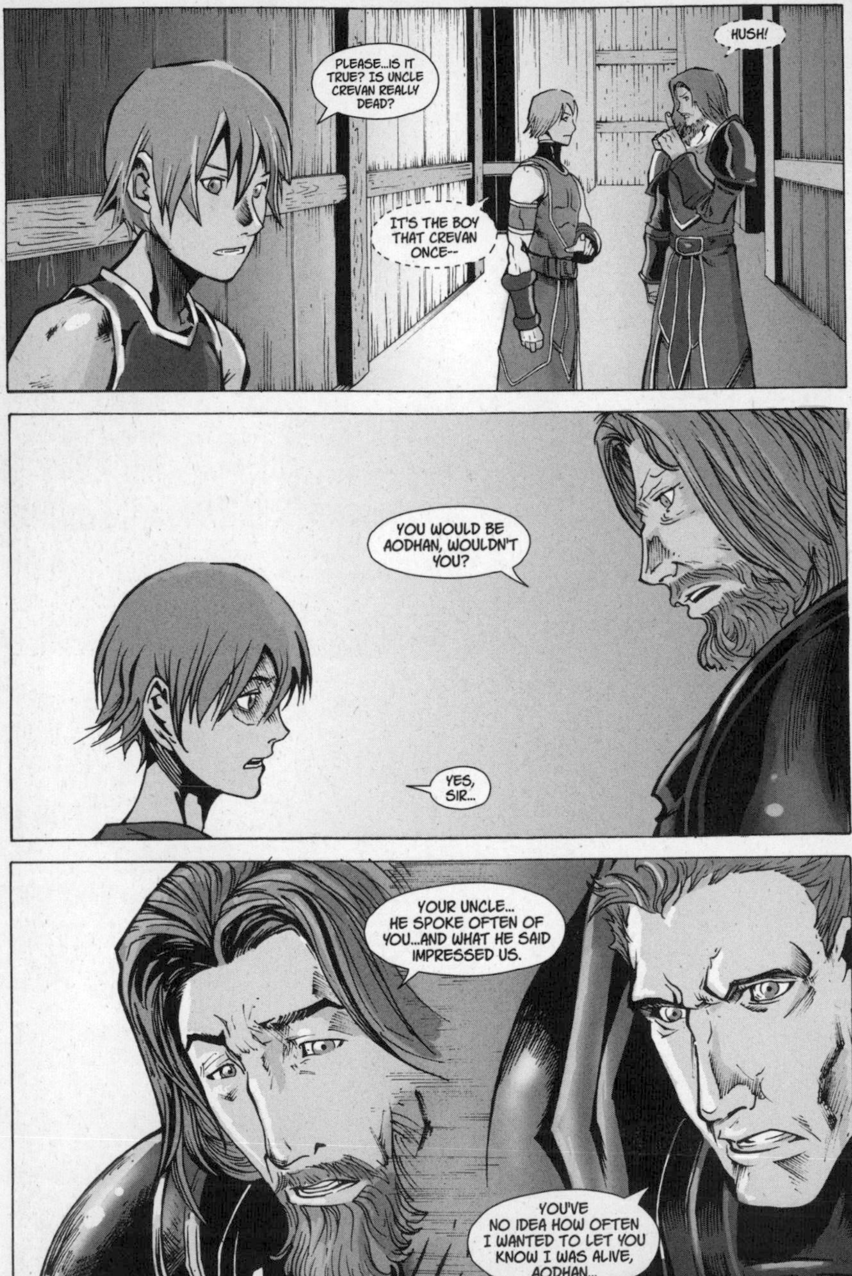
PLEASE...IS IT TRUE? IS UNCLE CREVAN REALLY DEAD?
IT'S THE BOY THAT CREVAN ONCE--
HUSH!
YOU WOULD BE AODHAN, WOULDN'T YOU?
YES, SIR...
YOUR UNCLE... HE SPOKE OFTEN OF YOU...AND WHAT HE SAID IMPRESSED US.
YOU'VE NO IDEA HOW OFTEN I WANTED TO LET YOU KNOW I WAS ALIVE, AODHAN...

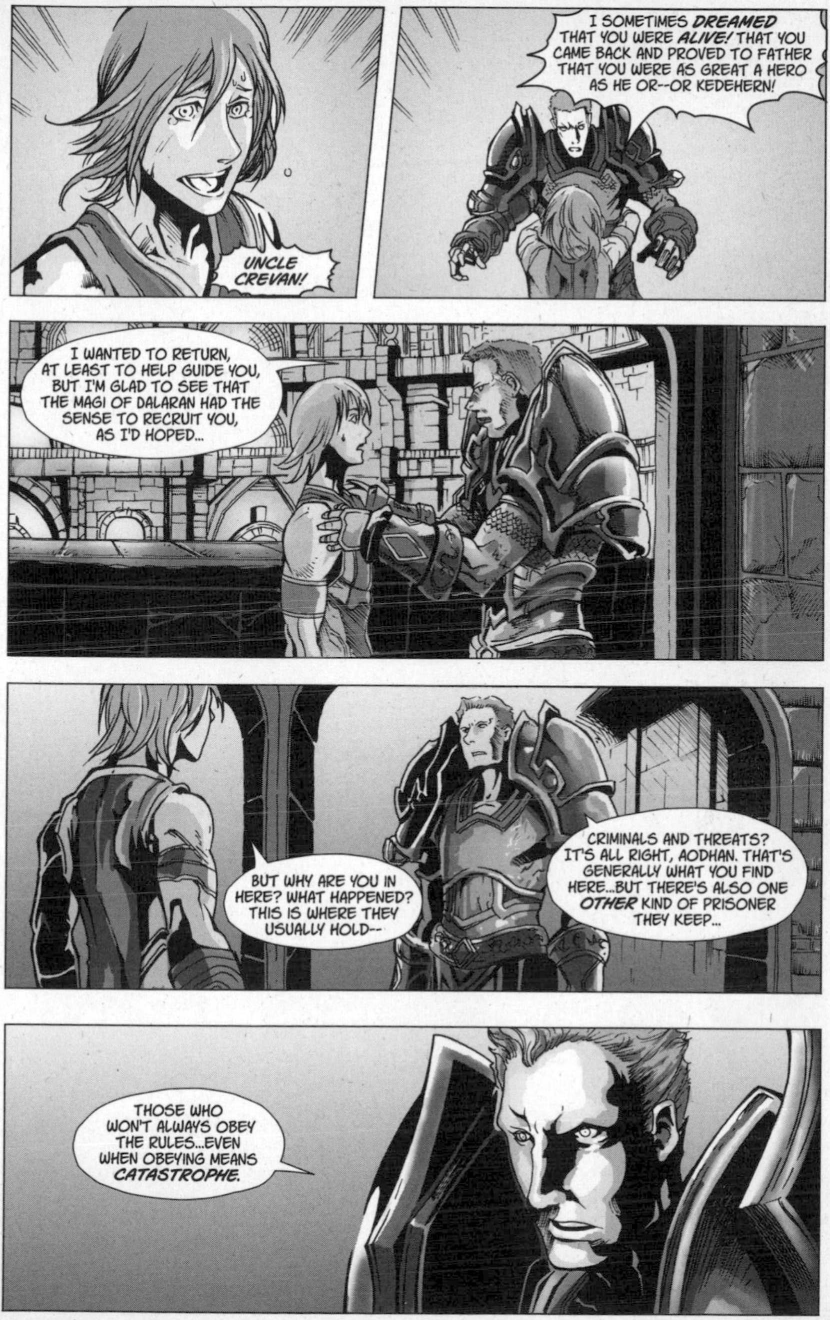
UNCLE CREVAN!
I SOMETIMES DREAMED THAT YOU WERE ALIVE! THAT YOU CAME BACK AND PROVED TO FATHER THAT YOU WERE AS GREAT A HERO AS HE OR--OR KEDEHERN!
I WANTED TO RETURN, AT LEAST TO HELP GUIDE YOU, BUT I'M GLAD TO SEE THAT THE MAGI OF DALARAN HAD THE SENSE TO RECRUIT YOU, AS I'D HOPED...
BUT WHY ARE YOU IN HERE? WHAT HAPPENED? THIS IS WHERE THEY USUALLY HOLD--
CRIMINALS AND THREATS? IT'S ALL RIGHT, AODHAN. THAT'S GENERALLY WHAT YOU FIND HERE...BUT THERE'S ALSO ONE OTHER KIND OF PRISONER THEY KEEP...
THOSE WHO WON'T ALWAYS OBEY THE RULES...EVEN WHEN OBEYING MEANS CATASTROPHE.

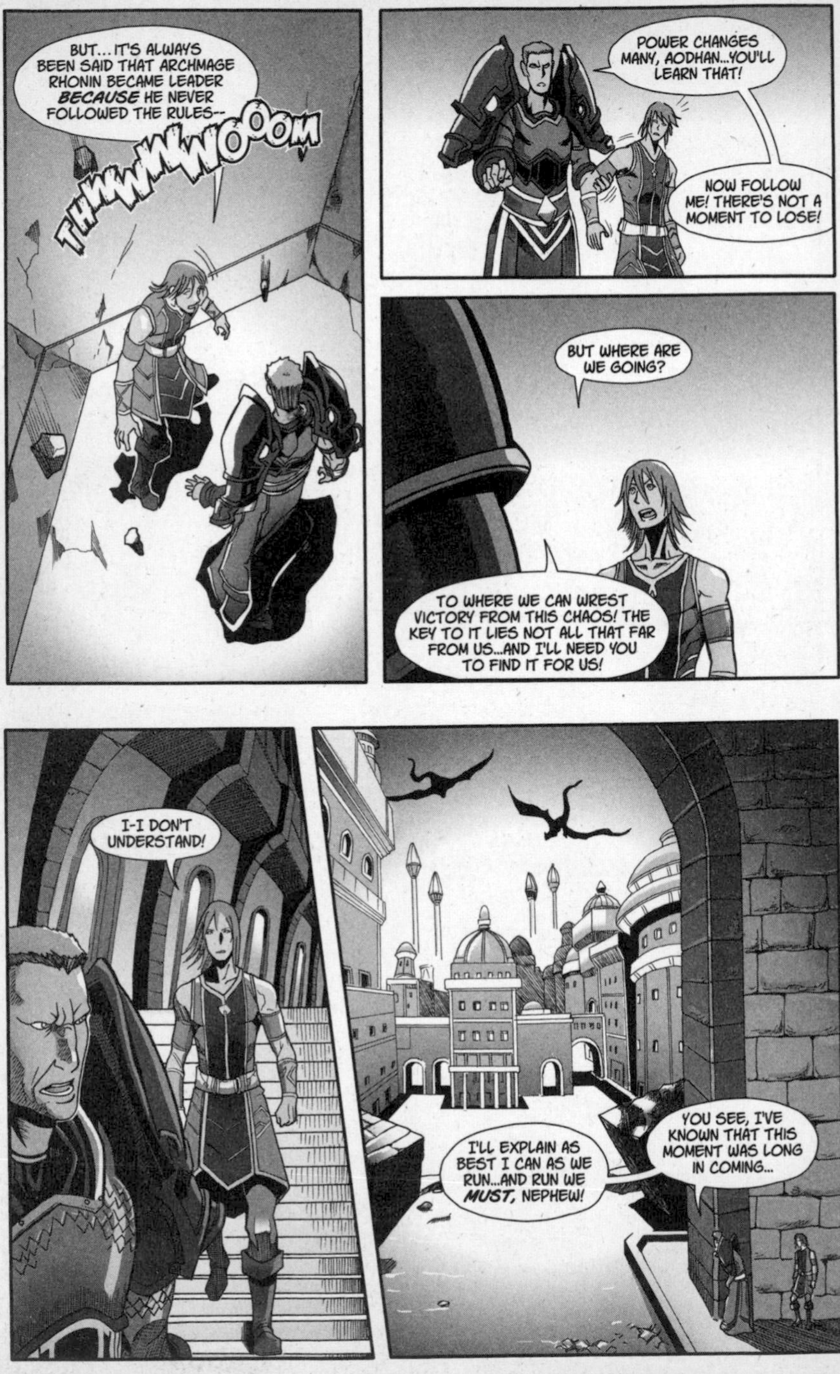
BUT... IT'S ALWAYS BEEN SAID THAT ARCHMAGE RHONIN BECAME LEADER *BECAUSE* HE NEVER FOLLOWED THE RULES--
THWWWWOOOM
POWER CHANGES MANY, AODHAN...YOU'LL LEARN THAT!
NOW FOLLOW ME! THERE'S NOT A MOMENT TO LOSE!
BUT WHERE ARE WE GOING?
TO WHERE WE CAN WREST VICTORY FROM THIS CHAOS! THE KEY TO IT LIES NOT ALL THAT FAR FROM US...AND I'LL NEED YOU TO FIND IT FOR US!
I-I DON'T UNDERSTAND!
I'LL EXPLAIN AS BEST I CAN AS WE RUN...AND RUN WE *MUST,* NEPHEW!
YOU SEE, I'VE KNOWN THAT THIS MOMENT WAS LONG IN COMING...

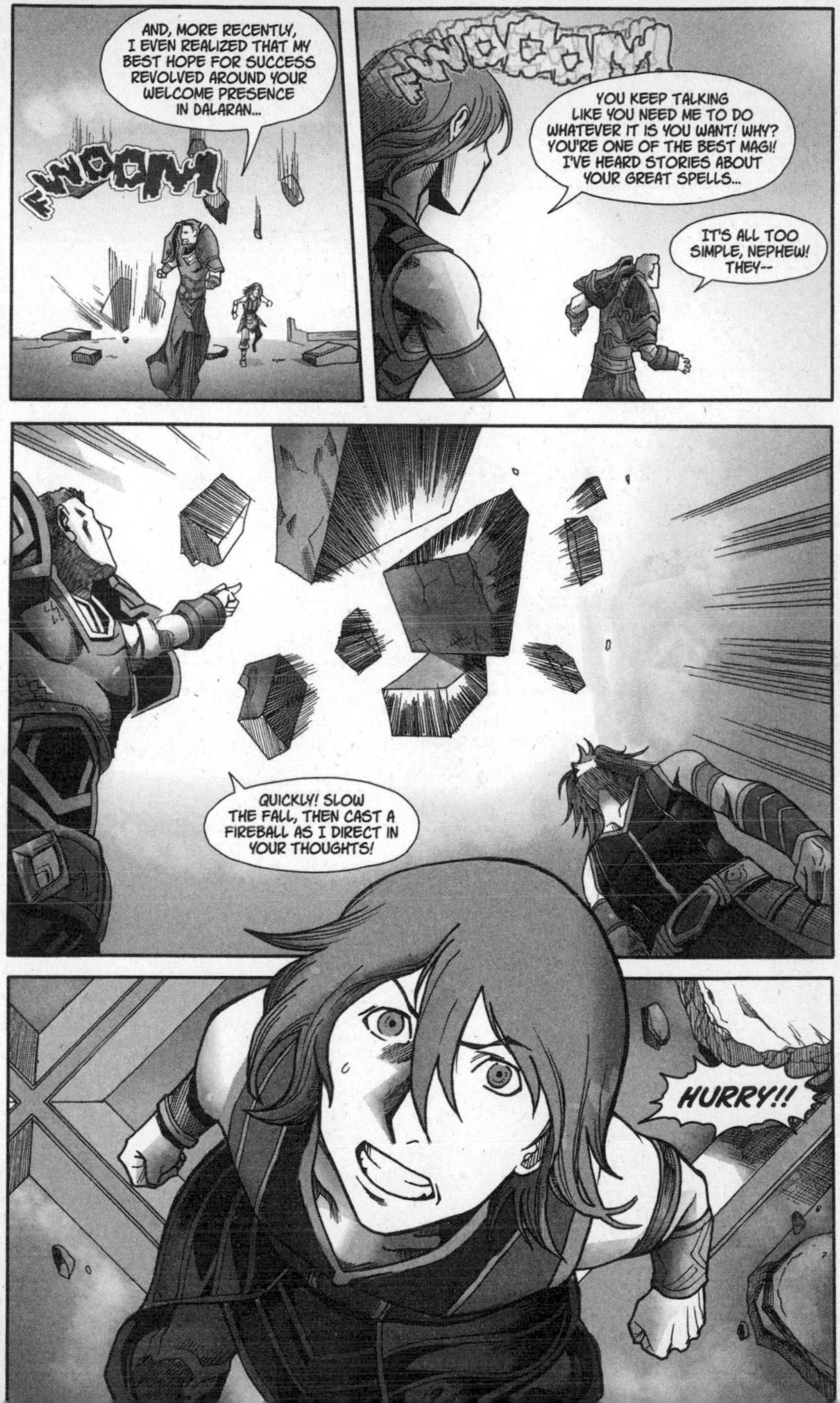
AND, MORE RECENTLY, I EVEN REALIZED THAT MY BEST HOPE FOR SUCCESS REVOLVED AROUND YOUR WELCOME PRESENCE IN DALARAN...
FWOOOM
FWOOOOM
YOU KEEP TALKING LIKE YOU NEED ME TO DO WHATEVER IT IS YOU WANT! WHY? YOU'RE ONE OF THE BEST MAGI! I'VE HEARD STORIES ABOUT YOUR GREAT SPELLS...
IT'S ALL TOO SIMPLE, NEPHEW! THEY--
QUICKLY! SLOW THE FALL, THEN CAST A FIREBALL AS I DIRECT IN YOUR THOUGHTS!
HURRY!!

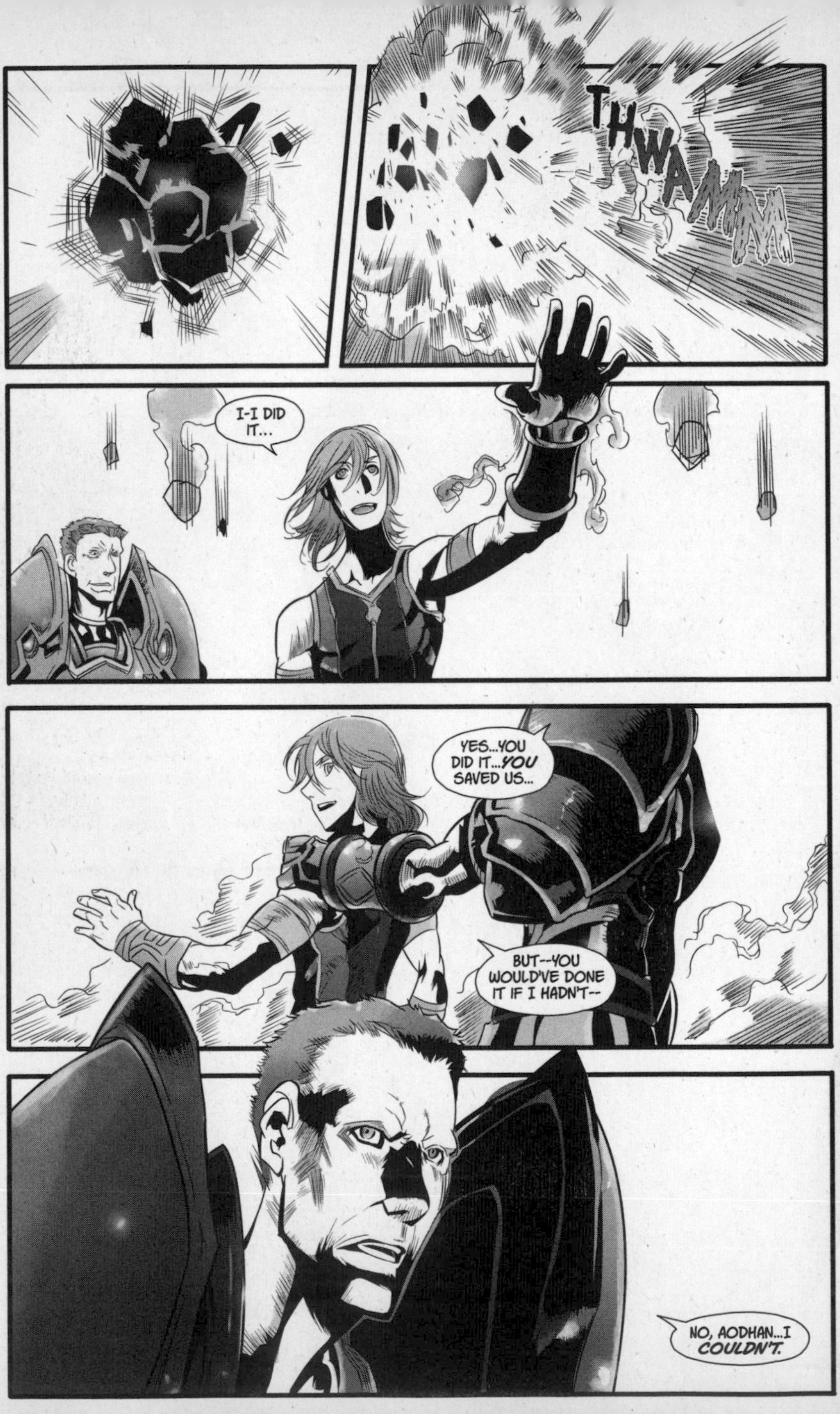
THWAMMM
I-I DID IT...
YES...YOU DID IT...YOU SAVED US...
BUT--YOU WOULD'VE DONE IT IF I HADN'T--
NO, AODHAN...I COULDN'T.

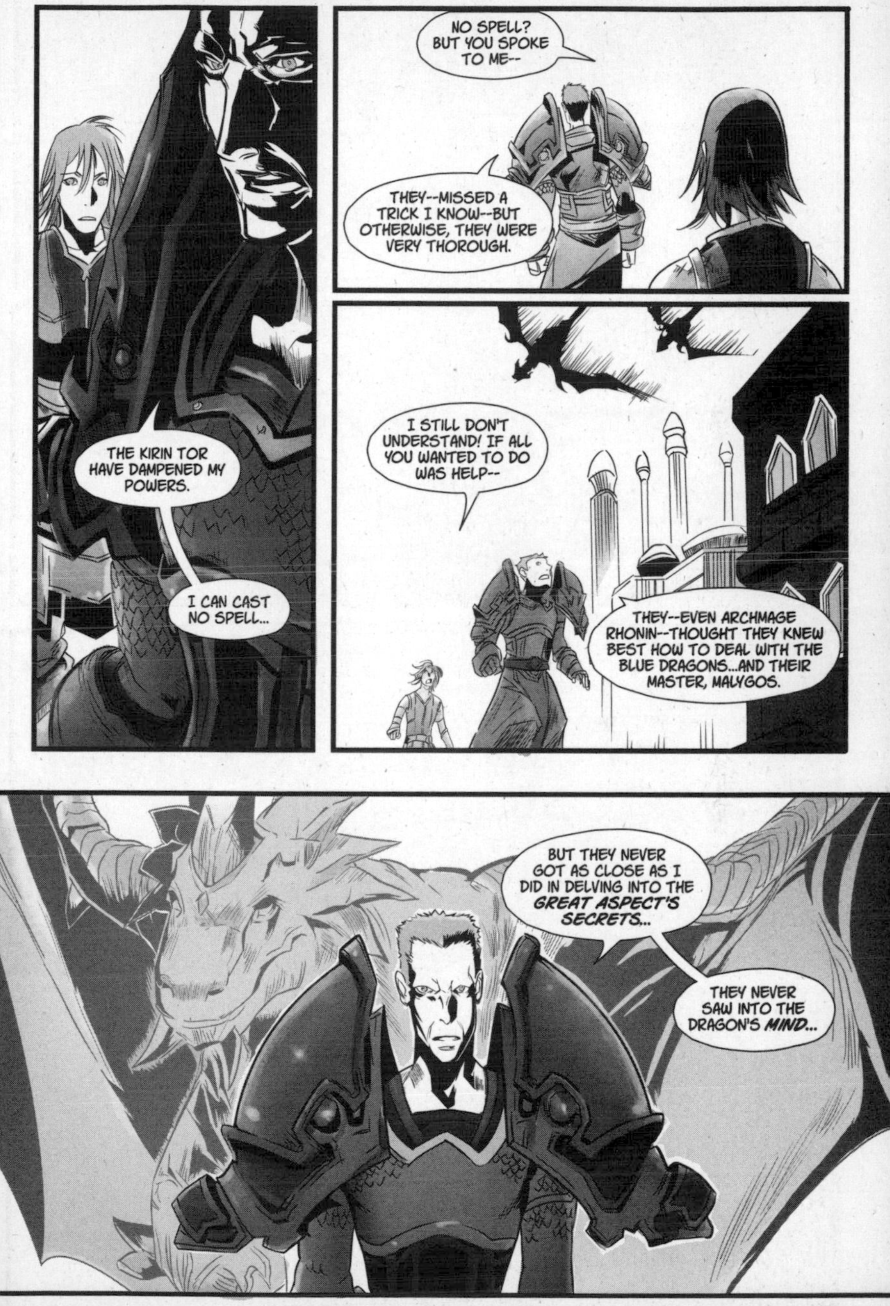
THE KIRIN TOR HAVE DAMPENED MY POWERS.
I CAN CAST NO SPELL...
NO SPELL? BUT YOU SPOKE TO ME--
THEY--MISSED A TRICK I KNOW--BUT OTHERWISE, THEY WERE VERY THOROUGH.
I STILL DON'T UNDERSTAND! IF ALL YOU WANTED TO DO WAS HELP--
THEY--EVEN ARCHMAGE RHONIN--THOUGHT THEY KNEW BEST HOW TO DEAL WITH THE BLUE DRAGONS...AND THEIR MASTER, MALYGOS.
BUT THEY NEVER GOT AS CLOSE AS I DID IN DELVING INTO THE ***GREAT ASPECT'S SECRETS...***
THEY NEVER SAW INTO THE DRAGON'S ***MIND...***

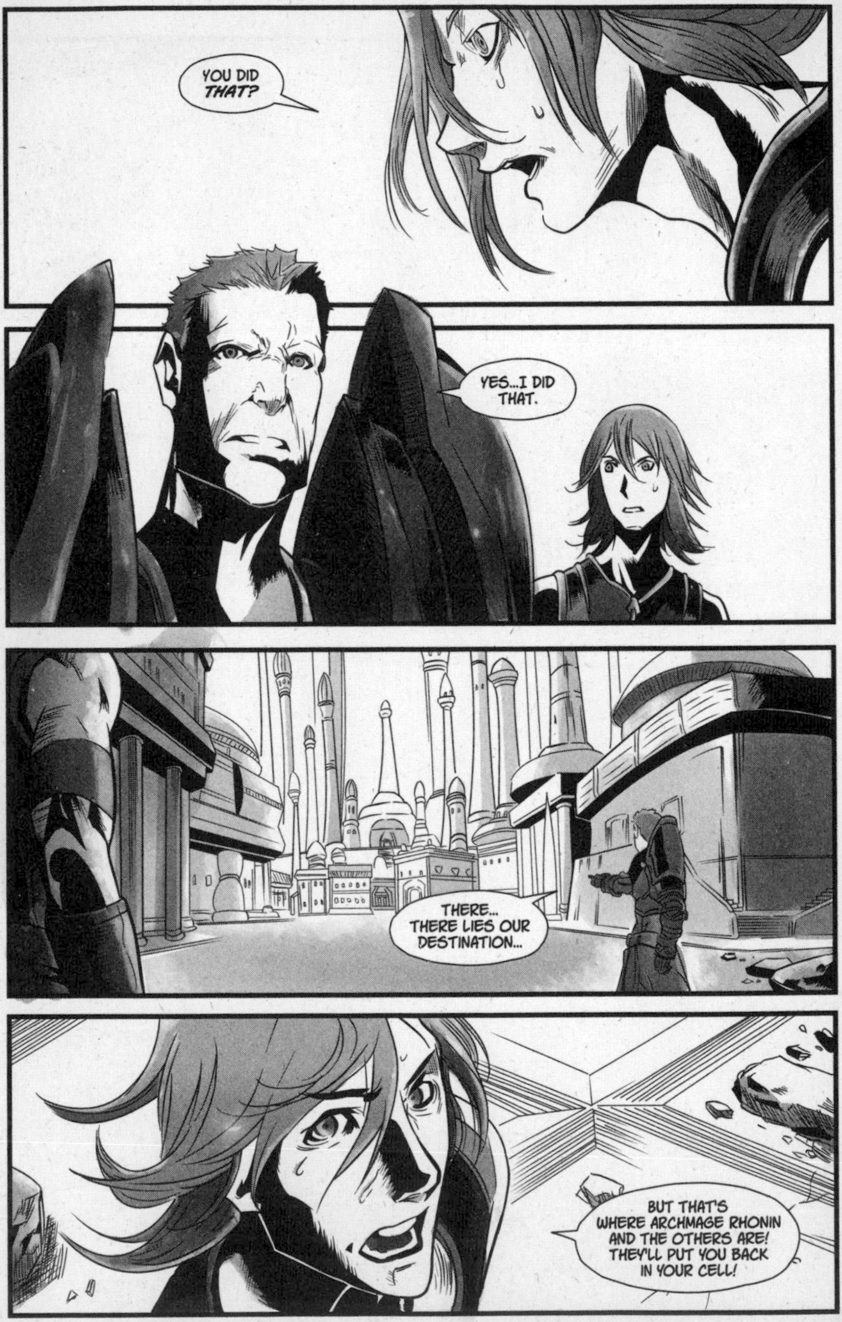

YOU DID *THAT?*
YES...I DID THAT.
THERE... THERE LIES OUR DESTINATION...
BUT THAT'S WHERE ARCHMAGE RHONIN AND THE OTHERS ARE! THEY'LL PUT YOU BACK IN YOUR CELL!

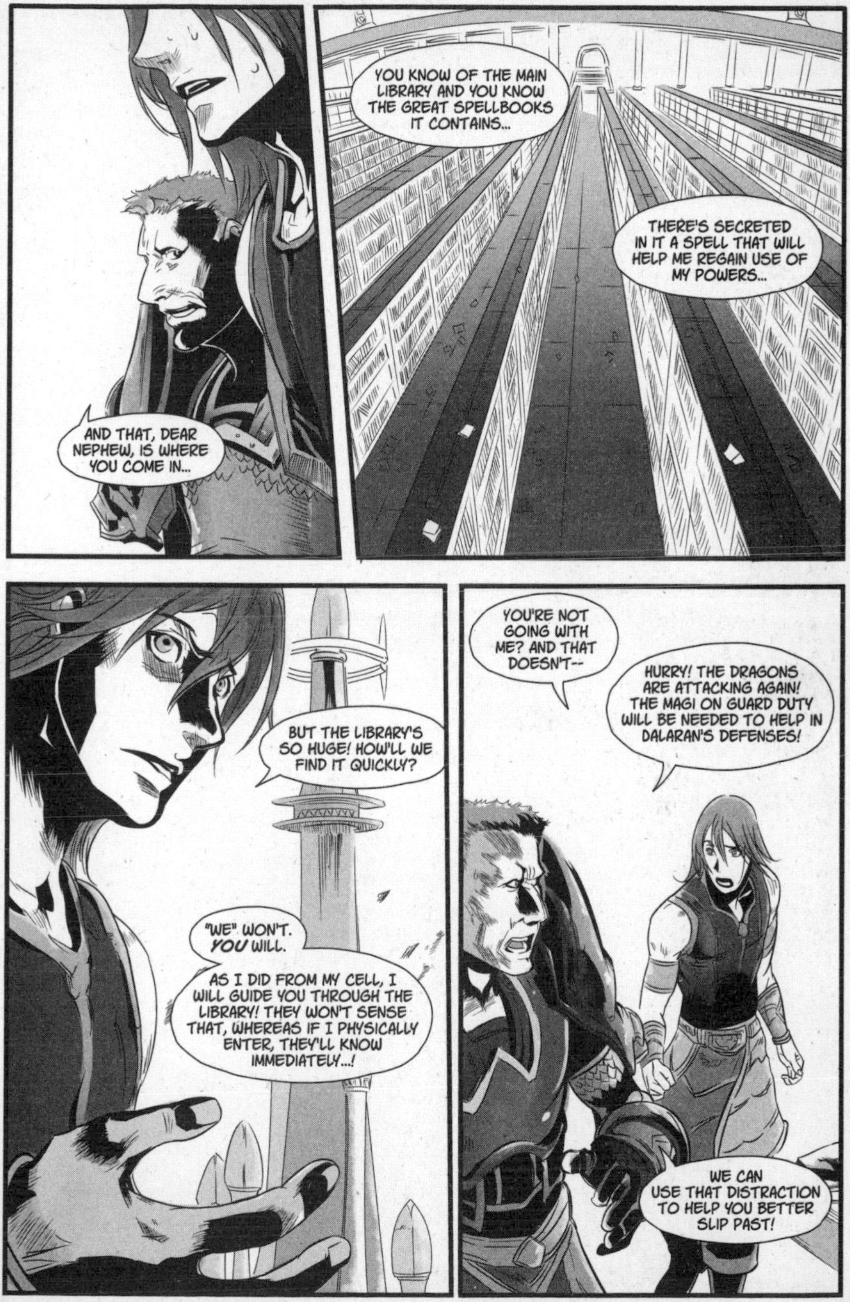
YOU KNOW OF THE MAIN LIBRARY AND YOU KNOW THE GREAT SPELLBOOKS IT CONTAINS...
THERE'S SECRETED IN IT A SPELL THAT WILL HELP ME REGAIN USE OF MY POWERS...
AND THAT, DEAR NEPHEW, IS WHERE YOU COME IN...
BUT THE LIBRARY'S SO HUGE! HOW'LL WE FIND IT QUICKLY?
"WE" WON'T. YOU WILL.
AS I DID FROM MY CELL, I WILL GUIDE YOU THROUGH THE LIBRARY! THEY WON'T SENSE THAT, WHEREAS IF I PHYSICALLY ENTER, THEY'LL KNOW IMMEDIATELY...!
YOU'RE NOT GOING WITH ME? AND THAT DOESN'T--
HURRY! THE DRAGONS ARE ATTACKING AGAIN! THE MAGI ON GUARD DUTY WILL BE NEEDED TO HELP IN DALARAN'S DEFENSES!
WE CAN USE THAT DISTRACTION TO HELP YOU BETTER SLIP PAST!

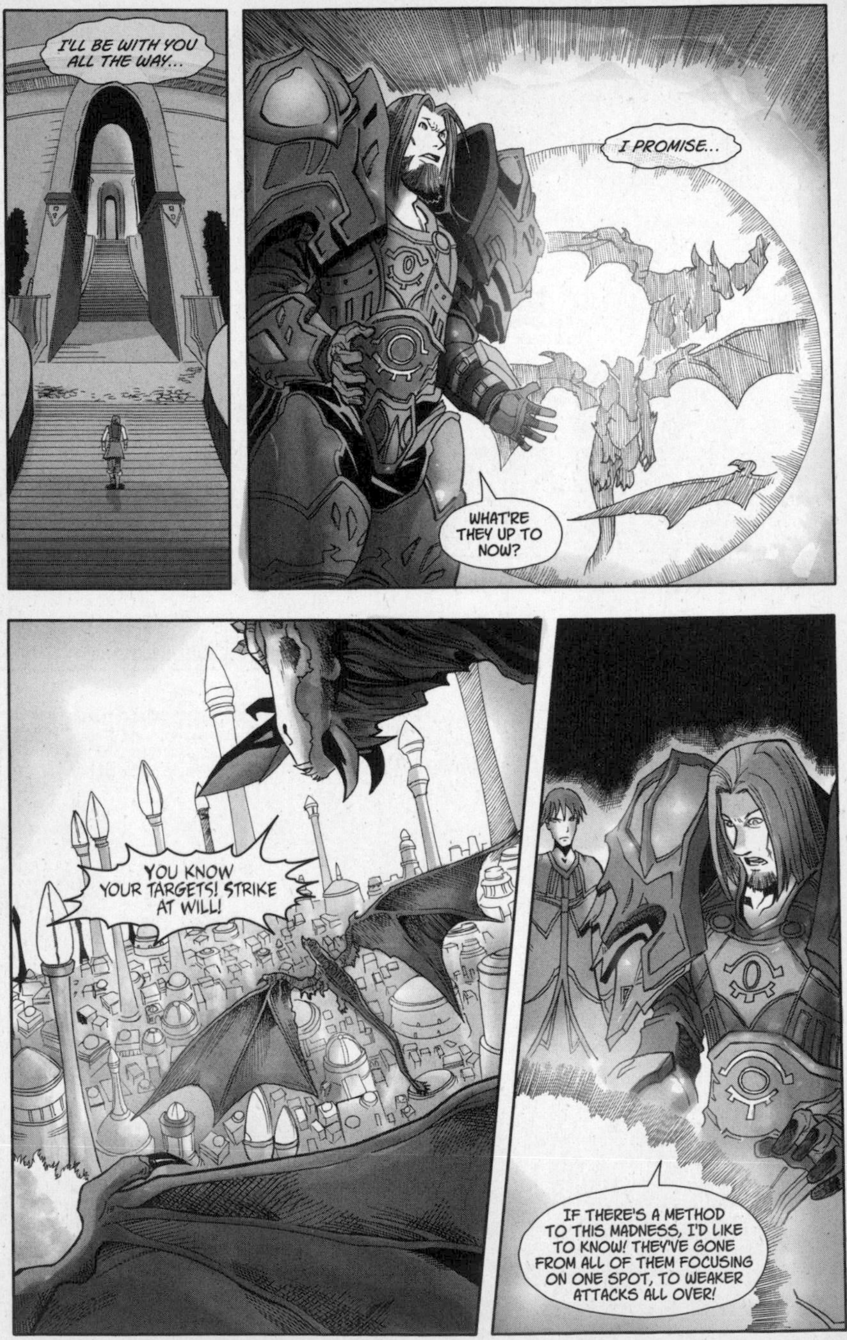
I'LL BE WITH YOU ALL THE WAY...
I PROMISE...
WHAT'RE THEY UP TO NOW?
YOU KNOW YOUR TARGETS! STRIKE AT WILL!
IF THERE'S A METHOD TO THIS MADNESS, I'D LIKE TO KNOW! THEY'VE GONE FROM ALL OF THEM FOCUSING ON ONE SPOT, TO WEAKER ATTACKS ALL OVER!

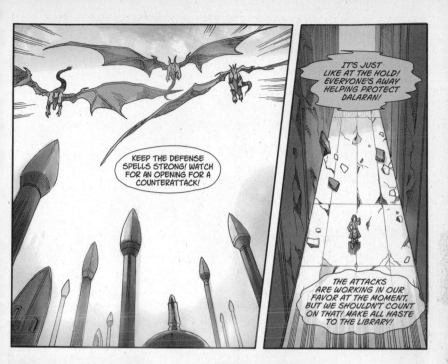

KEEP THE DEFENSE SPELLS STRONG! WATCH FOR AN OPENING FOR A COUNTERATTACK!

IT'S JUST LIKE AT THE HOLD! EVERYONE'S AWAY HELPING PROTECT DALARAN!

THE ATTACKS ARE WORKING IN OUR FAVOR AT THE MOMENT, BUT WE SHOULDN'T COUNT ON THAT! MAKE ALL HASTE TO THE LIBRARY!

THE ATTACK IS GETTING WORSE AGAIN!

WE'RE HERE, UNCLE!

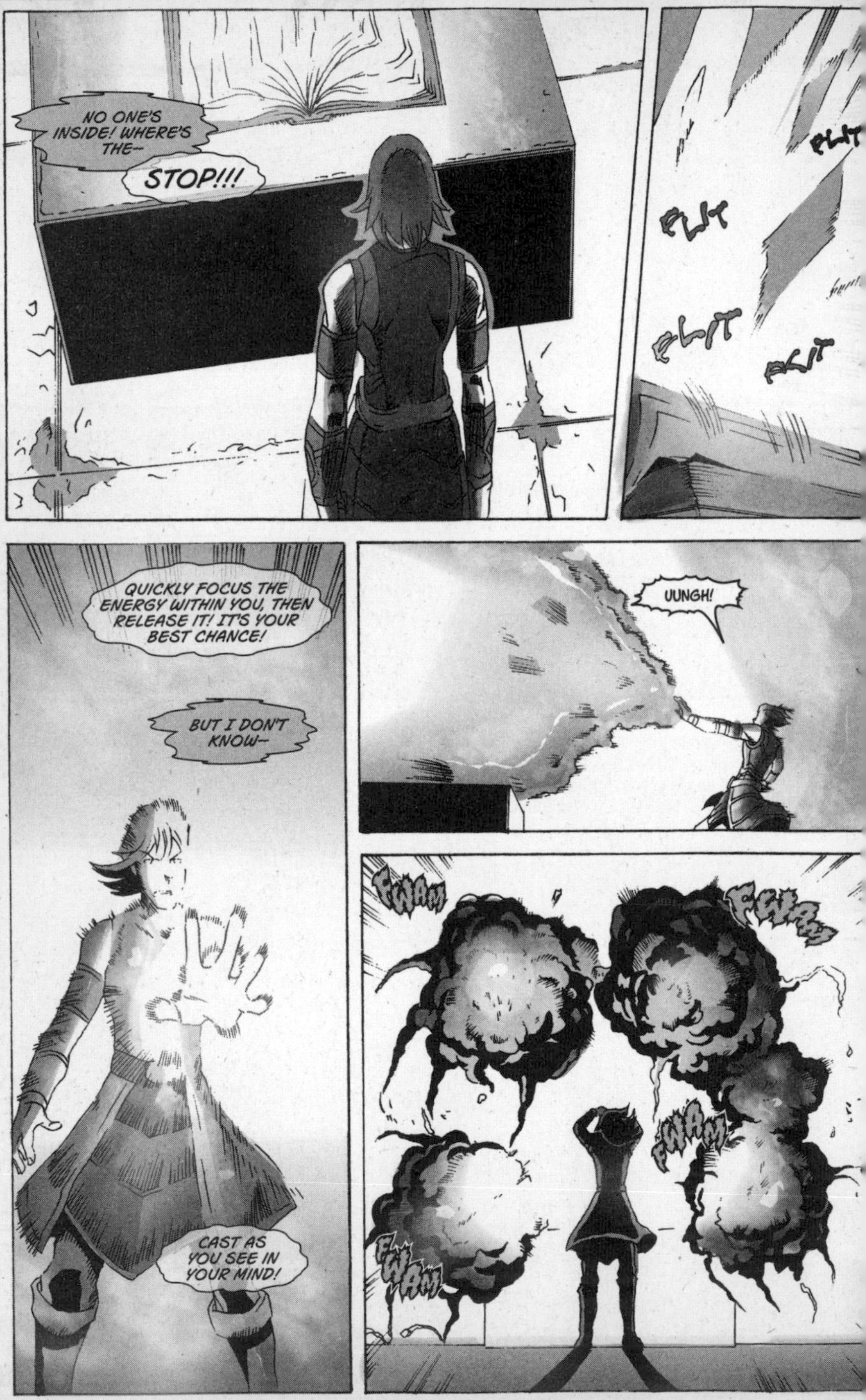
NO ONE'S INSIDE! WHERE'S THE–
STOP!!!
FLIT
FLIT
FLIT
FLIT
QUICKLY FOCUS THE ENERGY WITHIN YOU, THEN RELEASE IT! IT'S YOUR BEST CHANCE!
BUT I DON'T KNOW–
CAST AS YOU SEE IN YOUR MIND!
UUNGH!
FWAM
FWAM
FWAM
FWAM

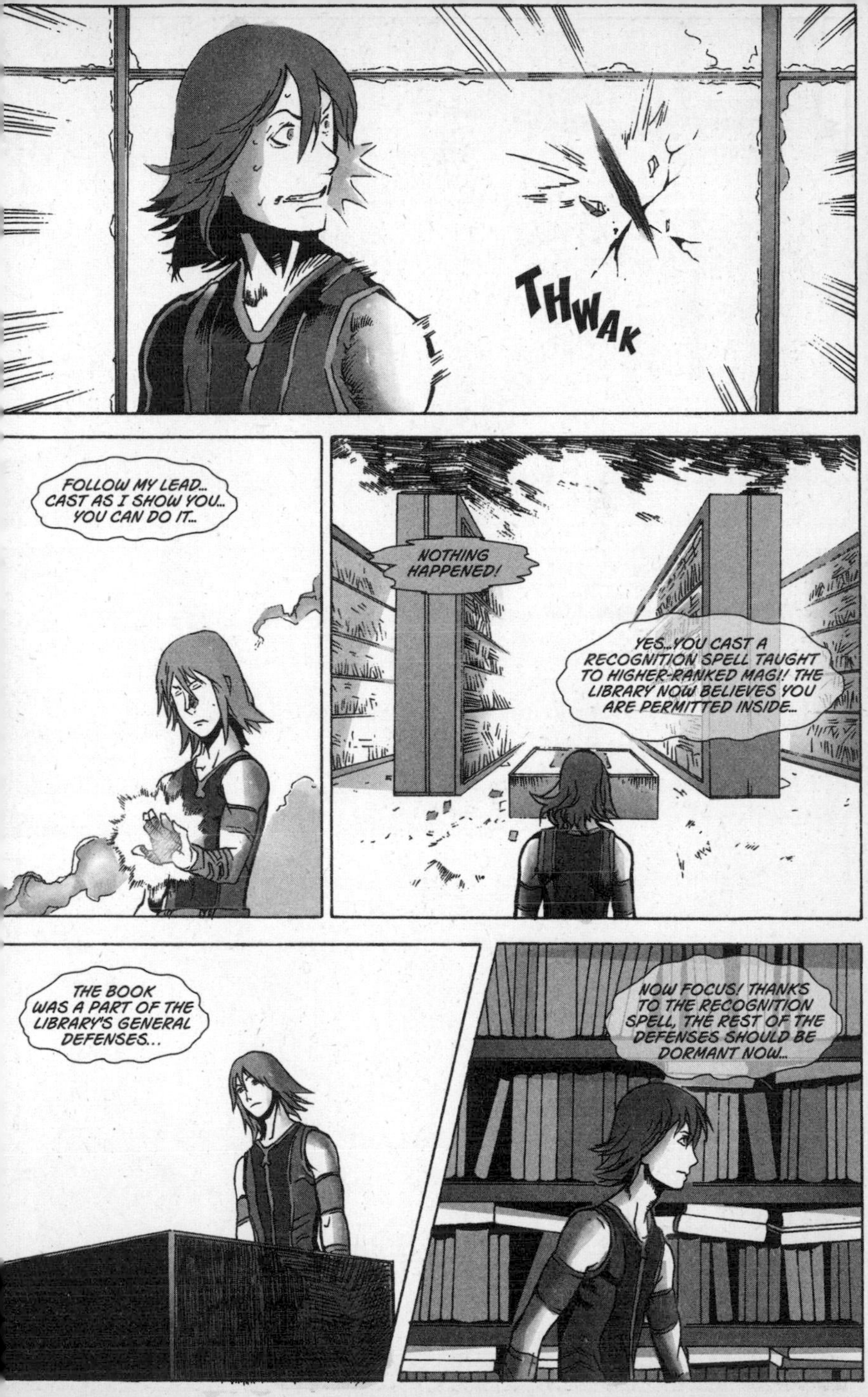
THWAK
FOLLOW MY LEAD... CAST AS I SHOW YOU... YOU CAN DO IT...
NOTHING HAPPENED!
YES...YOU CAST A RECOGNITION SPELL TAUGHT TO HIGHER-RANKED MAGI! THE LIBRARY NOW BELIEVES YOU ARE PERMITTED INSIDE...
THE BOOK WAS A PART OF THE LIBRARY'S GENERAL DEFENSES...
NOW FOCUS! THANKS TO THE RECOGNITION SPELL, THE REST OF THE DEFENSES SHOULD BE DORMANT NOW...

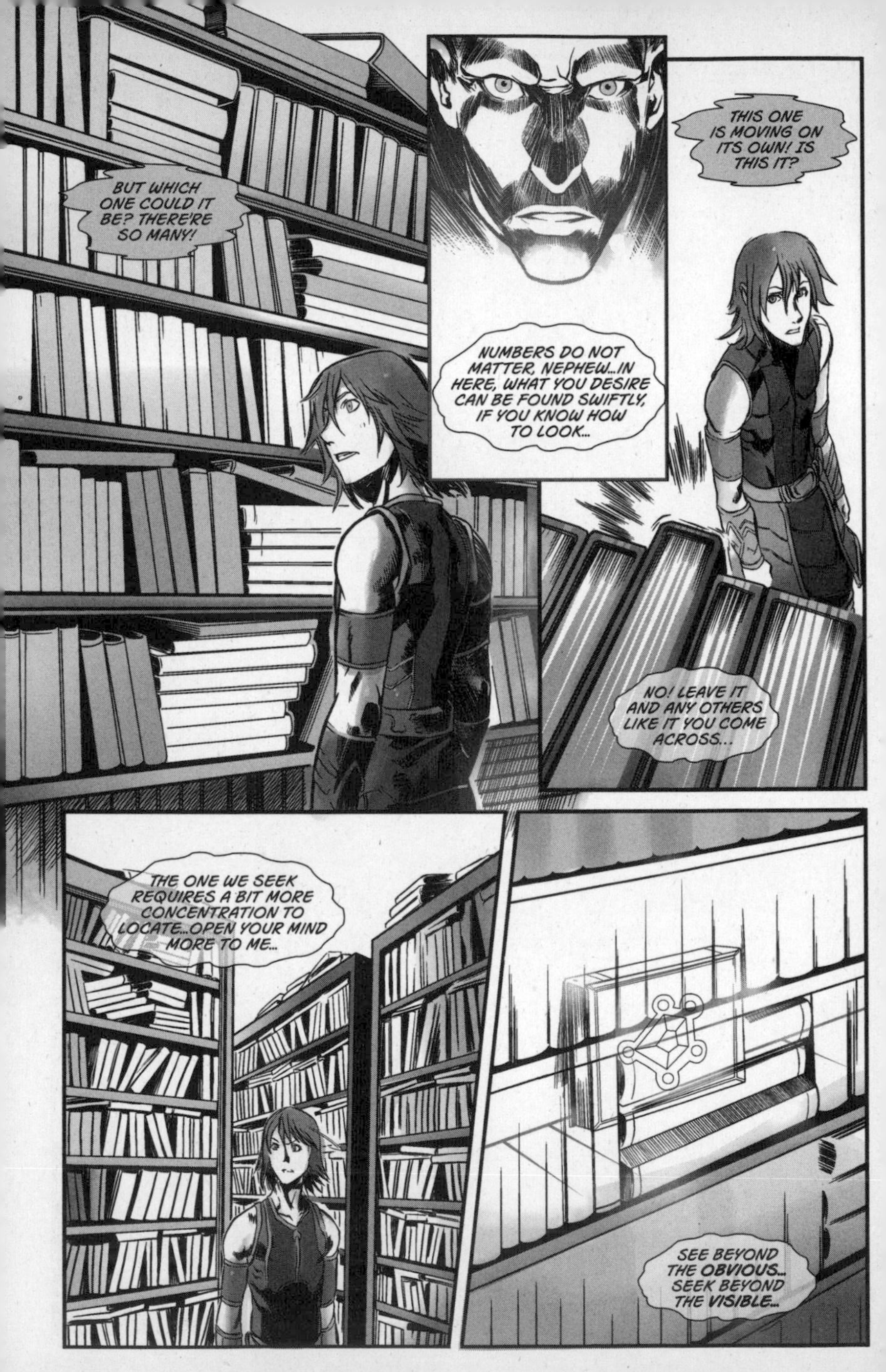
BUT WHICH ONE COULD IT BE? THERE'RE SO MANY!
NUMBERS DO NOT MATTER, NEPHEW...IN HERE, WHAT YOU DESIRE CAN BE FOUND SWIFTLY, IF YOU KNOW HOW TO LOOK...
THIS ONE IS MOVING ON ITS OWN! IS THIS IT?
NO! LEAVE IT AND ANY OTHERS LIKE IT YOU COME ACROSS...
THE ONE WE SEEK REQUIRES A BIT MORE CONCENTRATION TO LOCATE...OPEN YOUR MIND MORE TO ME...
SEE BEYOND THE OBVIOUS... SEEK BEYOND THE VISIBLE...

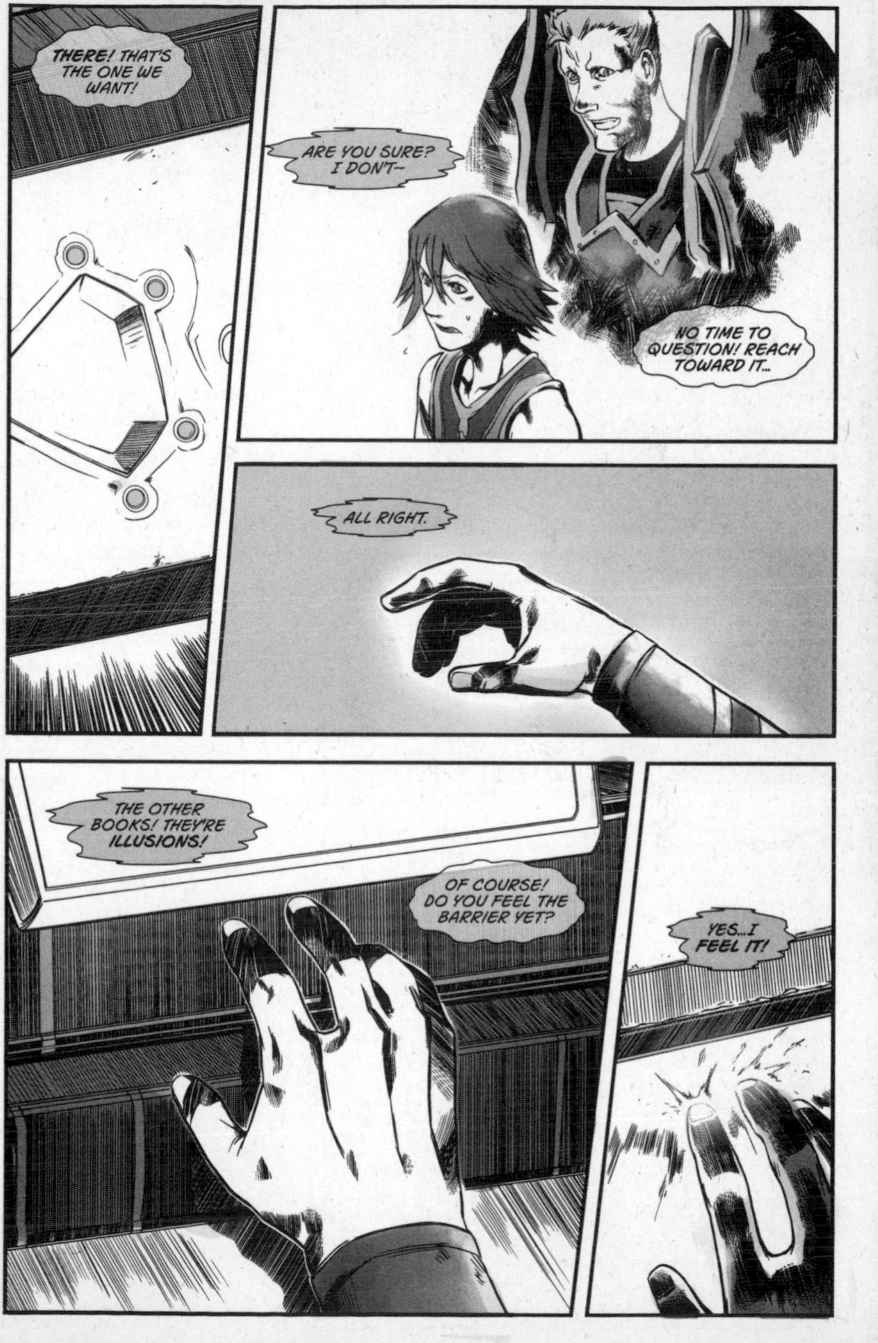
THERE! THAT'S THE ONE WE WANT!
ARE YOU SURE? I DON'T--
NO TIME TO QUESTION! REACH TOWARD IT...
ALL RIGHT.
THE OTHER BOOKS! THEY'RE ILLUSIONS!
OF COURSE! DO YOU FEEL THE BARRIER YET?
YES...I FEEL IT!

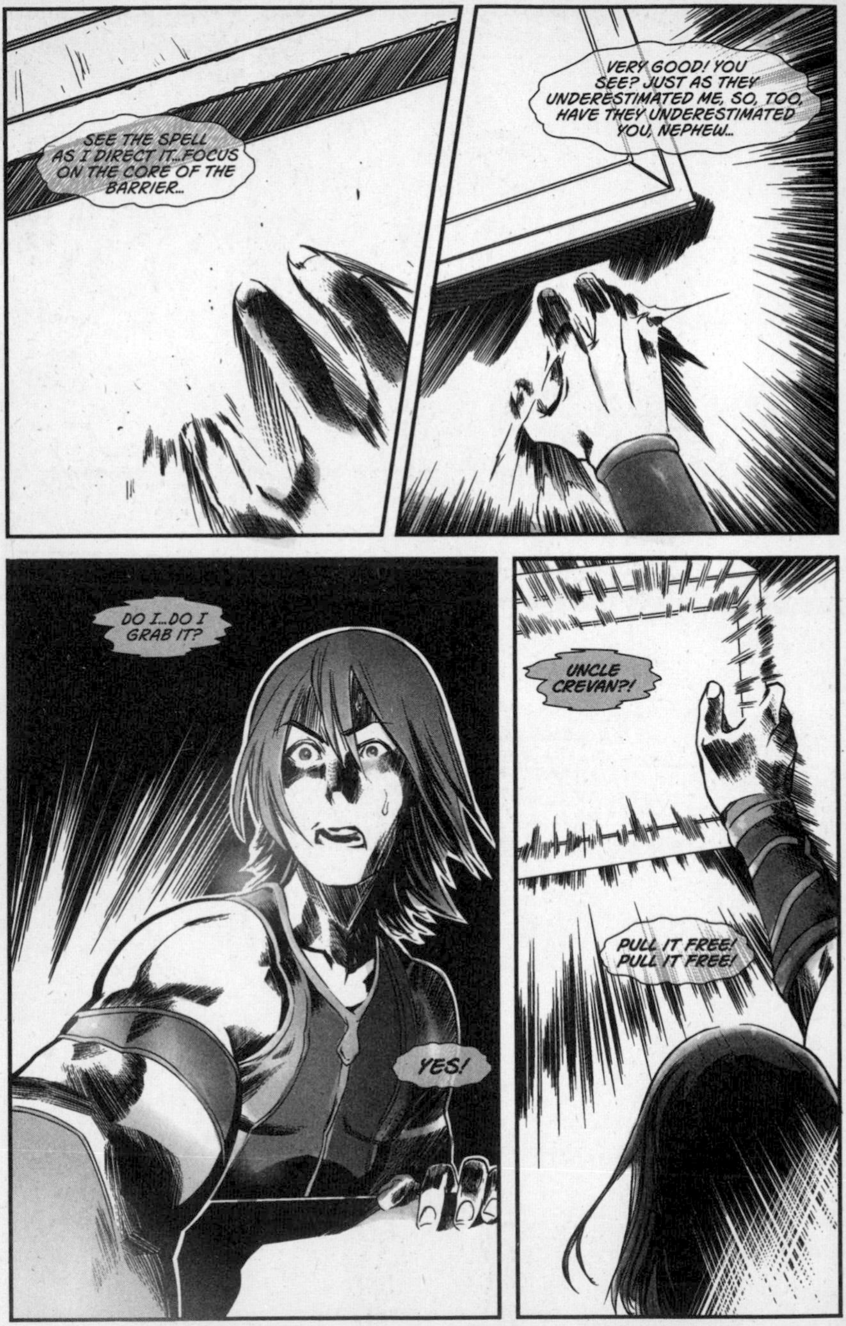
SEE THE SPELL AS I DIRECT IT...FOCUS ON THE CORE OF THE BARRIER...
VERY GOOD! YOU SEE? JUST AS THEY UNDERESTIMATED ME, SO, TOO, HAVE THEY UNDERESTIMATED YOU, NEPHEW...
DO I...DO I GRAB IT?
YES!
UNCLE CREVAN?!
PULL IT FREE! PULL IT FREE!

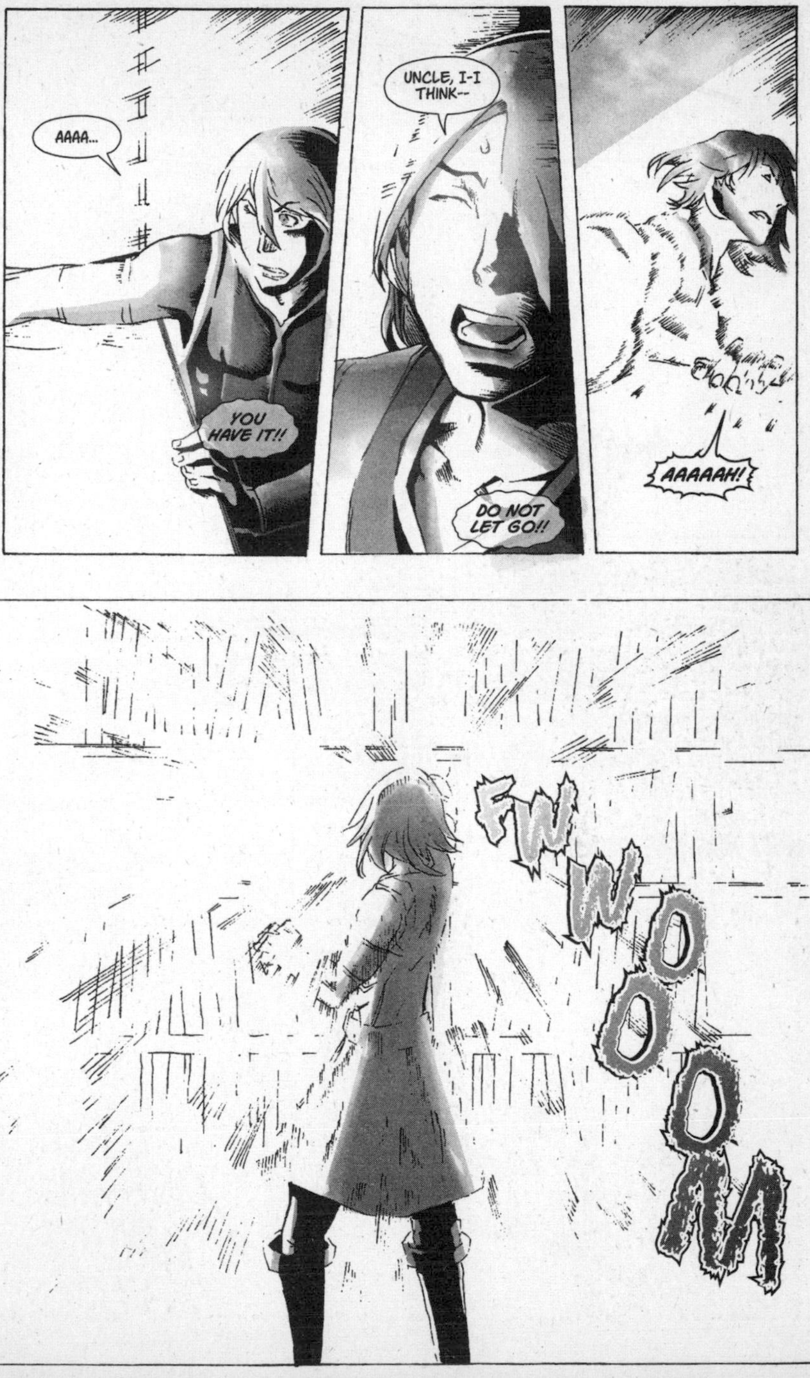
AAAA...
YOU HAVE IT!!
UNCLE, I-I THINK--
DO NOT LET GO!!
AAAAAH!
FWWOOOM

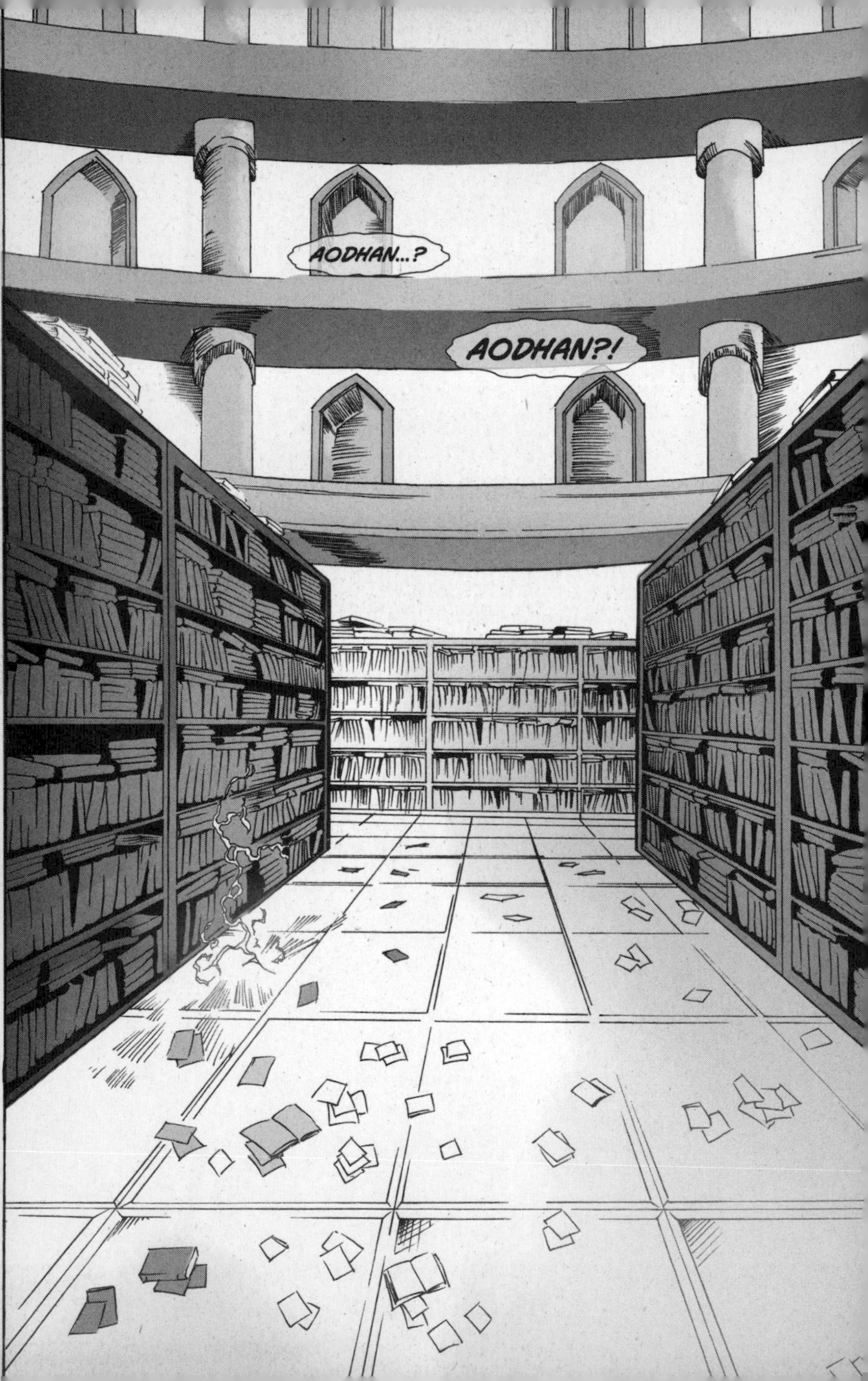
AODHAN...?
AODHAN?!

# CHAPTER THREE
# SPELLBOOK

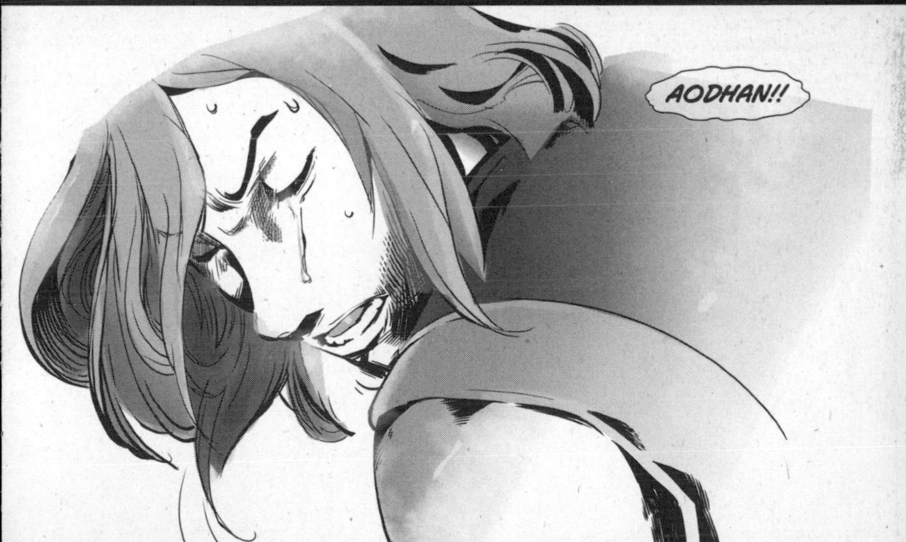
AODHAN!!

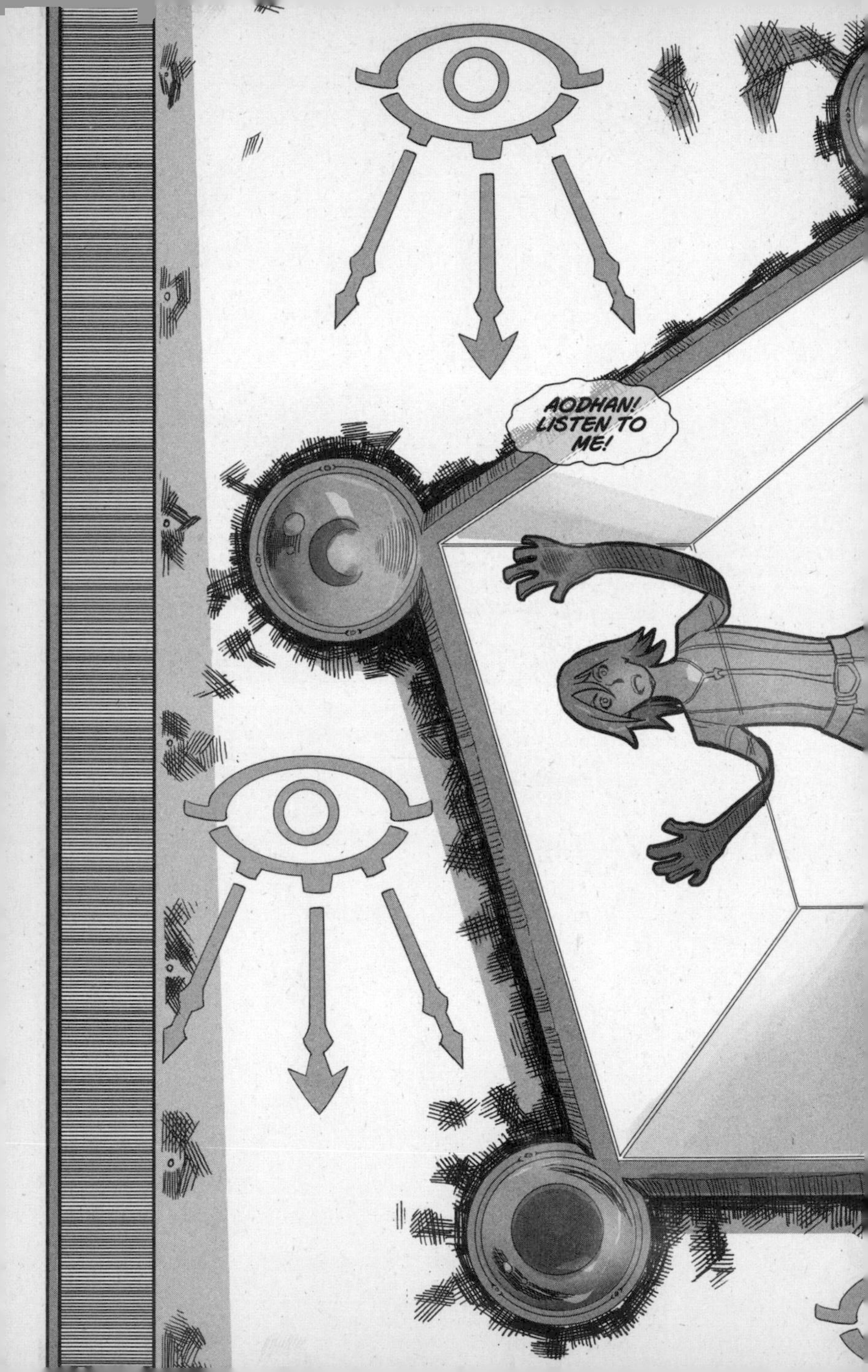
AODHAN! LISTEN TO ME!

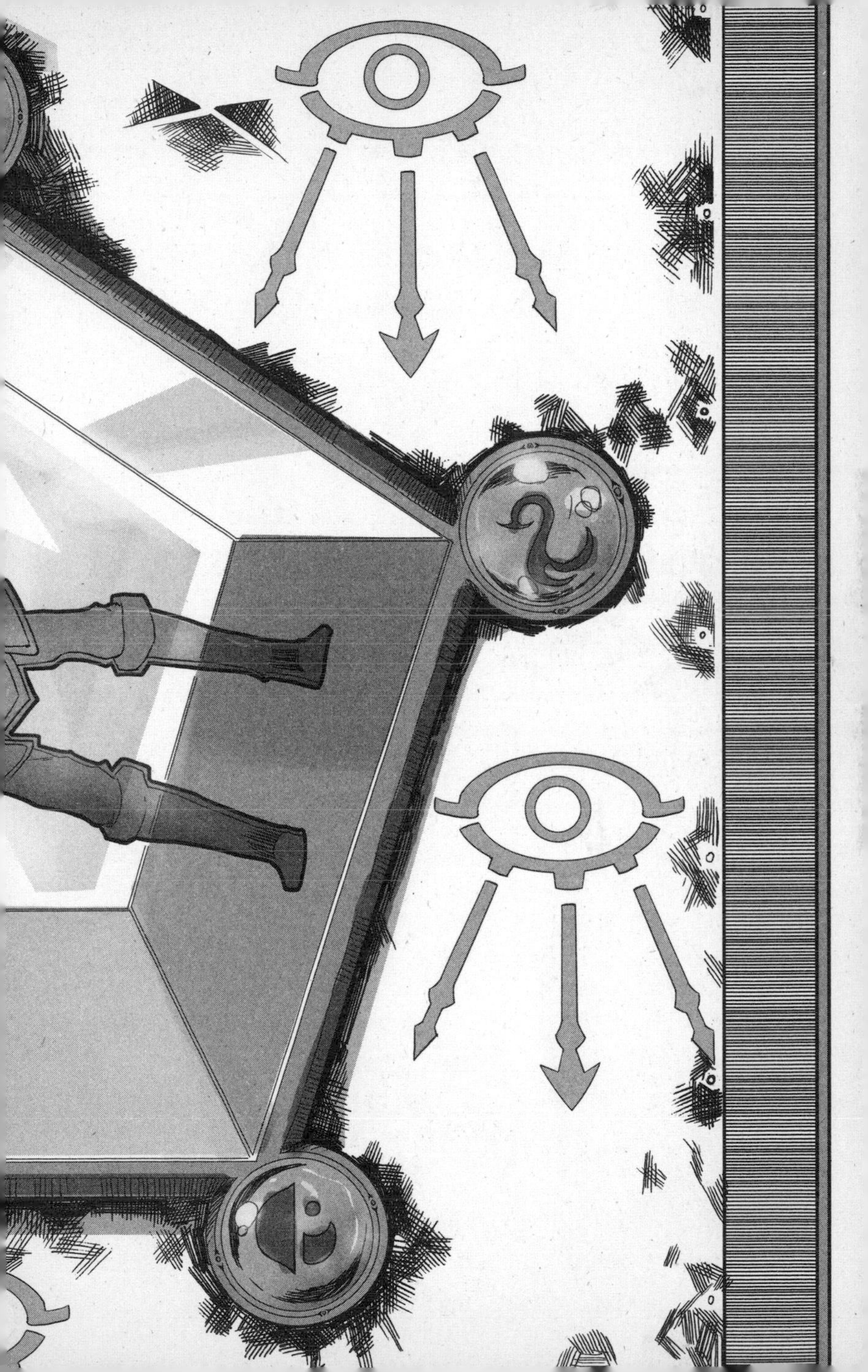

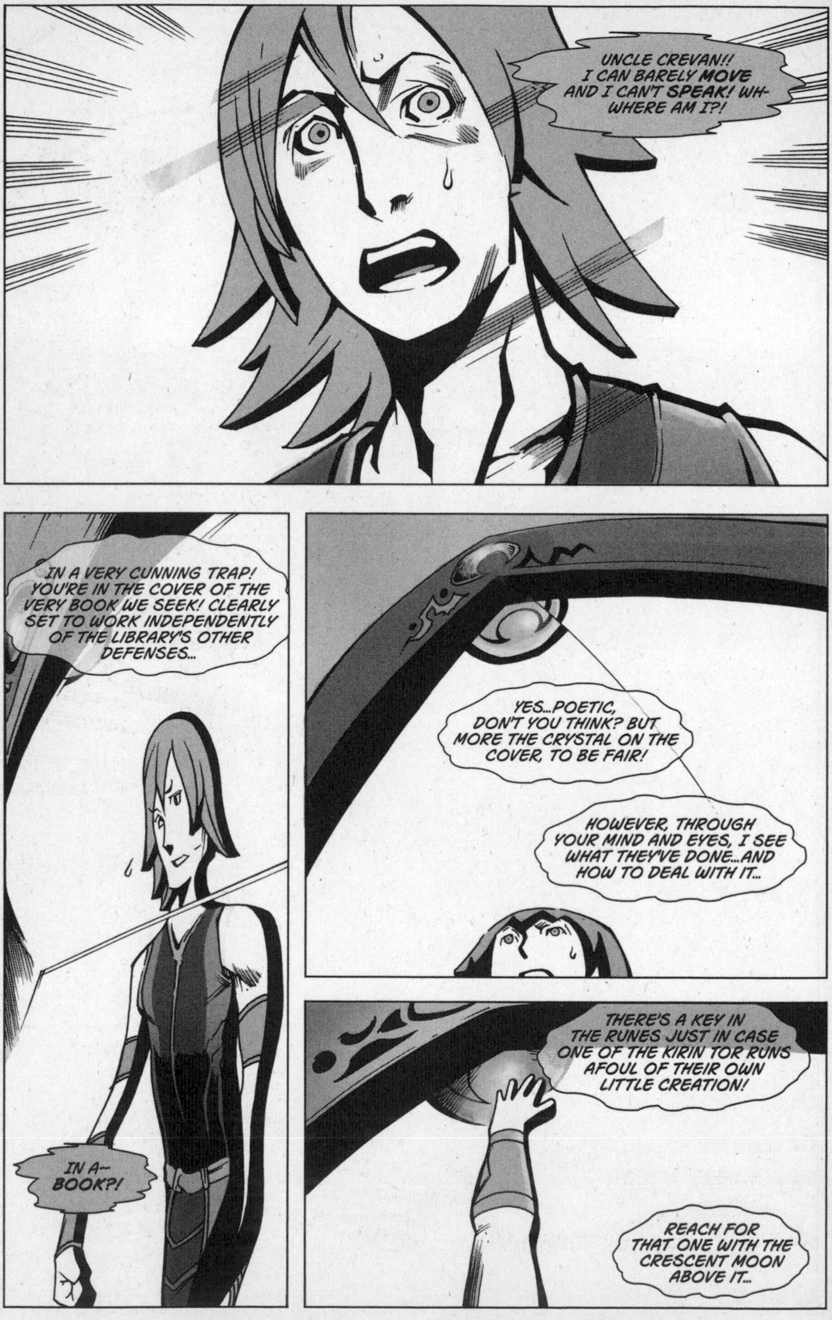
UNCLE CREVAN!! I CAN BARELY MOVE AND I CAN'T SPEAK! WH-WHERE AM I?!
IN A VERY CUNNING TRAP! YOU'RE IN THE COVER OF THE VERY BOOK WE SEEK! CLEARLY SET TO WORK INDEPENDENTLY OF THE LIBRARY'S OTHER DEFENSES...
IN A-- BOOK?!
YES...POETIC, DON'T YOU THINK? BUT MORE THE CRYSTAL ON THE COVER, TO BE FAIR!
HOWEVER, THROUGH YOUR MIND AND EYES, I SEE WHAT THEY'VE DONE...AND HOW TO DEAL WITH IT...
THERE'S A KEY IN THE RUNES JUST IN CASE ONE OF THE KIRIN TOR RUNS AFOUL OF THEIR OWN LITTLE CREATION!
REACH FOR THAT ONE WITH THE CRESCENT MOON ABOVE IT...

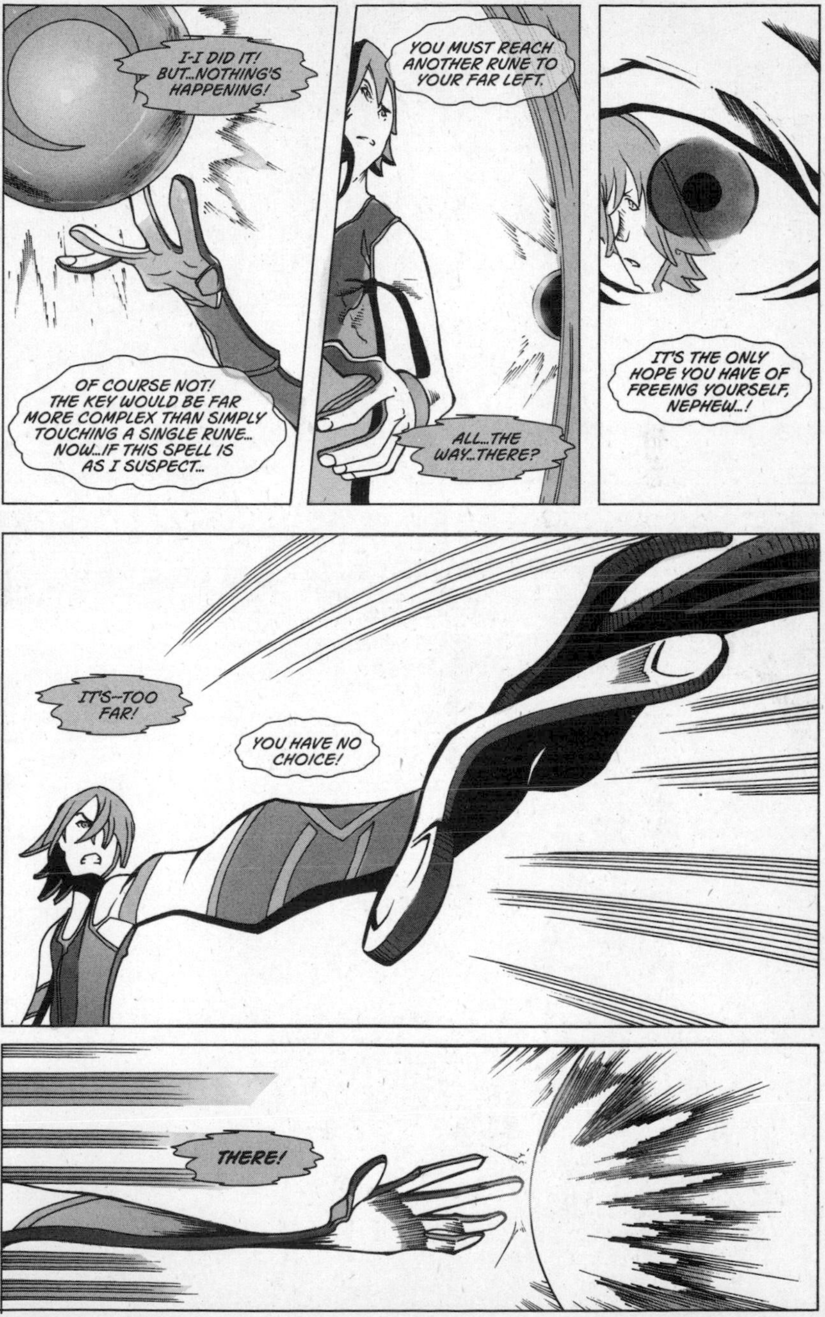
I-I DID IT! BUT...NOTHING'S HAPPENING!
OF COURSE NOT! THE KEY WOULD BE FAR MORE COMPLEX THAN SIMPLY TOUCHING A SINGLE RUNE... NOW...IF THIS SPELL IS AS I SUSPECT...
YOU MUST REACH ANOTHER RUNE TO YOUR FAR LEFT.
ALL...THE WAY...THERE?
IT'S THE ONLY HOPE YOU HAVE OF FREEING YOURSELF, NEPHEW...!
IT'S--TOO FAR!
YOU HAVE NO CHOICE!
THERE!

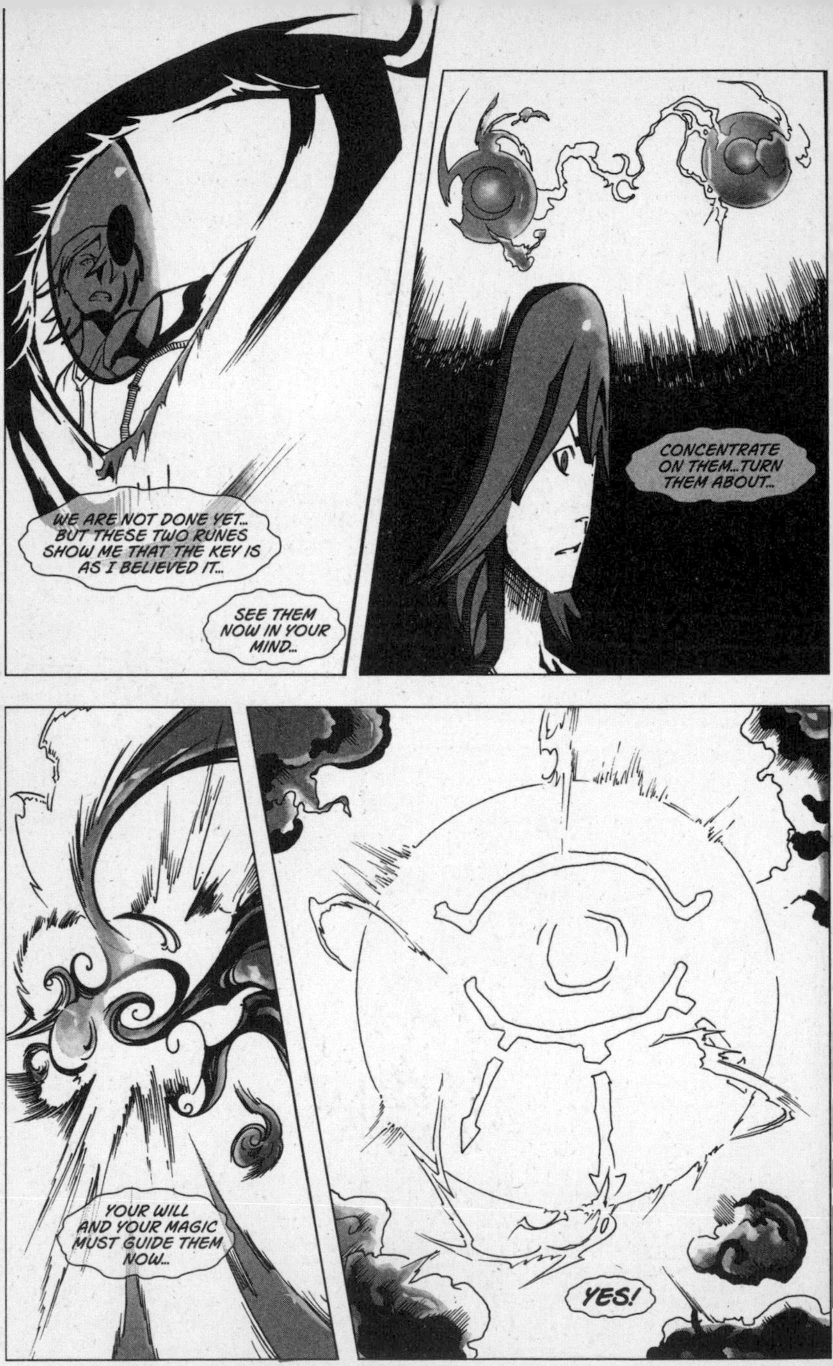
WE ARE NOT DONE YET... BUT THESE TWO RUNES SHOW ME THAT THE KEY IS AS I BELIEVED IT...
SEE THEM NOW IN YOUR MIND...
CONCENTRATE ON THEM...TURN THEM ABOUT...
YOUR WILL AND YOUR MAGIC MUST GUIDE THEM NOW...
YES!

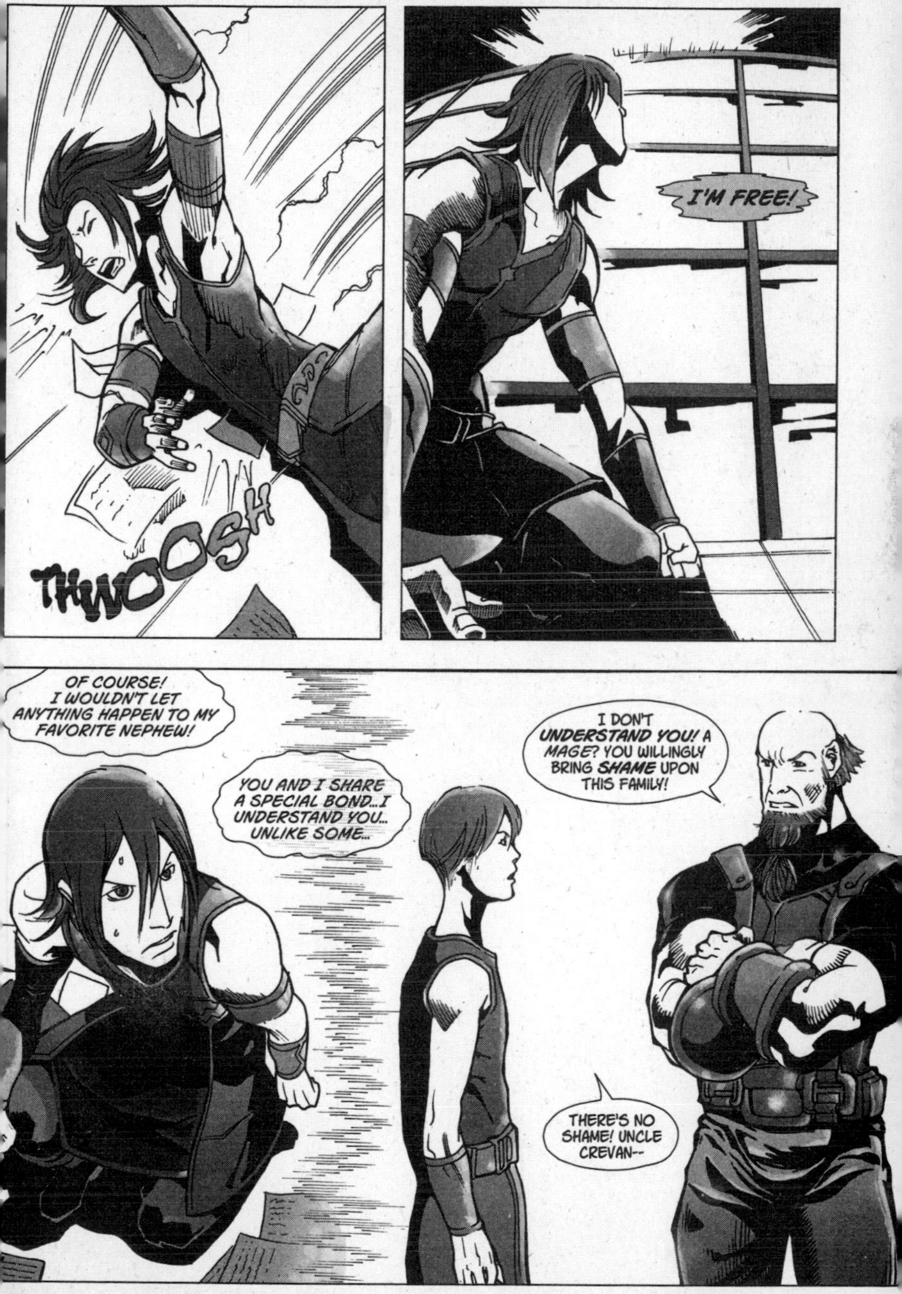
THWOOSH
I'M FREE!
OF COURSE! I WOULDN'T LET ANYTHING HAPPEN TO MY FAVORITE NEPHEW!
YOU AND I SHARE A SPECIAL BOND...I UNDERSTAND YOU... UNLIKE SOME...
I DON'T UNDERSTAND YOU! A MAGE? YOU WILLINGLY BRING SHAME UPON THIS FAMILY!
THERE'S NO SHAME! UNCLE CREVAN--

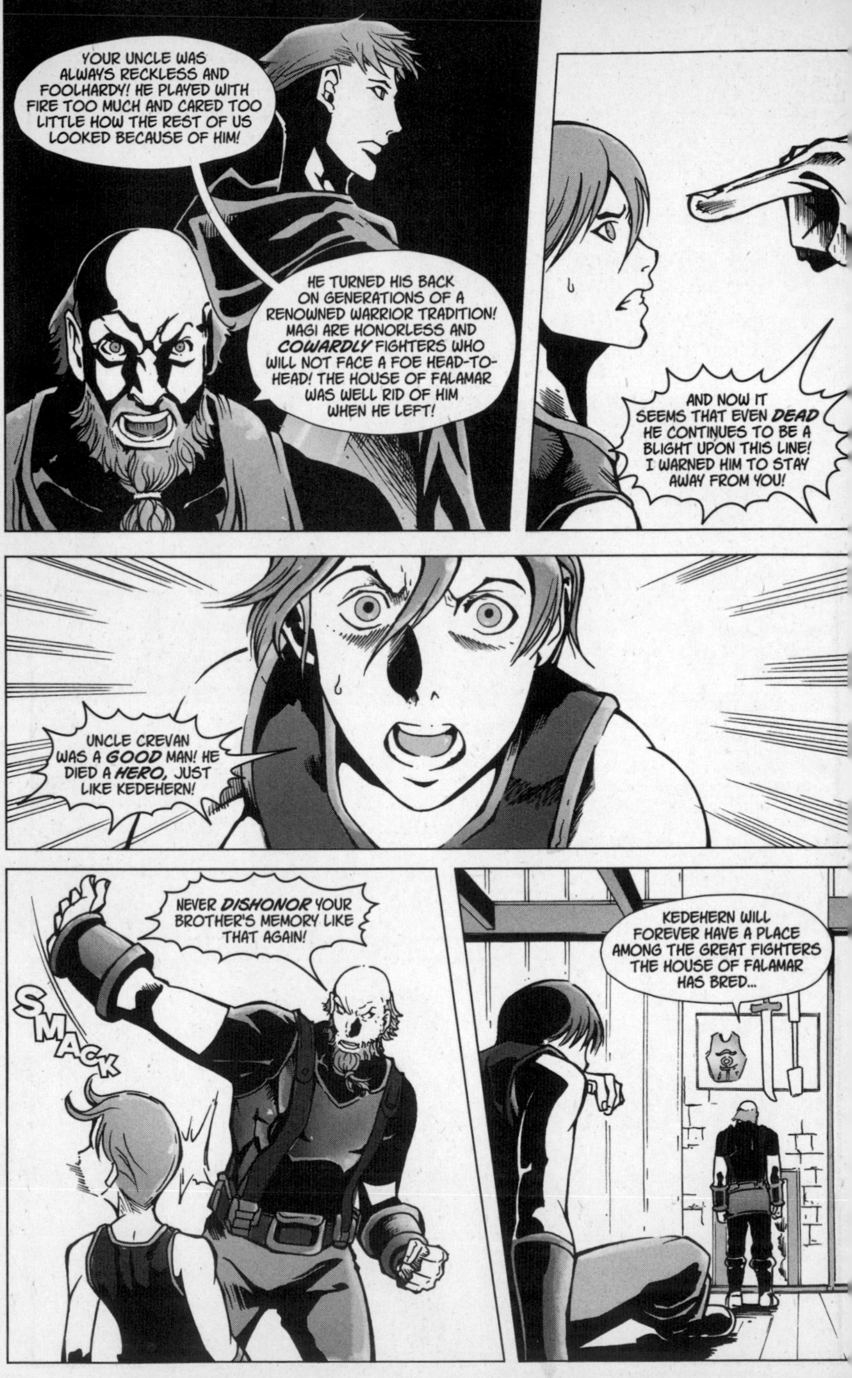
YOUR UNCLE WAS ALWAYS RECKLESS AND FOOLHARDY! HE PLAYED WITH FIRE TOO MUCH AND CARED TOO LITTLE HOW THE REST OF US LOOKED BECAUSE OF HIM!
HE TURNED HIS BACK ON GENERATIONS OF A RENOWNED WARRIOR TRADITION! MAGI ARE HONORLESS AND *COWARDLY* FIGHTERS WHO WILL NOT FACE A FOE HEAD-TO-HEAD! THE HOUSE OF FALAMAR WAS WELL RID OF HIM WHEN HE LEFT!
AND NOW IT SEEMS THAT EVEN *DEAD* HE CONTINUES TO BE A BLIGHT UPON THIS LINE! I WARNED HIM TO STAY AWAY FROM YOU!
UNCLE CREVAN WAS A *GOOD* MAN! HE DIED A *HERO,* JUST LIKE KEDEHERN!
SMACK
NEVER *DISHONOR* YOUR BROTHER'S MEMORY LIKE THAT AGAIN!
KEDEHERN WILL FOREVER HAVE A PLACE AMONG THE GREAT FIGHTERS THE HOUSE OF FALAMAR HAS BRED...

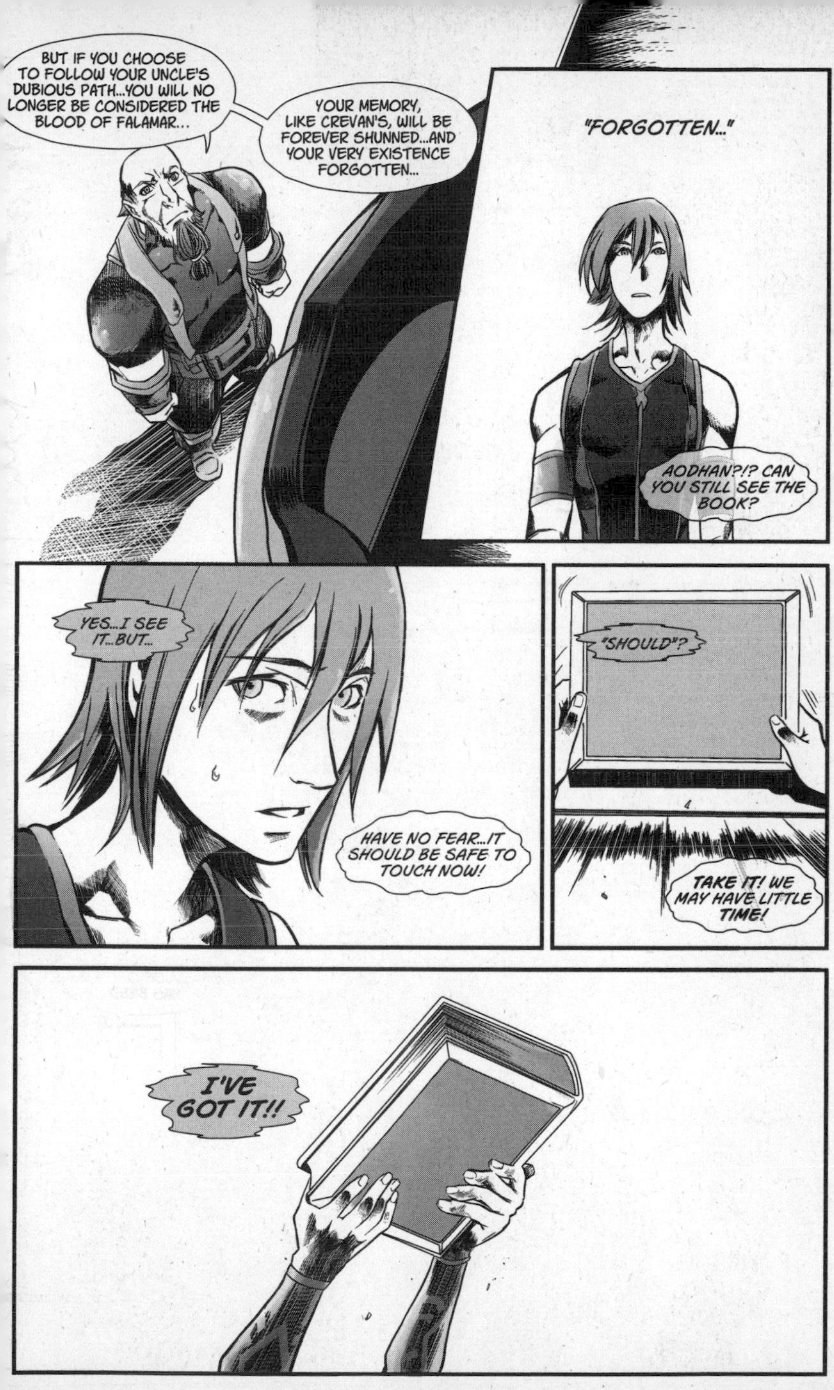
BUT IF YOU CHOOSE TO FOLLOW YOUR UNCLE'S DUBIOUS PATH...YOU WILL NO LONGER BE CONSIDERED THE BLOOD OF FALAMAR...
YOUR MEMORY, LIKE CREVAN'S, WILL BE FOREVER SHUNNED...AND YOUR VERY EXISTENCE FORGOTTEN...
"FORGOTTEN..."
AODHAN?!? CAN YOU STILL SEE THE BOOK?
YES...I SEE IT...BUT...
HAVE NO FEAR...IT SHOULD BE SAFE TO TOUCH NOW!
"SHOULD"?
TAKE IT! WE MAY HAVE LITTLE TIME!
I'VE GOT IT!!

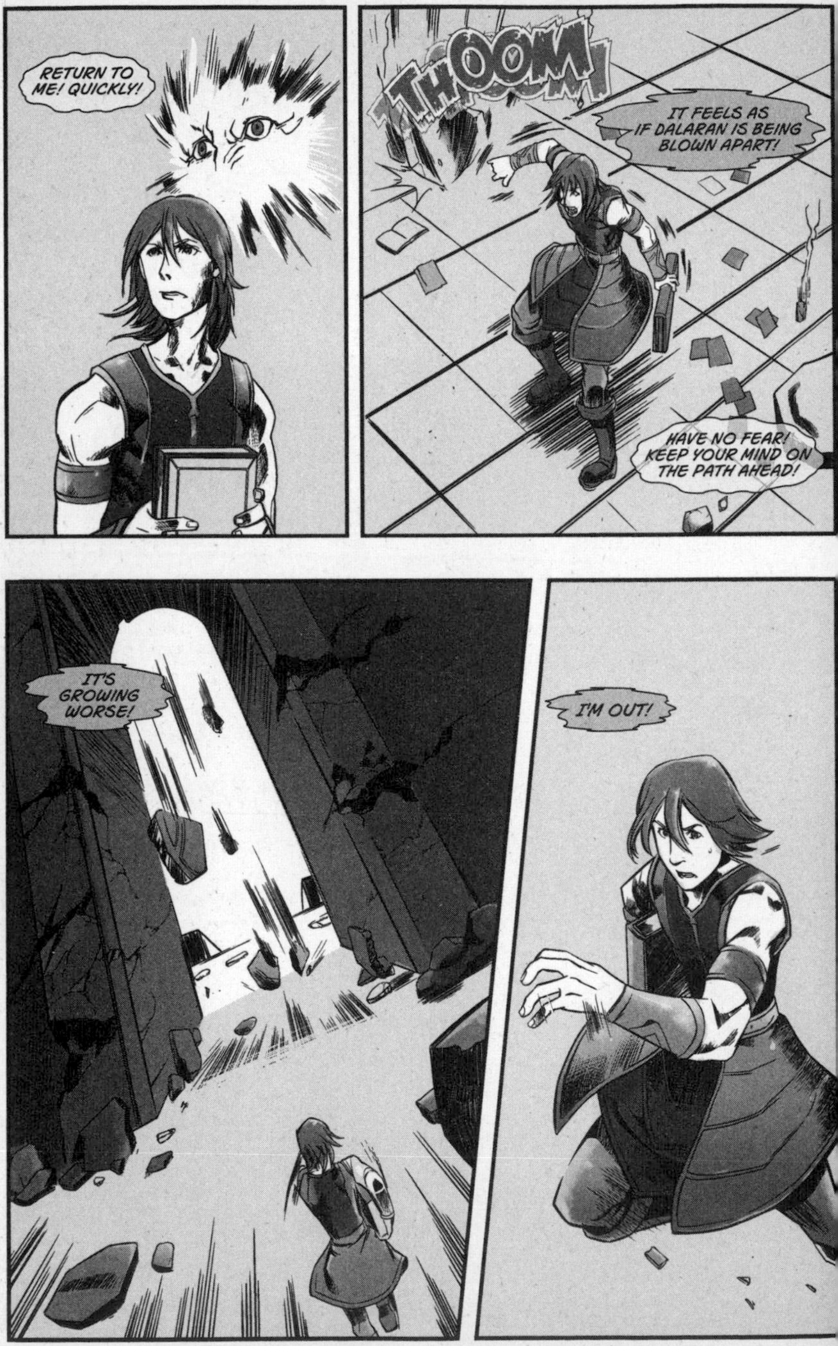
RETURN TO ME! QUICKLY!
THOOM!
IT FEELS AS IF DALARAN IS BEING BLOWN APART!
HAVE NO FEAR! KEEP YOUR MIND ON THE PATH AHEAD!
IT'S GROWING WORSE!
I'M OUT!

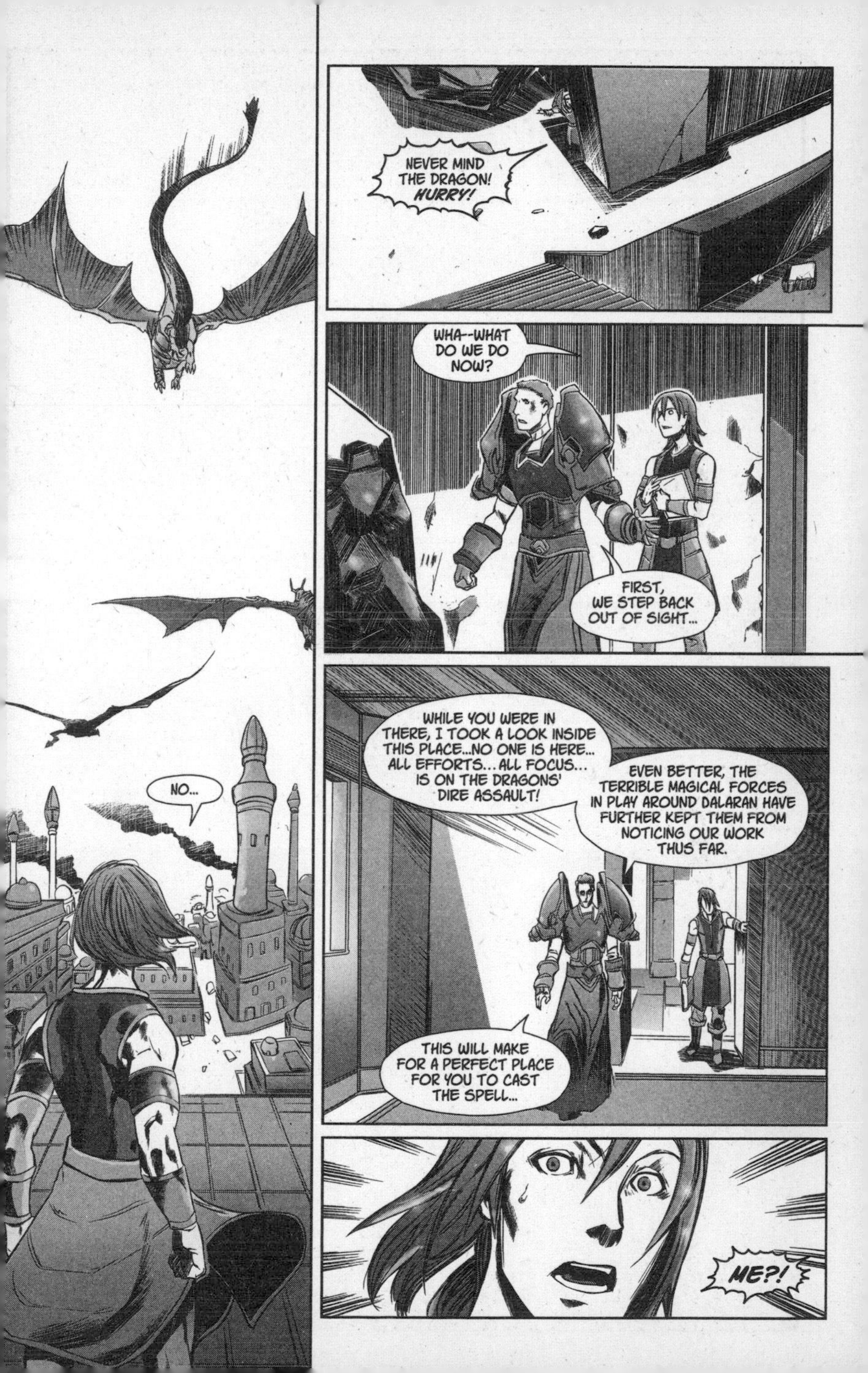
NO...
NEVER MIND THE DRAGON! HURRY!
WHA--WHAT DO WE DO NOW?
FIRST, WE STEP BACK OUT OF SIGHT...
WHILE YOU WERE IN THERE, I TOOK A LOOK INSIDE THIS PLACE...NO ONE IS HERE... ALL EFFORTS... ALL FOCUS... IS ON THE DRAGONS' DIRE ASSAULT!
EVEN BETTER, THE TERRIBLE MAGICAL FORCES IN PLAY AROUND DALARAN HAVE FURTHER KEPT THEM FROM NOTICING OUR WORK THUS FAR.
THIS WILL MAKE FOR A PERFECT PLACE FOR YOU TO CAST THE SPELL...
ME?!

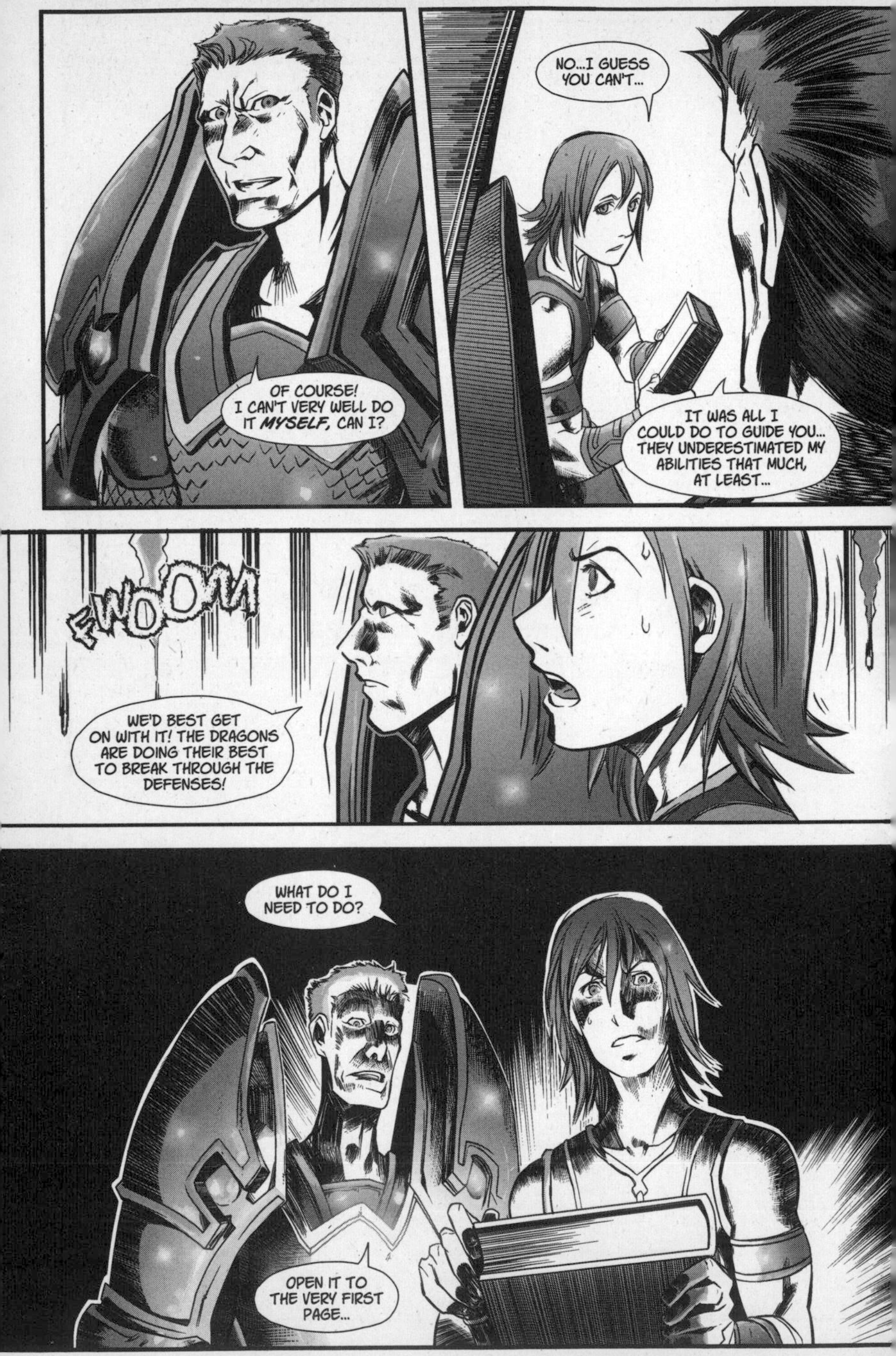
OF COURSE! I CAN'T VERY WELL DO IT *MYSELF*, CAN I?
NO...I GUESS YOU CAN'T...
IT WAS ALL I COULD DO TO GUIDE YOU... THEY UNDERESTIMATED MY ABILITIES THAT MUCH, AT LEAST...
FWOOM
WE'D BEST GET ON WITH IT! THE DRAGONS ARE DOING THEIR BEST TO BREAK THROUGH THE DEFENSES!
WHAT DO I NEED TO DO?
OPEN IT TO THE VERY FIRST PAGE...

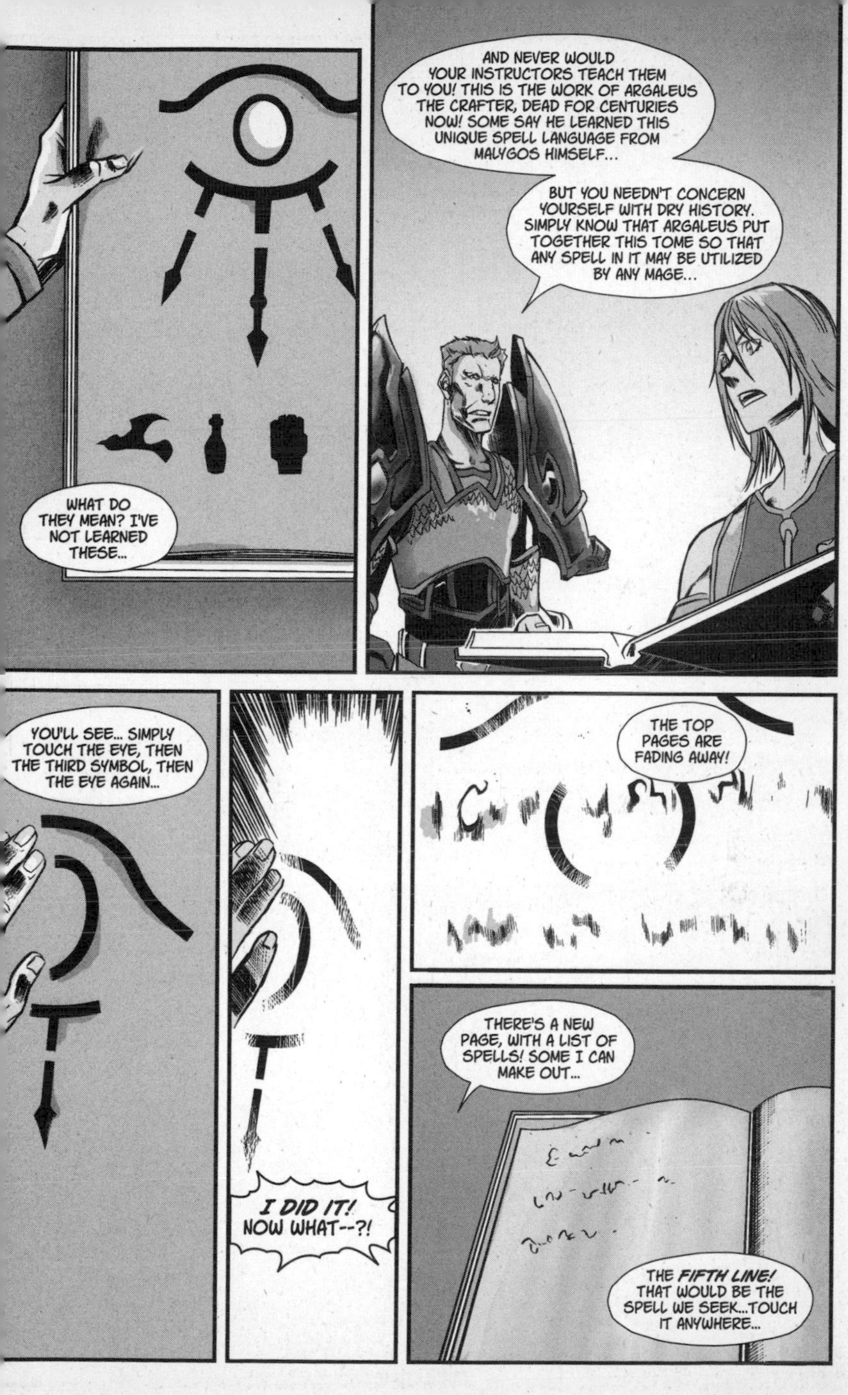
WHAT DO THEY MEAN? I'VE NOT LEARNED THESE...
AND NEVER WOULD YOUR INSTRUCTORS TEACH THEM TO YOU! THIS IS THE WORK OF ARGALEUS THE CRAFTER, DEAD FOR CENTURIES NOW! SOME SAY HE LEARNED THIS UNIQUE SPELL LANGUAGE FROM MALYGOS HIMSELF...
BUT YOU NEEDN'T CONCERN YOURSELF WITH DRY HISTORY. SIMPLY KNOW THAT ARGALEUS PUT TOGETHER THIS TOME SO THAT ANY SPELL IN IT MAY BE UTILIZED BY ANY MAGE...
YOU'LL SEE... SIMPLY TOUCH THE EYE, THEN THE THIRD SYMBOL, THEN THE EYE AGAIN...
I DID IT! NOW WHAT--?!
THE TOP PAGES ARE FADING AWAY!
THERE'S A NEW PAGE, WITH A LIST OF SPELLS! SOME I CAN MAKE OUT...
THE FIFTH LINE! THAT WOULD BE THE SPELL WE SEEK...TOUCH IT ANYWHERE...

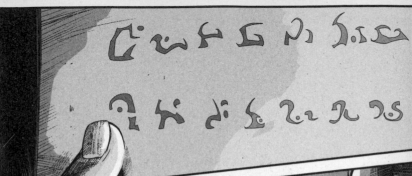

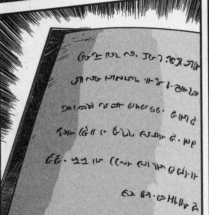

IS THIS IT?

YES! EXCELLENT, AODHAN!

NOW, IN YOUR MIND PICTURE THE IMAGE OF THE PAGE...AND THE SPELL WRITTEN IN IT...

IF THE SPELL FADES AWAY, THEN YOU'VE MEMORIZED IT! IT WON'T BE VISIBLE AGAIN UNTIL THE BOOK IS NEXT OPENED...ANOTHER OF ARGALEUS'S MANY UNIQUE TOUCHES...

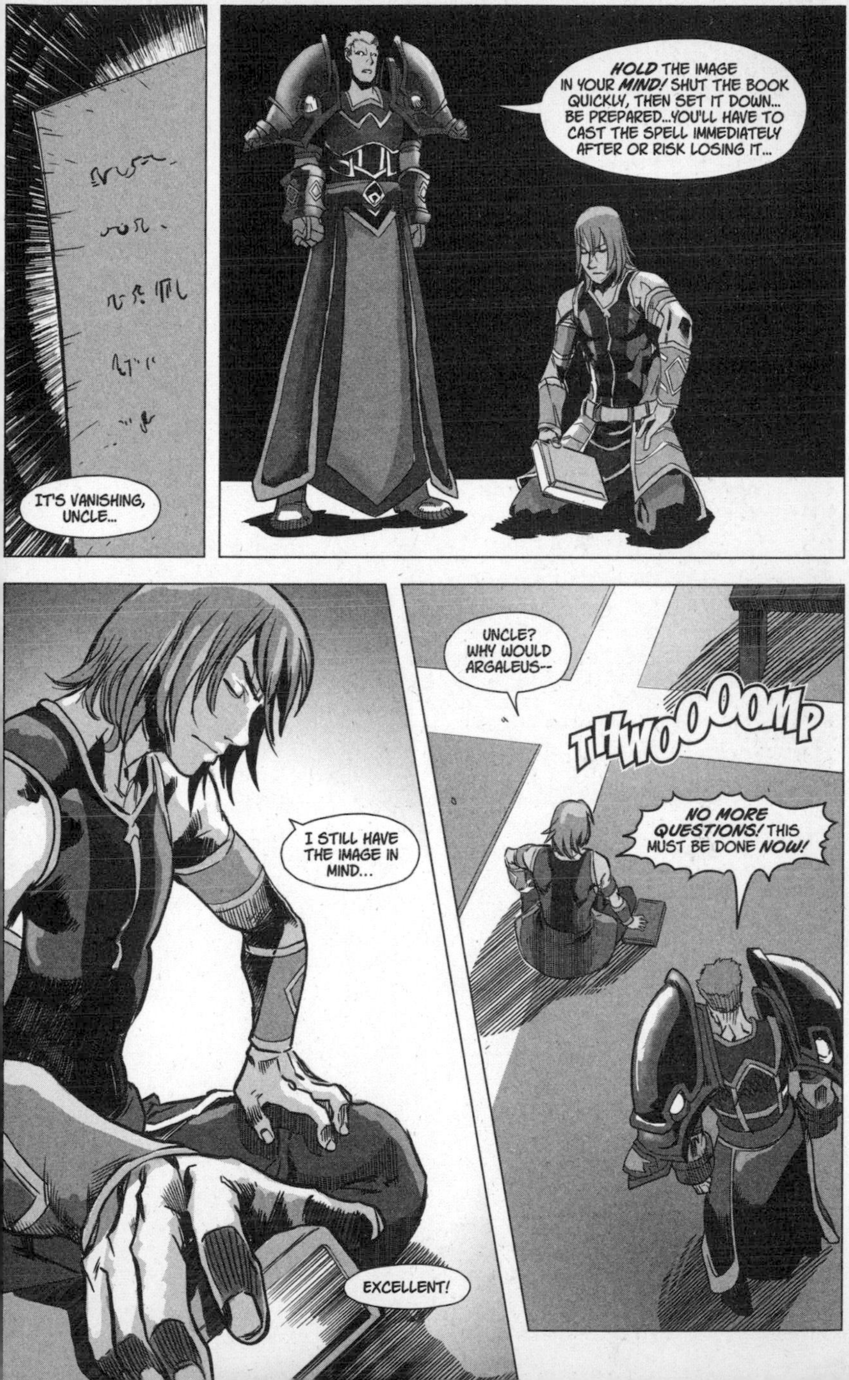
IT'S VANISHING, UNCLE...
HOLD THE IMAGE IN YOUR MIND! SHUT THE BOOK QUICKLY, THEN SET IT DOWN... BE PREPARED...YOU'LL HAVE TO CAST THE SPELL IMMEDIATELY AFTER OR RISK LOSING IT...
I STILL HAVE THE IMAGE IN MIND...
EXCELLENT!
UNCLE? WHY WOULD ARGALEUS--
THWOOOOMP
NO MORE QUESTIONS! THIS MUST BE DONE NOW!

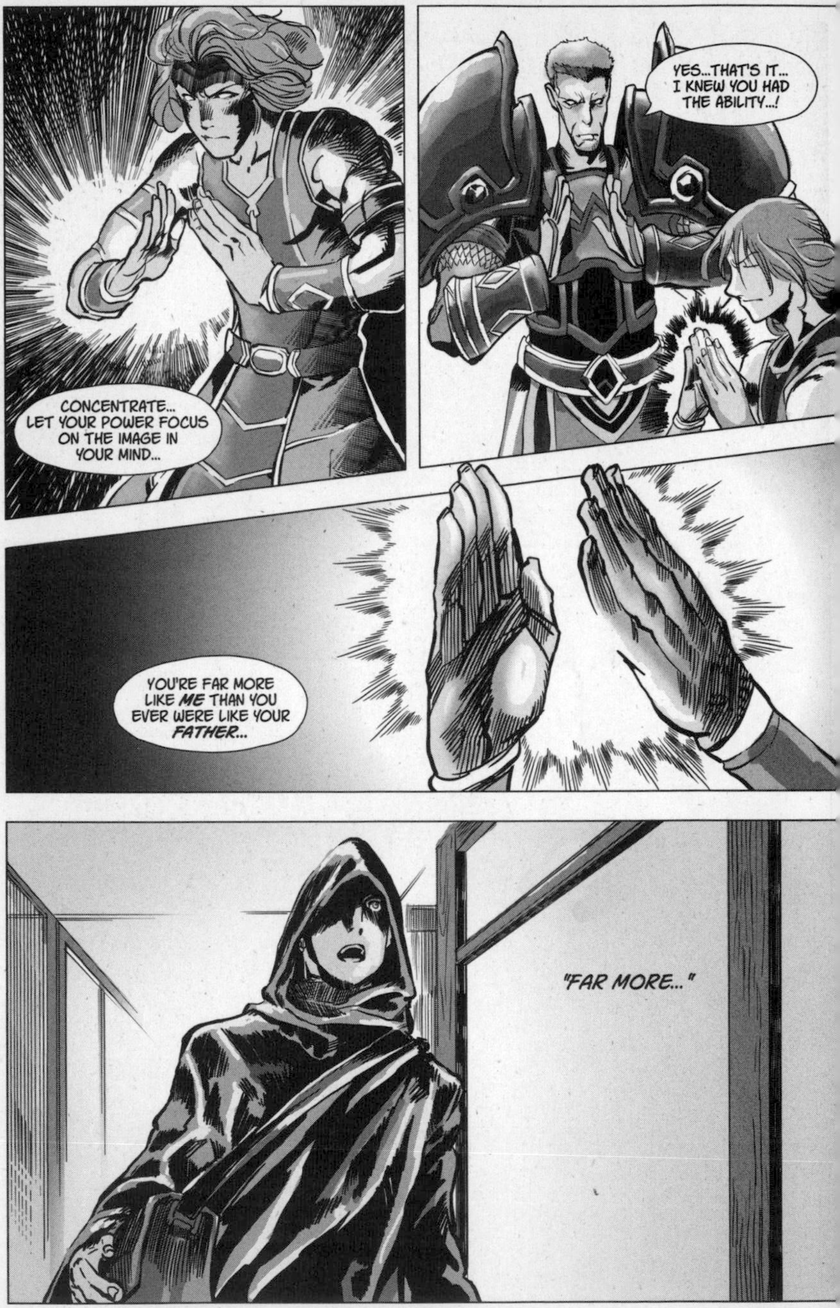
CONCENTRATE... LET YOUR POWER FOCUS ON THE IMAGE IN YOUR MIND...
YES...THAT'S IT... I KNEW YOU HAD THE ABILITY...!
YOU'RE FAR MORE LIKE *ME* THAN YOU EVER WERE LIKE YOUR *FATHER*...
"FAR MORE..."

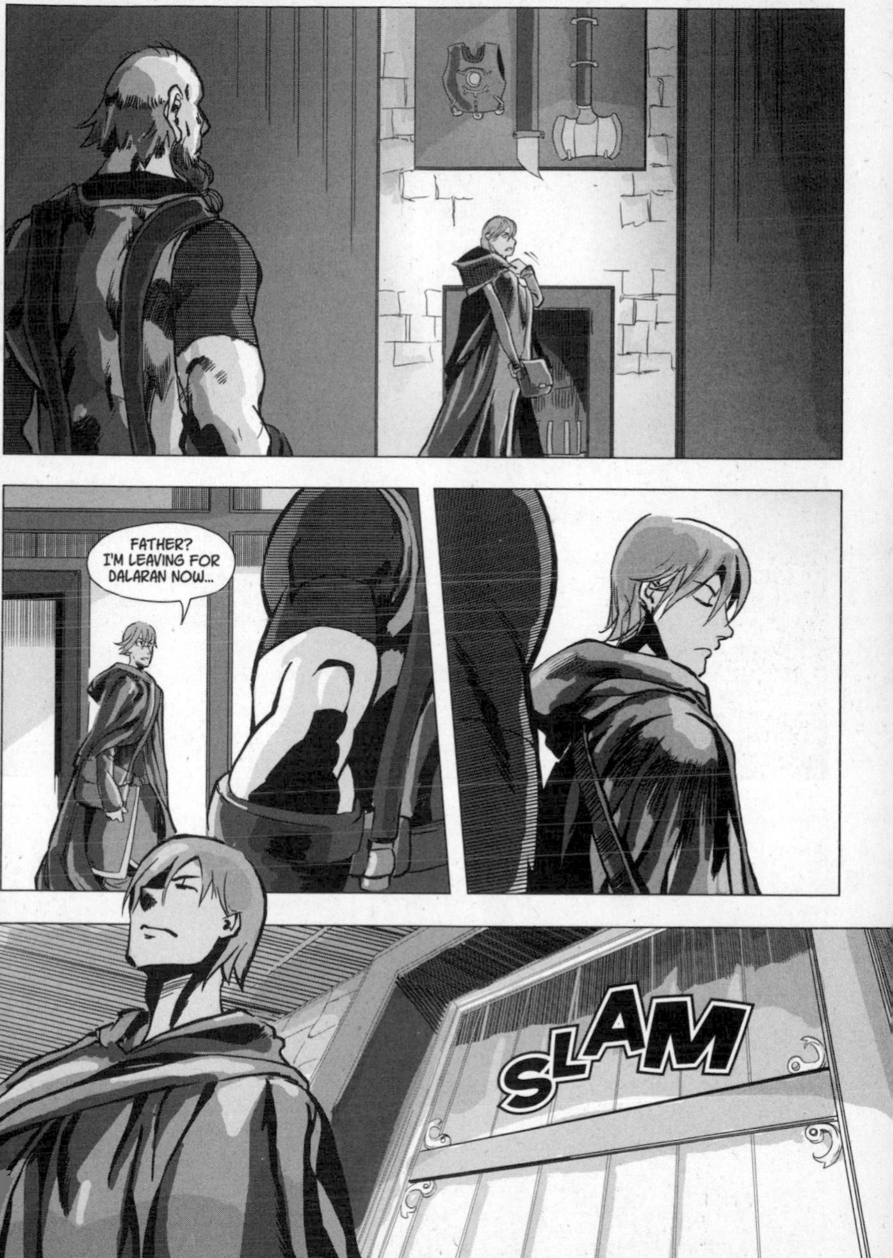
FATHER? I'M LEAVING FOR DALARAN NOW...
SLAM

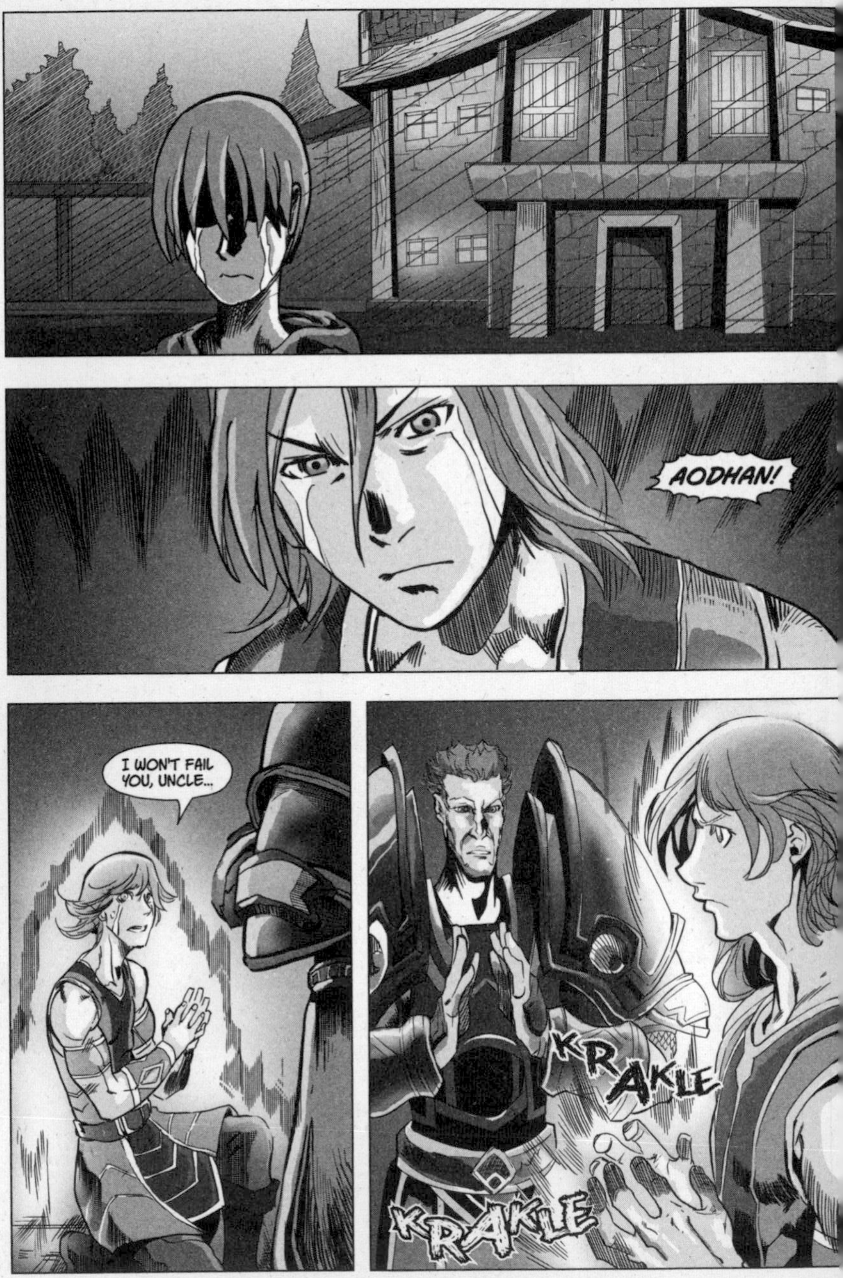
AODHAN!
I WON'T FAIL YOU, UNCLE...
KRAKLE
KRAKLE

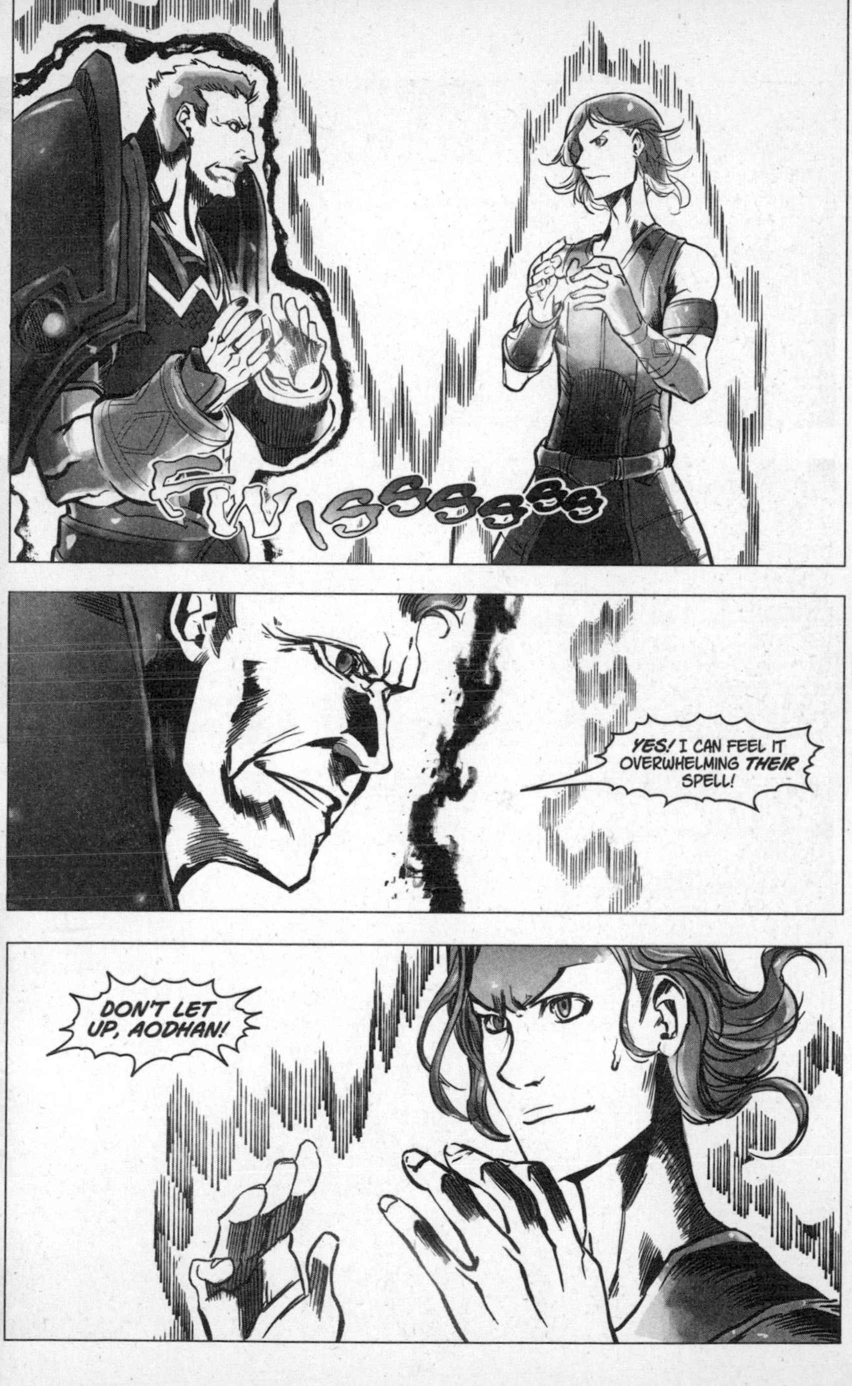
FWISSSSSSS
YES! I CAN FEEL IT OVERWHELMING THEIR SPELL!
DON'T LET UP, AODHAN!

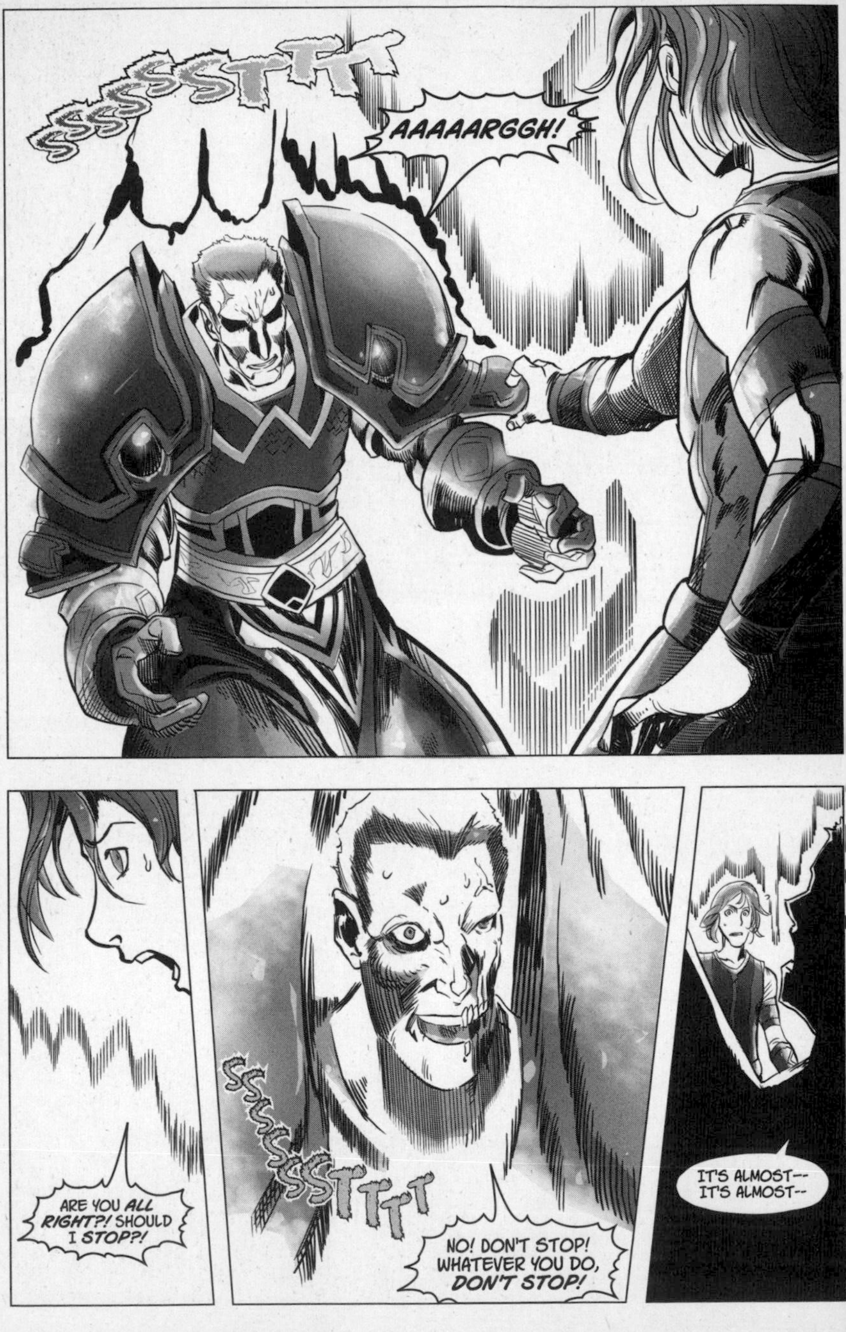
SSSSSSTTT
AAAAARGGH!
ARE YOU ALL RIGHT?! SHOULD I STOP?!
SSSSSSTTTT
NO! DON'T STOP! WHATEVER YOU DO, DON'T STOP!
IT'S ALMOST-- IT'S ALMOST--

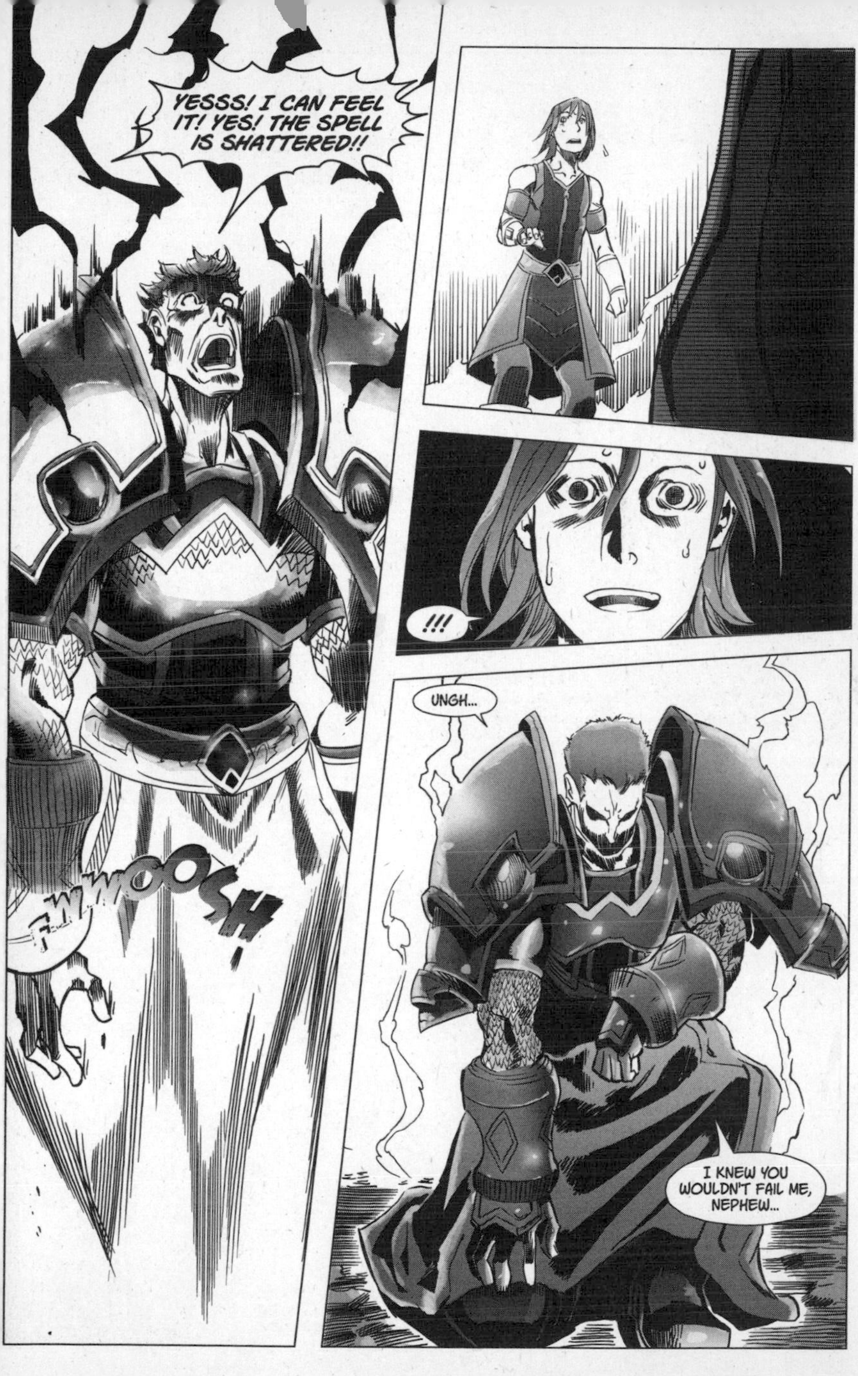
YESSS! I CAN FEEL IT! YES! THE SPELL IS SHATTERED!!
FWWOOSH
!!!
UNGH...
I KNEW YOU WOULDN'T FAIL ME, NEPHEW...

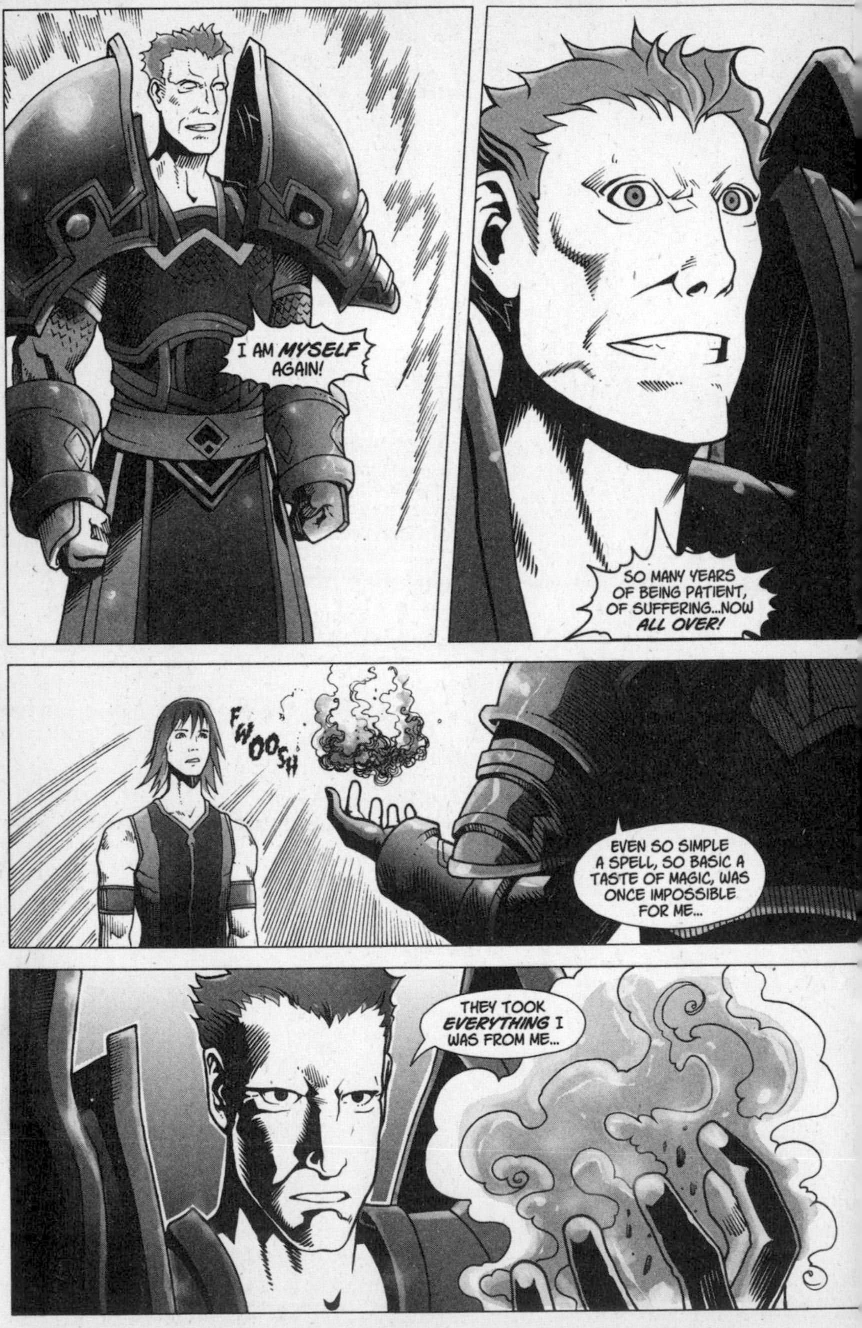
I AM *MYSELF* AGAIN!
SO MANY YEARS OF BEING PATIENT, OF SUFFERING...NOW *ALL OVER!*
FWOOSH
EVEN SO SIMPLE A SPELL, SO BASIC A TASTE OF MAGIC, WAS ONCE IMPOSSIBLE FOR ME...
THEY TOOK *EVERYTHING* I WAS FROM ME...

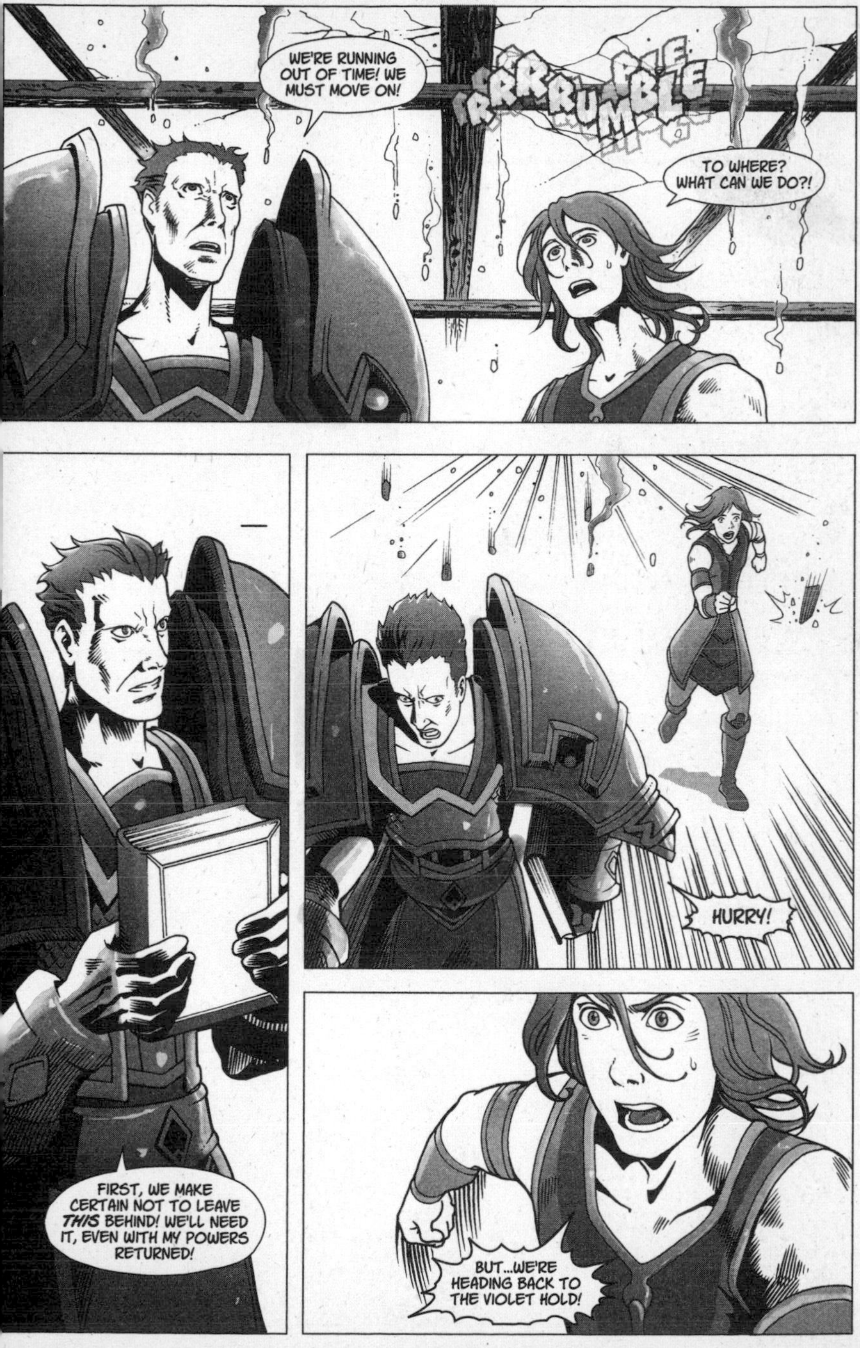
WE'RE RUNNING OUT OF TIME! WE MUST MOVE ON!
RRRRUMBLE
TO WHERE? WHAT CAN WE DO?!
FIRST, WE MAKE CERTAIN NOT TO LEAVE *THIS* BEHIND! WE'LL NEED IT, EVEN WITH MY POWERS RETURNED!
HURRY!
BUT...WE'RE HEADING BACK TO THE VIOLET HOLD!

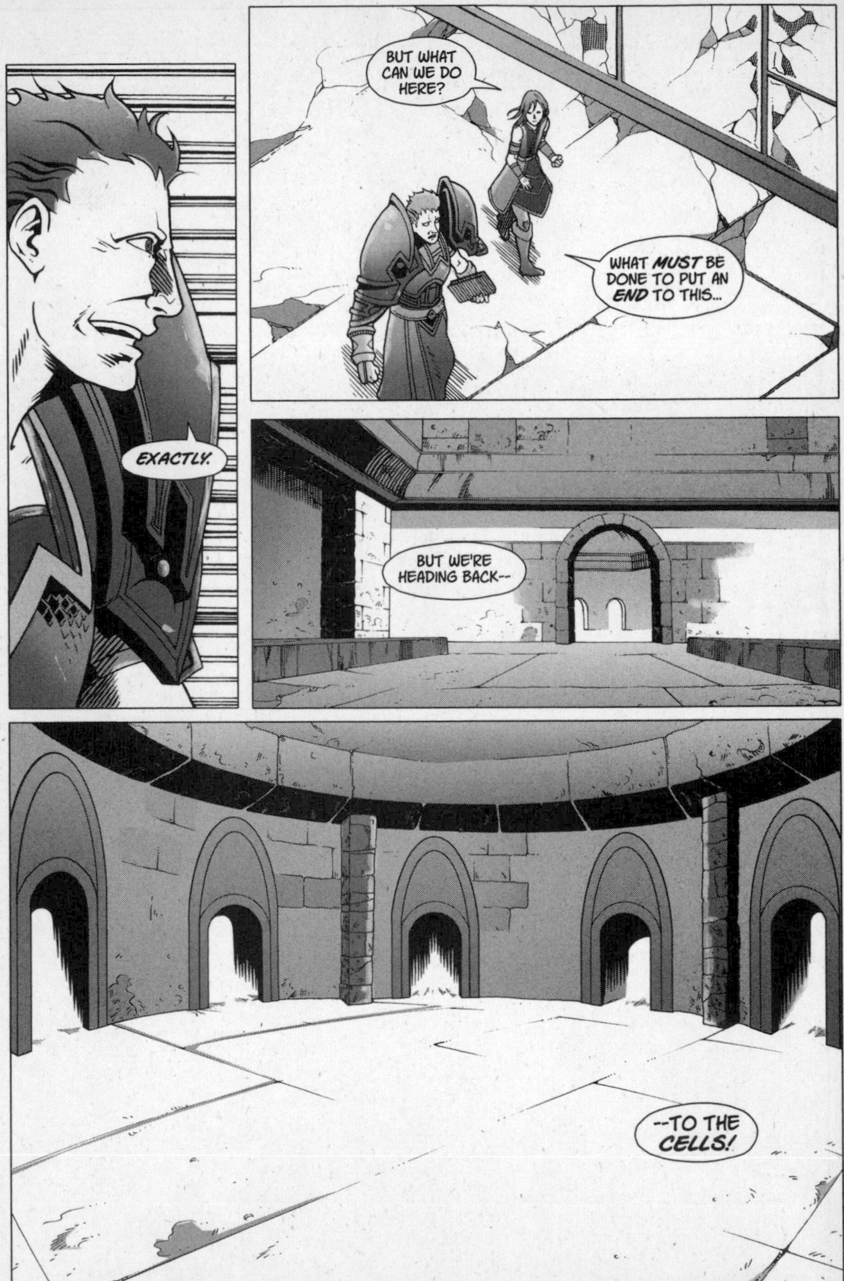
BUT WHAT CAN WE DO HERE?
WHAT MUST BE DONE TO PUT AN END TO THIS...
EXACTLY.
BUT WE'RE HEADING BACK--
--TO THE CELLS!

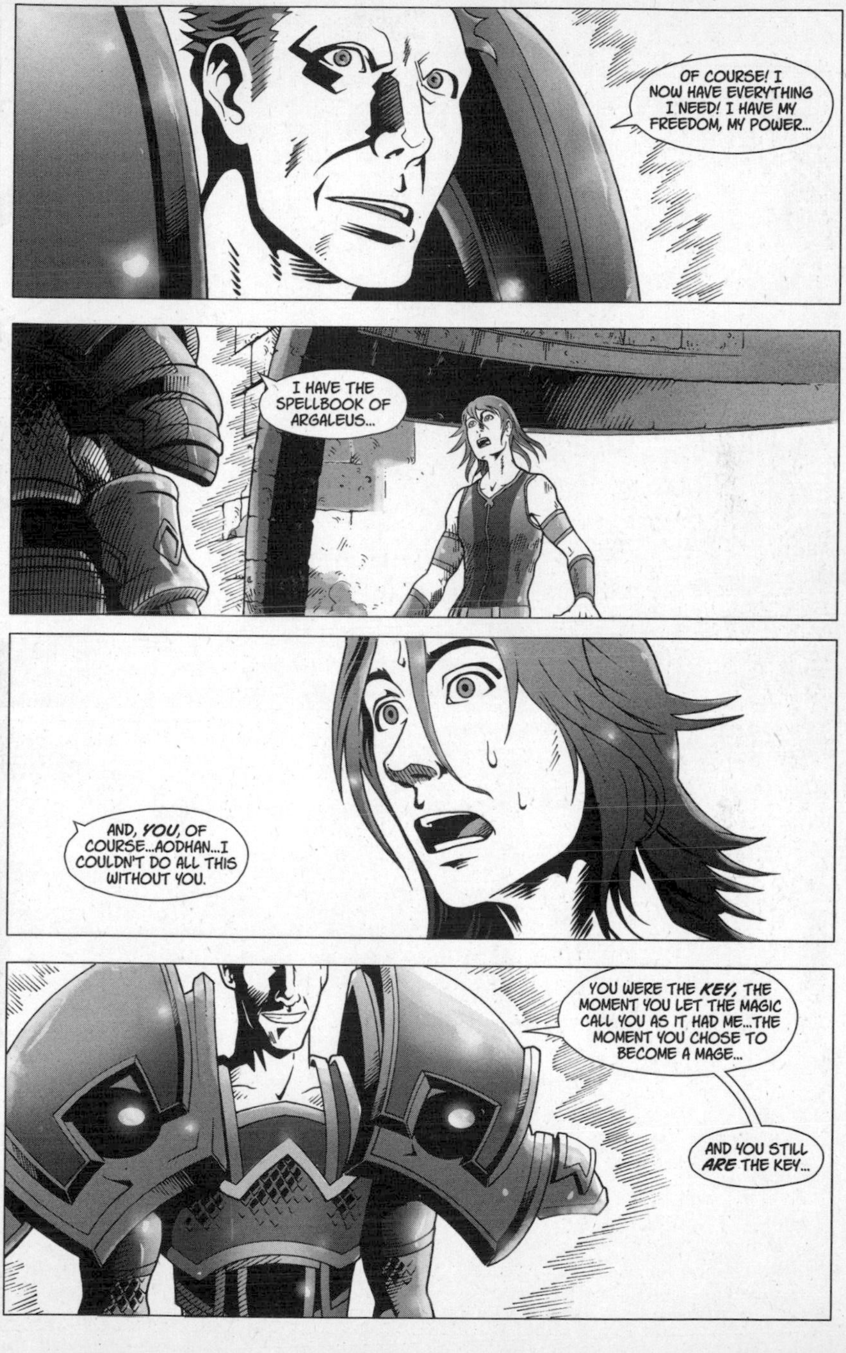
OF COURSE! I NOW HAVE EVERYTHING I NEED! I HAVE MY FREEDOM, MY POWER...
I HAVE THE SPELLBOOK OF ARGALEUS...
AND, YOU, OF COURSE...AODHAN...I COULDN'T DO ALL THIS WITHOUT YOU.
YOU WERE THE KEY, THE MOMENT YOU LET THE MAGIC CALL YOU AS IT HAD ME...THE MOMENT YOU CHOSE TO BECOME A MAGE...
AND YOU STILL ARE THE KEY...

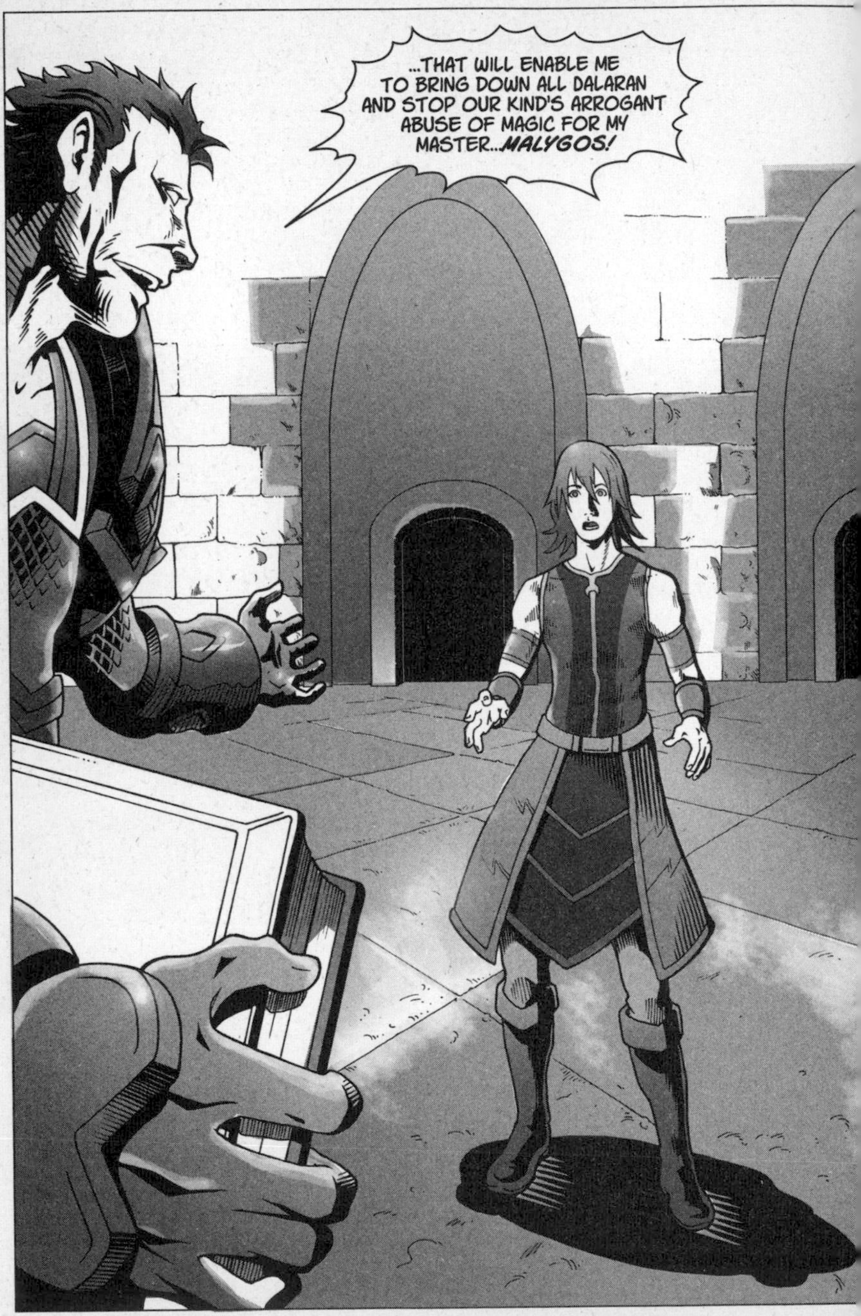
...THAT WILL ENABLE ME TO BRING DOWN ALL DALARAN AND STOP OUR KIND'S ARROGANT ABUSE OF MAGIC FOR MY MASTER...MALYGOS!

# CHAPTER FOUR
# BY BLOOD BETRAYED

OUR INSTRUMENT IS IN PLACE!

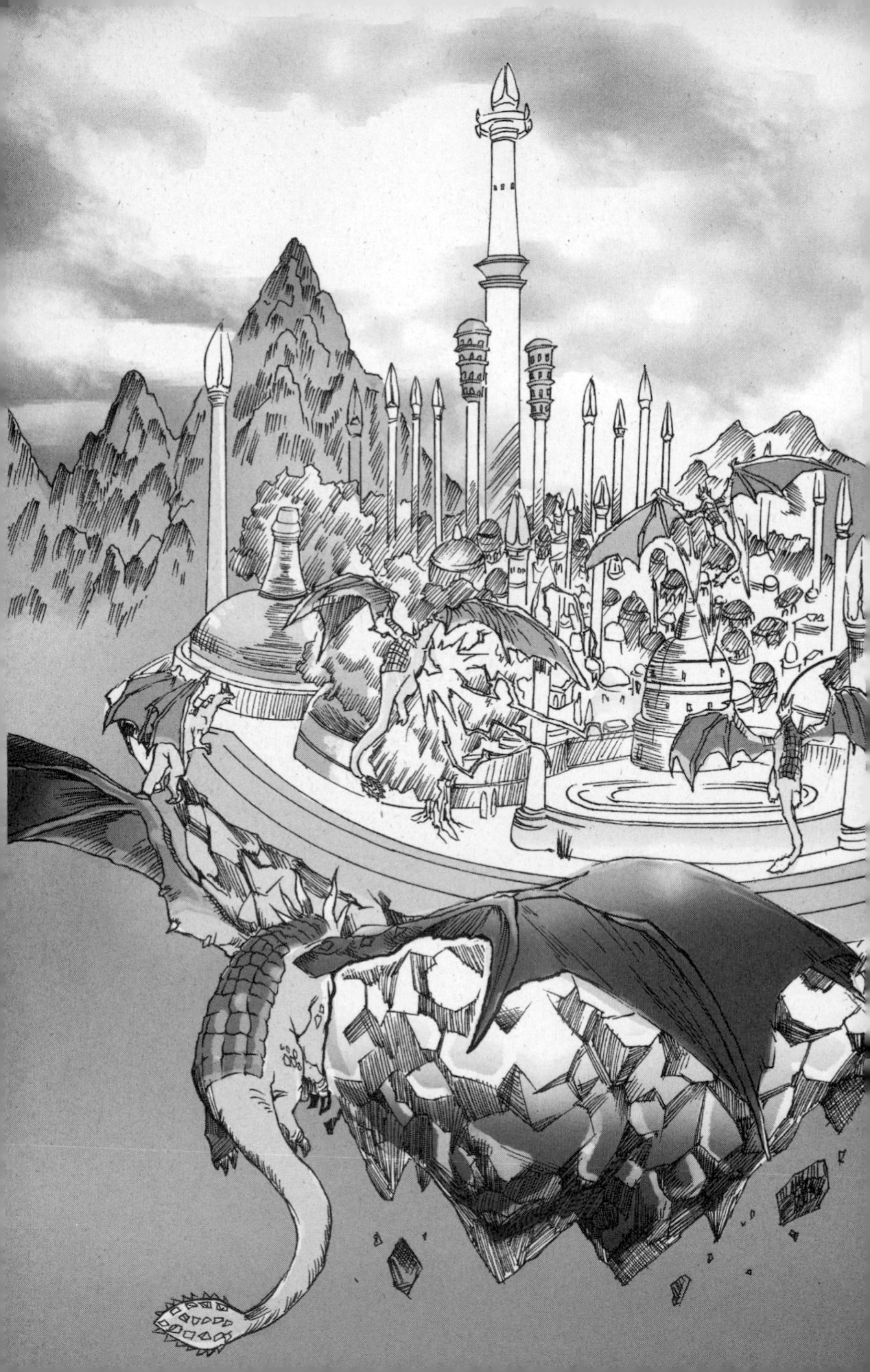

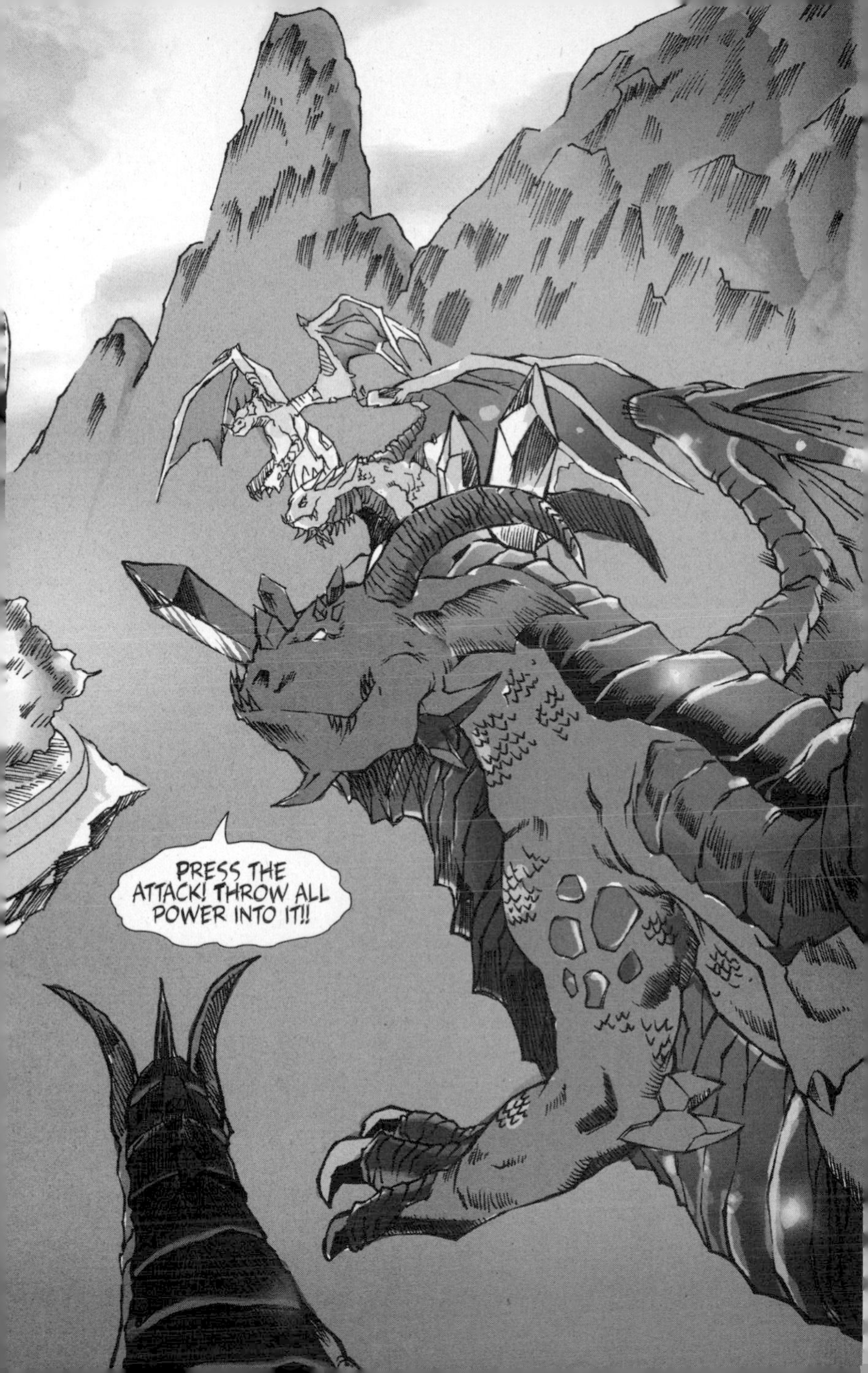
PRESS THE ATTACK! THROW ALL POWER INTO IT!!

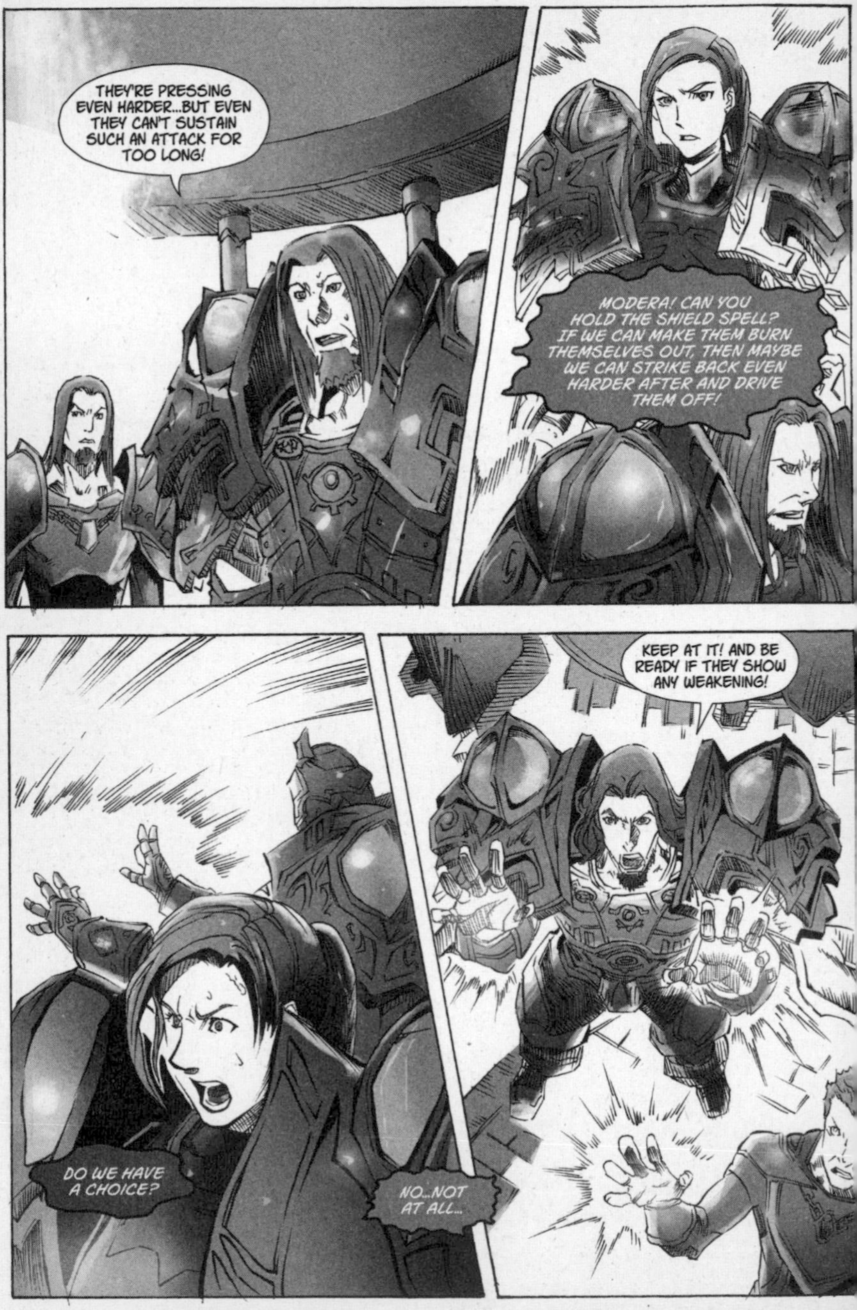
THEY'RE PRESSING EVEN HARDER...BUT EVEN THEY CAN'T SUSTAIN SUCH AN ATTACK FOR TOO LONG!
MODERA! CAN YOU HOLD THE SHIELD SPELL? IF WE CAN MAKE THEM BURN THEMSELVES OUT, THEN MAYBE WE CAN STRIKE BACK EVEN HARDER AFTER AND DRIVE THEM OFF!
DO WE HAVE A CHOICE?
NO...NOT AT ALL...
KEEP AT IT! AND BE READY IF THEY SHOW ANY WEAKENING!

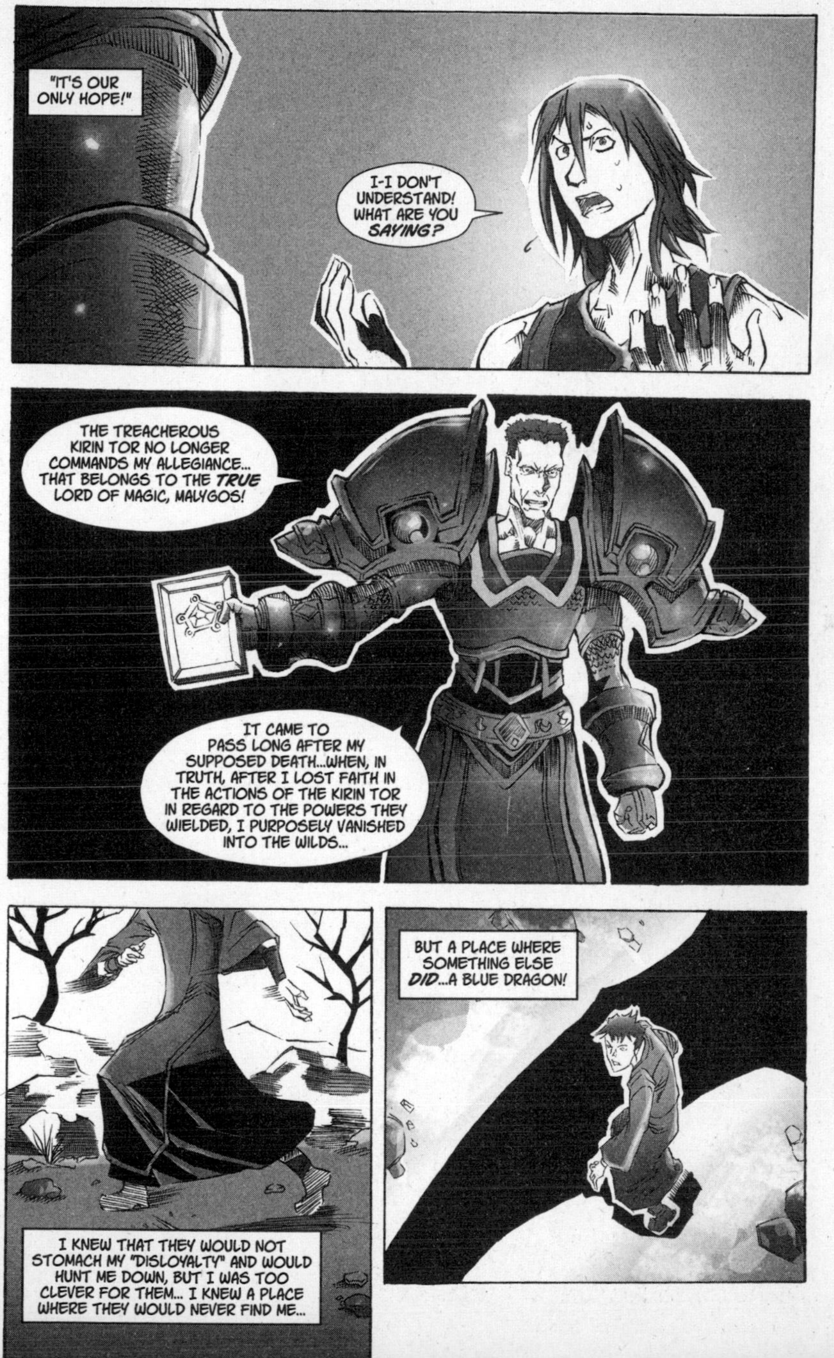
"IT'S OUR ONLY HOPE!"
I-I DON'T UNDERSTAND! WHAT ARE YOU SAYING?
THE TREACHEROUS KIRIN TOR NO LONGER COMMANDS MY ALLEGIANCE... THAT BELONGS TO THE TRUE LORD OF MAGIC, MALYGOS!
IT CAME TO PASS LONG AFTER MY SUPPOSED DEATH...WHEN, IN TRUTH, AFTER I LOST FAITH IN THE ACTIONS OF THE KIRIN TOR IN REGARD TO THE POWERS THEY WIELDED, I PURPOSELY VANISHED INTO THE WILDS...
I KNEW THAT THEY WOULD NOT STOMACH MY "DISLOYALTY" AND WOULD HUNT ME DOWN, BUT I WAS TOO CLEVER FOR THEM... I KNEW A PLACE WHERE THEY WOULD NEVER FIND ME...
BUT A PLACE WHERE SOMETHING ELSE DID...A BLUE DRAGON!

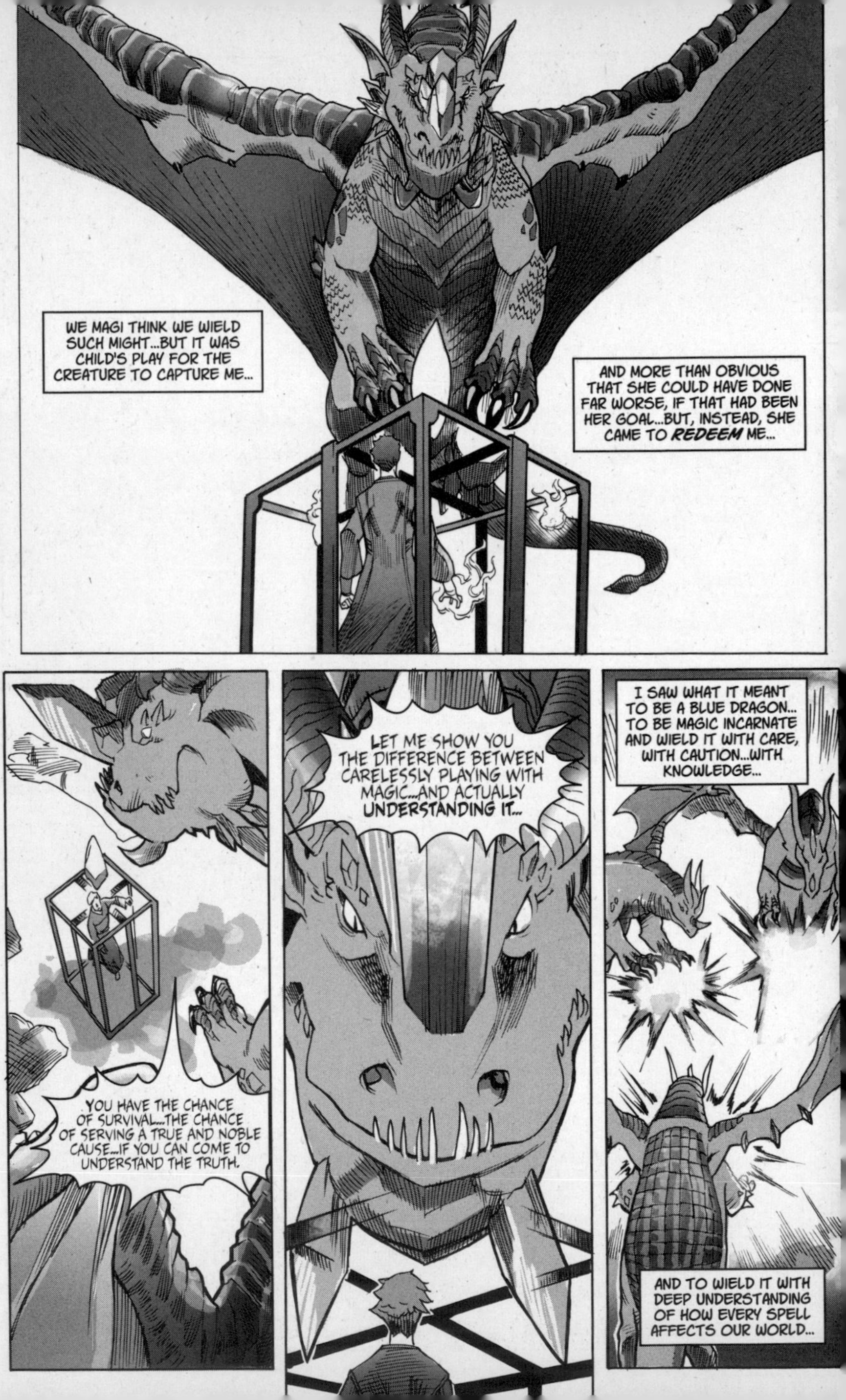
WE MAGI THINK WE WIELD SUCH MIGHT...BUT IT WAS CHILD'S PLAY FOR THE CREATURE TO CAPTURE ME...
AND MORE THAN OBVIOUS THAT SHE COULD HAVE DONE FAR WORSE, IF THAT HAD BEEN HER GOAL...BUT, INSTEAD, SHE CAME TO *REDEEM* ME...
YOU HAVE THE CHANCE OF SURVIVAL...THE CHANCE OF SERVING A TRUE AND NOBLE CAUSE...IF YOU CAN COME TO UNDERSTAND THE TRUTH.
LET ME SHOW YOU THE DIFFERENCE BETWEEN CARELESSLY PLAYING WITH MAGIC...AND ACTUALLY **UNDERSTANDING IT**...
I SAW WHAT IT MEANT TO BE A BLUE DRAGON... TO BE MAGIC INCARNATE AND WIELD IT WITH CARE, WITH CAUTION...WITH KNOWLEDGE...
AND TO WIELD IT WITH DEEP UNDERSTANDING OF HOW EVERY SPELL AFFECTS OUR WORLD...

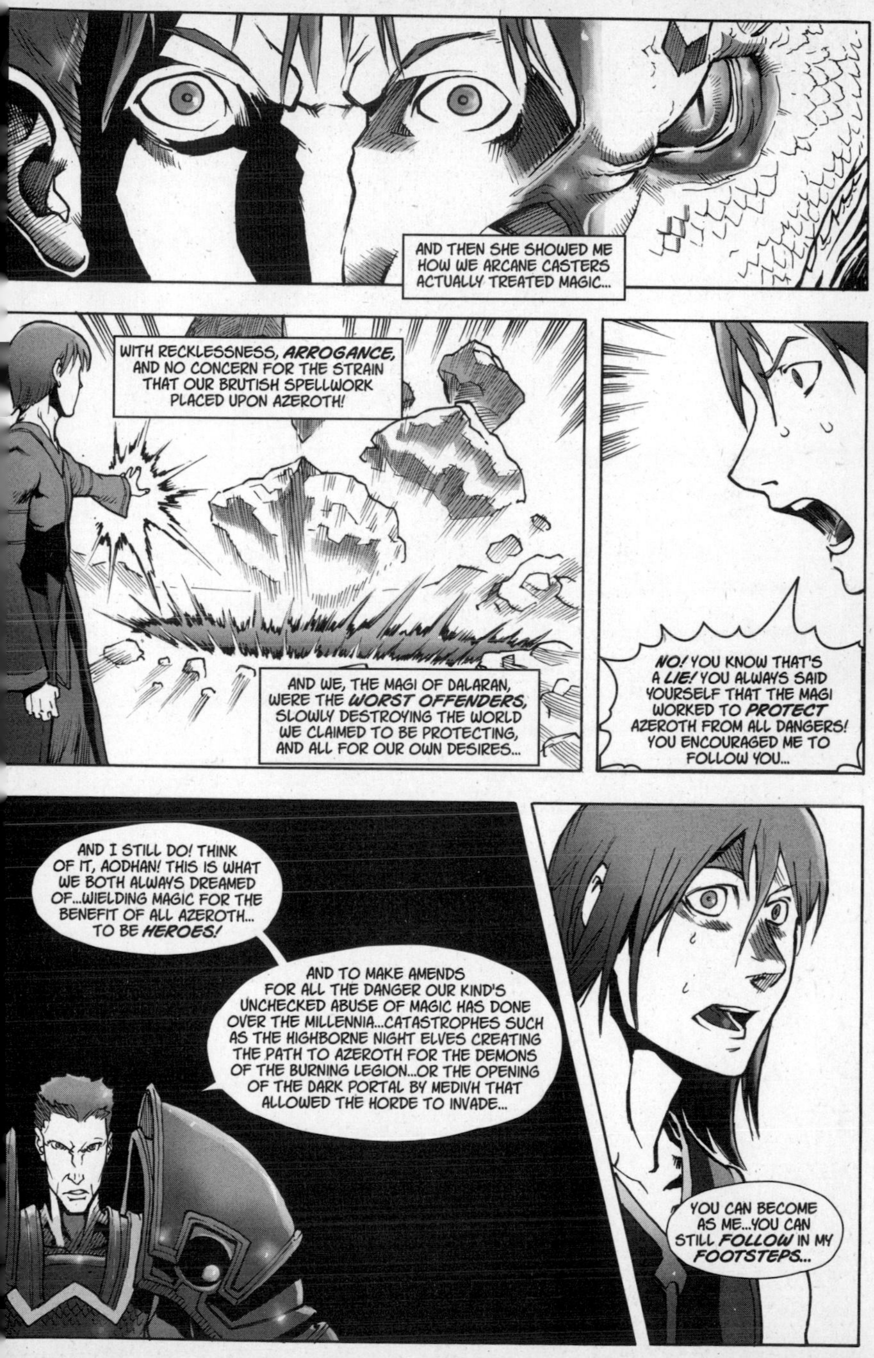
AND THEN SHE SHOWED ME HOW WE ARCANE CASTERS ACTUALLY TREATED MAGIC...
WITH RECKLESSNESS, ARROGANCE, AND NO CONCERN FOR THE STRAIN THAT OUR BRUTISH SPELLWORK PLACED UPON AZEROTH!
AND WE, THE MAGI OF DALARAN, WERE THE WORST OFFENDERS, SLOWLY DESTROYING THE WORLD WE CLAIMED TO BE PROTECTING, AND ALL FOR OUR OWN DESIRES...
NO! YOU KNOW THAT'S A LIE! YOU ALWAYS SAID YOURSELF THAT THE MAGI WORKED TO PROTECT AZEROTH FROM ALL DANGERS! YOU ENCOURAGED ME TO FOLLOW YOU...
AND I STILL DO! THINK OF IT, AODHAN! THIS IS WHAT WE BOTH ALWAYS DREAMED OF...WIELDING MAGIC FOR THE BENEFIT OF ALL AZEROTH... TO BE HEROES!
AND TO MAKE AMENDS FOR ALL THE DANGER OUR KIND'S UNCHECKED ABUSE OF MAGIC HAS DONE OVER THE MILLENNIA...CATASTROPHES SUCH AS THE HIGHBORNE NIGHT ELVES CREATING THE PATH TO AZEROTH FOR THE DEMONS OF THE BURNING LEGION...OR THE OPENING OF THE DARK PORTAL BY MEDIVH THAT ALLOWED THE HORDE TO INVADE...
YOU CAN BECOME AS ME...YOU CAN STILL FOLLOW IN MY FOOTSTEPS...

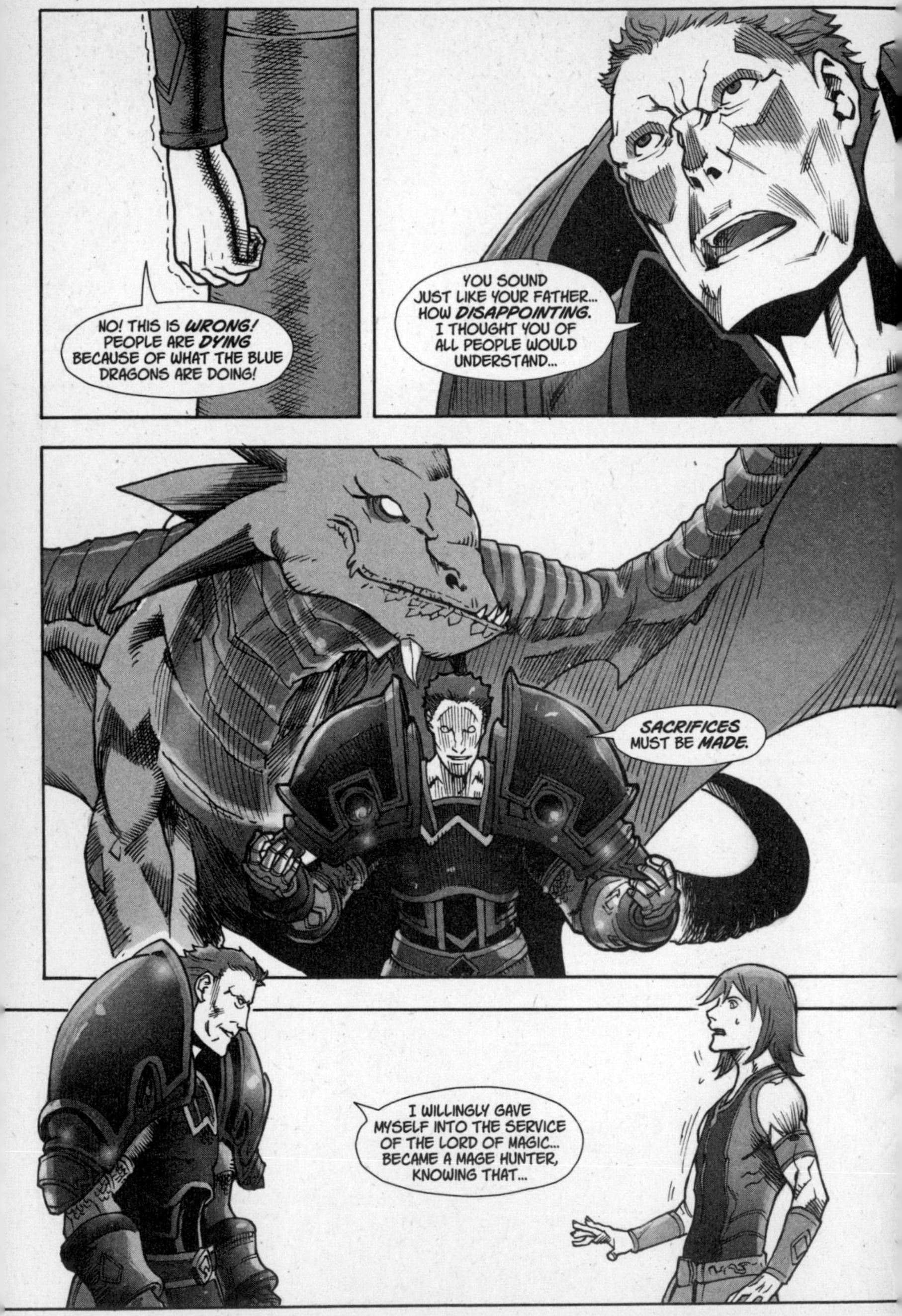
NO! THIS IS WRONG! PEOPLE ARE DYING BECAUSE OF WHAT THE BLUE DRAGONS ARE DOING!
YOU SOUND JUST LIKE YOUR FATHER... HOW DISAPPOINTING. I THOUGHT YOU OF ALL PEOPLE WOULD UNDERSTAND...
SACRIFICES MUST BE MADE.
I WILLINGLY GAVE MYSELF INTO THE SERVICE OF THE LORD OF MAGIC... BECAME A MAGE HUNTER, KNOWING THAT...

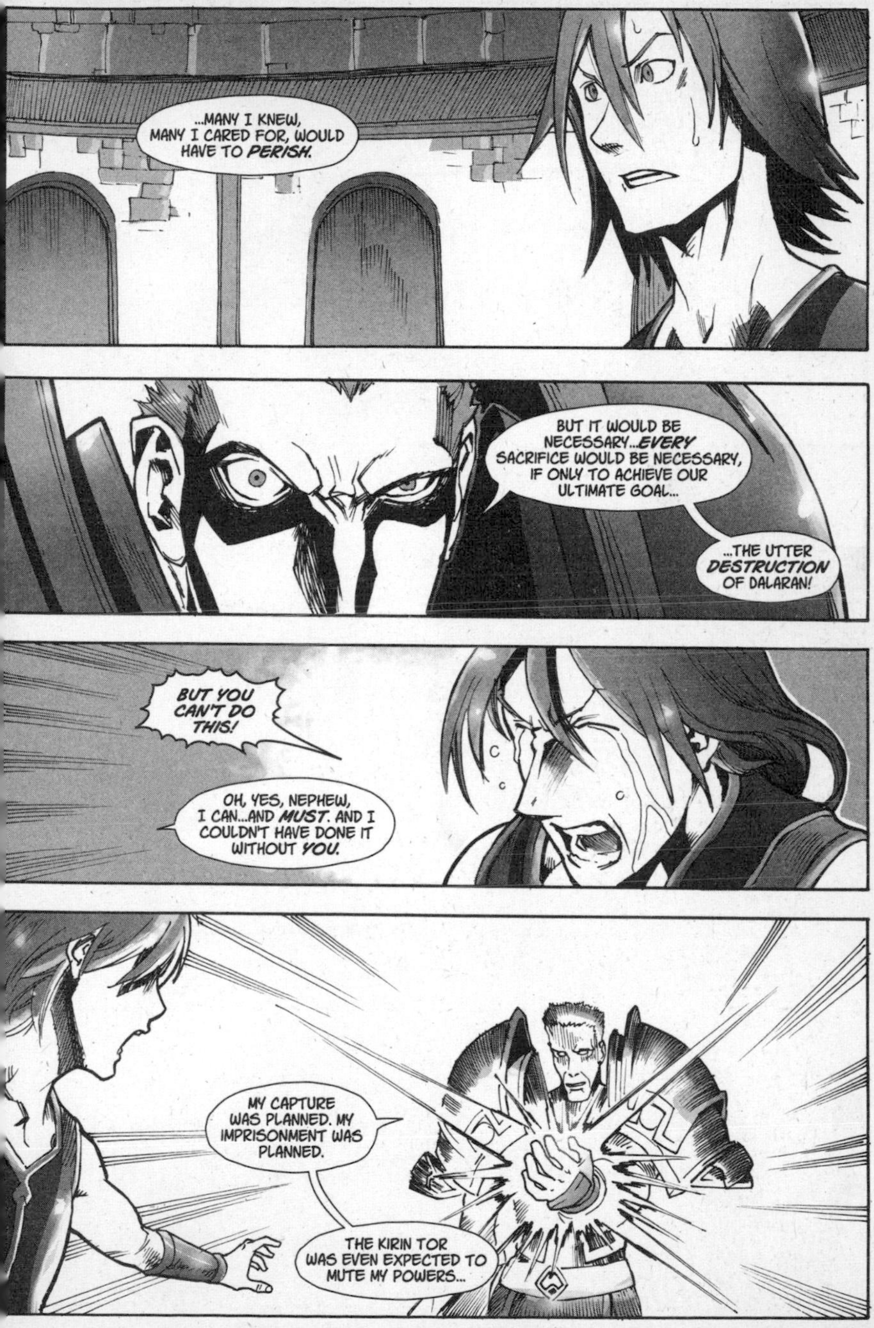
...MANY I KNEW, MANY I CARED FOR, WOULD HAVE TO PERISH.
BUT IT WOULD BE NECESSARY...EVERY SACRIFICE WOULD BE NECESSARY, IF ONLY TO ACHIEVE OUR ULTIMATE GOAL...
...THE UTTER DESTRUCTION OF DALARAN!
BUT YOU CAN'T DO THIS!
OH, YES, NEPHEW, I CAN...AND MUST. AND I COULDN'T HAVE DONE IT WITHOUT YOU.
MY CAPTURE WAS PLANNED. MY IMPRISONMENT WAS PLANNED.
THE KIRIN TOR WAS EVEN EXPECTED TO MUTE MY POWERS...

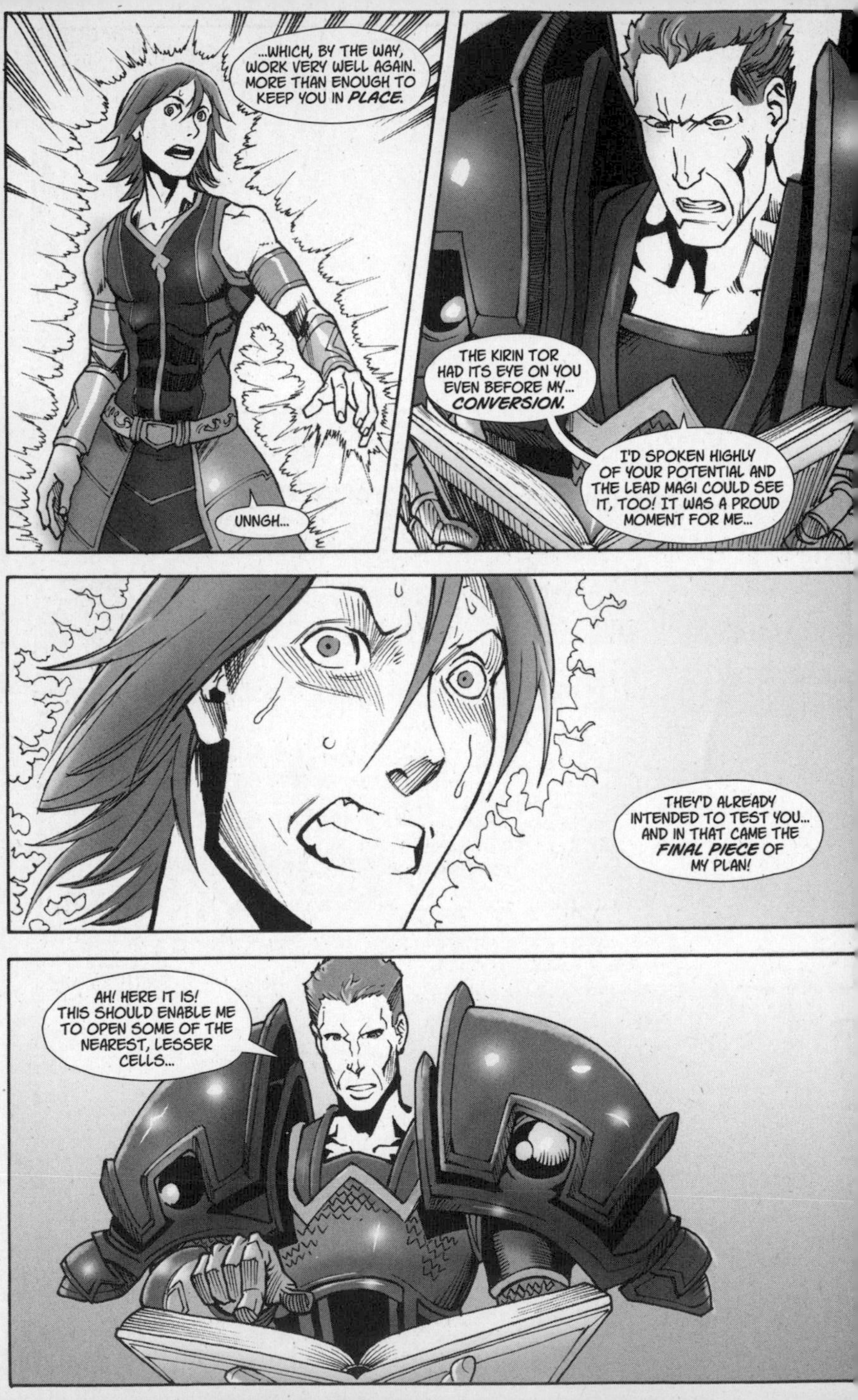
...WHICH, BY THE WAY, WORK VERY WELL AGAIN. MORE THAN ENOUGH TO KEEP YOU IN *PLACE*.
UNNGH...
THE KIRIN TOR HAD ITS EYE ON YOU EVEN BEFORE MY... *CONVERSION*.
I'D SPOKEN HIGHLY OF YOUR POTENTIAL AND THE LEAD MAGI COULD SEE IT, TOO! IT WAS A PROUD MOMENT FOR ME...
THEY'D ALREADY INTENDED TO TEST YOU... AND IN THAT CAME THE *FINAL PIECE* OF MY PLAN!
AH! HERE IT IS! THIS SHOULD ENABLE ME TO OPEN SOME OF THE NEAREST, LESSER CELLS...

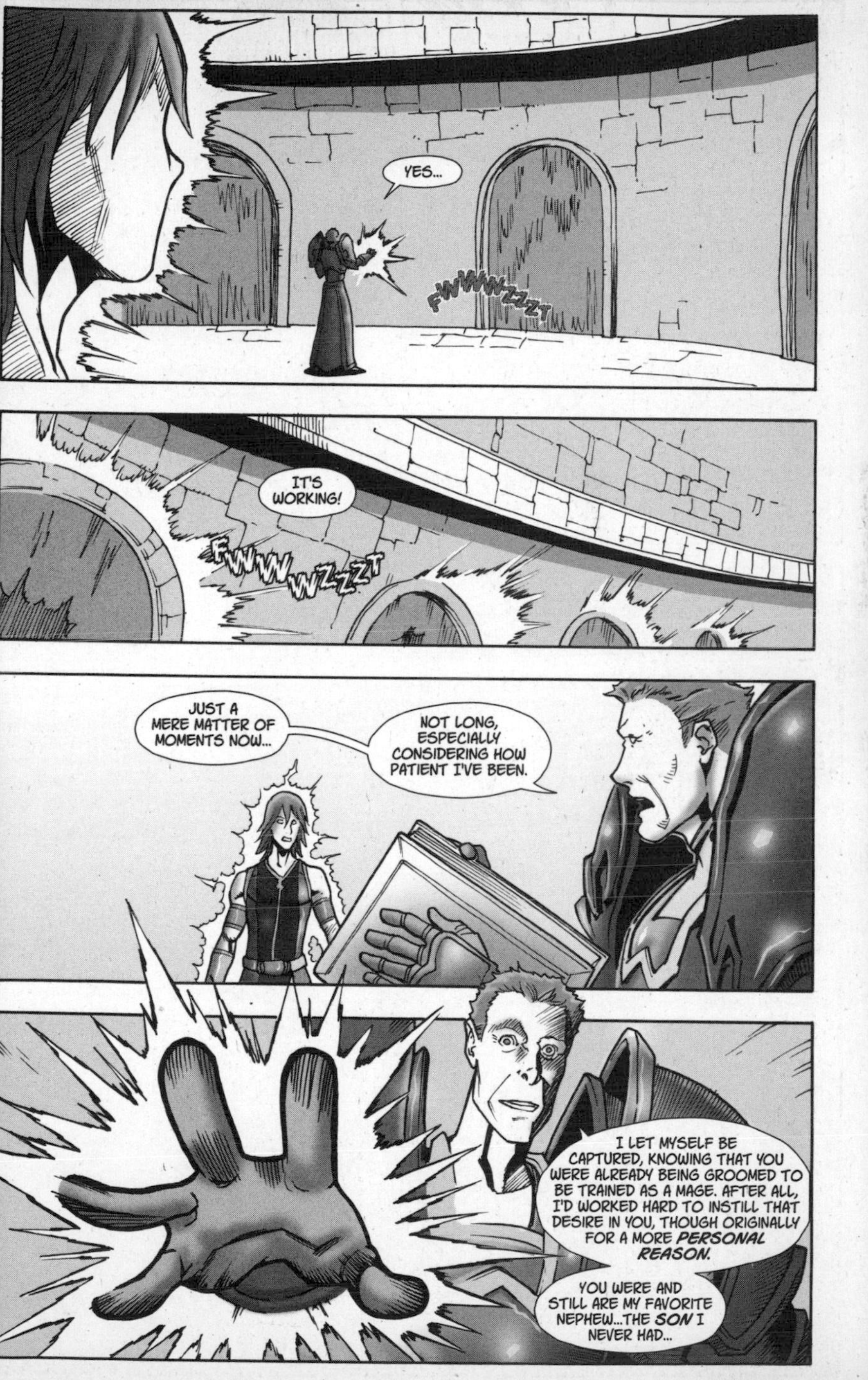
YES...
FWWWWZZZT
IT'S WORKING!
FWWWWWZZZT
JUST A MERE MATTER OF MOMENTS NOW...
NOT LONG, ESPECIALLY CONSIDERING HOW PATIENT I'VE BEEN.
I LET MYSELF BE CAPTURED, KNOWING THAT YOU WERE ALREADY BEING GROOMED TO BE TRAINED AS A MAGE. AFTER ALL, I'D WORKED HARD TO INSTILL THAT DESIRE IN YOU, THOUGH ORIGINALLY FOR A MORE *PERSONAL REASON*.
YOU WERE AND STILL ARE MY FAVORITE NEPHEW...THE *SON* I NEVER HAD...

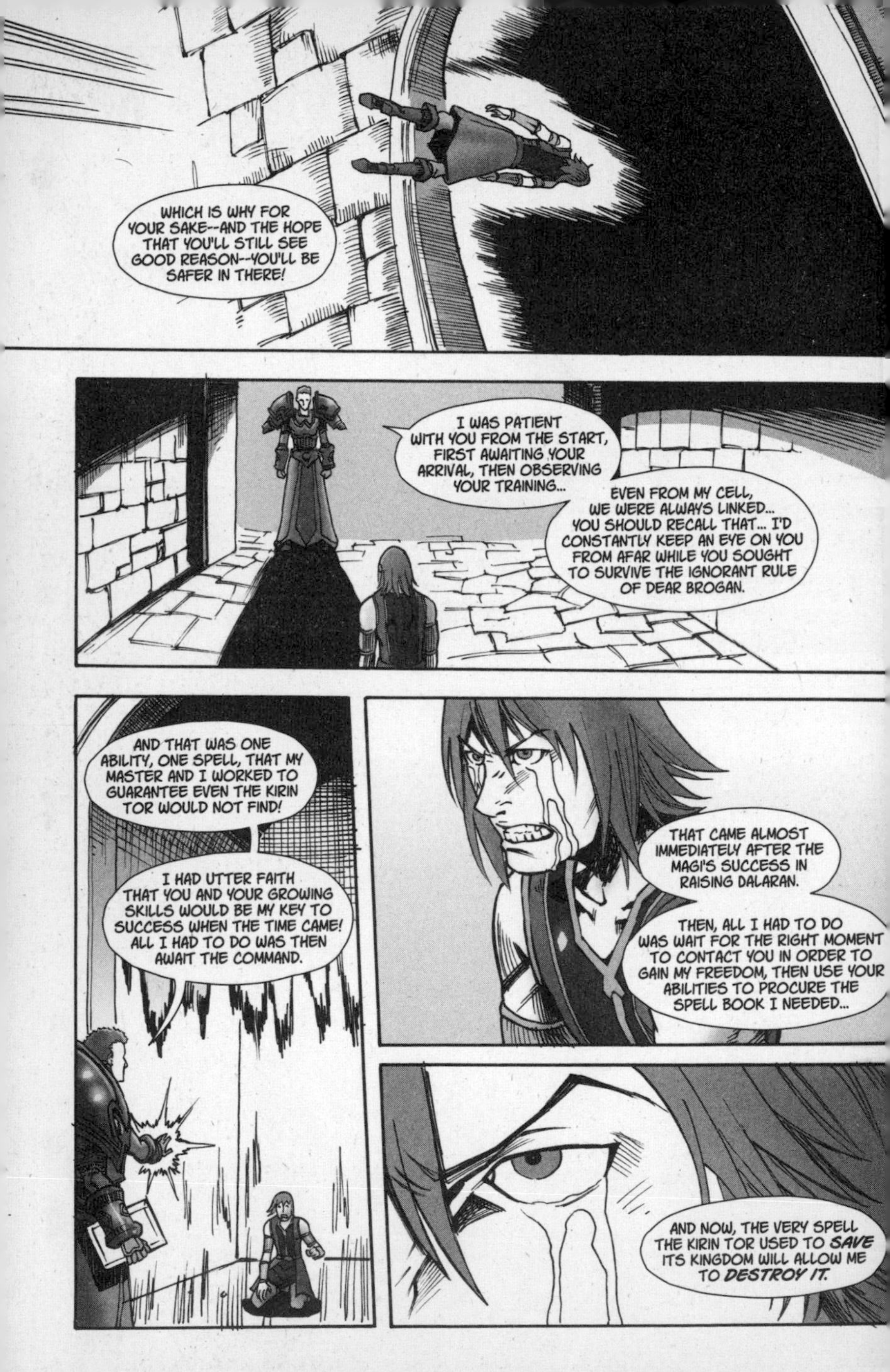
WHICH IS WHY FOR YOUR SAKE--AND THE HOPE THAT YOU'LL STILL SEE GOOD REASON--YOU'LL BE SAFER IN THERE!
I WAS PATIENT WITH YOU FROM THE START, FIRST AWAITING YOUR ARRIVAL, THEN OBSERVING YOUR TRAINING...
EVEN FROM MY CELL, WE WERE ALWAYS LINKED... YOU SHOULD RECALL THAT... I'D CONSTANTLY KEEP AN EYE ON YOU FROM AFAR WHILE YOU SOUGHT TO SURVIVE THE IGNORANT RULE OF DEAR BROGAN.
AND THAT WAS ONE ABILITY, ONE SPELL, THAT MY MASTER AND I WORKED TO GUARANTEE EVEN THE KIRIN TOR WOULD NOT FIND!
I HAD UTTER FAITH THAT YOU AND YOUR GROWING SKILLS WOULD BE MY KEY TO SUCCESS WHEN THE TIME CAME! ALL I HAD TO DO WAS THEN AWAIT THE COMMAND.
THAT CAME ALMOST IMMEDIATELY AFTER THE MAGI'S SUCCESS IN RAISING DALARAN.
THEN, ALL I HAD TO DO WAS WAIT FOR THE RIGHT MOMENT TO CONTACT YOU IN ORDER TO GAIN MY FREEDOM, THEN USE YOUR ABILITIES TO PROCURE THE SPELL BOOK I NEEDED...
AND NOW, THE VERY SPELL THE KIRIN TOR USED TO *SAVE* ITS KINGDOM WILL ALLOW ME TO ***DESTROY IT.***

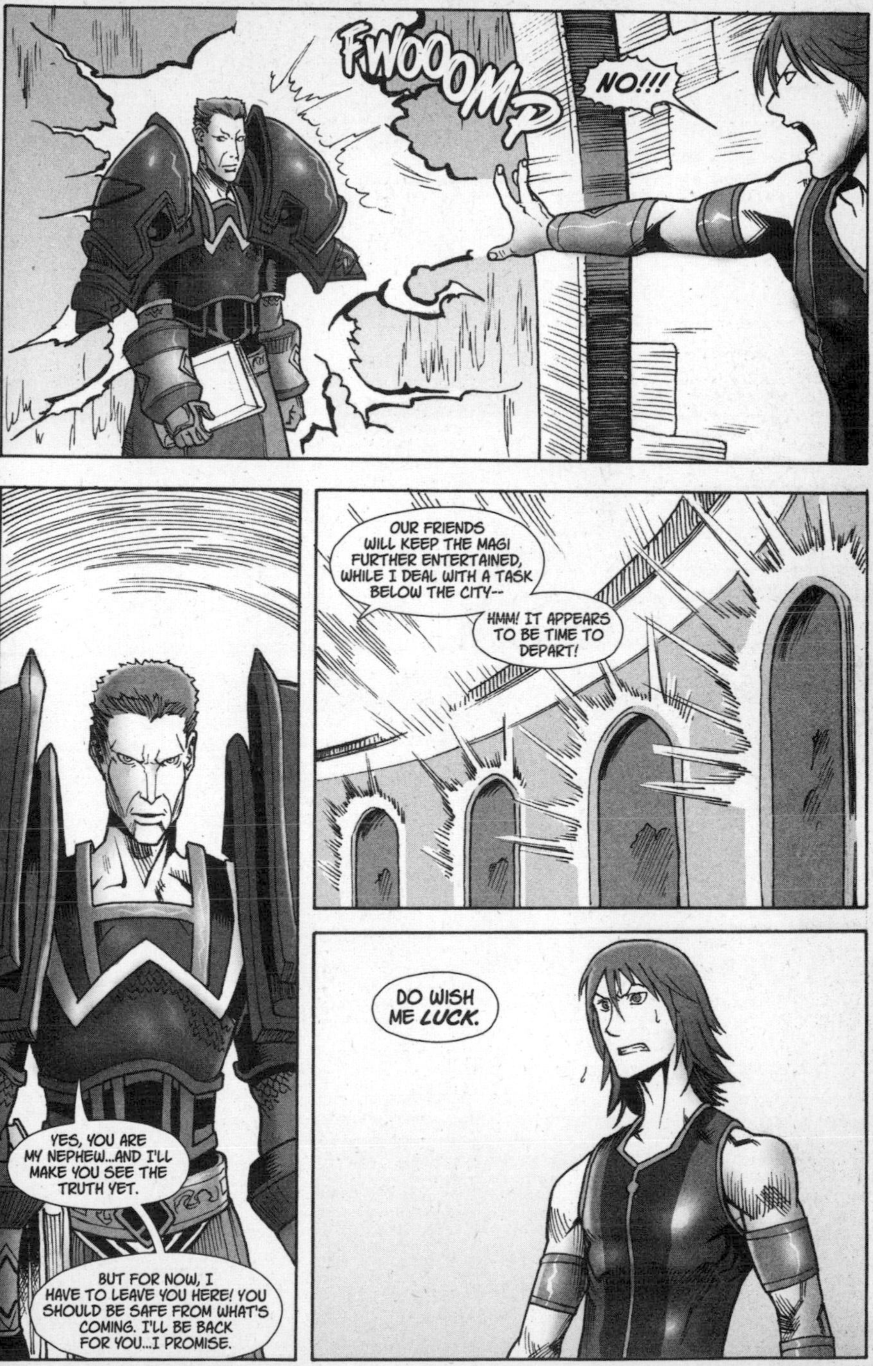
FWOOOMP
NO!!!
YES, YOU ARE MY NEPHEW...AND I'LL MAKE YOU SEE THE TRUTH YET.
BUT FOR NOW, I HAVE TO LEAVE YOU HERE! YOU SHOULD BE SAFE FROM WHAT'S COMING. I'LL BE BACK FOR YOU...I PROMISE.
OUR FRIENDS WILL KEEP THE MAGI FURTHER ENTERTAINED, WHILE I DEAL WITH A TASK BELOW THE CITY--
HMM! IT APPEARS TO BE TIME TO DEPART!
DO WISH ME LUCK.

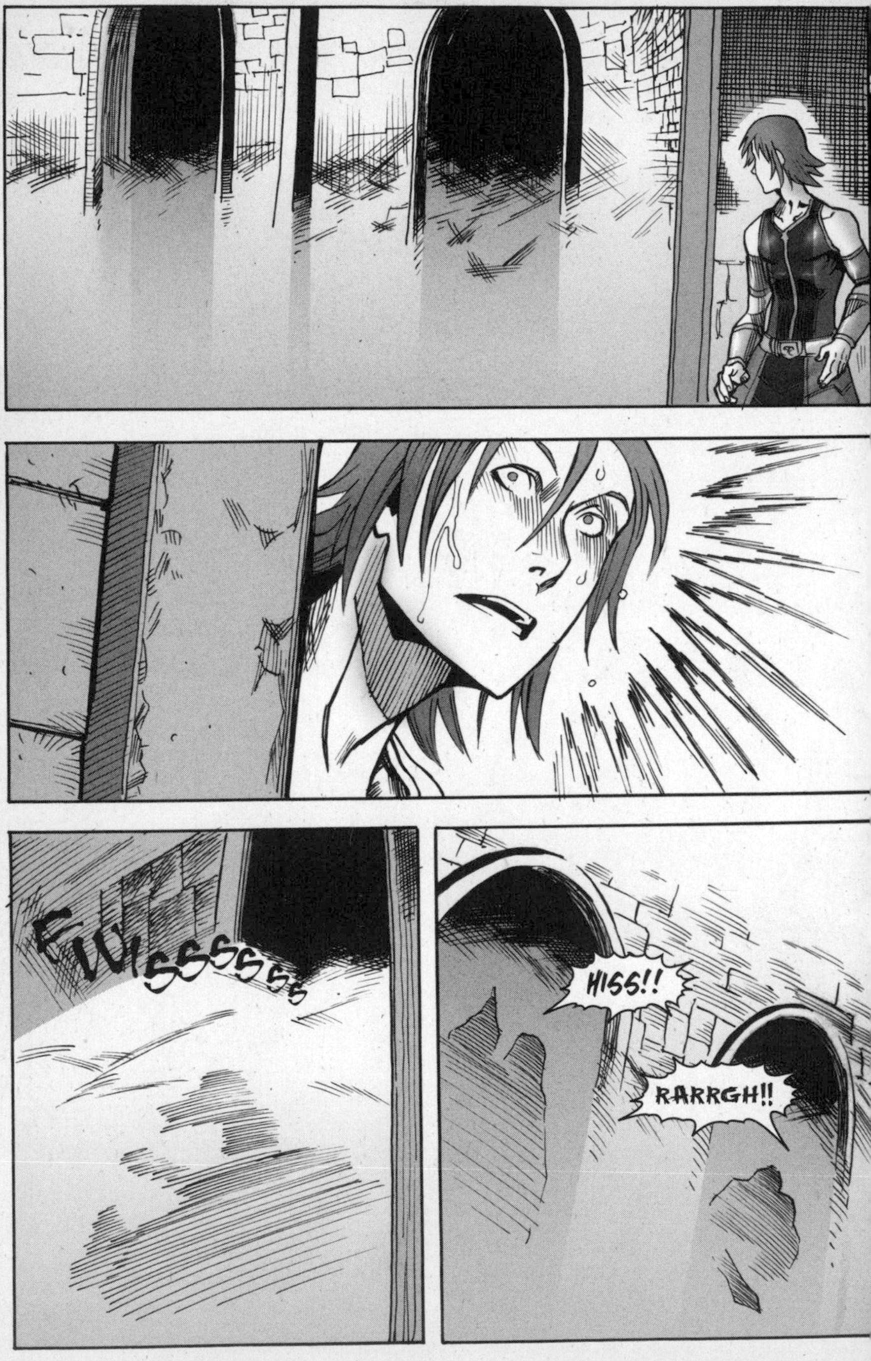
EWISSSSSS
HISS!!
RARRGH!!

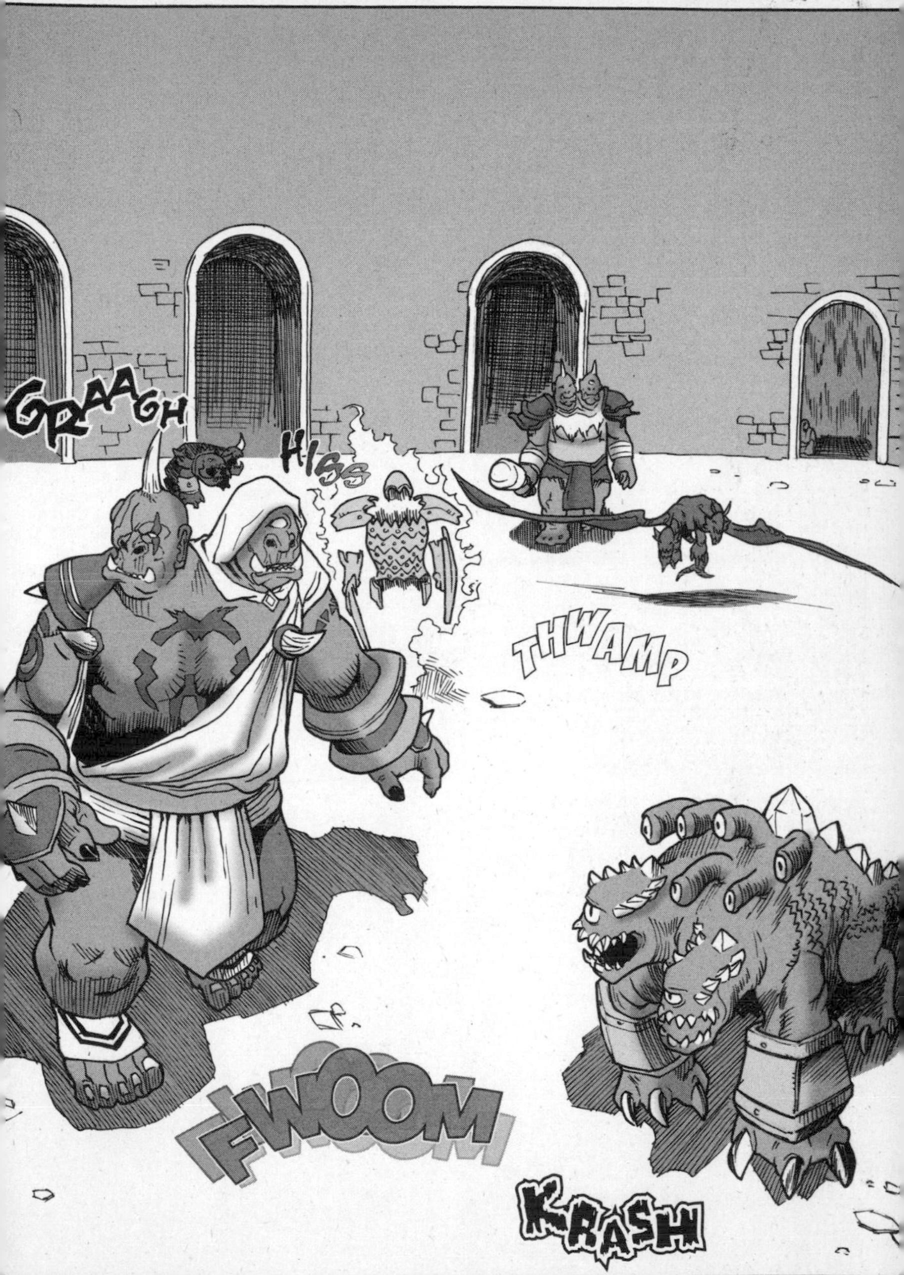
GRAAGH
HISS
THWAMP
FWOOM
KRASH

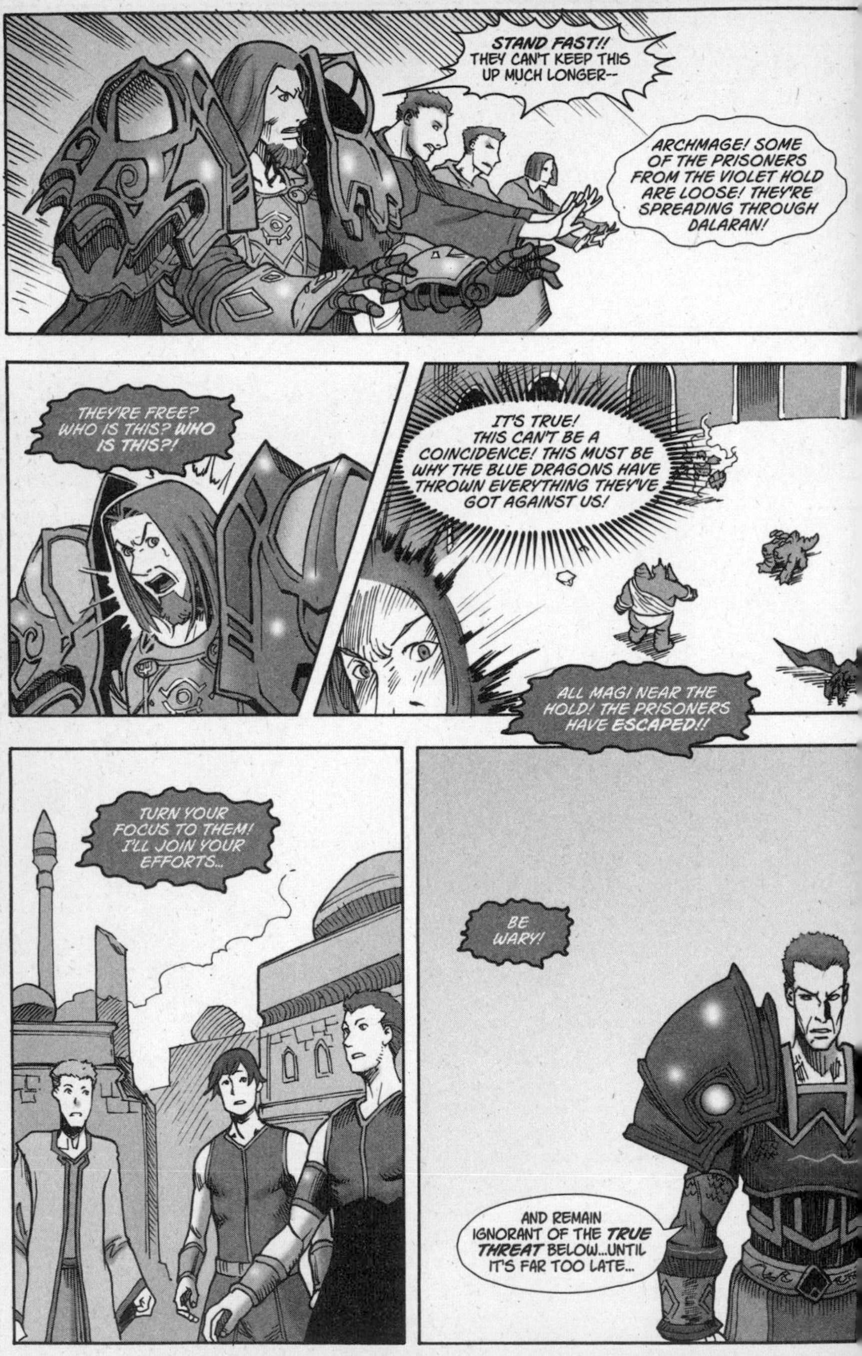
STAND FAST!! THEY CAN'T KEEP THIS UP MUCH LONGER--
ARCHMAGE! SOME OF THE PRISONERS FROM THE VIOLET HOLD ARE LOOSE! THEY'RE SPREADING THROUGH DALARAN!
THEY'RE FREE? WHO IS THIS? WHO IS THIS?!
IT'S TRUE! THIS CAN'T BE A COINCIDENCE! THIS MUST BE WHY THE BLUE DRAGONS HAVE THROWN EVERYTHING THEY'VE GOT AGAINST US!
ALL MAGI NEAR THE HOLD! THE PRISONERS HAVE ESCAPED!!
TURN YOUR FOCUS TO THEM! I'LL JOIN YOUR EFFORTS...
BE WARY!
AND REMAIN IGNORANT OF THE TRUE THREAT BELOW...UNTIL IT'S FAR TOO LATE...

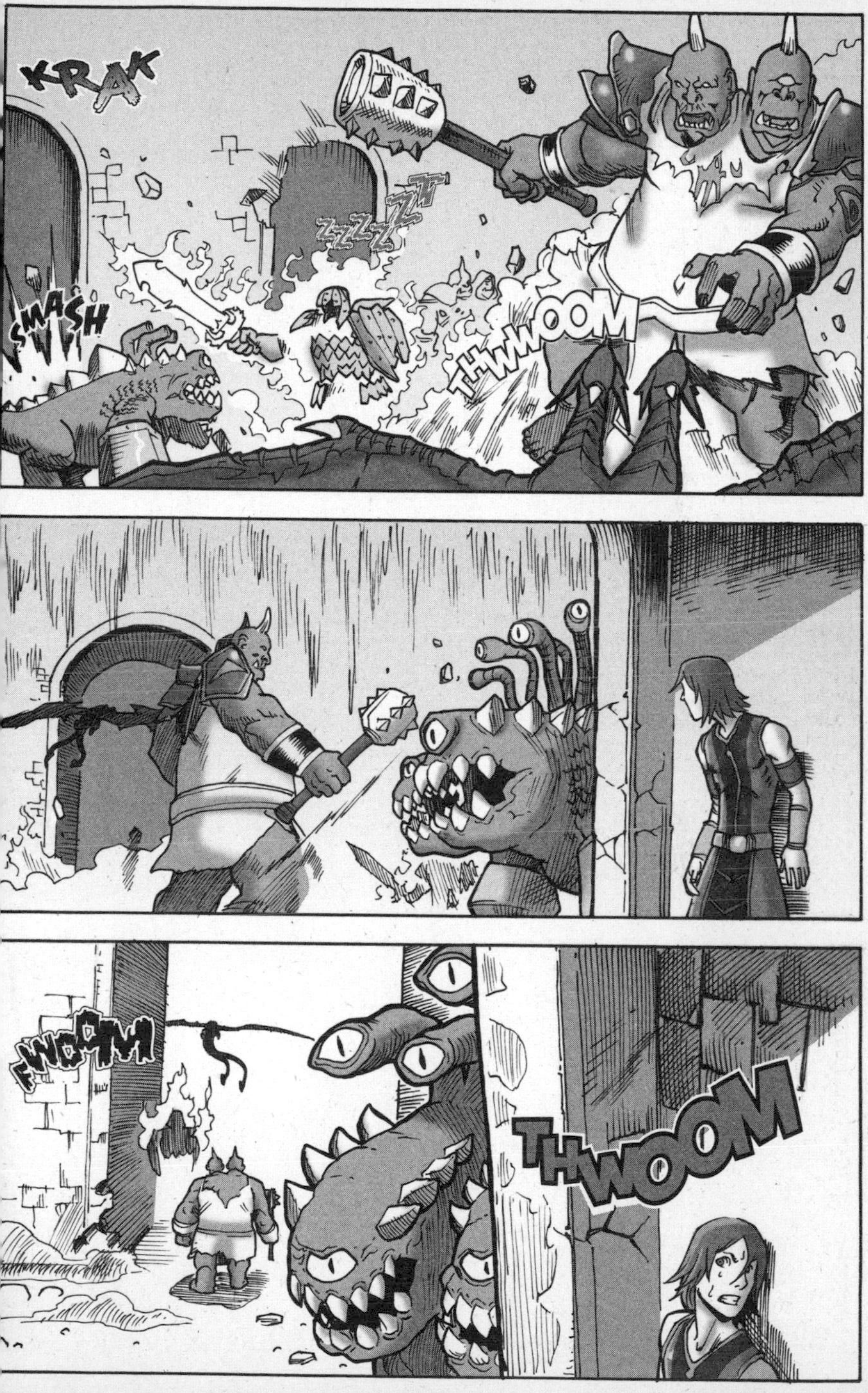
KRAK
ZZZZZT
SMASH
THWOOM
FWOOM
THWOOM

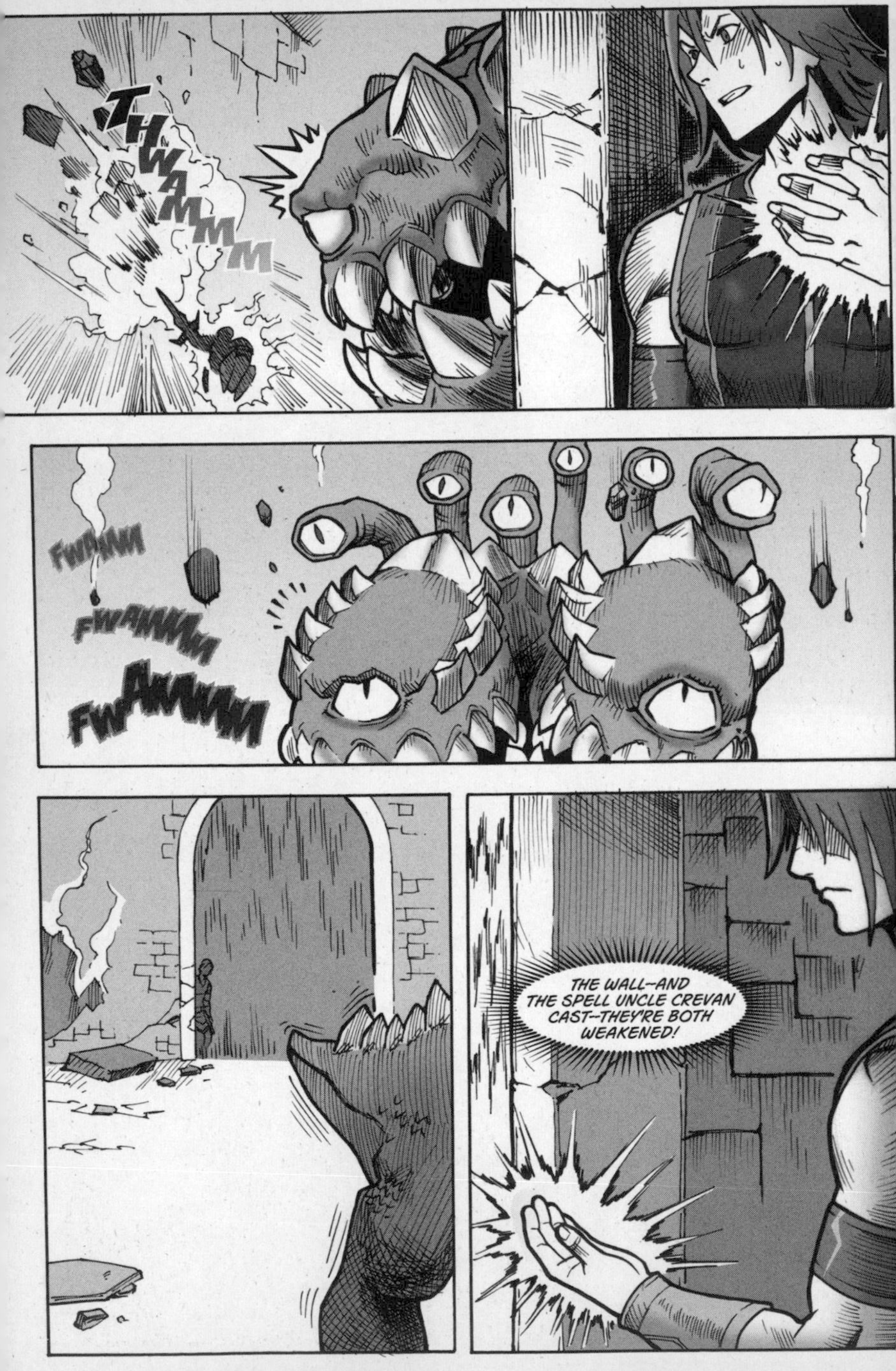
THWAMMMM
FWAAAA
FWAAAAAA
FWAAAAAA
THE WALL--AND THE SPELL UNCLE CREVAN CAST--THEY'RE BOTH WEAKENED!

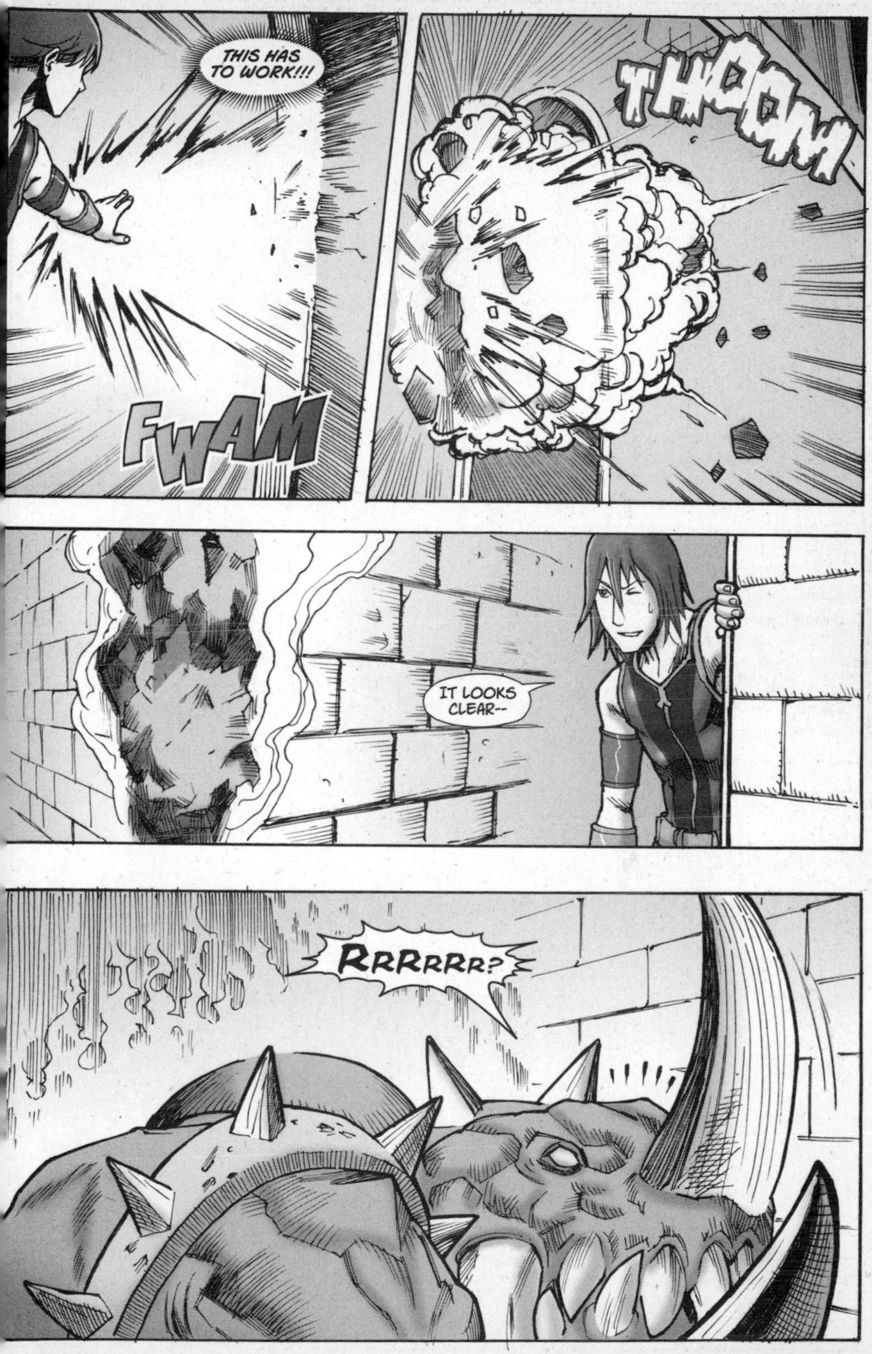
THIS HAS TO WORK!!!
FWAM
THOOM
IT LOOKS CLEAR--
RRRRRR?

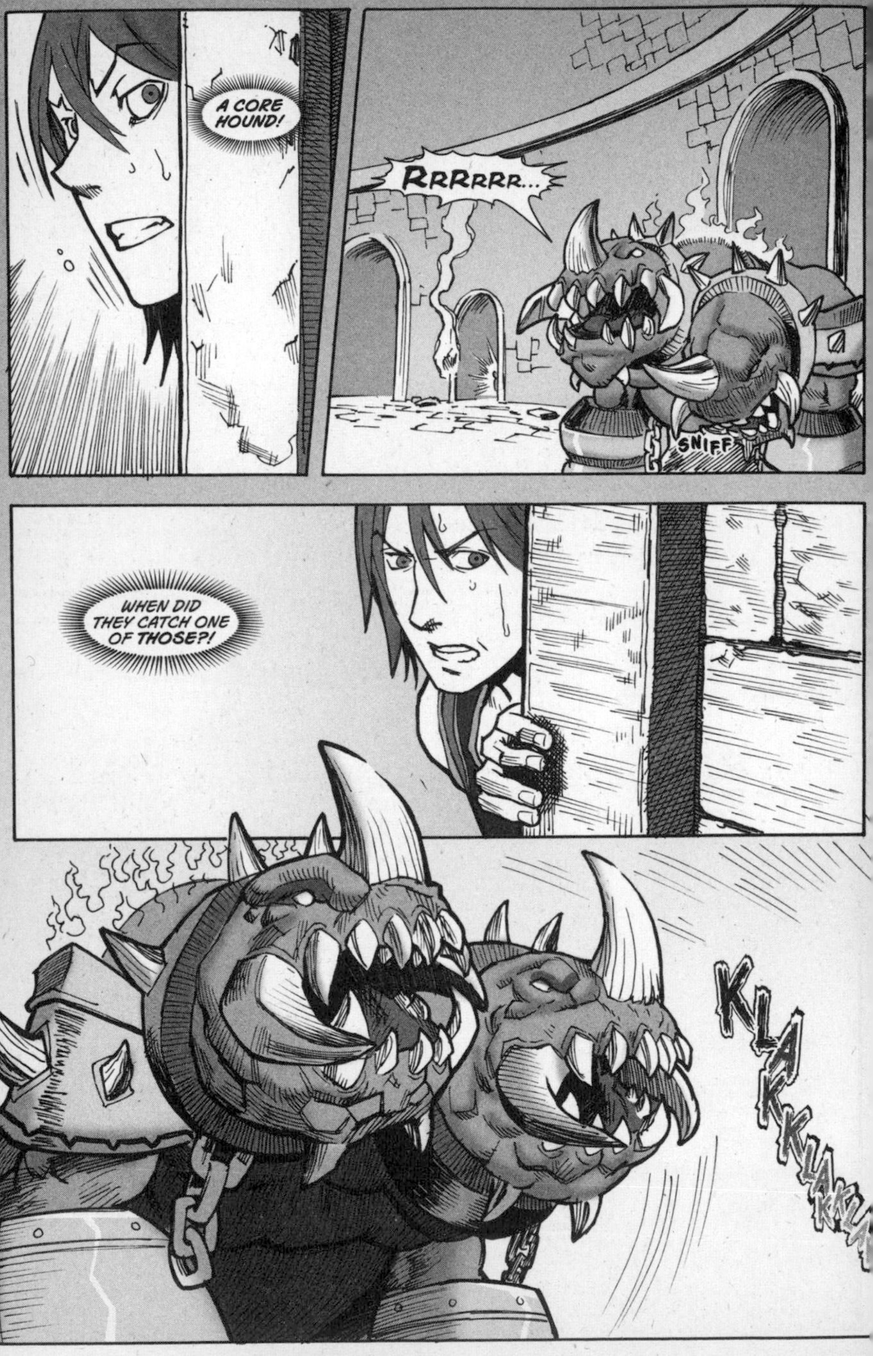
A CORE HOUND!
RRRRRRR...
SNIFF
WHEN DID THEY CATCH ONE OF THOSE?!
KLAKKLAKKLA

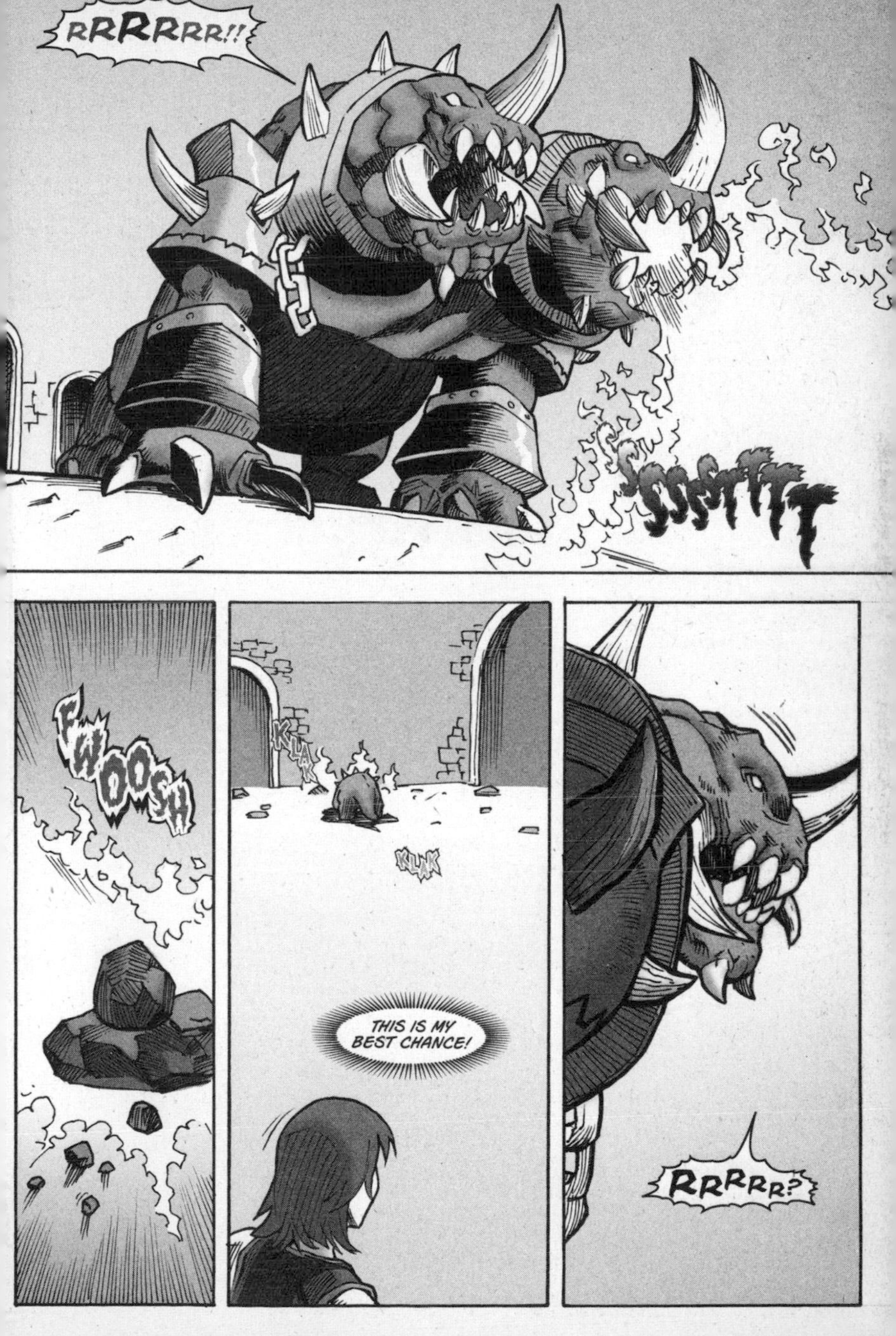
RRRRRRR!!
SSSSTTTT
FWOOSH
KLAK
KLAK
THIS IS MY BEST CHANCE!
RRRRR?

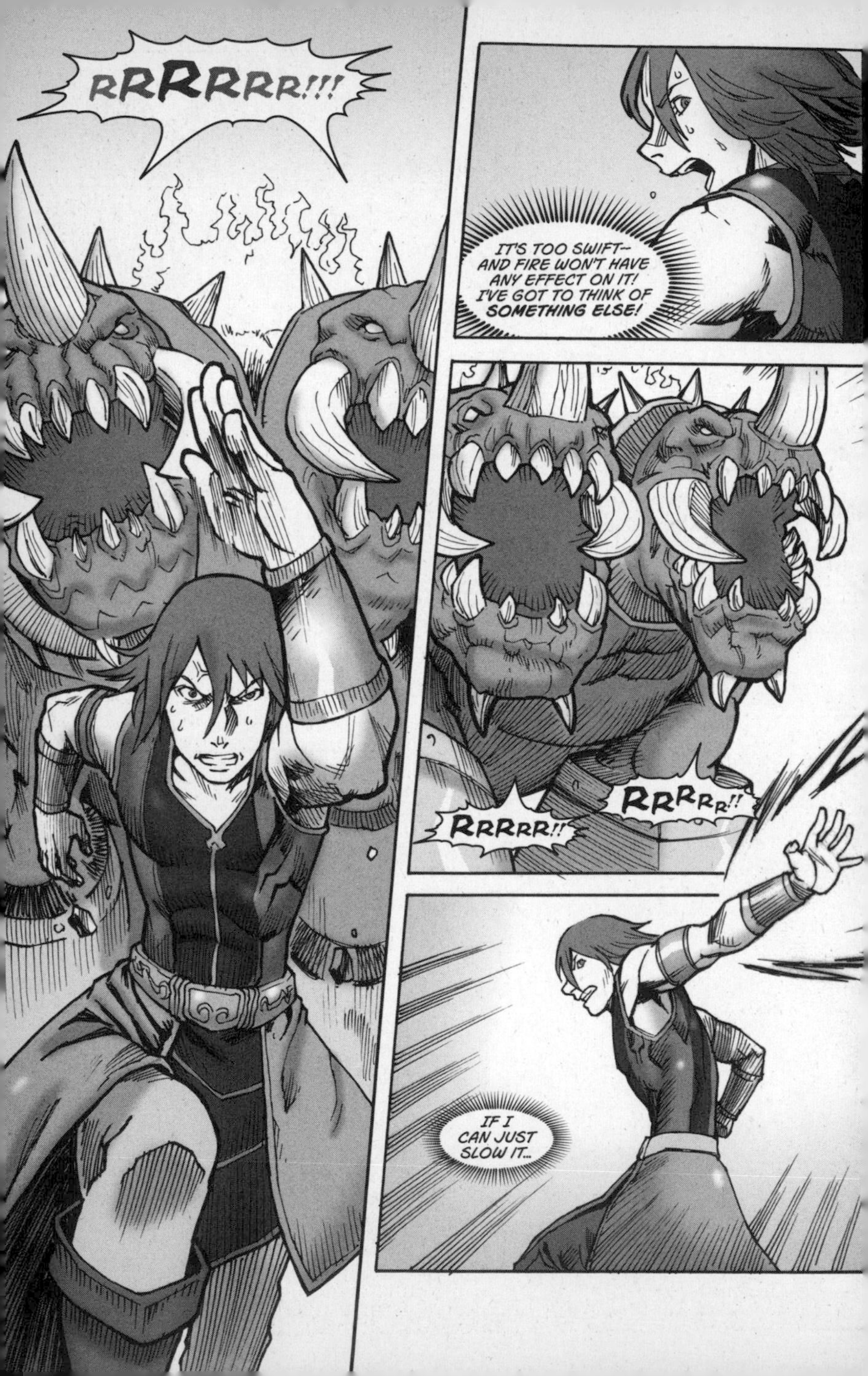
RRRRRRR!!!
IT'S TOO SWIFT--
AND FIRE WON'T HAVE
ANY EFFECT ON IT!
I'VE GOT TO THINK OF
SOMETHING ELSE!
RRRRR!!
RRRRR!!
IF I
CAN JUST
SLOW IT...

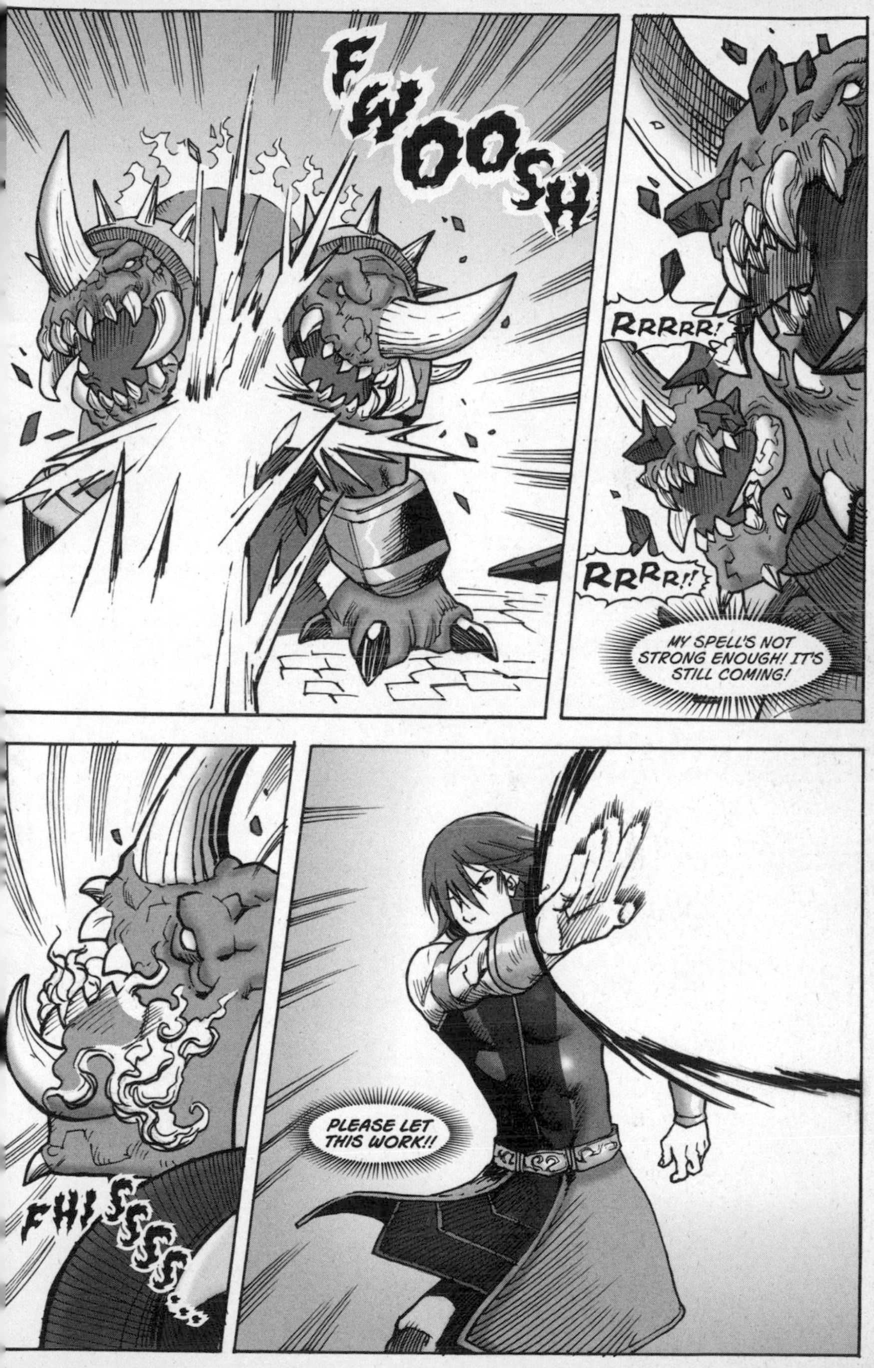
FWOOSH
RRRRR!
RRRR!!
MY SPELL'S NOT STRONG ENOUGH! IT'S STILL COMING!
FHISSSS...
PLEASE LET THIS WORK!!

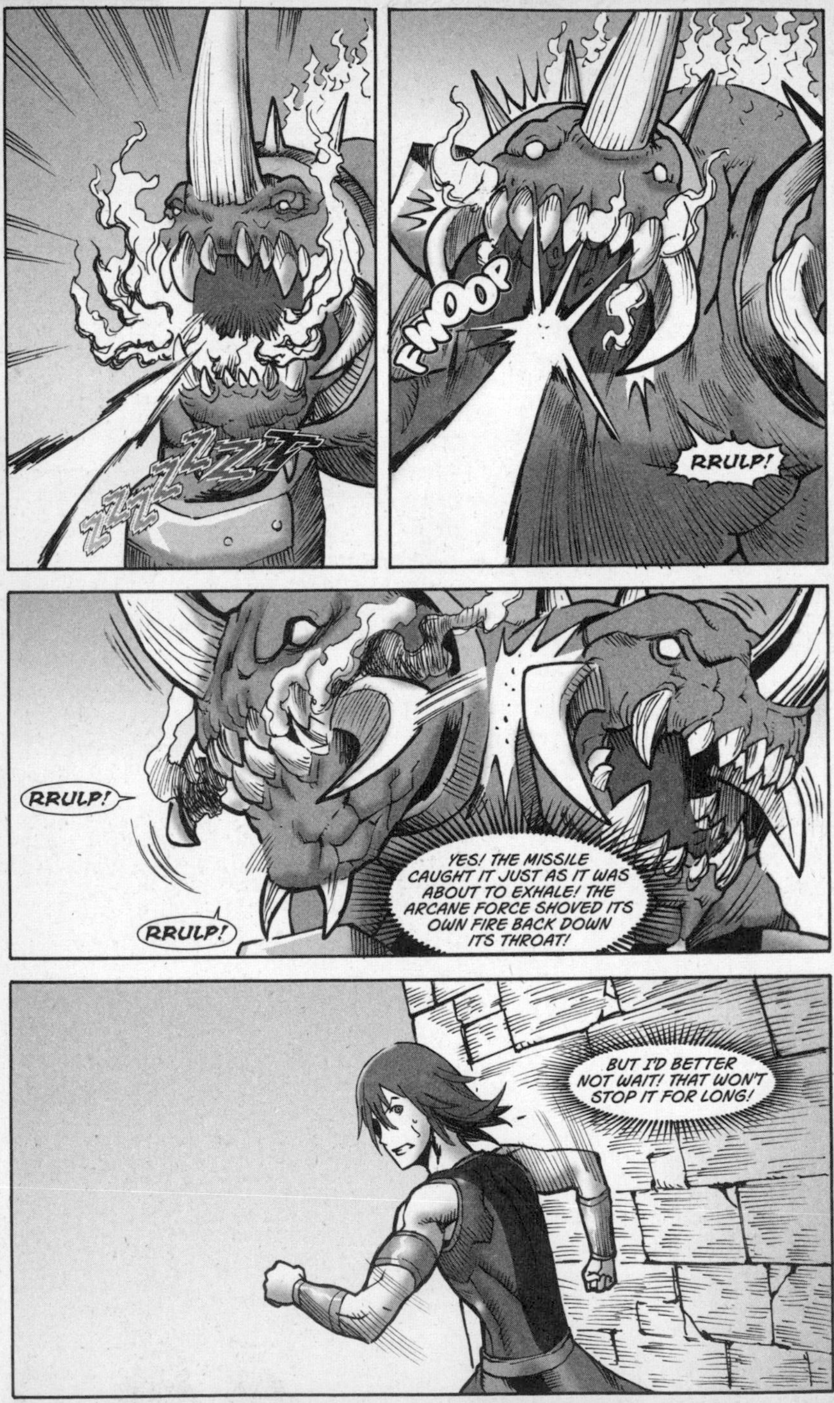
ZZZZZZT
FWOOP
RRULP!
RRULP!
RRULP!
YES! THE MISSILE CAUGHT IT JUST AS IT WAS ABOUT TO EXHALE! THE ARCANE FORCE SHOVED ITS OWN FIRE BACK DOWN ITS THROAT!
BUT I'D BETTER NOT WAIT! THAT WON'T STOP IT FOR LONG!

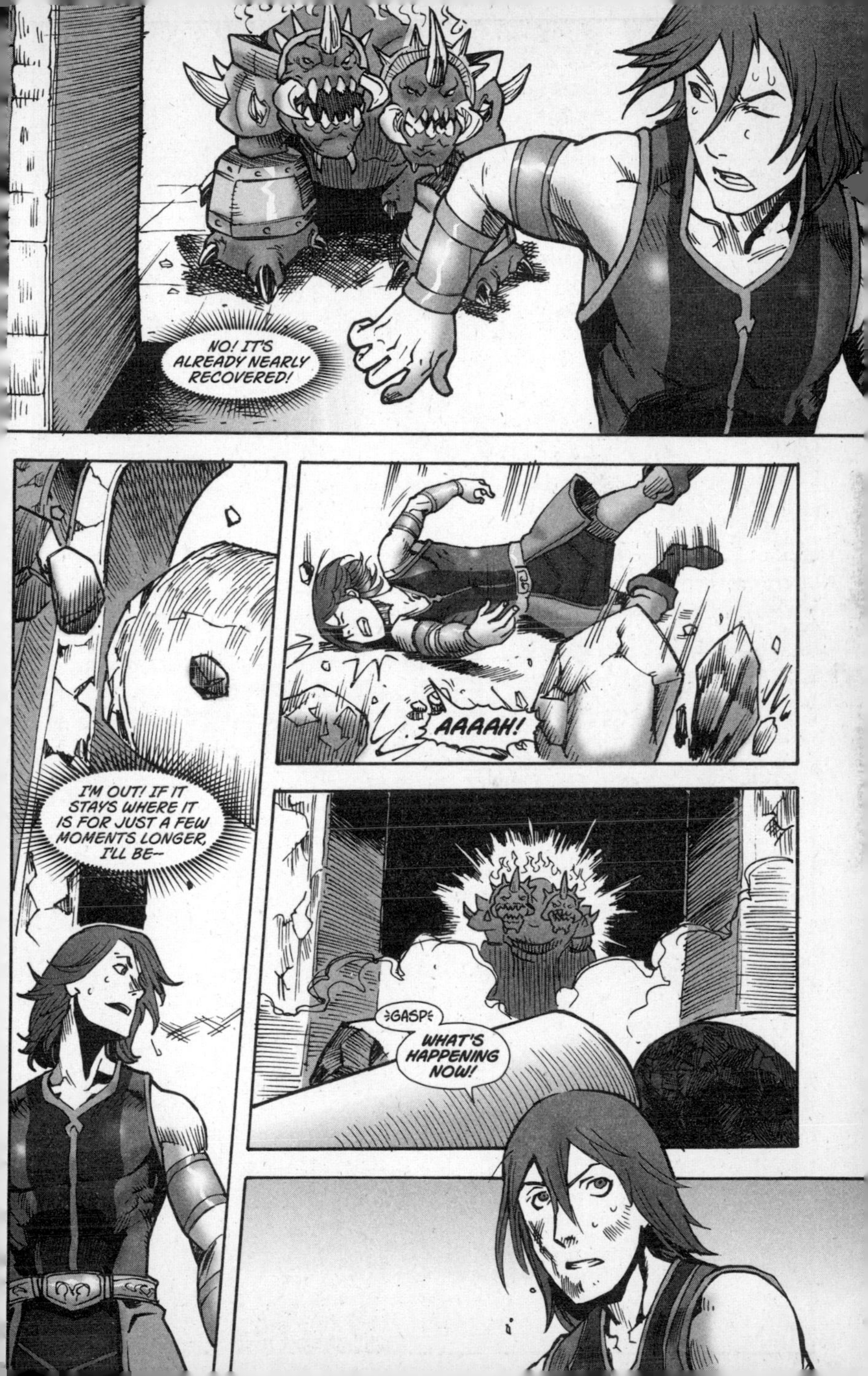
NO! IT'S ALREADY NEARLY RECOVERED!
AAAAH!
I'M OUT! IF IT STAYS WHERE IT IS FOR JUST A FEW MOMENTS LONGER, I'LL BE--
GASP
WHAT'S HAPPENING NOW!

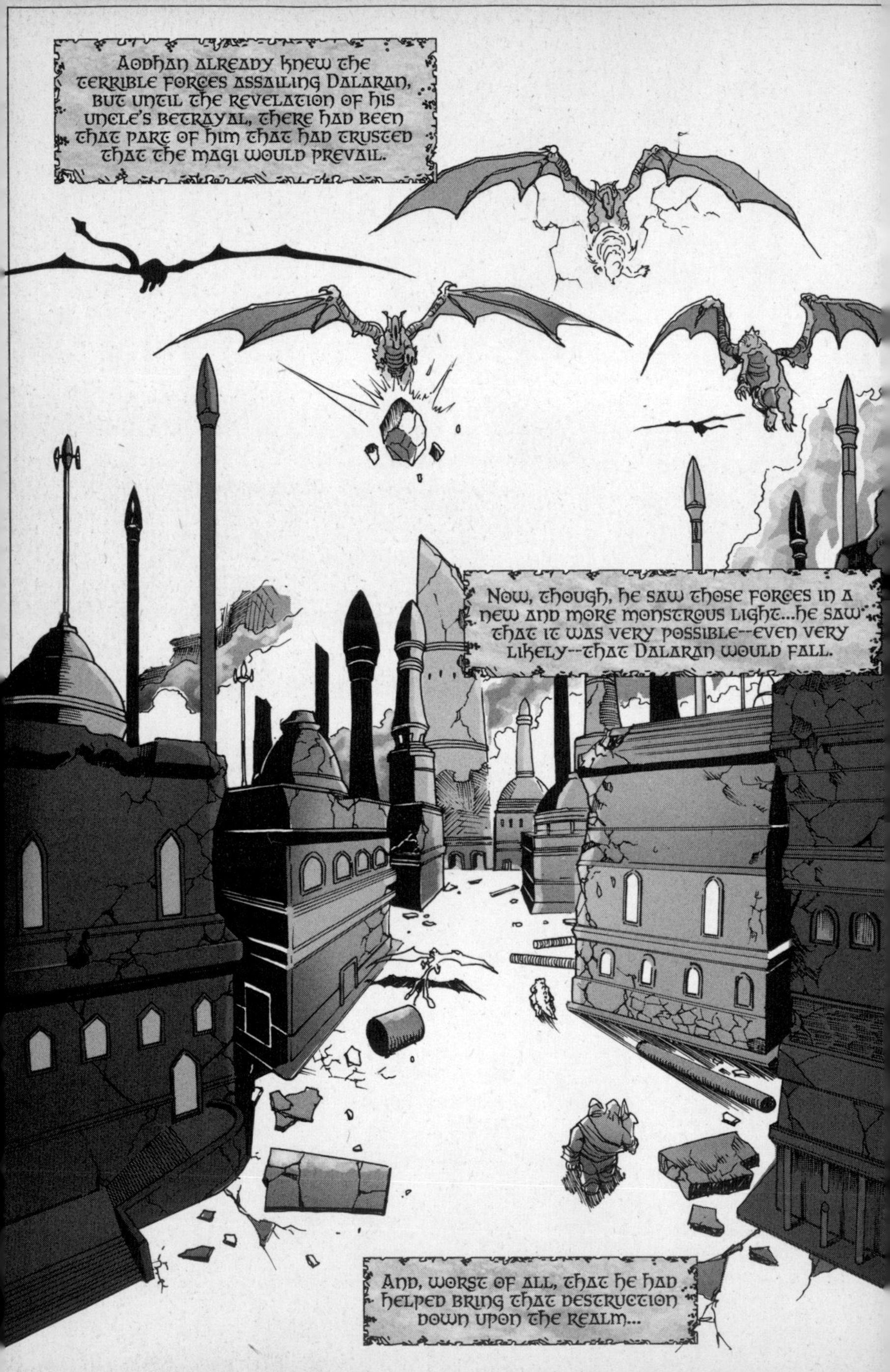
Aodhan already knew the terrible forces assailing Dalaran, but until the revelation of his uncle's betrayal, there had been that part of him that had trusted that the magi would prevail.
Now, though, he saw those forces in a new and more monstrous light...he saw that it was very possible--even very likely--that Dalaran would fall.
And, worst of all, that he had helped bring that destruction down upon the realm...

# CHAPTER FIVE
# DECISION & DISASTER

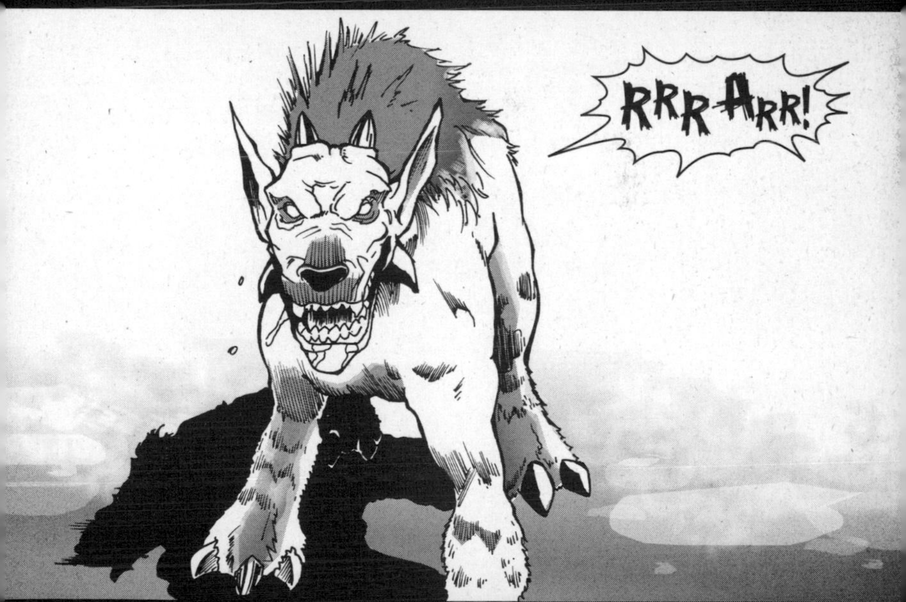
RRR ARR!

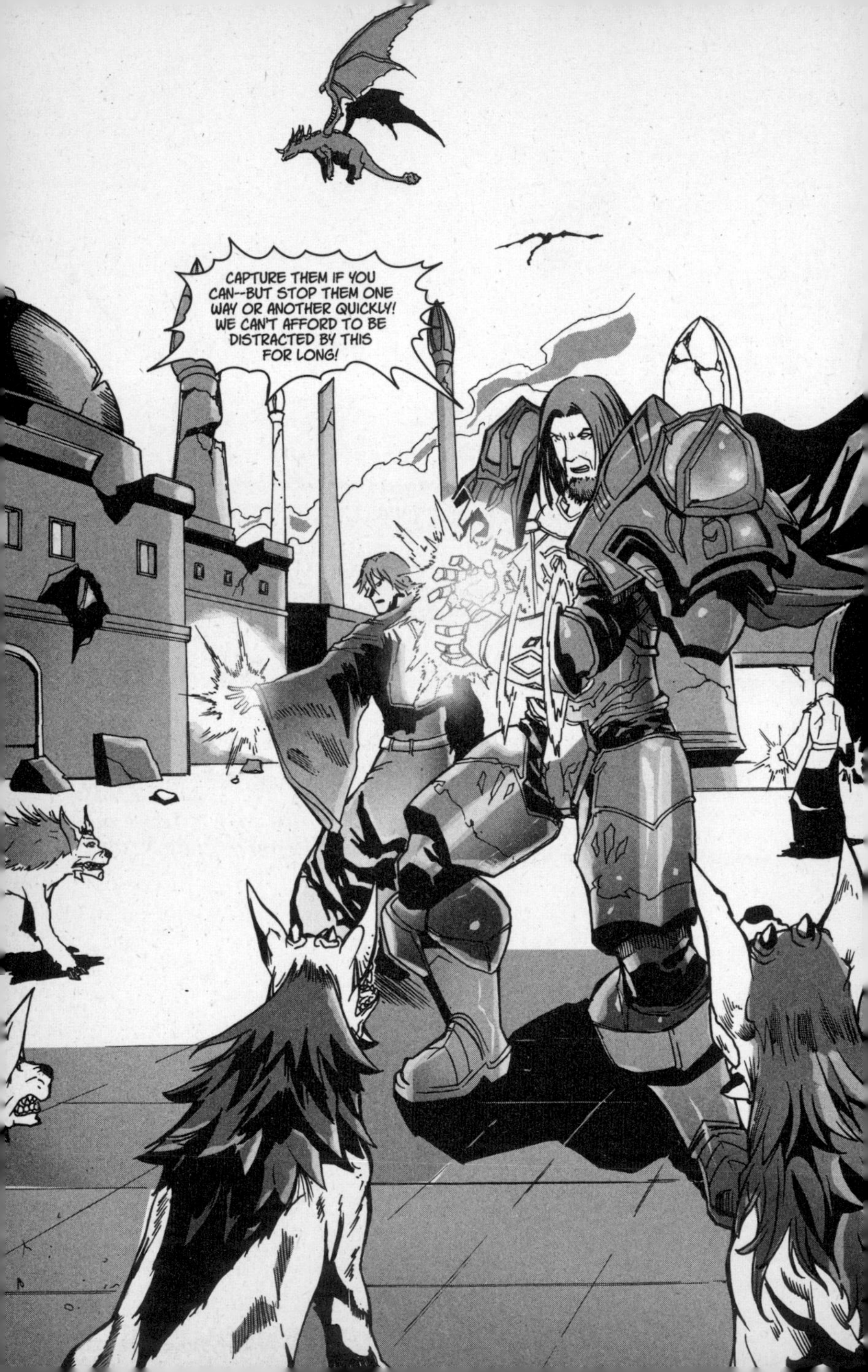
CAPTURE THEM IF YOU CAN--BUT STOP THEM ONE WAY OR ANOTHER QUICKLY! WE CAN'T AFFORD TO BE DISTRACTED BY THIS FOR LONG!

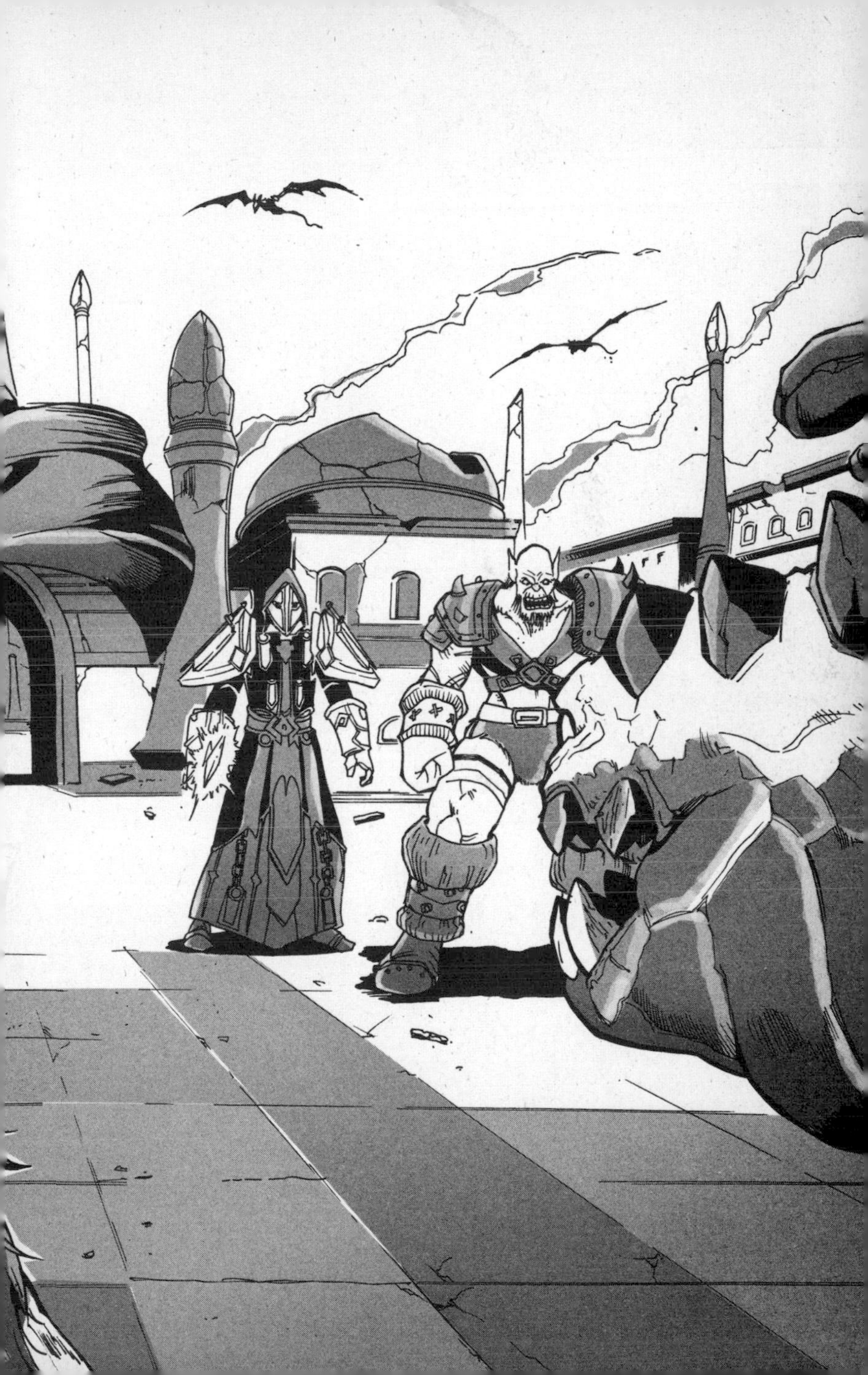

AND I CAN'T HELP THINKING THIS IS NO COINCIDENCE! THE DRAGONS MUST BE UP TO SOMETHING...

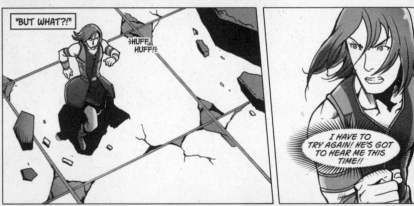

"BUT WHAT?!"

*HUFF...*
*HUFF!!*

I HAVE TO TRY AGAIN! HE'S GOT TO HEAR ME THIS TIME!!

ARCHMAGE RHONIN! ANYONE! THERE'S A MAGE HUNTER LOOSE IN DALARAN! HE'S GONE BELOW THE CITY! THERE'S—

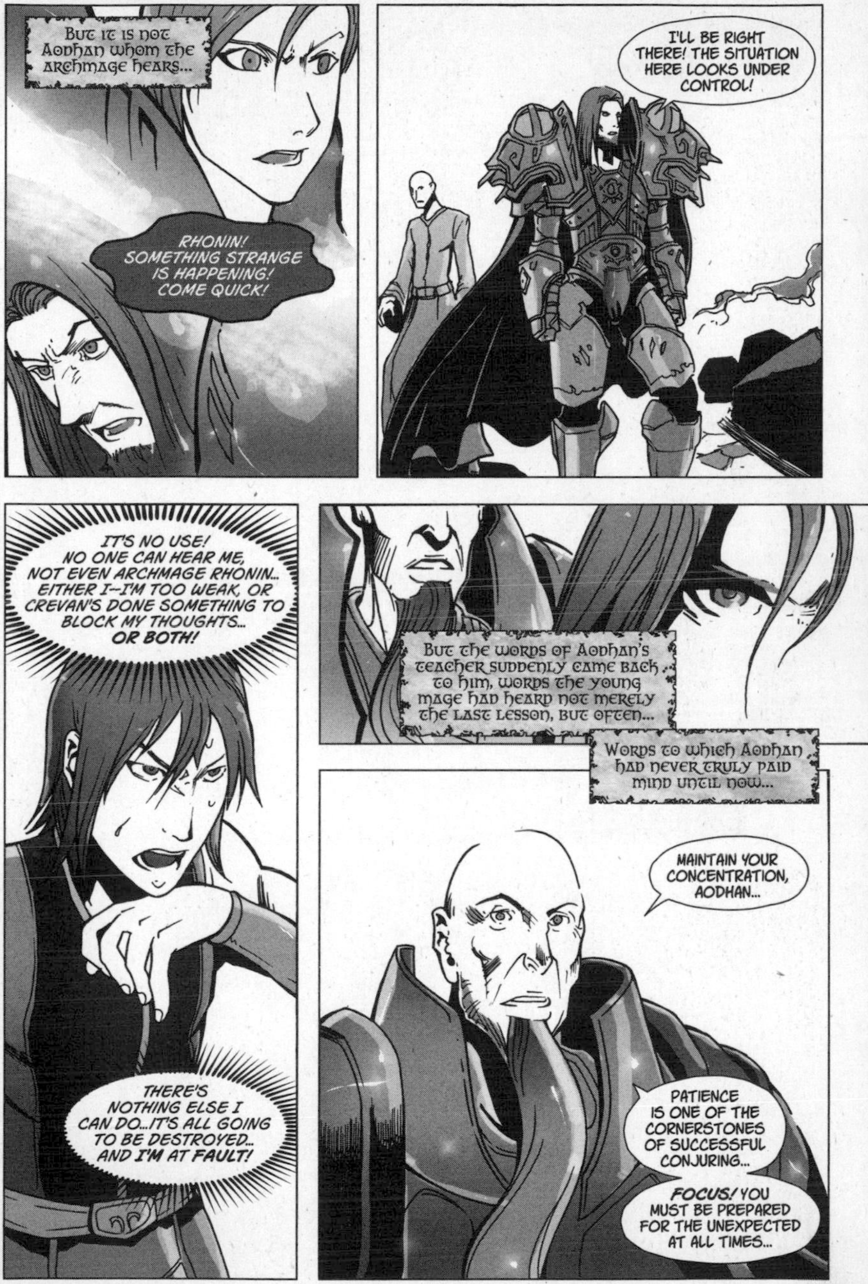
But it is not Aodhan whom the archmage hears...
RHONIN! SOMETHING STRANGE IS HAPPENING! COME QUICK!
I'LL BE RIGHT THERE! THE SITUATION HERE LOOKS UNDER CONTROL!
IT'S NO USE! NO ONE CAN HEAR ME, NOT EVEN ARCHMAGE RHONIN... EITHER I--I'M TOO WEAK, OR CREVAN'S DONE SOMETHING TO BLOCK MY THOUGHTS... OR BOTH!
THERE'S NOTHING ELSE I CAN DO...IT'S ALL GOING TO BE DESTROYED... AND I'M AT FAULT!
But the words of Aodhan's teacher suddenly came back to him, words the young mage had heard not merely the last lesson, but often...
Words to which Aodhan had never truly paid mind until now...
MAINTAIN YOUR CONCENTRATION, AODHAN...
PATIENCE IS ONE OF THE CORNERSTONES OF SUCCESSFUL CONJURING...
FOCUS! YOU MUST BE PREPARED FOR THE UNEXPECTED AT ALL TIMES...

"PATIENCE... FOCUS..."

I HAVE TO FOLLOW CREVAN... BUT HOW? THERE'S NO NEARBY PATH LEADING DOWN--

PATIENCE AND FOCUS...BUT IT'S ONE THING TO TEACH AND ANOTHER TO BE IN THE MIDDLE OF ALL THIS!

BUT--I HAVE TO DO SOMETHING!

MAYBE...

ALMOST THERE...!

THE DRAGONS! THEY LOOK LIKE THEY'RE--

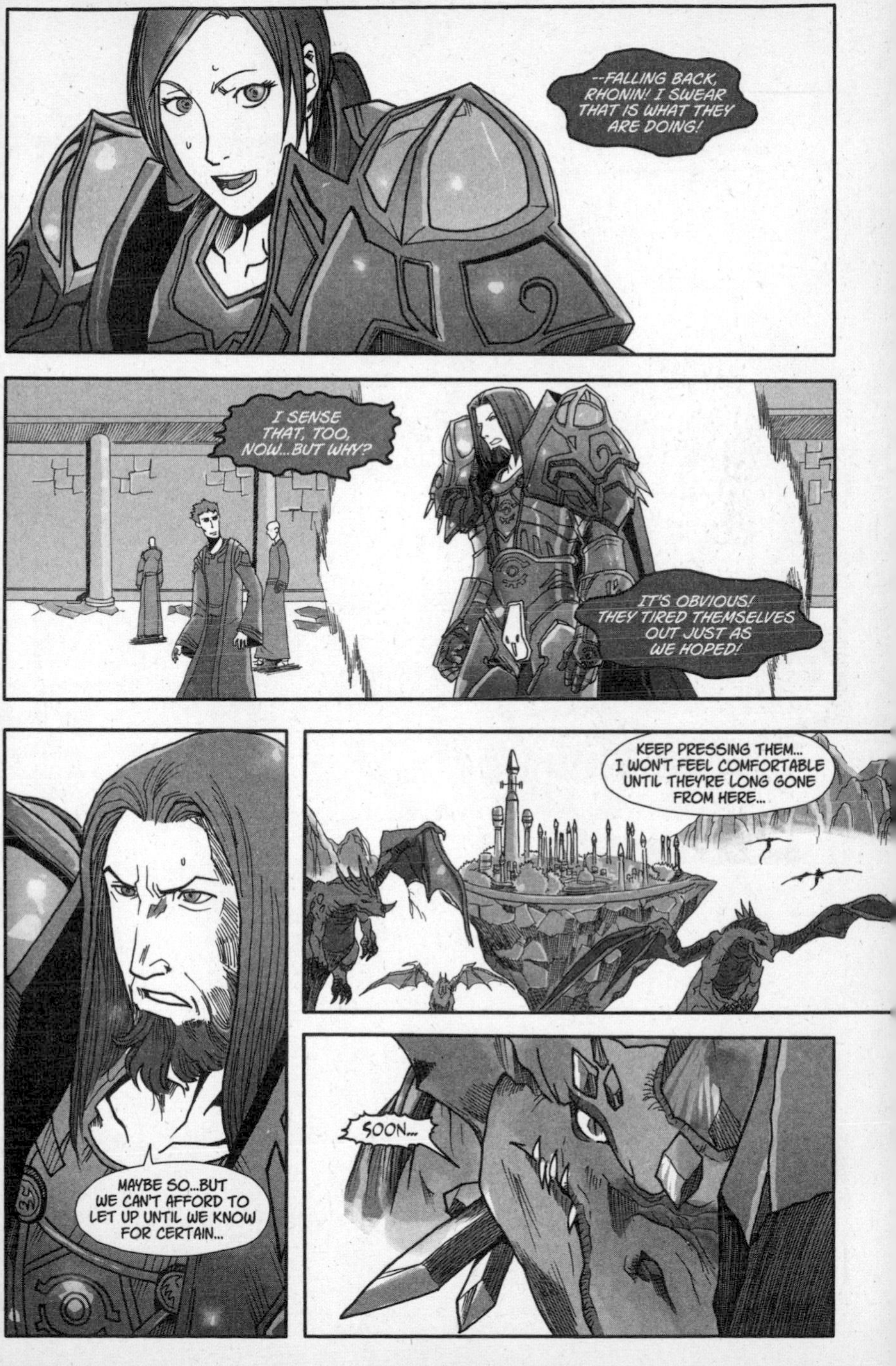
--FALLING BACK, RHONIN! I SWEAR THAT IS WHAT THEY ARE DOING!
I SENSE THAT, TOO, NOW...BUT WHY?
IT'S OBVIOUS! THEY TIRED THEMSELVES OUT JUST AS WE HOPED!
MAYBE SO...BUT WE CAN'T AFFORD TO LET UP UNTIL WE KNOW FOR CERTAIN...
KEEP PRESSING THEM... I WON'T FEEL COMFORTABLE UNTIL THEY'RE LONG GONE FROM HERE...
SOON...

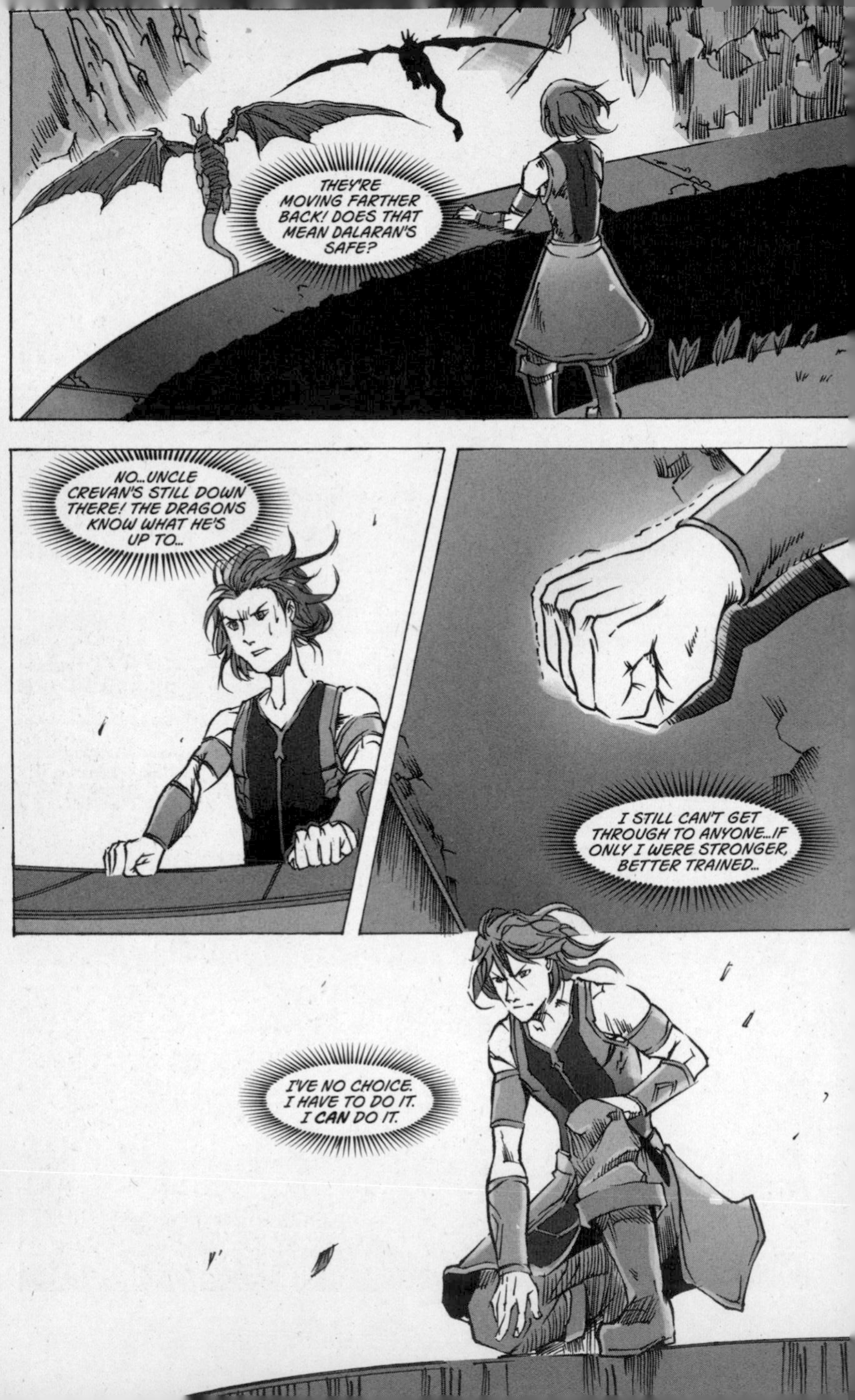
THEY'RE MOVING FARTHER BACK! DOES THAT MEAN DALARAN'S SAFE?
NO...UNCLE CREVAN'S STILL DOWN THERE! THE DRAGONS KNOW WHAT HE'S UP TO...
I STILL CAN'T GET THROUGH TO ANYONE...IF ONLY I WERE STRONGER, BETTER TRAINED...
I'VE NO CHOICE. I HAVE TO DO IT. I **CAN** DO IT.

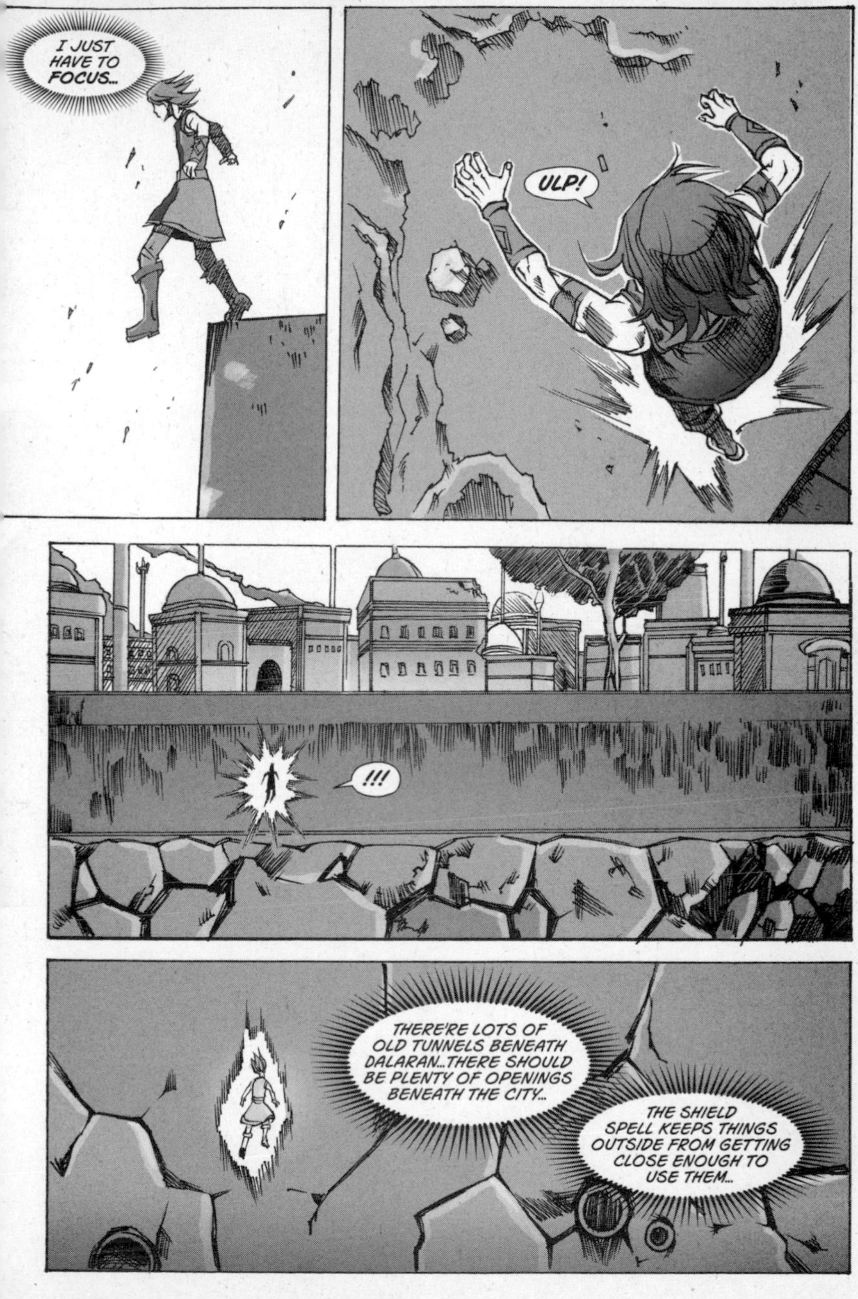
I JUST HAVE TO FOCUS...
ULP!
!!!
THERE'RE LOTS OF OLD TUNNELS BENEATH DALARAN...THERE SHOULD BE PLENTY OF OPENINGS BENEATH THE CITY...
THE SHIELD SPELL KEEPS THINGS OUTSIDE FROM GETTING CLOSE ENOUGH TO USE THEM...

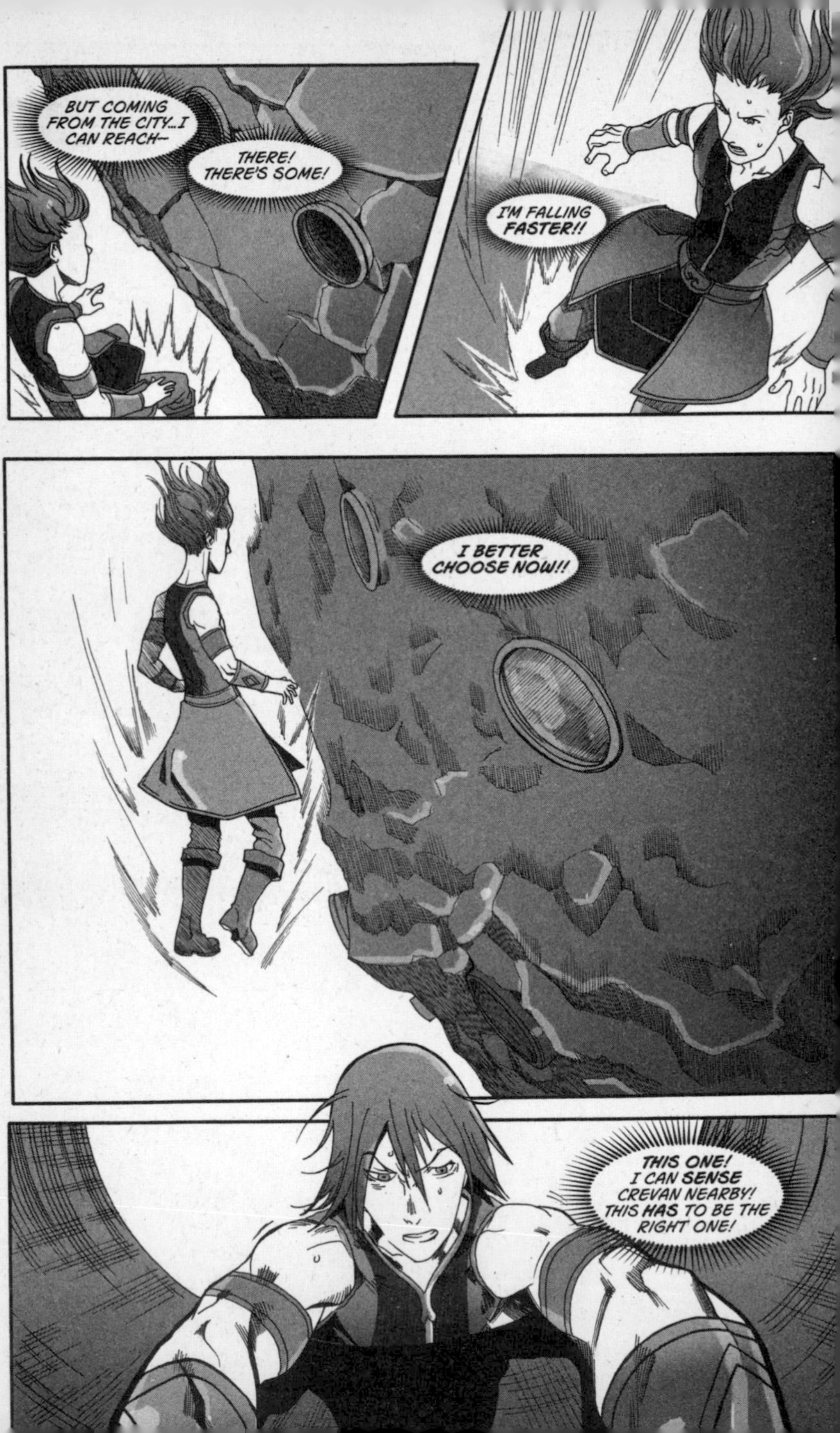
BUT COMING FROM THE CITY...I CAN REACH–
THERE! THERE'S SOME!
I'M FALLING FASTER!!
I BETTER CHOOSE NOW!!
THIS ONE! I CAN SENSE CREVAN NEARBY! THIS HAS TO BE THE RIGHT ONE!

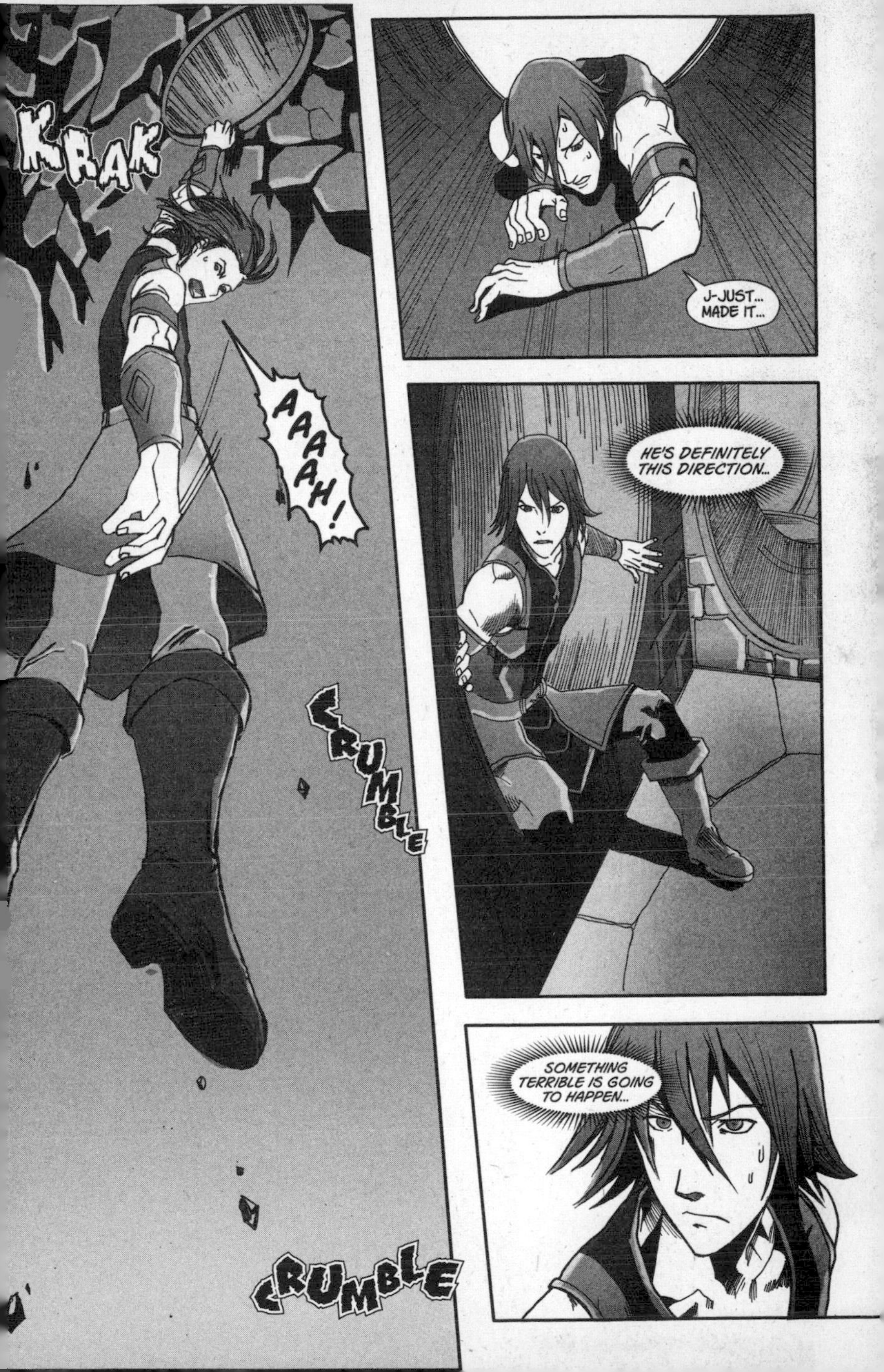
KRAK
AAAAH!
CRUMBLE
CRUMBLE
J-JUST...
MADE IT...
HE'S DEFINITELY
THIS DIRECTION...
SOMETHING
TERRIBLE IS GOING
TO HAPPEN...

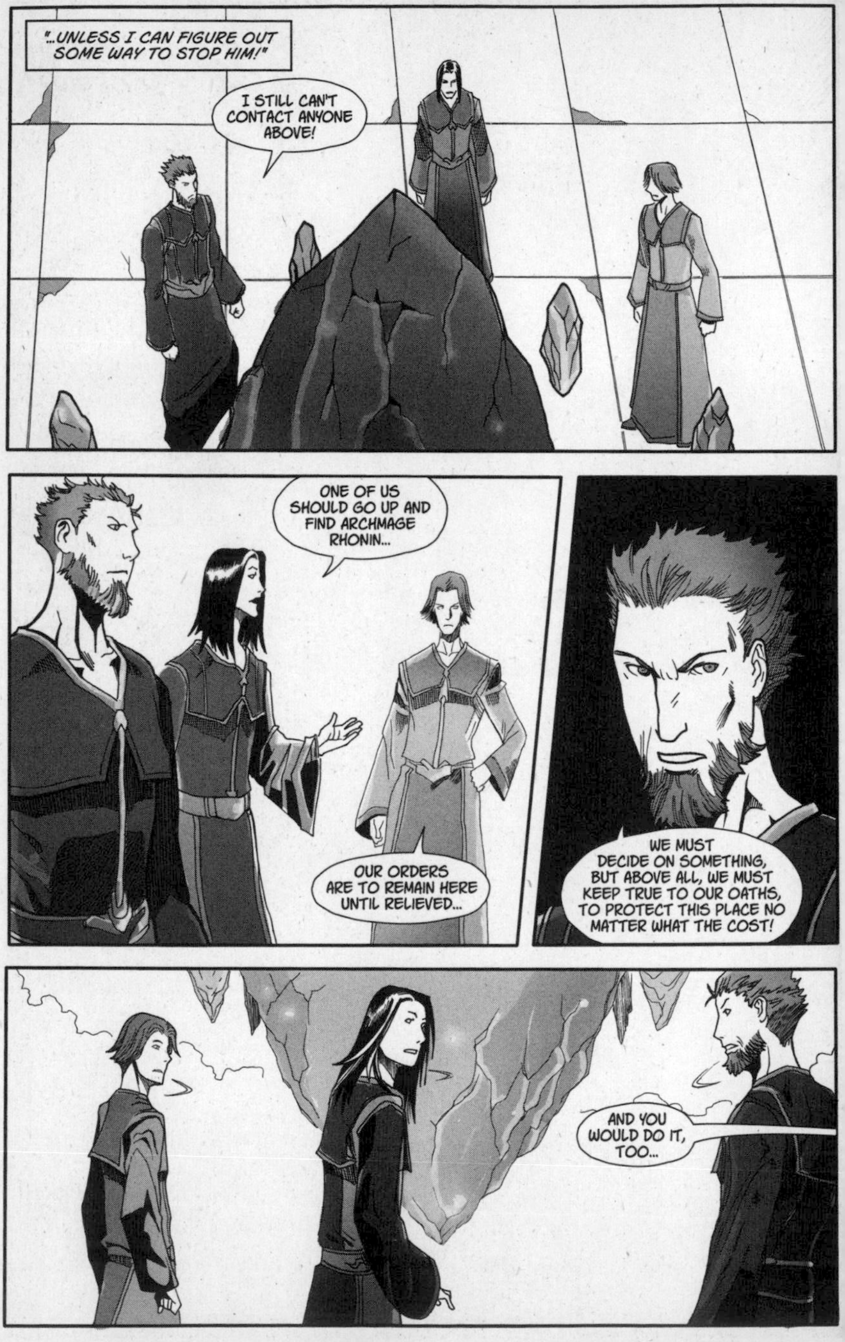
"...UNLESS I CAN FIGURE OUT SOME WAY TO STOP HIM!"
I STILL CAN'T CONTACT ANYONE ABOVE!
ONE OF US SHOULD GO UP AND FIND ARCHMAGE RHONIN...
OUR ORDERS ARE TO REMAIN HERE UNTIL RELIEVED...
WE MUST DECIDE ON SOMETHING, BUT ABOVE ALL, WE MUST KEEP TRUE TO OUR OATHS, TO PROTECT THIS PLACE NO MATTER WHAT THE COST!
AND YOU WOULD DO IT, TOO...

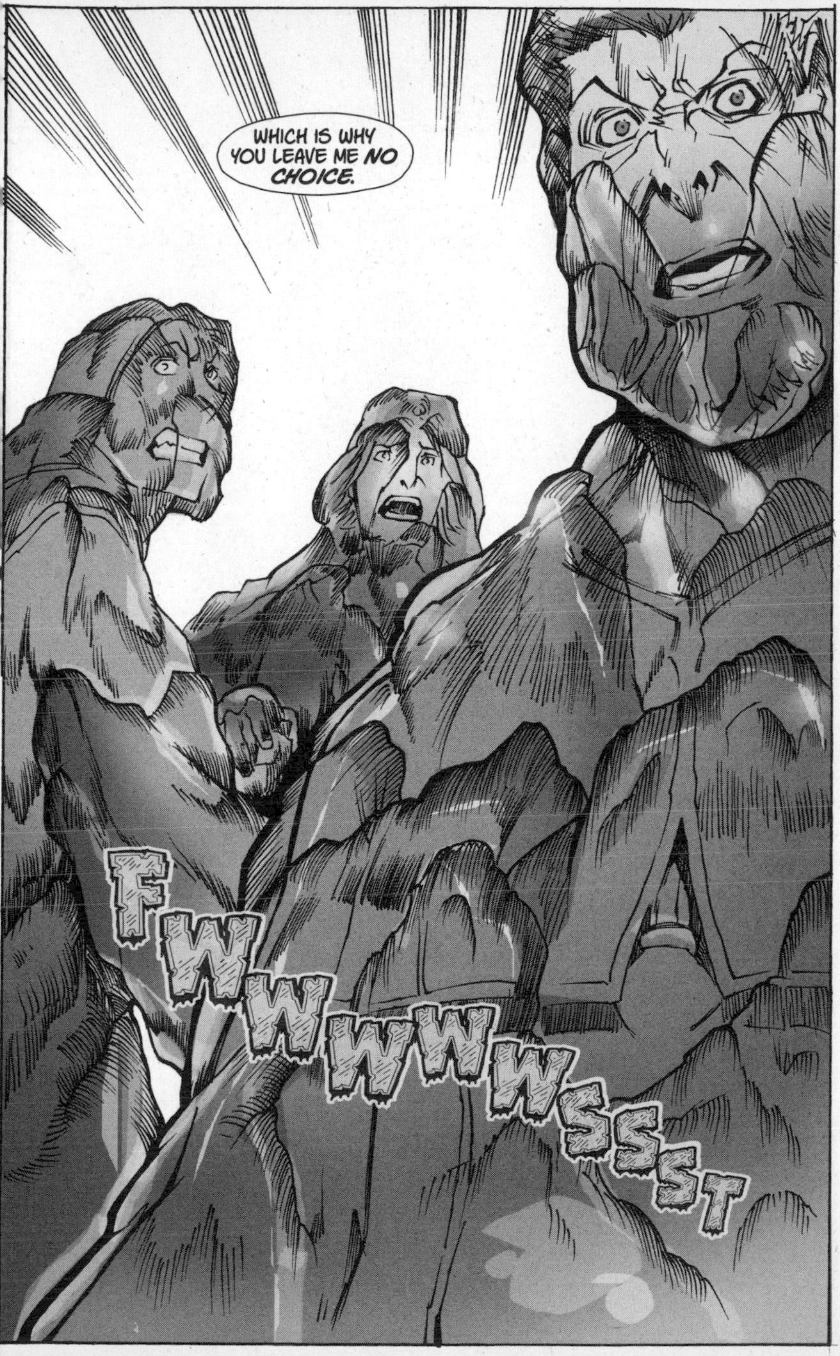
WHICH IS WHY YOU LEAVE ME *NO CHOICE.*
FWWWWWSSST

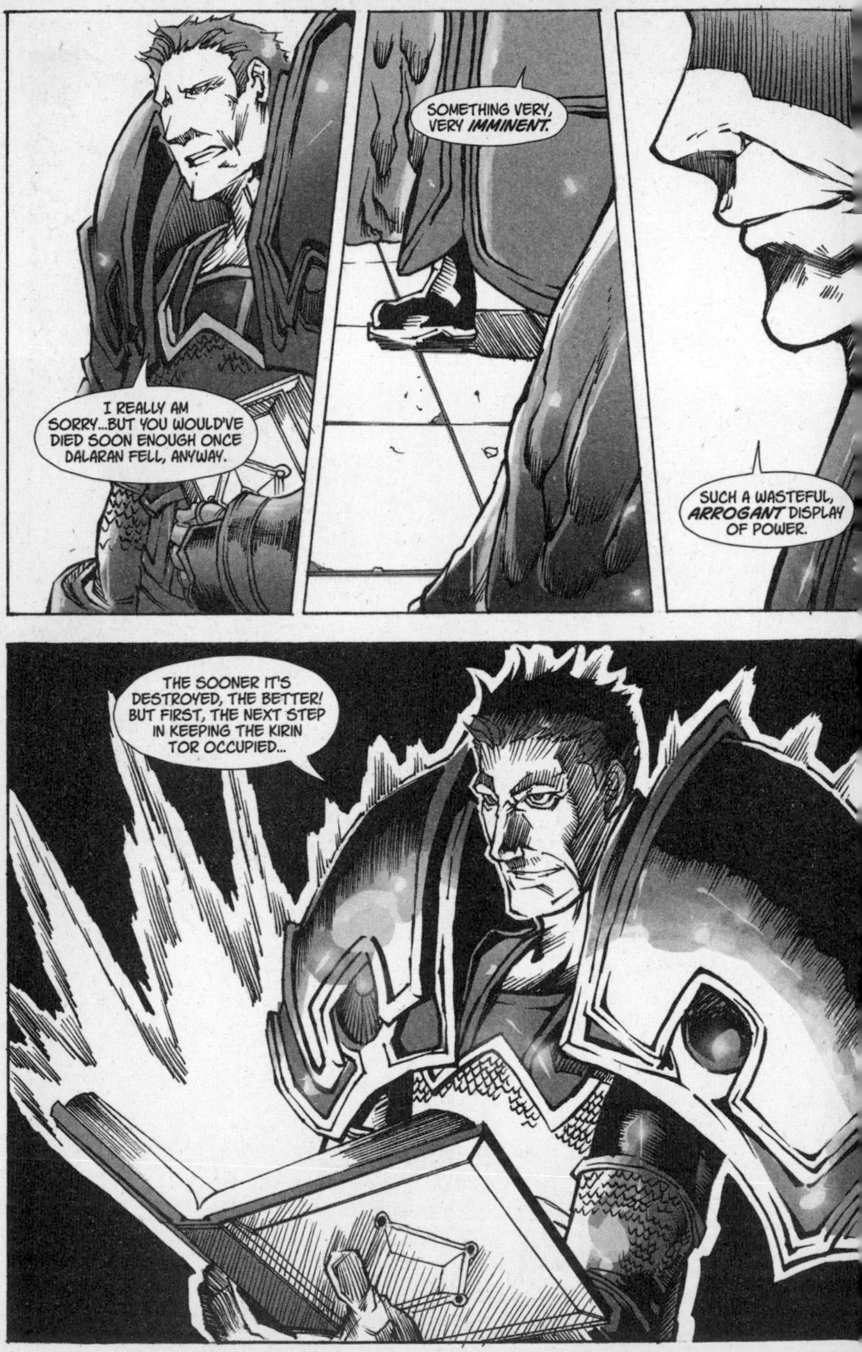
I REALLY AM SORRY...BUT YOU WOULD'VE DIED SOON ENOUGH ONCE DALARAN FELL, ANYWAY.
SOMETHING VERY, VERY *IMMINENT.*
SUCH A WASTEFUL, ***ARROGANT*** DISPLAY OF POWER.
THE SOONER IT'S DESTROYED, THE BETTER! BUT FIRST, THE NEXT STEP IN KEEPING THE KIRIN TOR OCCUPIED...

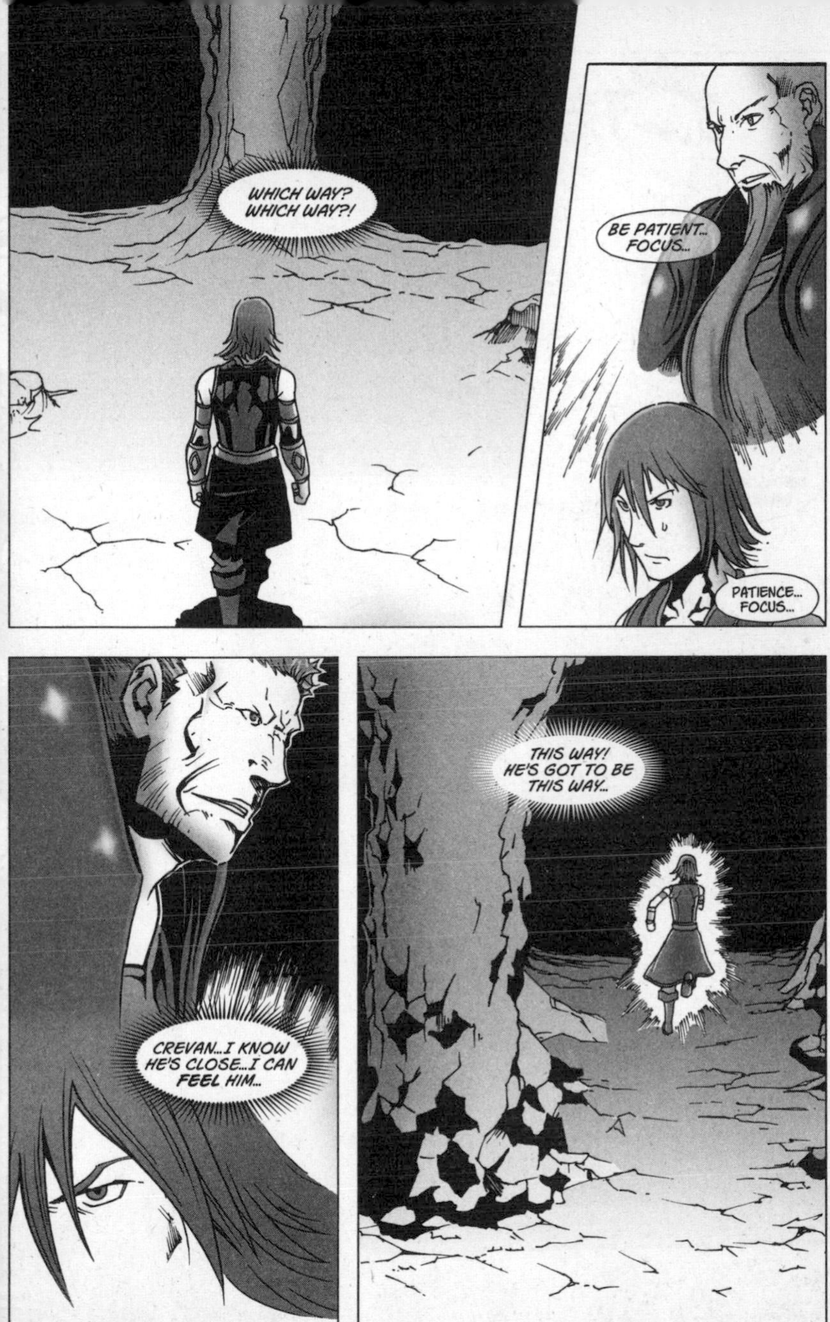
WHICH WAY? WHICH WAY?!
BE PATIENT... FOCUS...
PATIENCE... FOCUS...
CREVAN...I KNOW HE'S CLOSE...I CAN FEEL HIM...
THIS WAY! HE'S GOT TO BE THIS WAY...

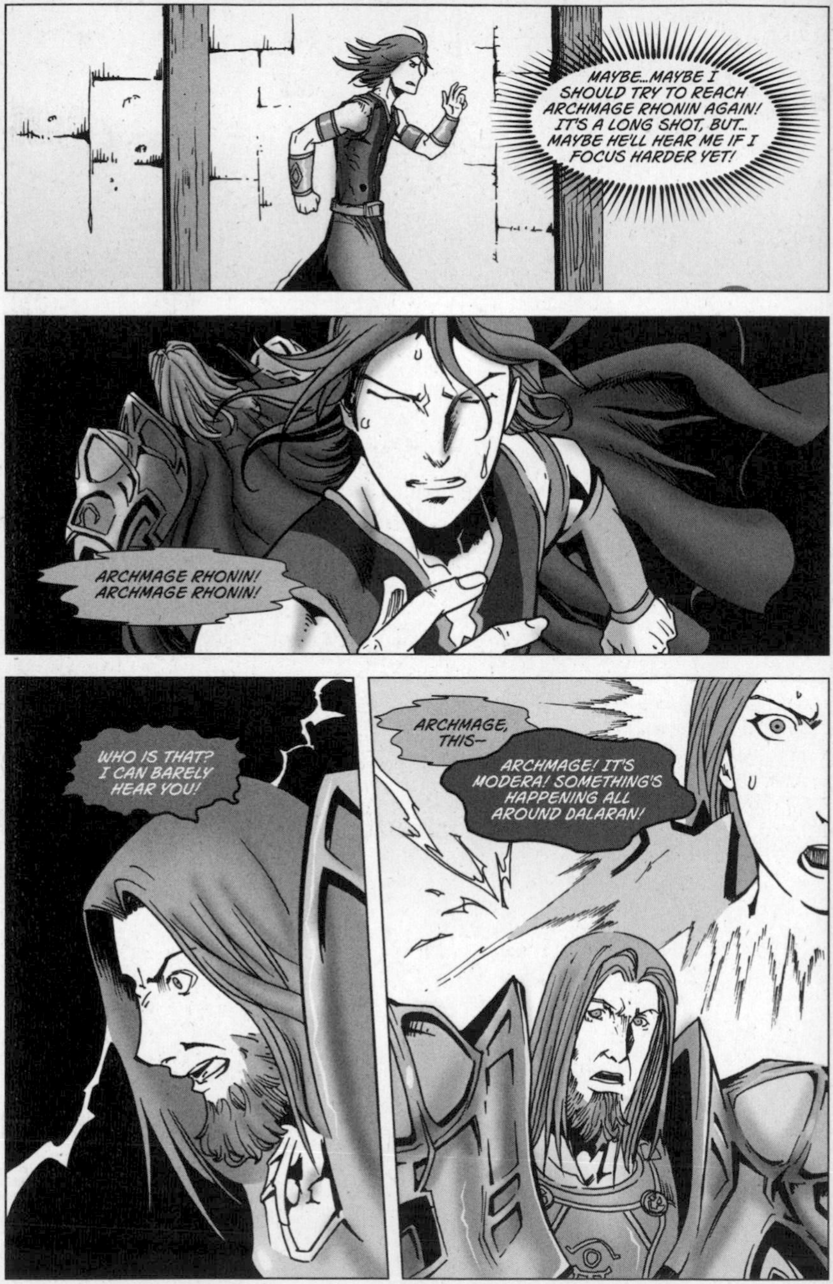
MAYBE...MAYBE I SHOULD TRY TO REACH ARCHMAGE RHONIN AGAIN! IT'S A LONG SHOT, BUT... MAYBE HE'LL HEAR ME IF I FOCUS HARDER YET!
ARCHMAGE RHONIN! ARCHMAGE RHONIN!
WHO IS THAT? I CAN BARELY HEAR YOU!
ARCHMAGE, THIS—
ARCHMAGE! IT'S MODERA! SOMETHING'S HAPPENING ALL AROUND DALARAN!

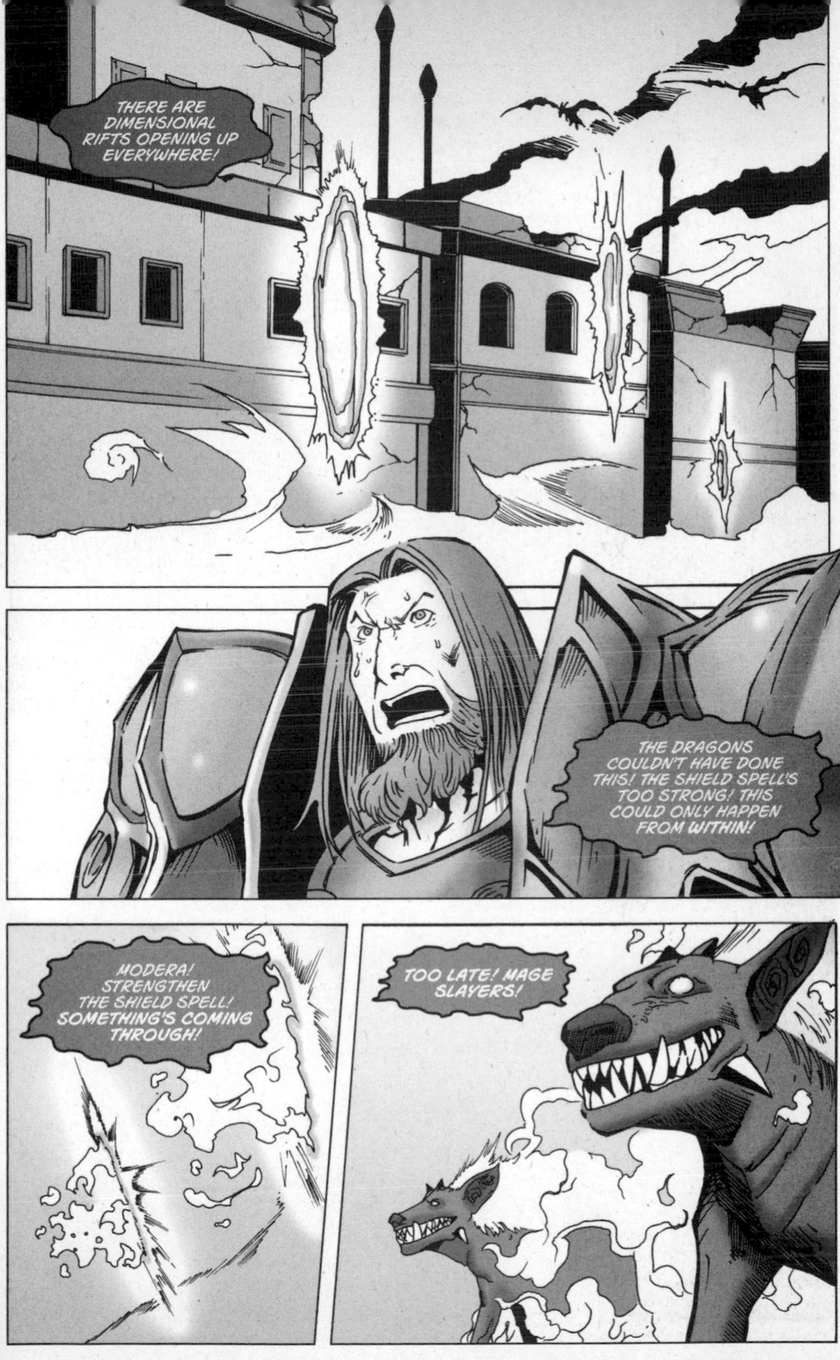

THERE ARE DIMENSIONAL RIFTS OPENING UP EVERYWHERE!
THE DRAGONS COULDN'T HAVE DONE THIS! THE SHIELD SPELL'S TOO STRONG! THIS COULD ONLY HAPPEN FROM WITHIN!
MODERA! STRENGTHEN THE SHIELD SPELL! SOMETHING'S COMING THROUGH!
TOO LATE! MAGE SLAYERS!

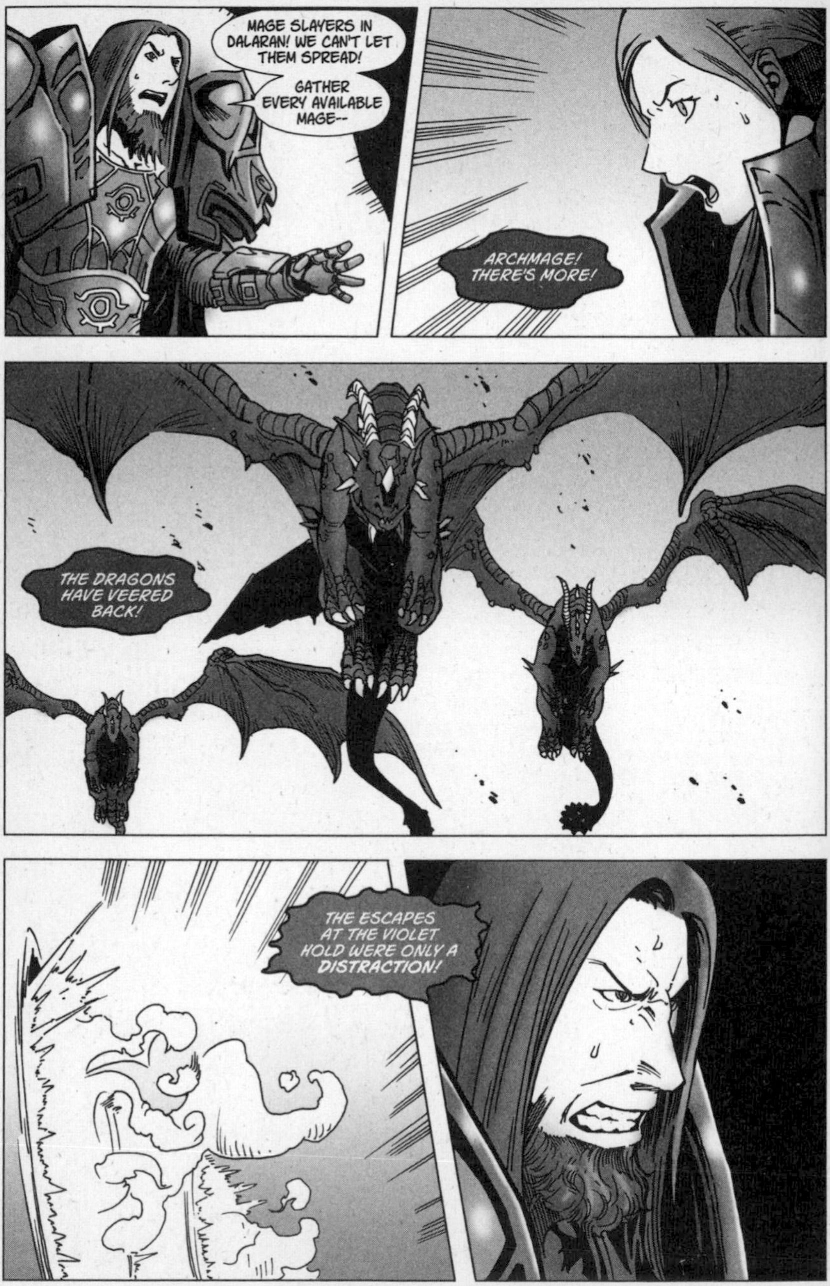
MAGE SLAYERS IN DALARAN! WE CAN'T LET THEM SPREAD!
GATHER EVERY AVAILABLE MAGE--
ARCHMAGE! THERE'S MORE!
THE DRAGONS HAVE VEERED BACK!
THE ESCAPES AT THE VIOLET HOLD WERE ONLY A DISTRACTION!

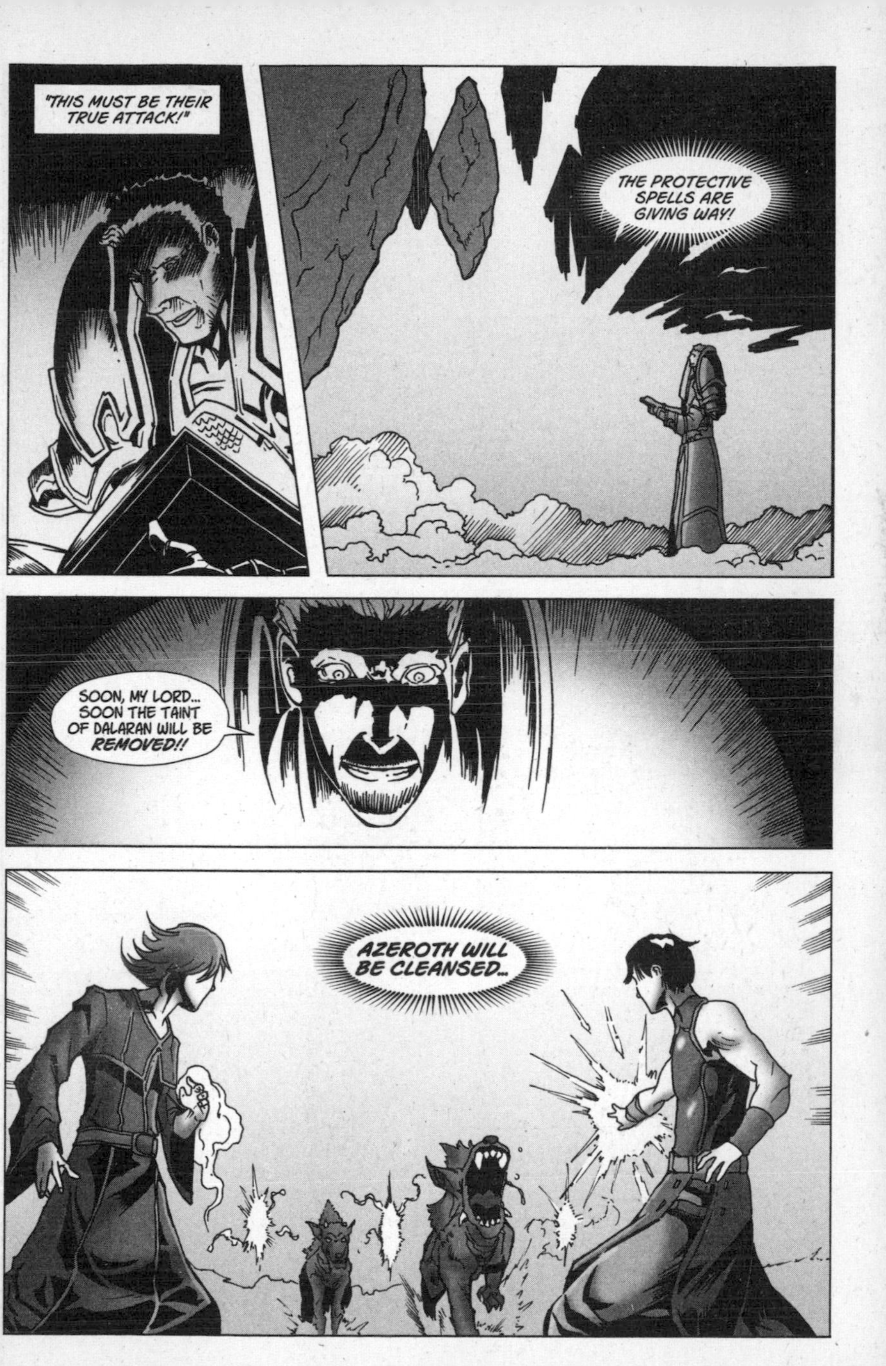
"THIS MUST BE THEIR TRUE ATTACK!"
THE PROTECTIVE SPELLS ARE GIVING WAY!
SOON, MY LORD... SOON THE TAINT OF DALARAN WILL BE *REMOVED!!*
AZEROTH WILL BE CLEANSED...

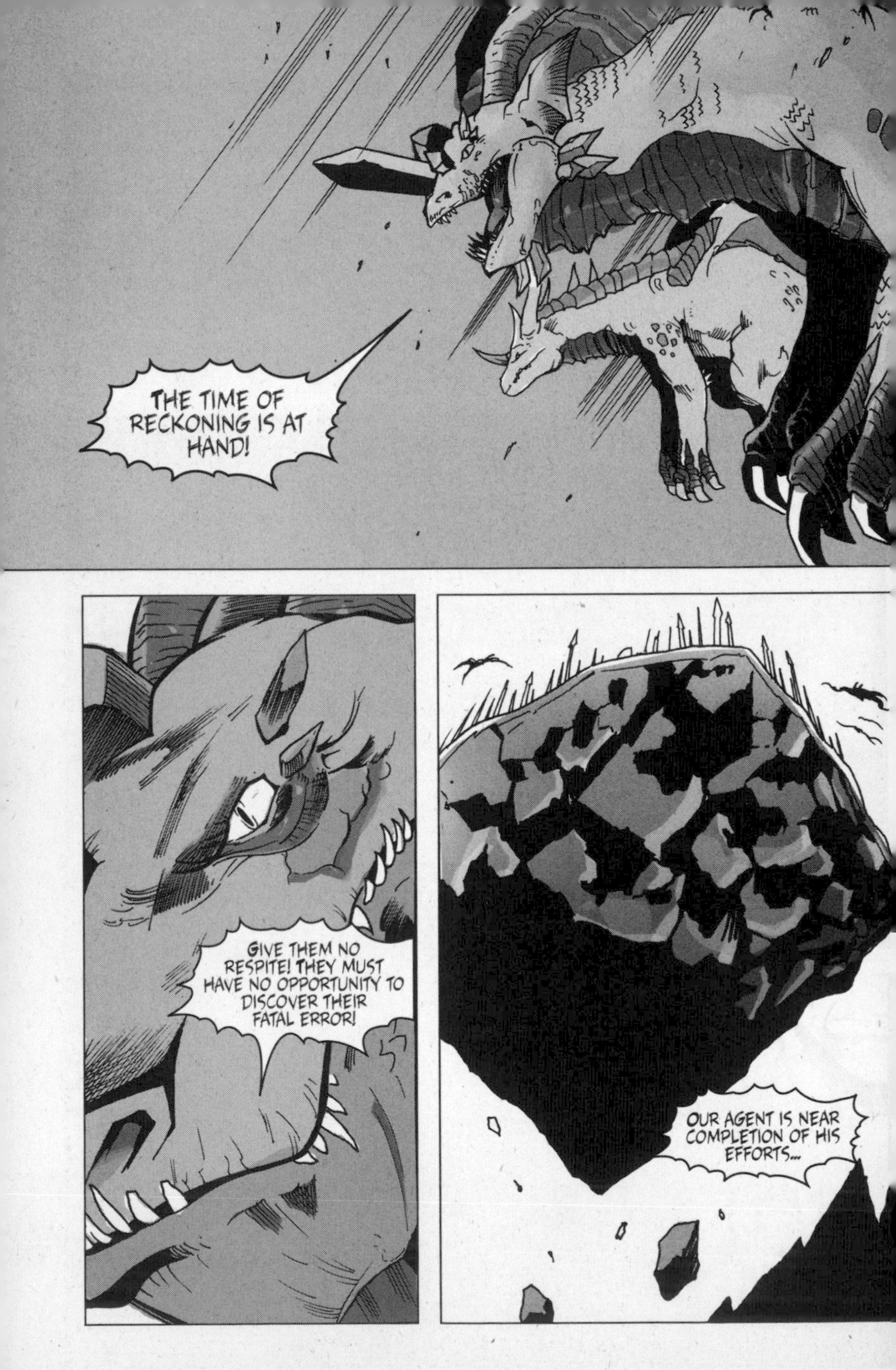
THE TIME OF RECKONING IS AT HAND!
GIVE THEM NO RESPITE! THEY MUST HAVE NO OPPORTUNITY TO DISCOVER THEIR FATAL ERROR!
OUR AGENT IS NEAR COMPLETION OF HIS EFFORTS...

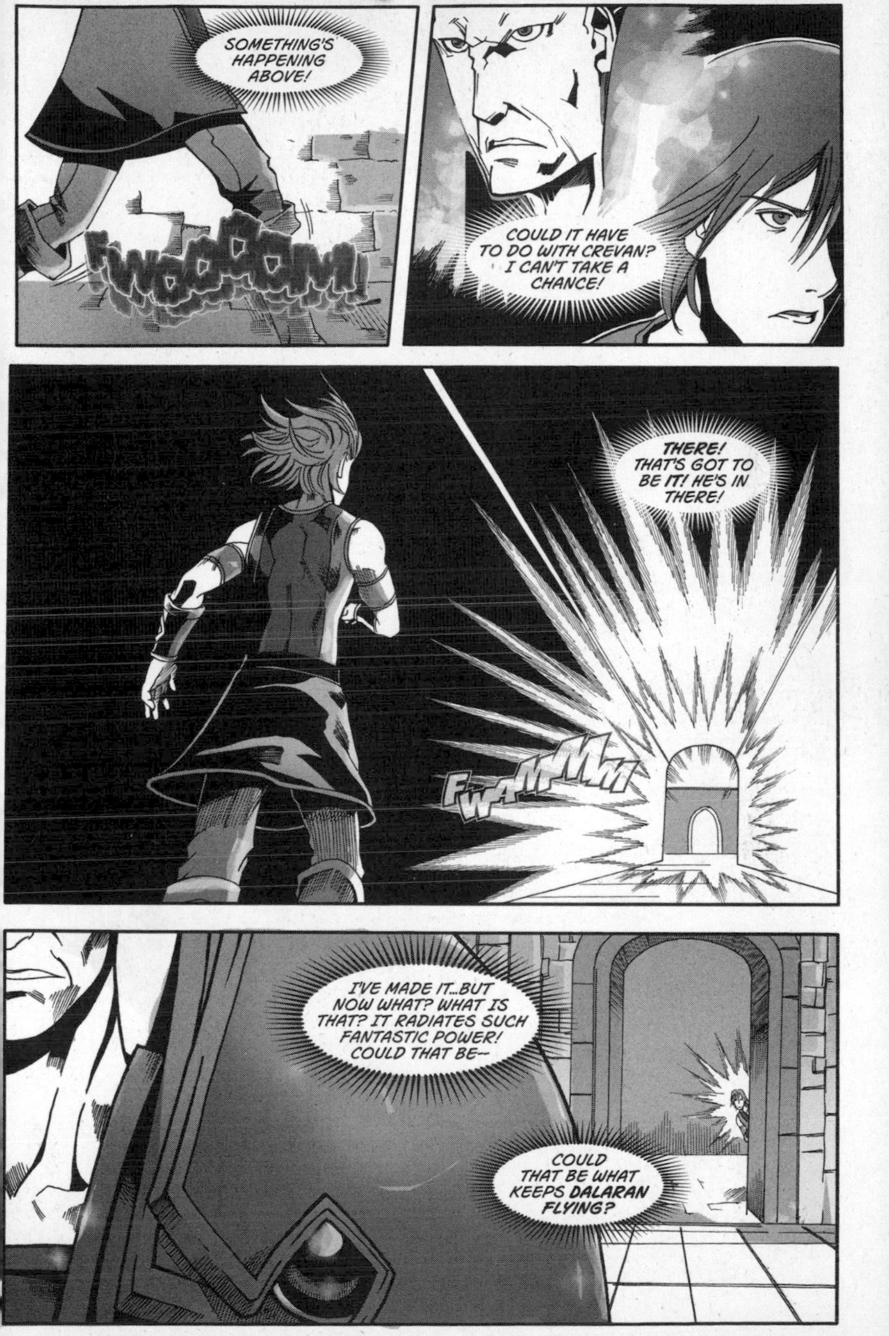
SOMETHING'S HAPPENING ABOVE!
FWOOOOM!
COULD IT HAVE TO DO WITH CREVAN? I CAN'T TAKE A CHANCE!
THERE! THAT'S GOT TO BE IT! HE'S IN THERE!
FWAMMMM
I'VE MADE IT...BUT NOW WHAT? WHAT IS THAT? IT RADIATES SUCH FANTASTIC POWER! COULD THAT BE--
COULD THAT BE WHAT KEEPS DALARAN FLYING?

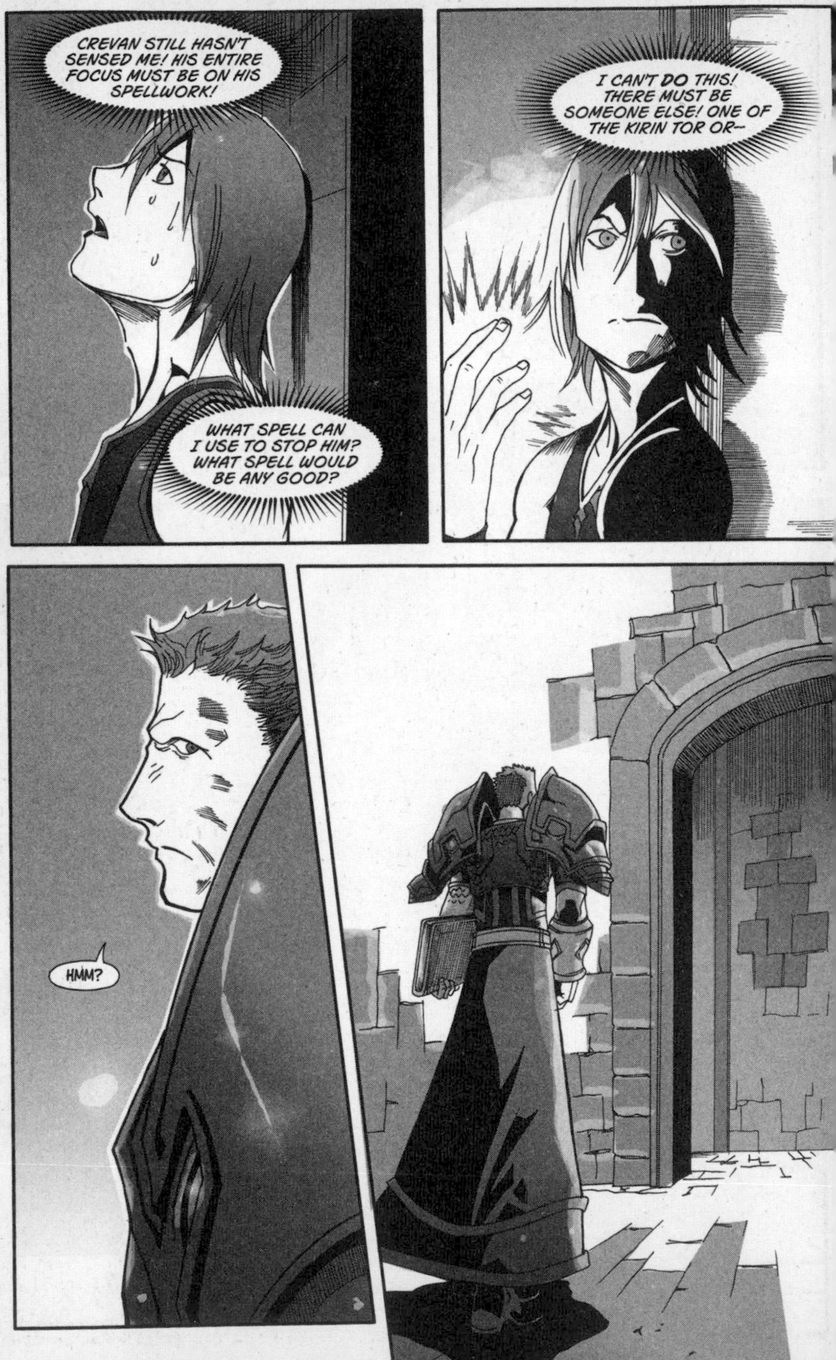
CREVAN STILL HASN'T SENSED ME! HIS ENTIRE FOCUS MUST BE ON HIS SPELLWORK!
WHAT SPELL CAN I USE TO STOP HIM? WHAT SPELL WOULD BE ANY GOOD?
I CAN'T DO THIS! THERE MUST BE SOMEONE ELSE! ONE OF THE KIRIN TOR OR--
HMM?

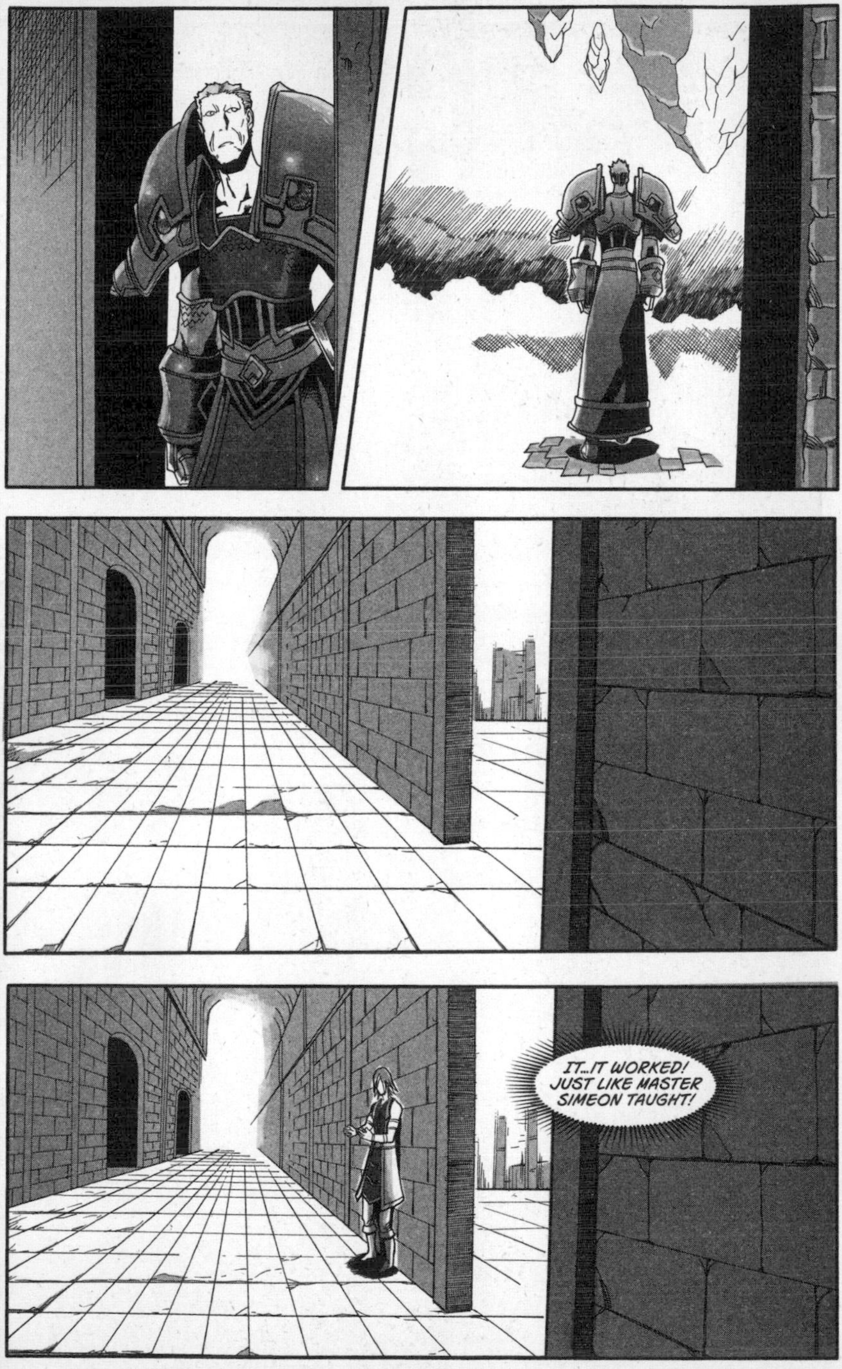
IT...IT WORKED! JUST LIKE MASTER SIMEON TAUGHT!

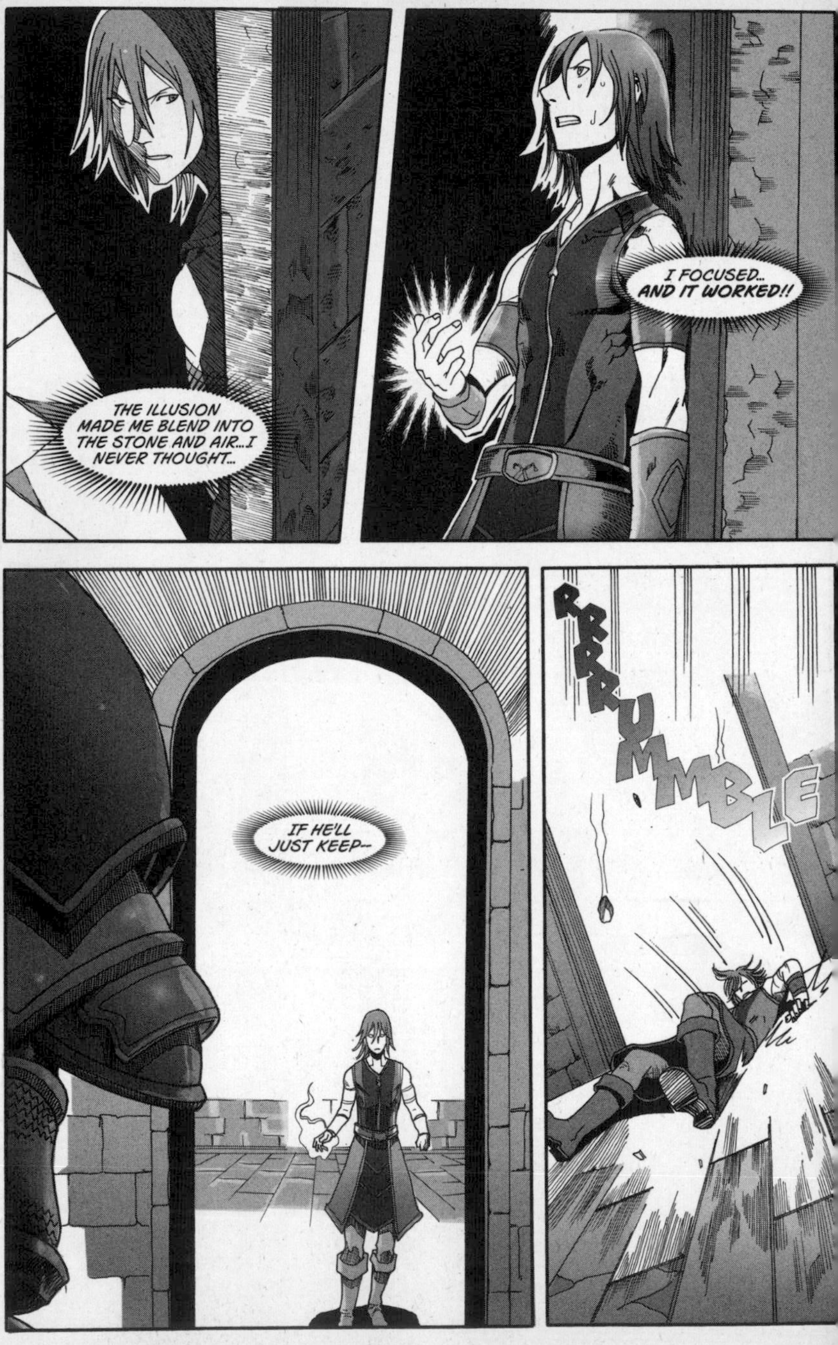
THE ILLUSION MADE ME BLEND INTO THE STONE AND AIR...I NEVER THOUGHT...
I FOCUSED... AND IT WORKED!!
IF HE'LL JUST KEEP--
RRRRUMMBLE

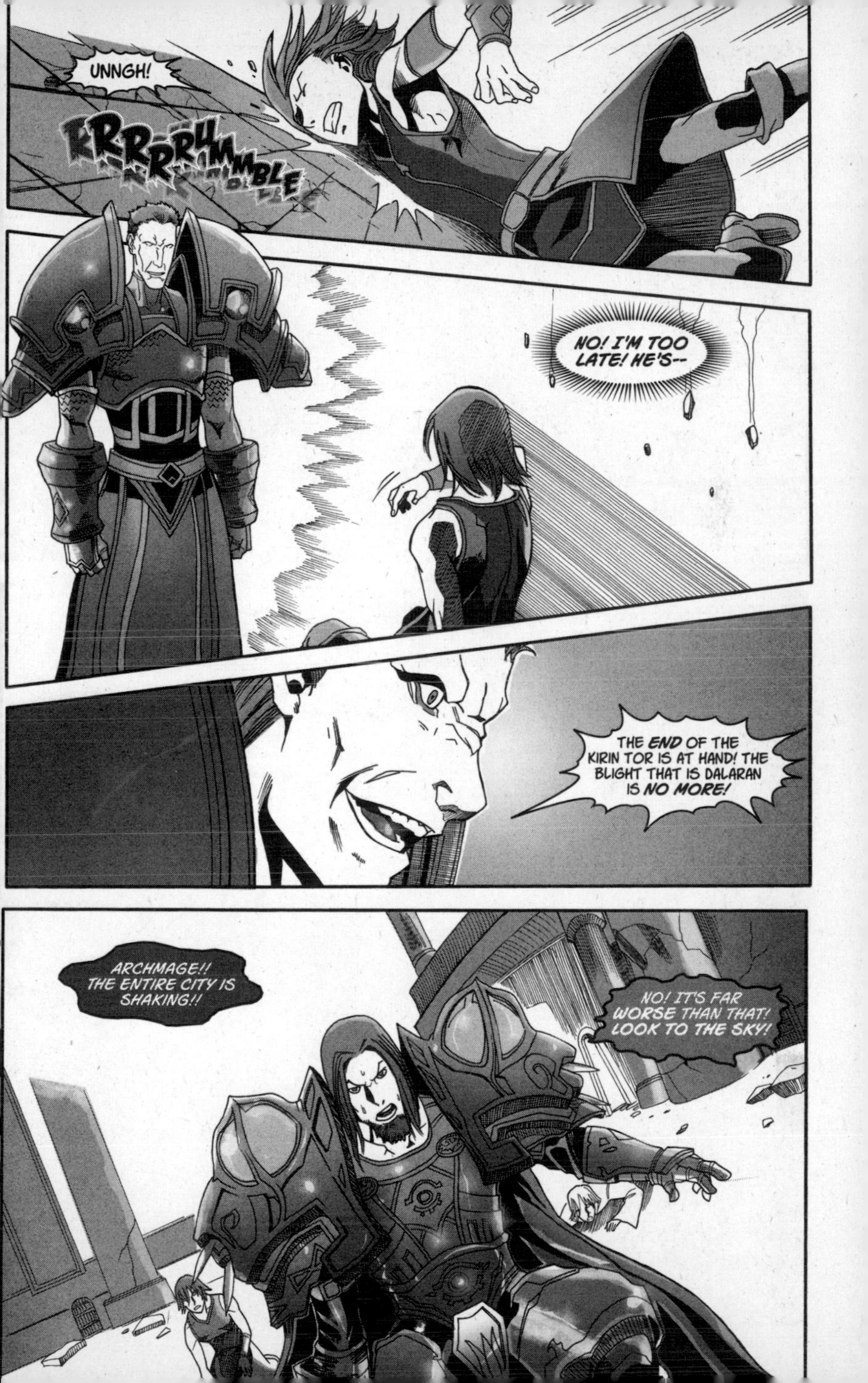
UNNGH!
RRRRRRUMMBLE
NO! I'M TOO LATE! HE'S--
THE END OF THE KIRIN TOR IS AT HAND! THE BLIGHT THAT IS DALARAN IS NO MORE!
ARCHMAGE!! THE ENTIRE CITY IS SHAKING!!
NO! IT'S FAR WORSE THAN THAT! LOOK TO THE SKY!

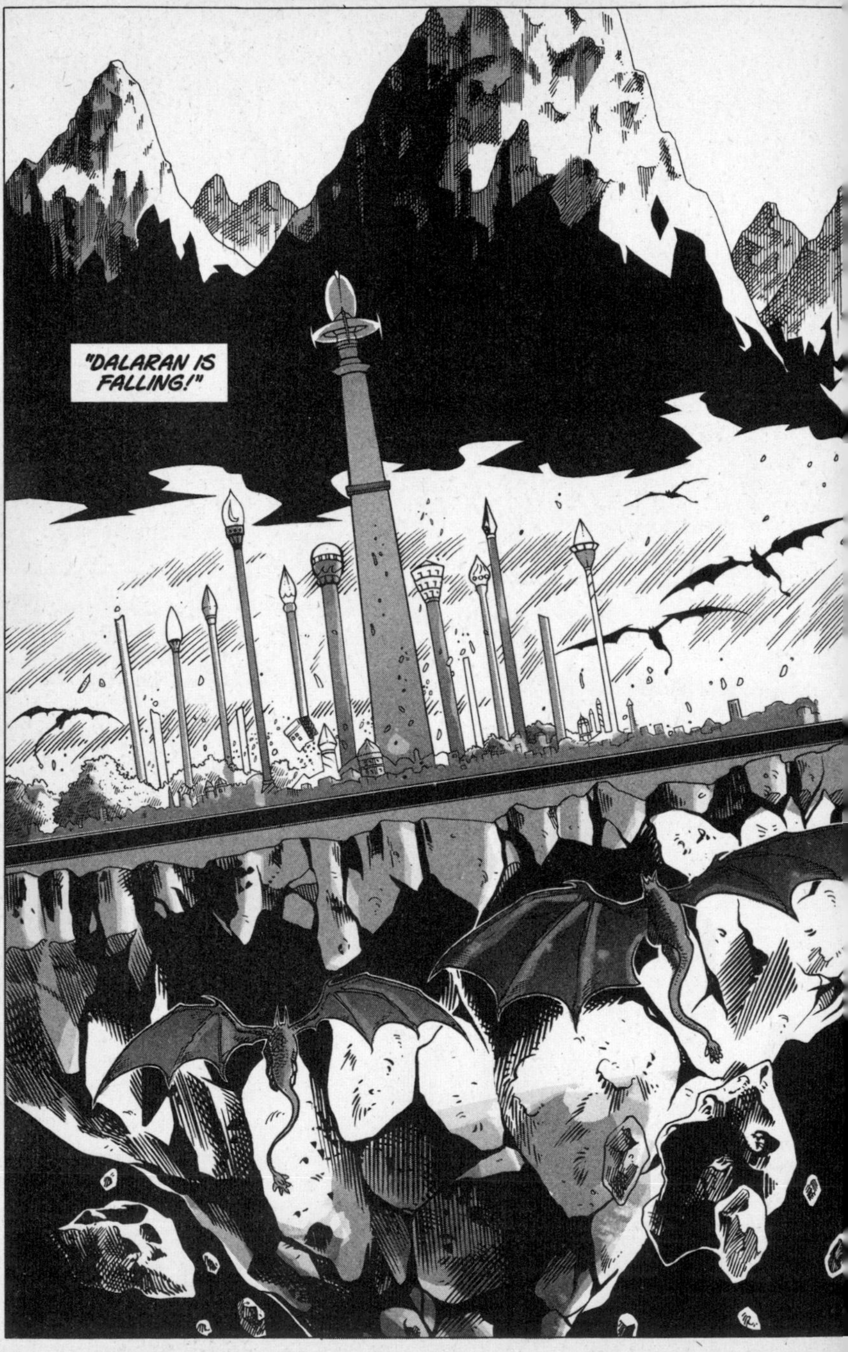
"DALARAN IS FALLING!"

# CHAPTER SIX

# FATAL PATH

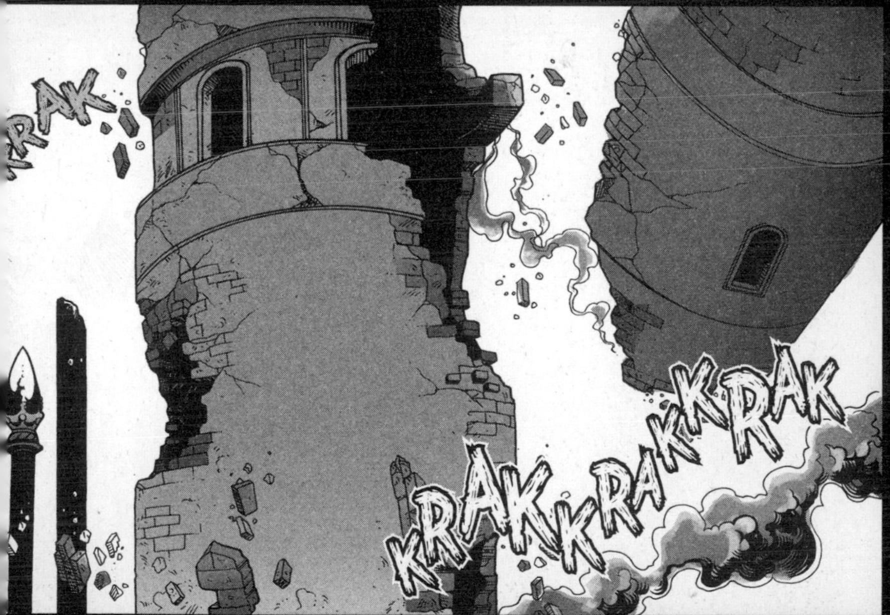
RAK
KRAKKRAKKRAKKRAK

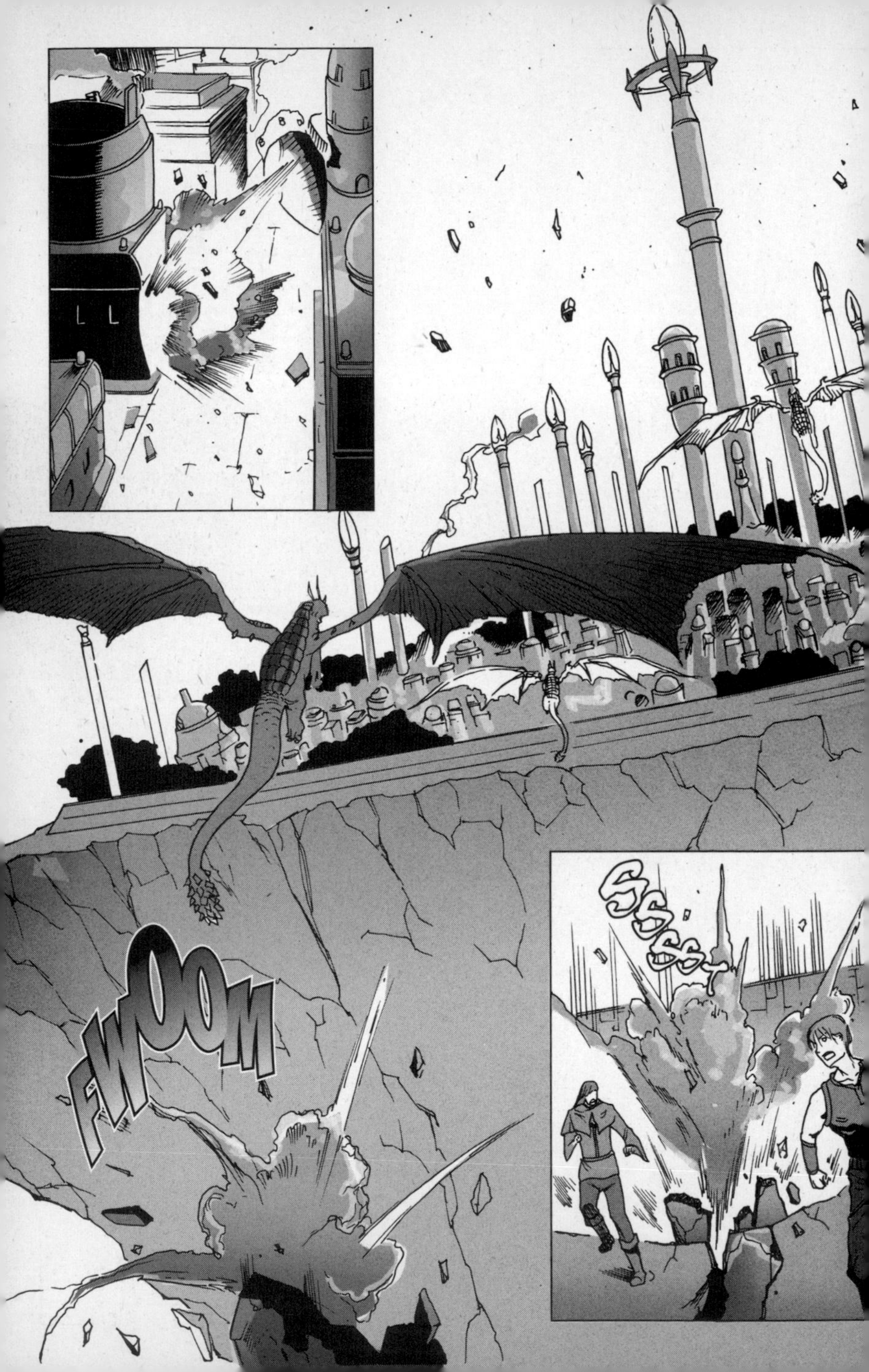
FWOOM
SSSST

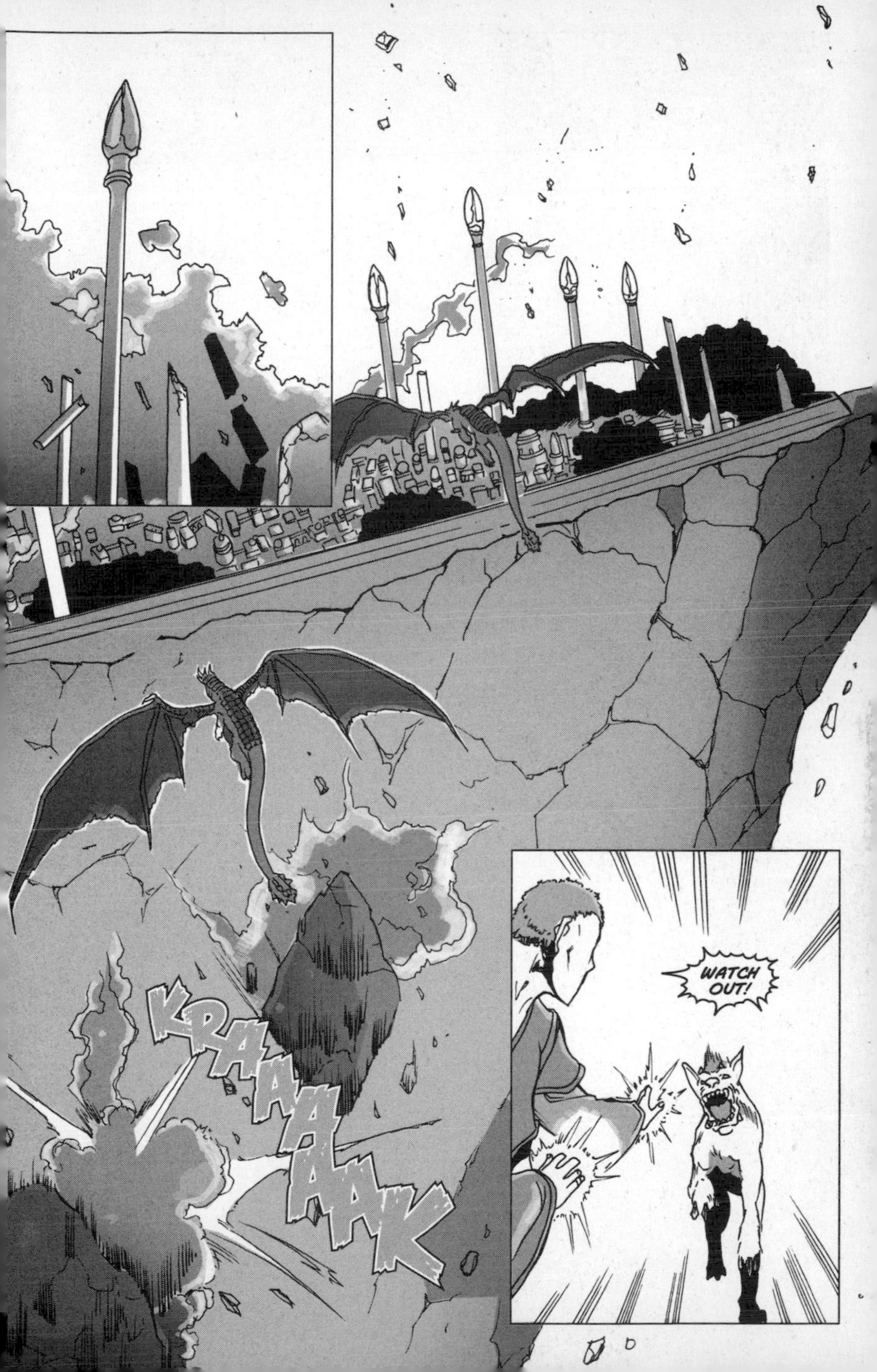
KRAAAAAK
WATCH OUT!

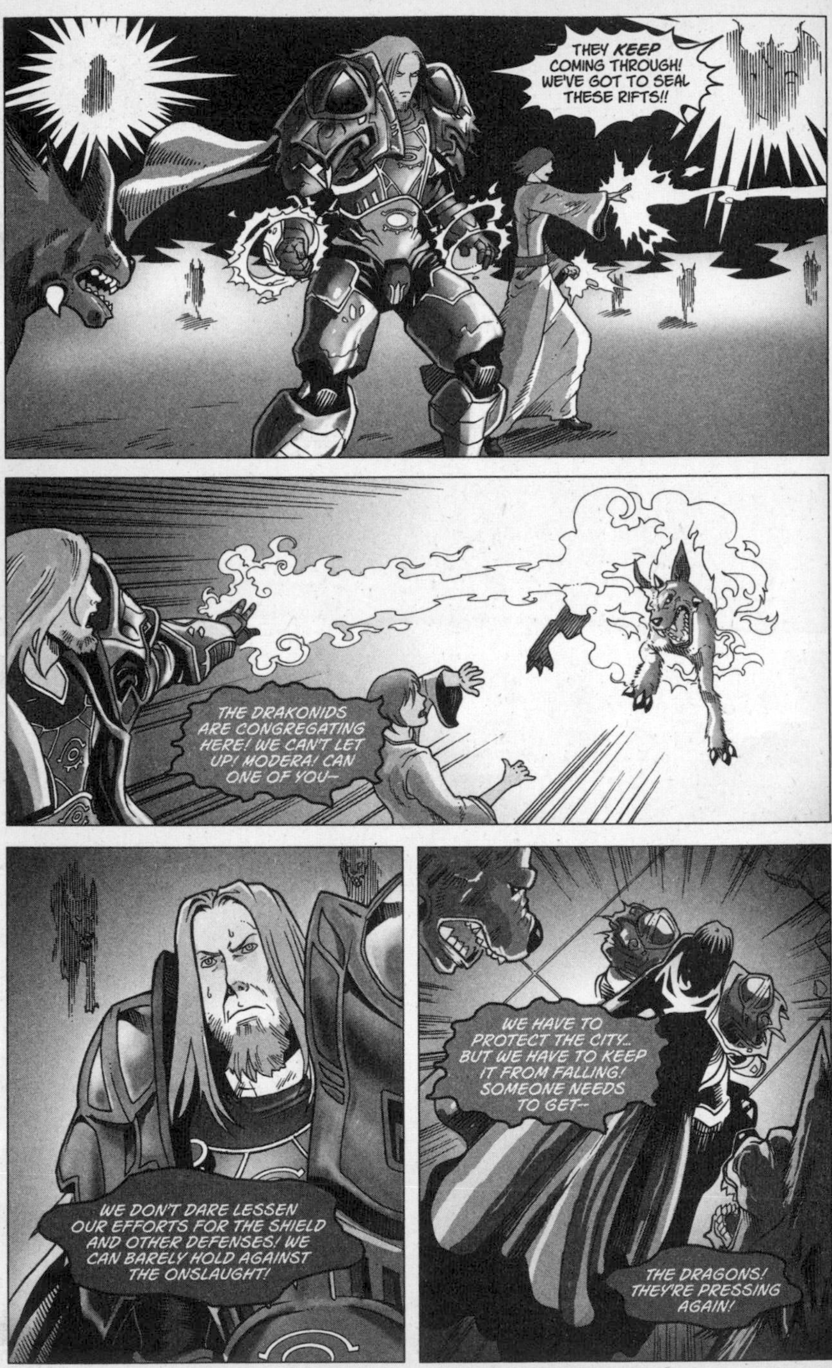
THEY *KEEP* COMING THROUGH! WE'VE GOT TO SEAL THESE RIFTS!!
THE DRAKONIDS ARE CONGREGATING HERE! WE CAN'T LET UP! MODERA! CAN ONE OF YOU--
WE DON'T DARE LESSEN OUR EFFORTS FOR THE SHIELD AND OTHER DEFENSES! WE CAN BARELY HOLD AGAINST THE ONSLAUGHT!
WE HAVE TO PROTECT THE CITY... BUT WE HAVE TO KEEP IT FROM FALLING! SOMEONE NEEDS TO GET--
THE DRAGONS! THEY'RE PRESSING AGAIN!

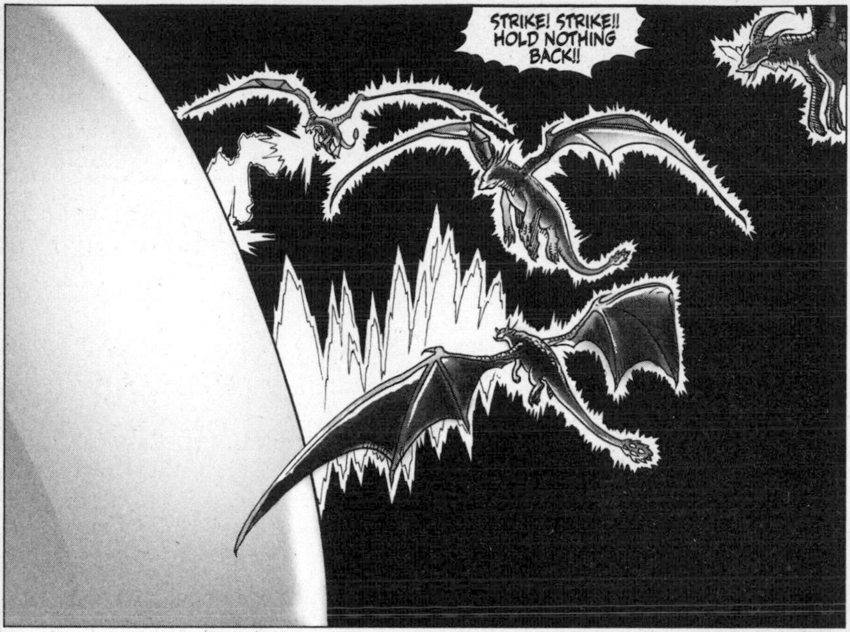
STRIKE! STRIKE!! HOLD NOTHING BACK!!

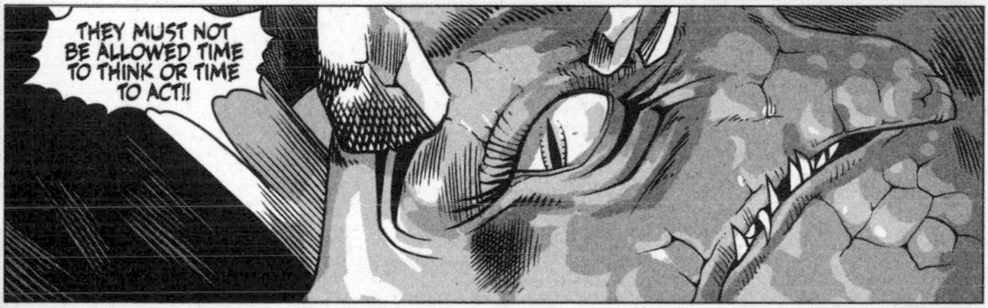
THEY MUST NOT BE ALLOWED TIME TO THINK OR TIME TO ACT!!

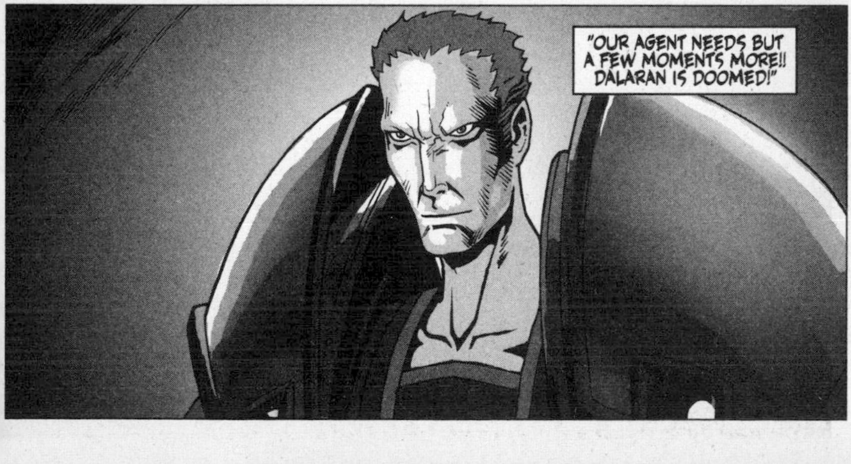
"OUR AGENT NEEDS BUT A FEW MOMENTS MORE!! DALARAN IS DOOMED!"

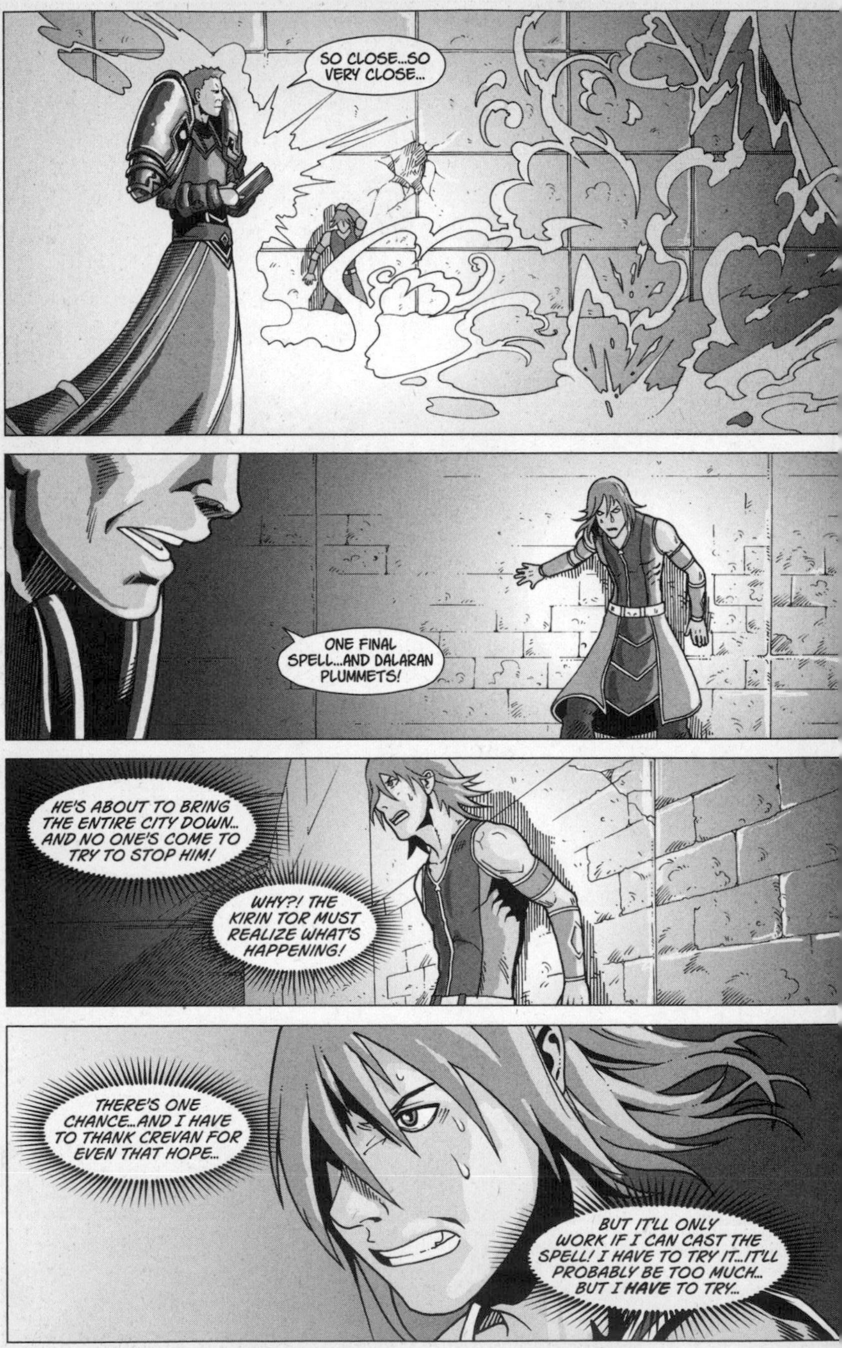
SO CLOSE...SO VERY CLOSE...
ONE FINAL SPELL...AND DALARAN PLUMMETS!
HE'S ABOUT TO BRING THE ENTIRE CITY DOWN... AND NO ONE'S COME TO TRY TO STOP HIM!
WHY?! THE KIRIN TOR MUST REALIZE WHAT'S HAPPENING!
THERE'S ONE CHANCE...AND I HAVE TO THANK CREVAN FOR EVEN THAT HOPE...
BUT IT'LL ONLY WORK IF I CAN CAST THE SPELL! I HAVE TO TRY IT...IT'LL PROBABLY BE TOO MUCH... BUT I HAVE TO TRY...

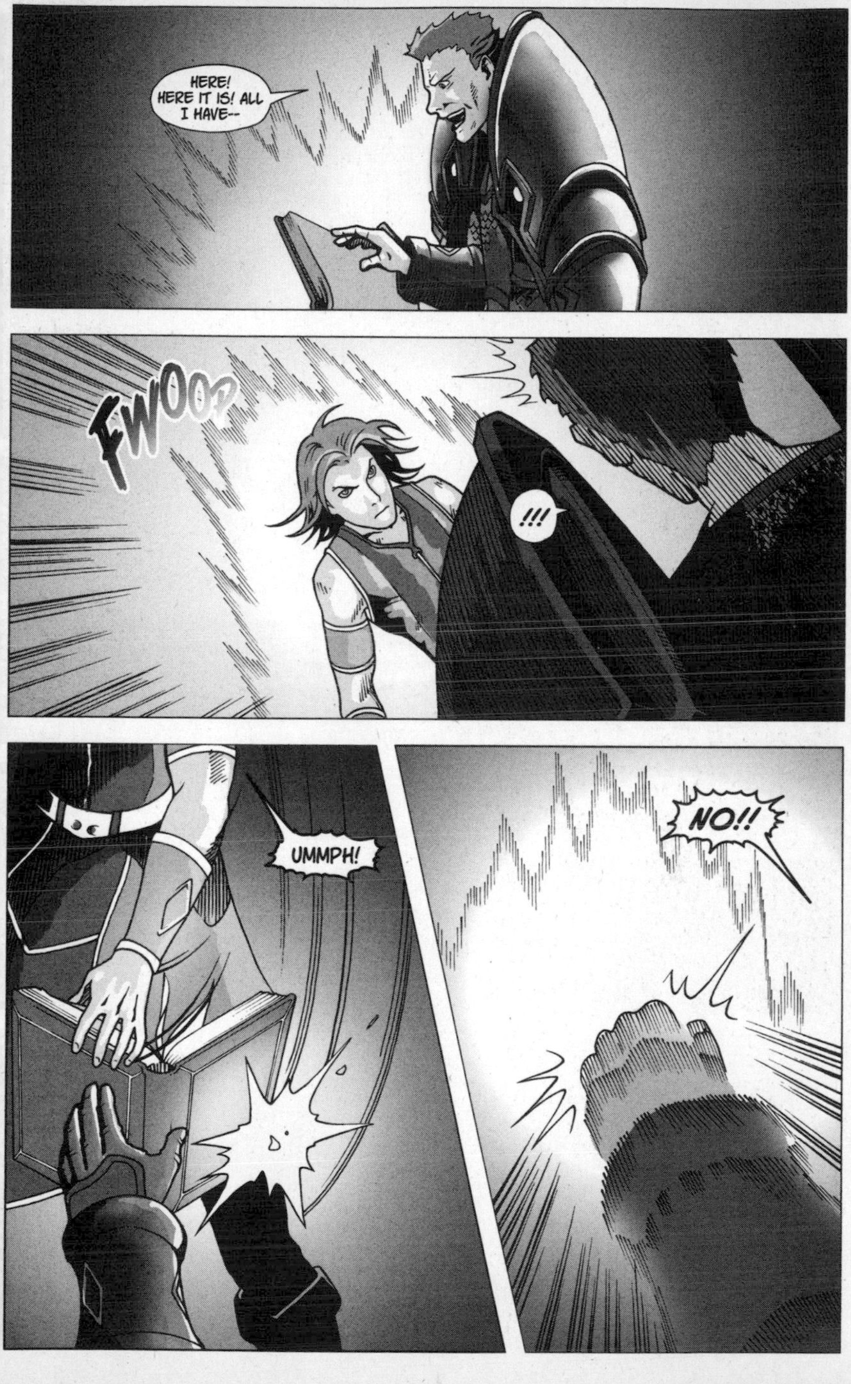
HERE! HERE IT IS! ALL I HAVE--
FWOOP
!!!
UMMPH!
NO!!

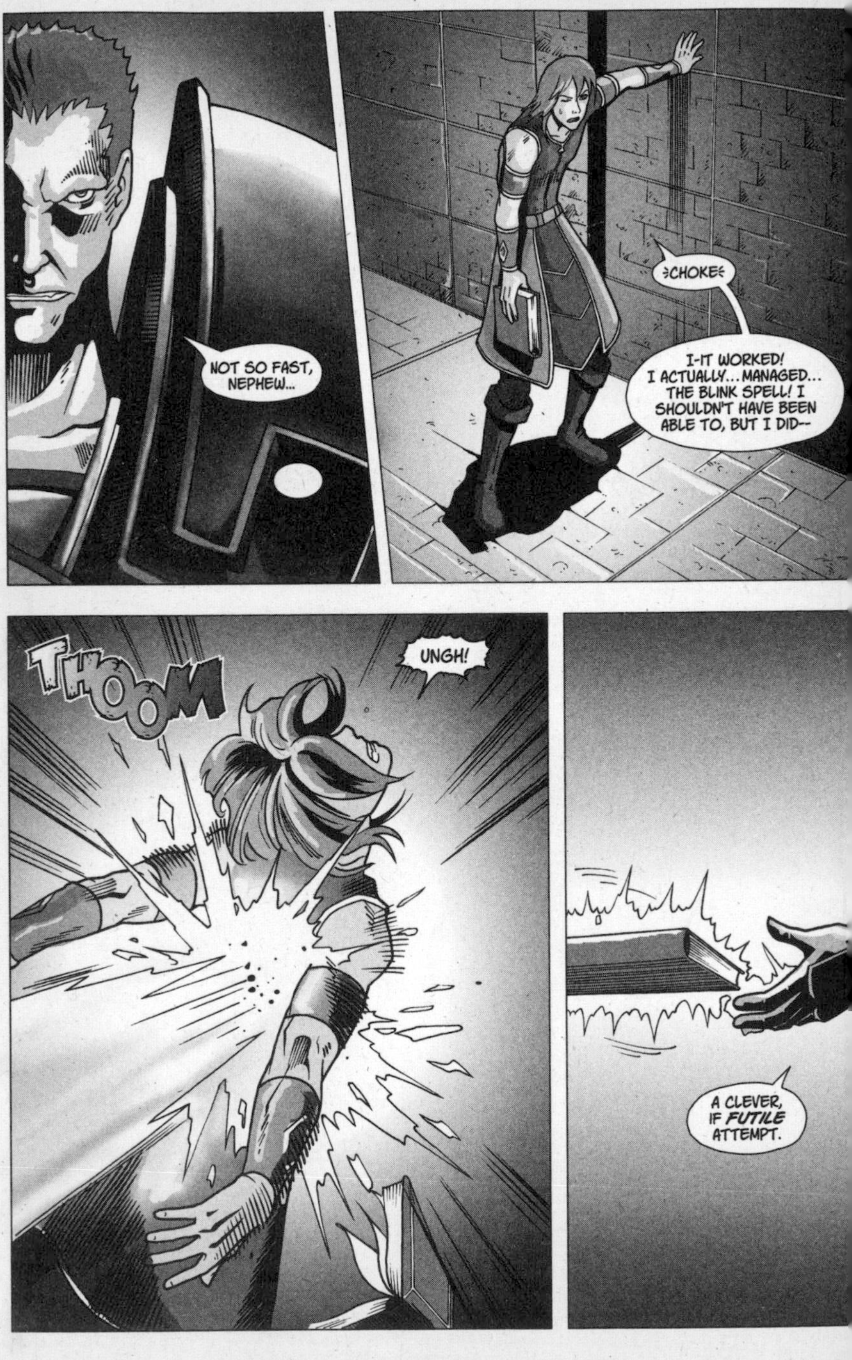
NOT SO FAST, NEPHEW...
CHOKE
I-IT WORKED! I ACTUALLY... MANAGED... THE BLINK SPELL! I SHOULDN'T HAVE BEEN ABLE TO, BUT I DID--
THOOM
UNGH!
A CLEVER, IF *FUTILE* ATTEMPT.

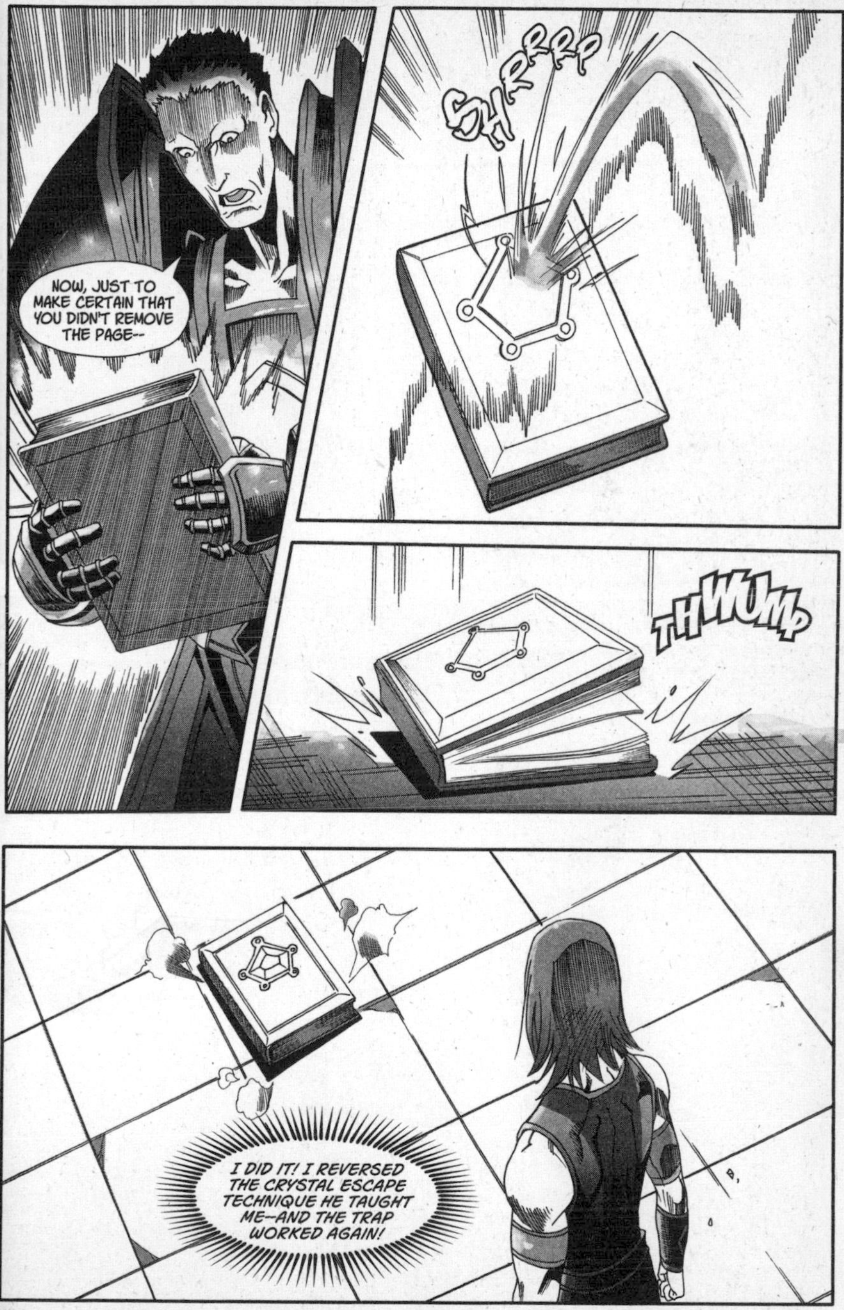
NOW, JUST TO MAKE CERTAIN THAT YOU DIDN'T REMOVE THE PAGE--
SHRRRP
THWUMP
I DID IT! I REVERSED THE CRYSTAL ESCAPE TECHNIQUE HE TAUGHT ME--AND THE TRAP WORKED AGAIN!

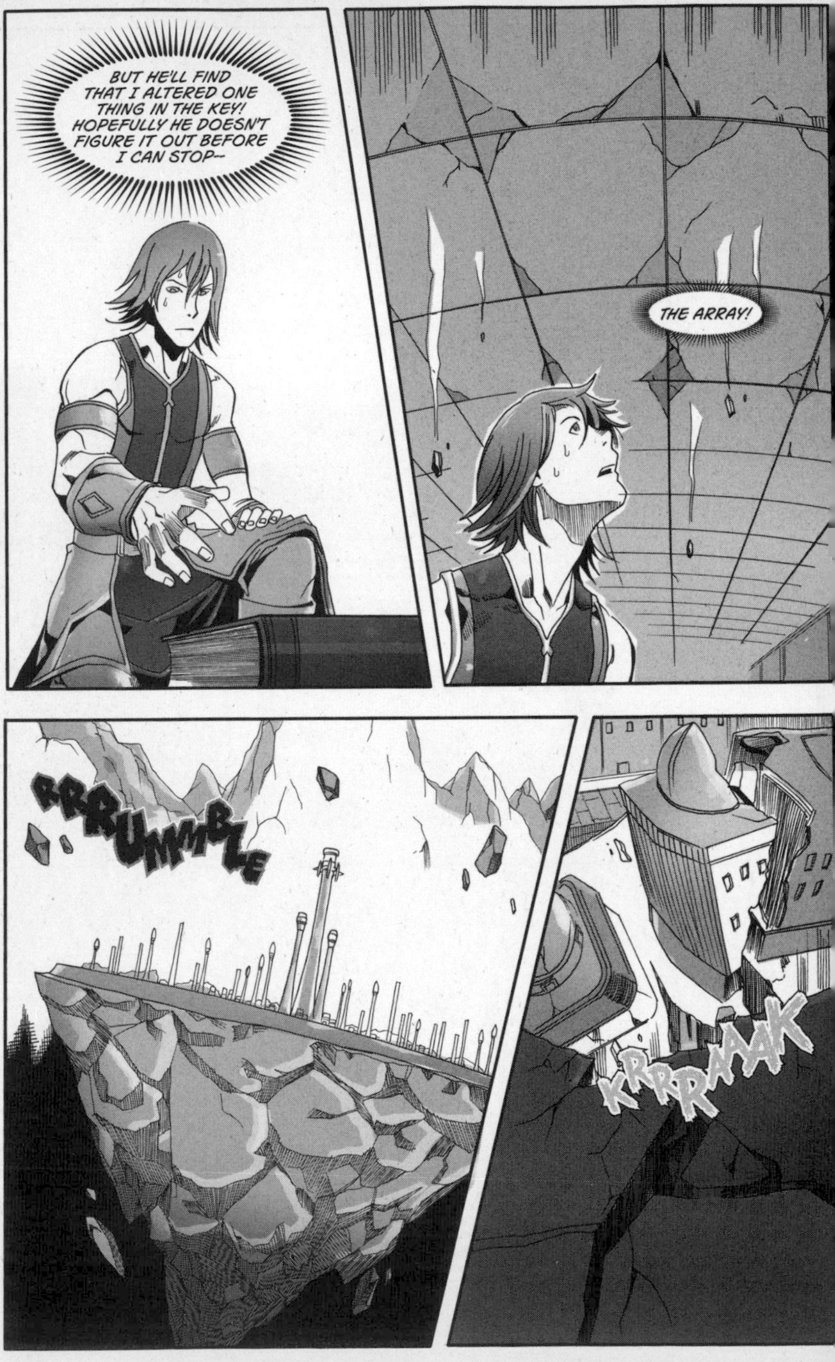
BUT HE'LL FIND THAT I ALTERED ONE THING IN THE KEY! HOPEFULLY HE DOESN'T FIGURE IT OUT BEFORE I CAN STOP--
THE ARRAY!
RRRUMMBLE
KRRRAAAK

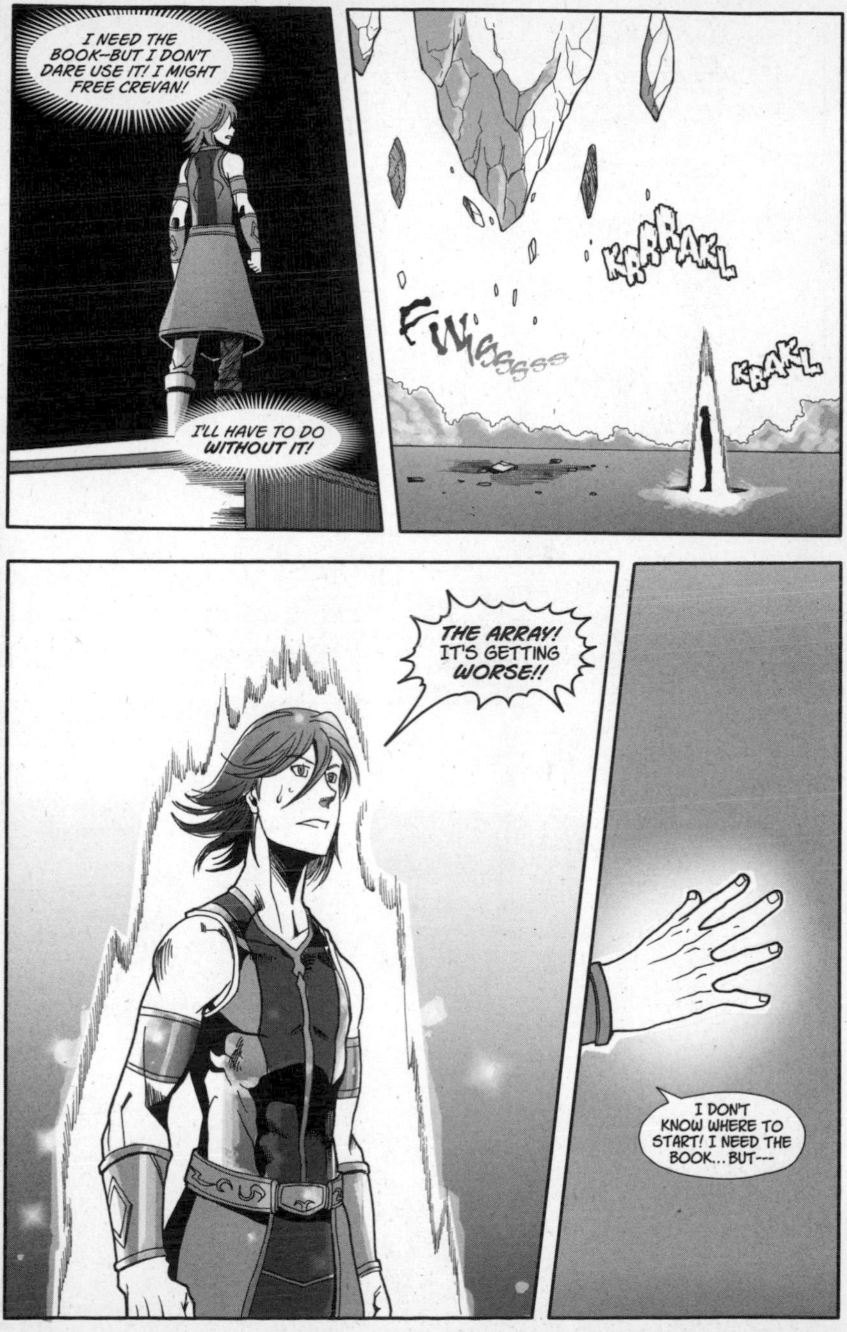
I NEED THE BOOK--BUT I DON'T DARE USE IT! I MIGHT FREE CREVAN!
I'LL HAVE TO DO WITHOUT IT!
KRRRRAKL
FWISSSSS
KRAKL
THE ARRAY! IT'S GETTING WORSE!!
I DON'T KNOW WHERE TO START! I NEED THE BOOK... BUT---

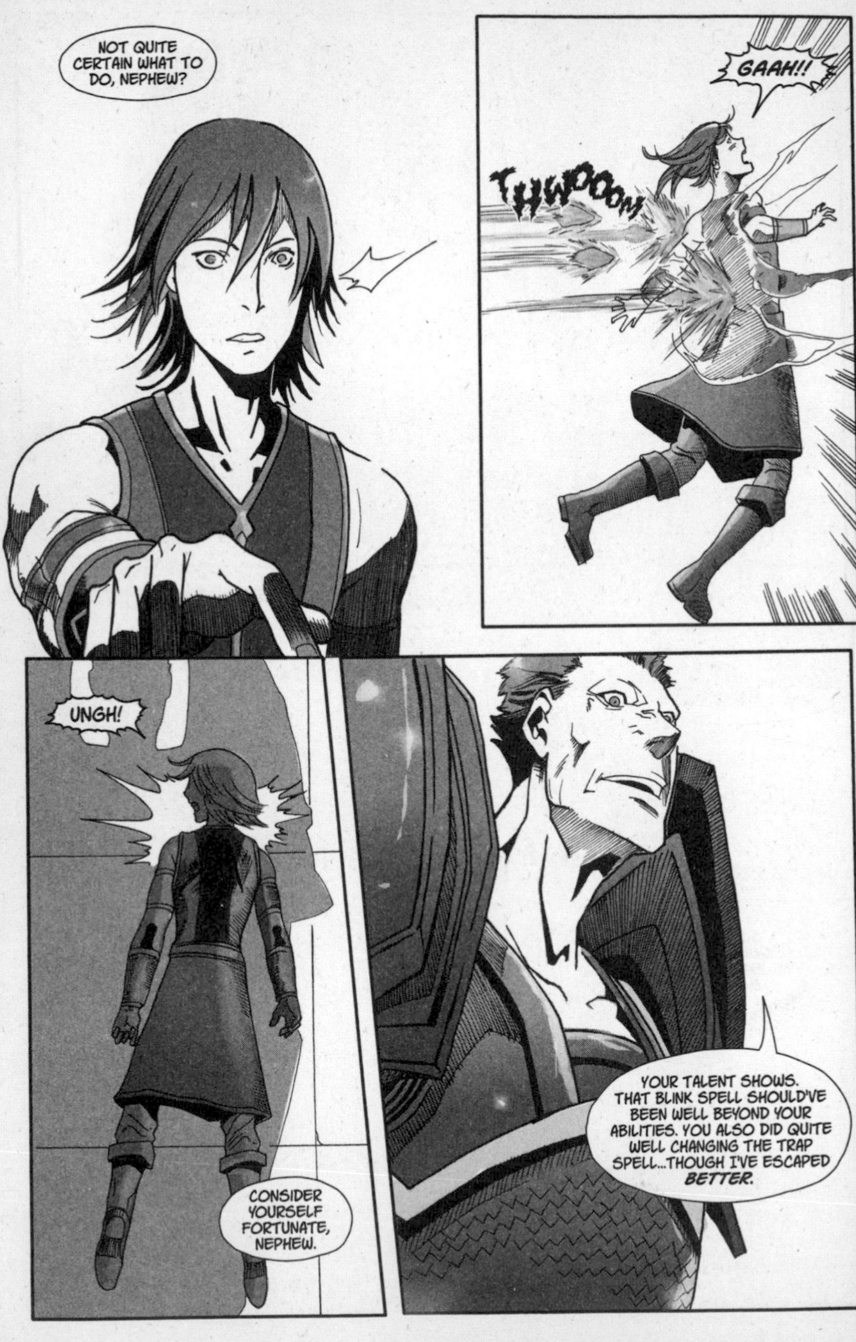
NOT QUITE CERTAIN WHAT TO DO, NEPHEW?
GAAH!!
THWOOOM
UNGH!
CONSIDER YOURSELF FORTUNATE, NEPHEW.
YOUR TALENT SHOWS. THAT BLINK SPELL SHOULD'VE BEEN WELL BEYOND YOUR ABILITIES. YOU ALSO DID QUITE WELL CHANGING THE TRAP SPELL...THOUGH I'VE ESCAPED *BETTER*.

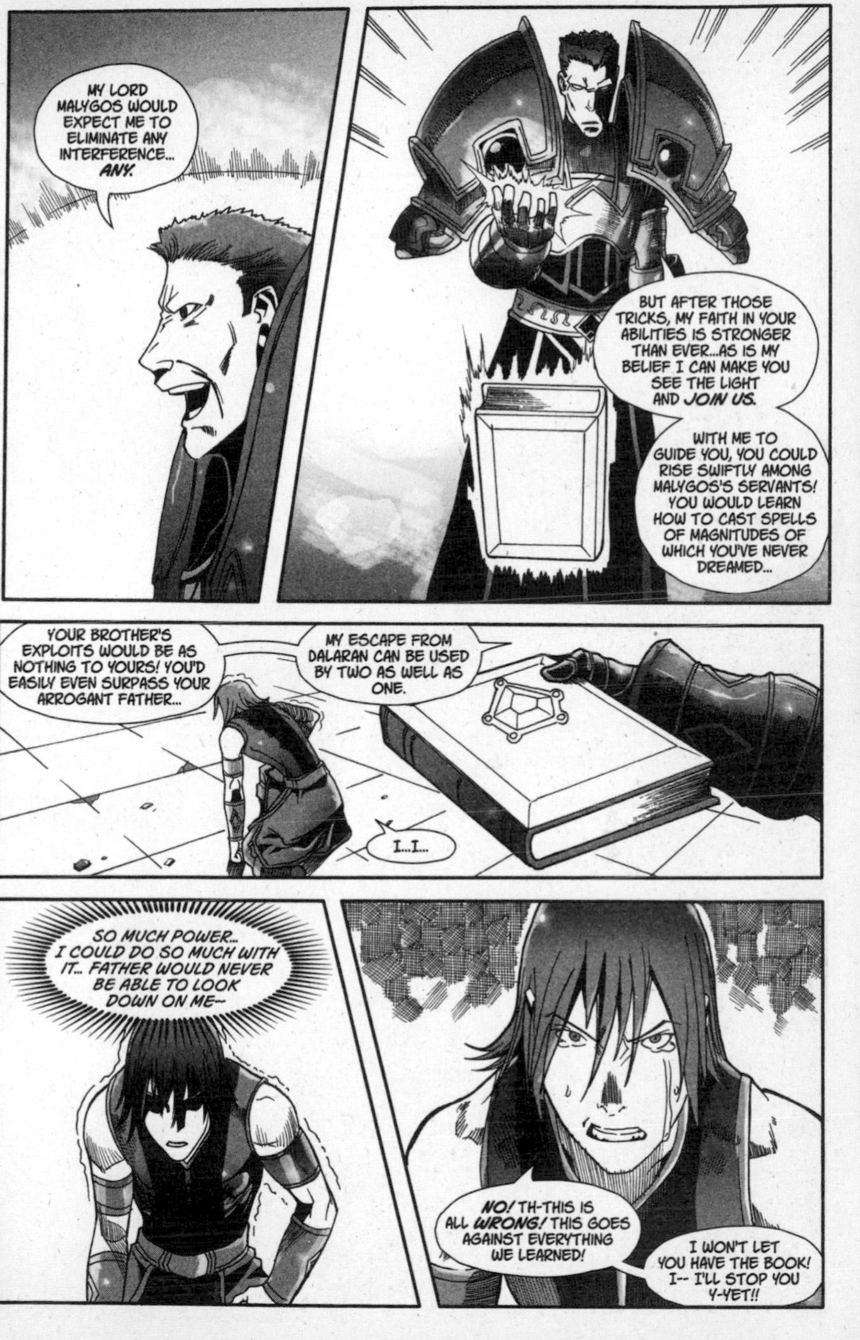
MY LORD MALYGOS WOULD EXPECT ME TO ELIMINATE ANY INTERFERENCE... *ANY.*
BUT AFTER THOSE TRICKS, MY FAITH IN YOUR ABILITIES IS STRONGER THAN EVER...AS IS MY BELIEF I CAN MAKE YOU SEE THE LIGHT AND *JOIN US.*
WITH ME TO GUIDE YOU, YOU COULD RISE SWIFTLY AMONG MALYGOS'S SERVANTS! YOU WOULD LEARN HOW TO CAST SPELLS OF MAGNITUDES OF WHICH YOU'VE NEVER DREAMED...
YOUR BROTHER'S EXPLOITS WOULD BE AS NOTHING TO YOURS! YOU'D EASILY EVEN SURPASS YOUR ARROGANT FATHER...
MY ESCAPE FROM DALARAN CAN BE USED BY TWO AS WELL AS ONE.
I...I...
*SO MUCH POWER... I COULD DO SO MUCH WITH IT... FATHER WOULD NEVER BE ABLE TO LOOK DOWN ON ME--*
*NO!* TH-THIS IS ALL *WRONG!* THIS GOES AGAINST EVERYTHING WE LEARNED!
I WON'T LET YOU HAVE THE BOOK! I-- I'LL STOP YOU Y-YET!!

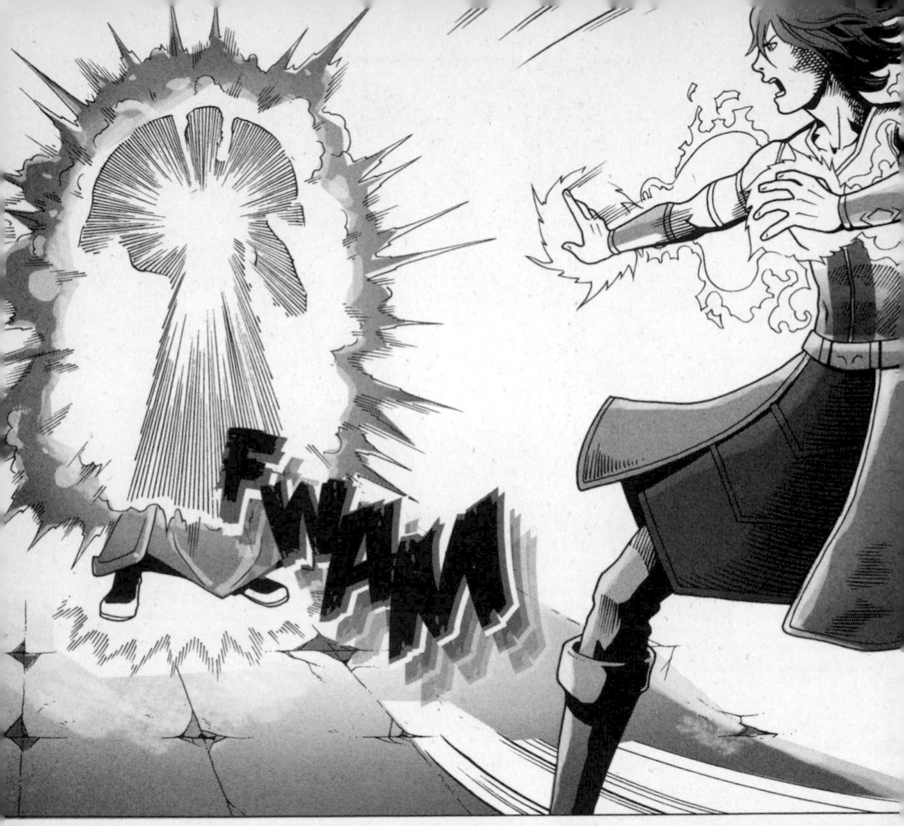
FWAM
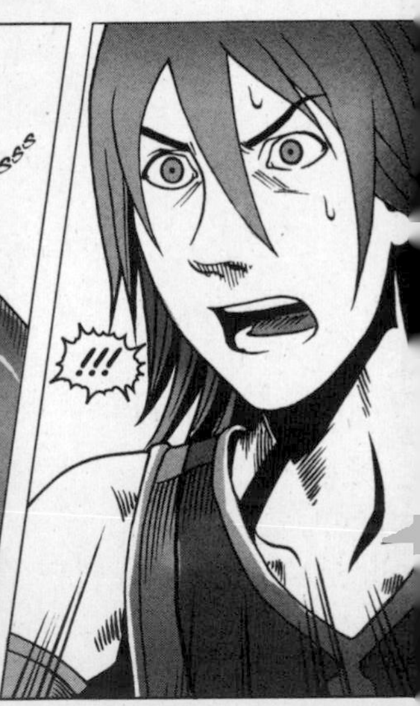
!!!
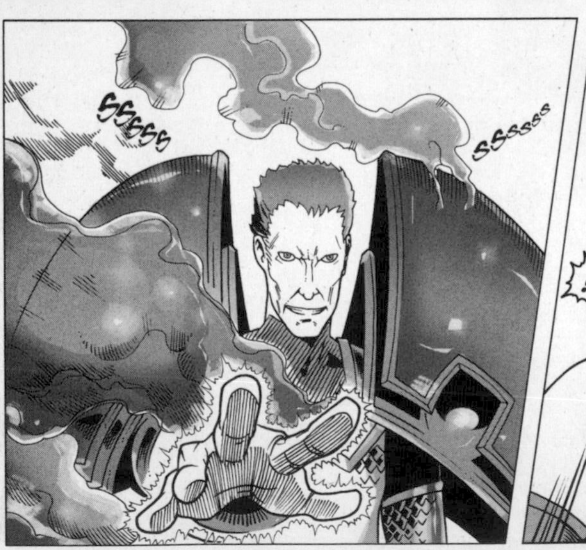
SSSSS
SSSSSS

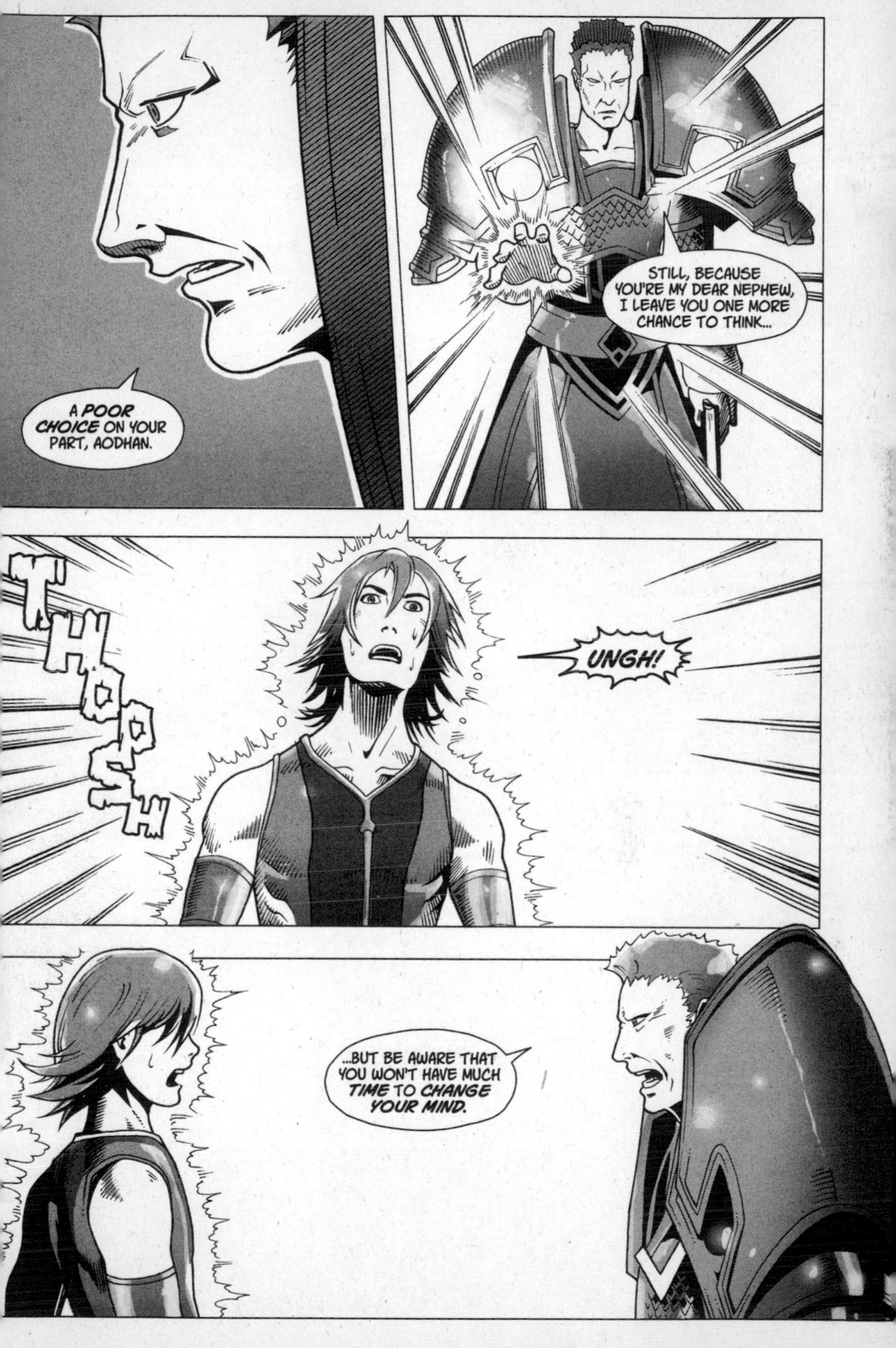
A POOR CHOICE ON YOUR PART, AODHAN.
STILL, BECAUSE YOU'RE MY DEAR NEPHEW, I LEAVE YOU ONE MORE CHANCE TO THINK...
THOOPSH
UNGH!
...BUT BE AWARE THAT YOU WON'T HAVE MUCH TIME TO CHANGE YOUR MIND.

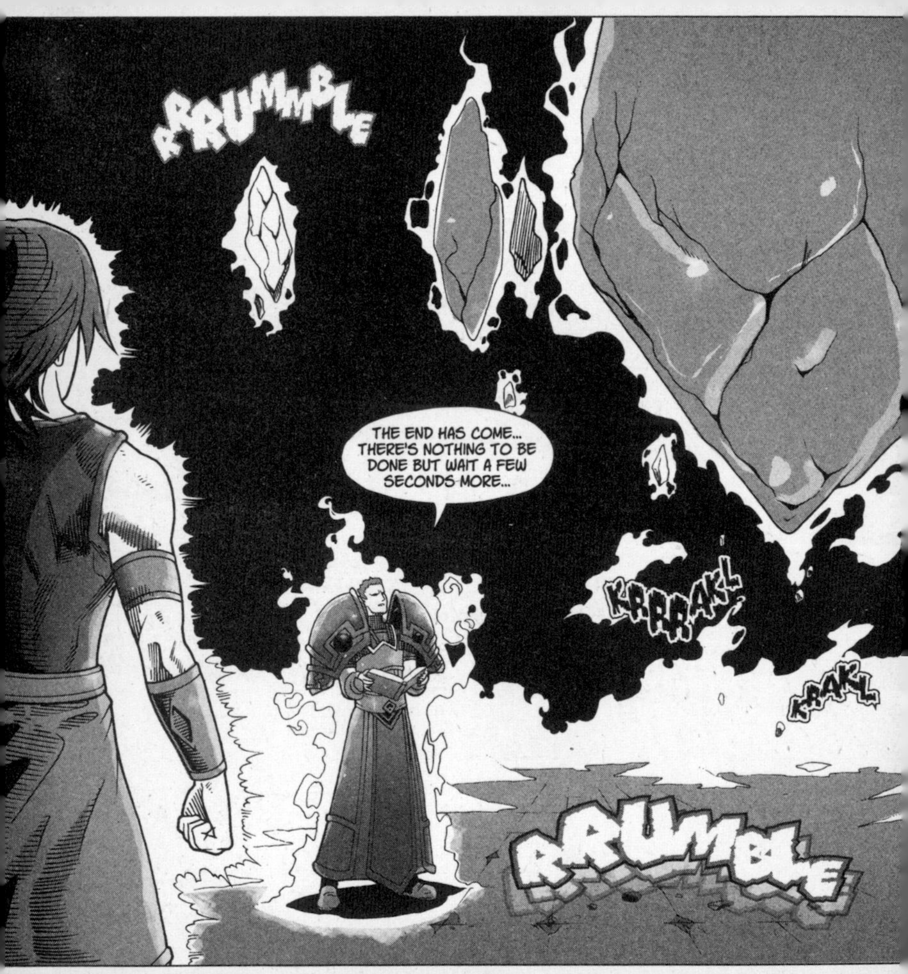
RRUMMBLE
THE END HAS COME... THERE'S NOTHING TO BE DONE BUT WAIT A FEW SECONDS MORE...
KRRRRAKL
KRAKL
RRUMBLE

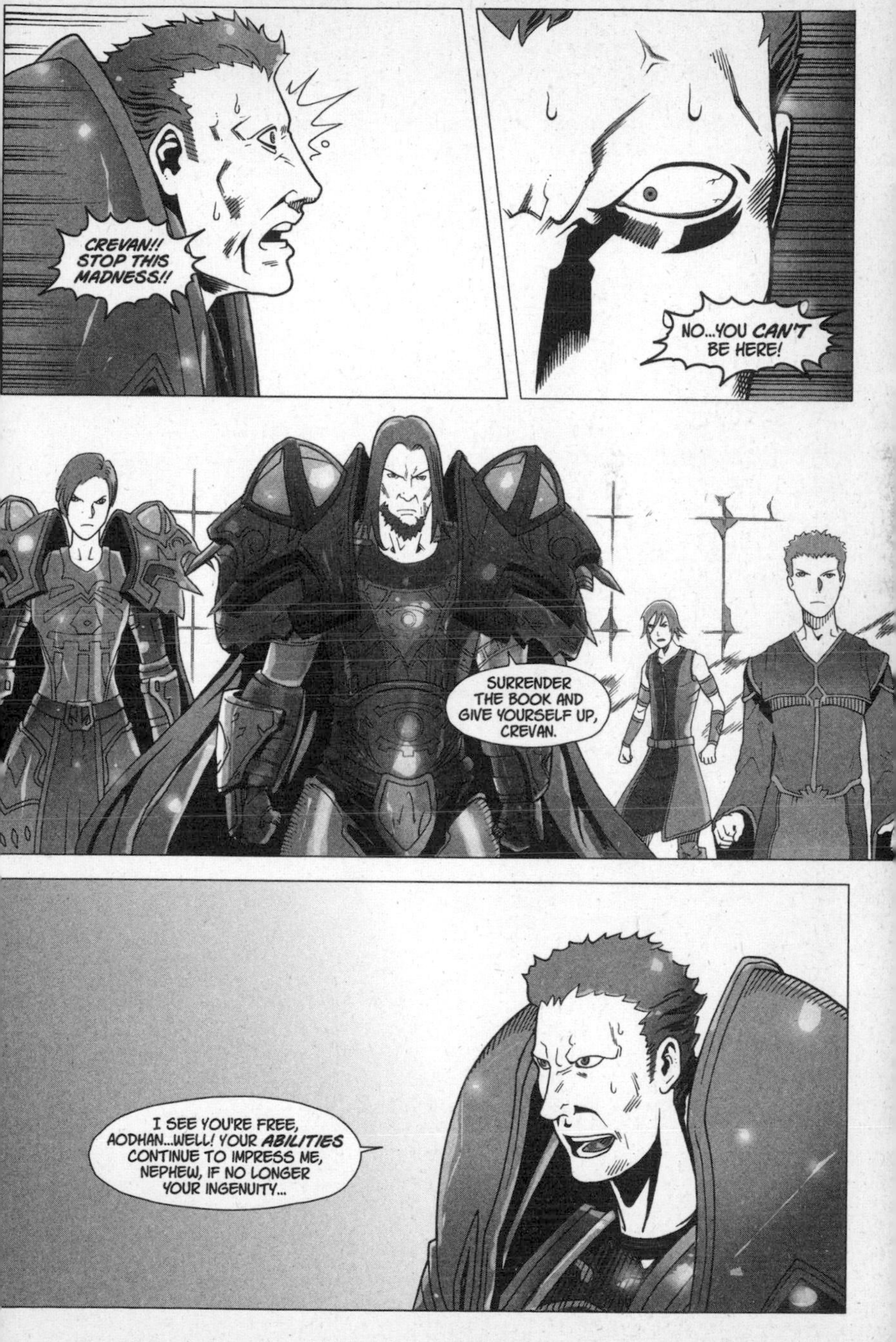
CREVAN!! STOP THIS MADNESS!!
NO...YOU CAN'T BE HERE!
SURRENDER THE BOOK AND GIVE YOURSELF UP, CREVAN.
I SEE YOU'RE FREE, AODHAN...WELL! YOUR ABILITIES CONTINUE TO IMPRESS ME, NEPHEW, IF NO LONGER YOUR INGENUITY...

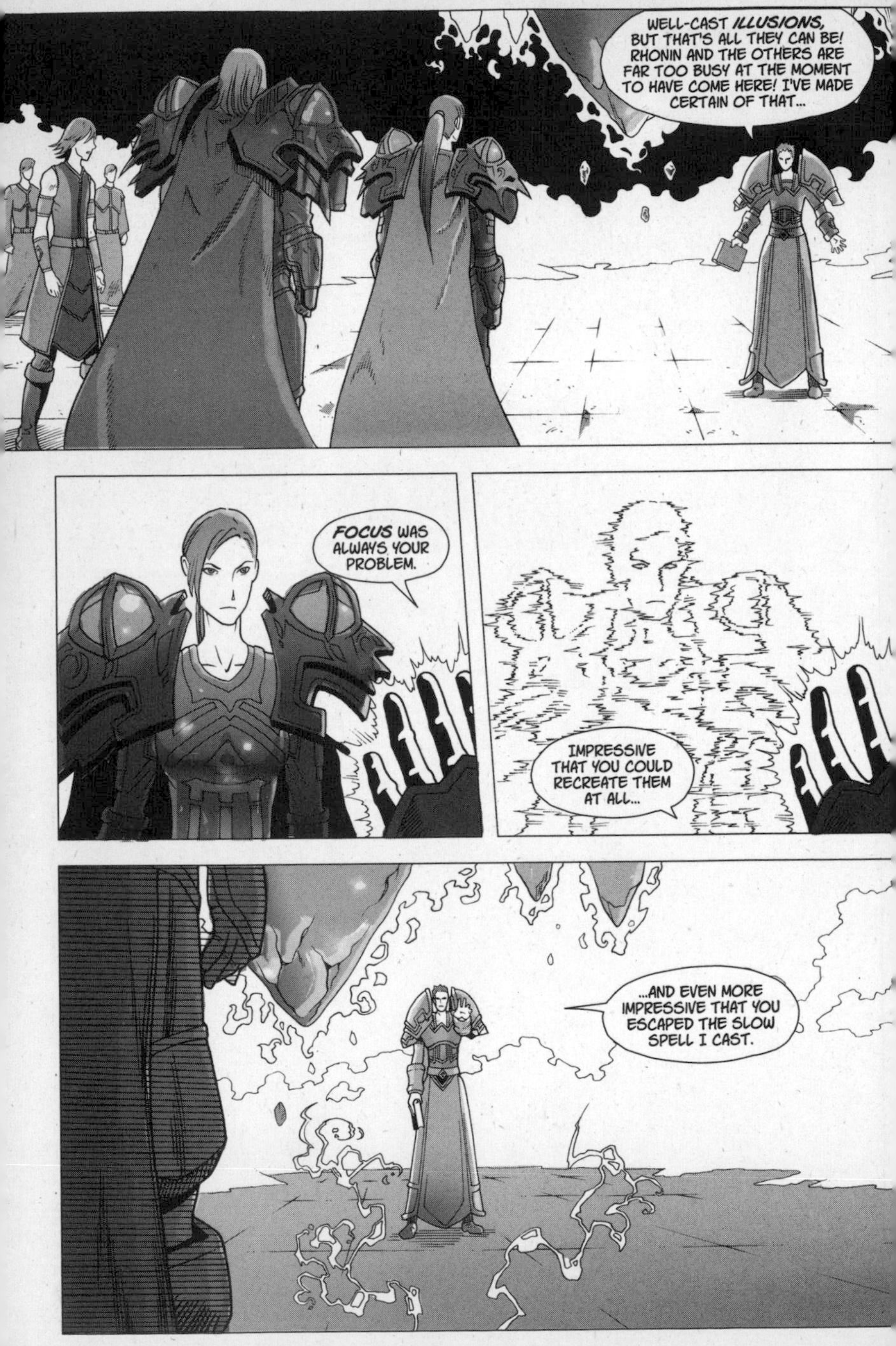
WELL-CAST ILLUSIONS, BUT THAT'S ALL THEY CAN BE! RHONIN AND THE OTHERS ARE FAR TOO BUSY AT THE MOMENT TO HAVE COME HERE! I'VE MADE CERTAIN OF THAT...
FOCUS WAS ALWAYS YOUR PROBLEM.
IMPRESSIVE THAT YOU COULD RECREATE THEM AT ALL...
...AND EVEN MORE IMPRESSIVE THAT YOU ESCAPED THE SLOW SPELL I CAST.

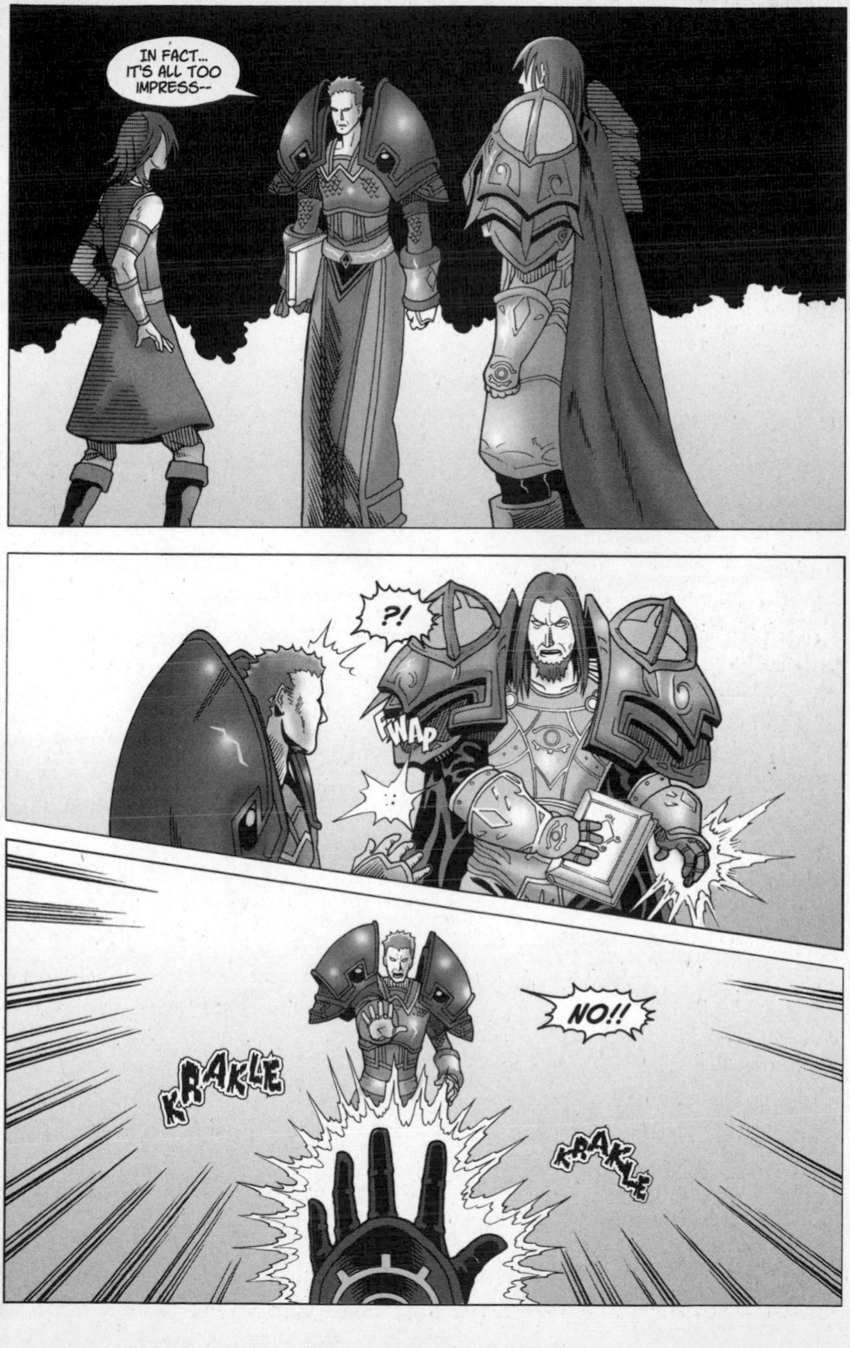
IN FACT... IT'S ALL TOO IMPRESS--
?!
FWAP
NO!!
KRAKLE
KRAKLE

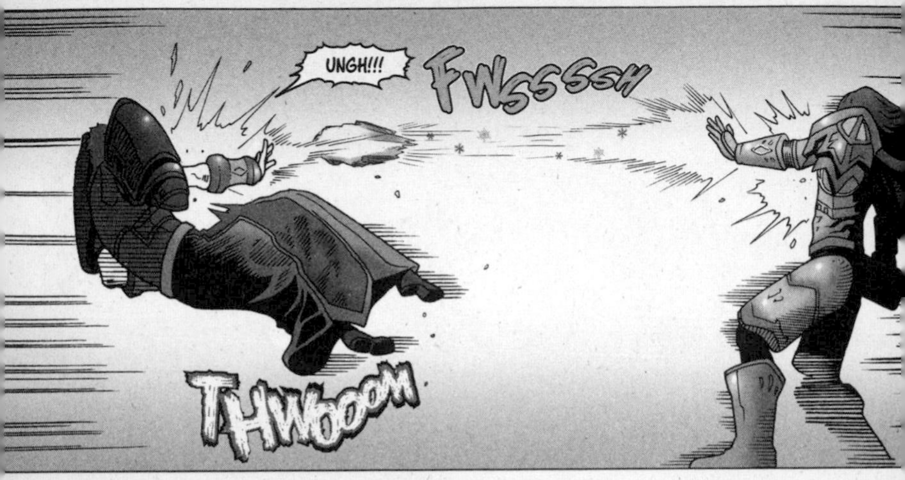
UNGH!!!
FWSSSSH
THWOOOM
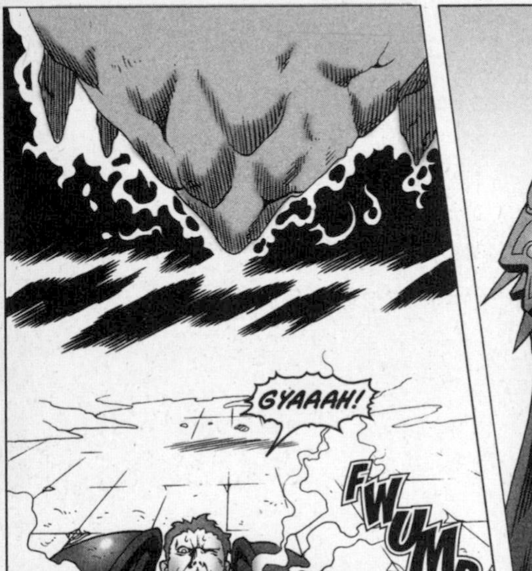
GYAAAH!
FWUMP
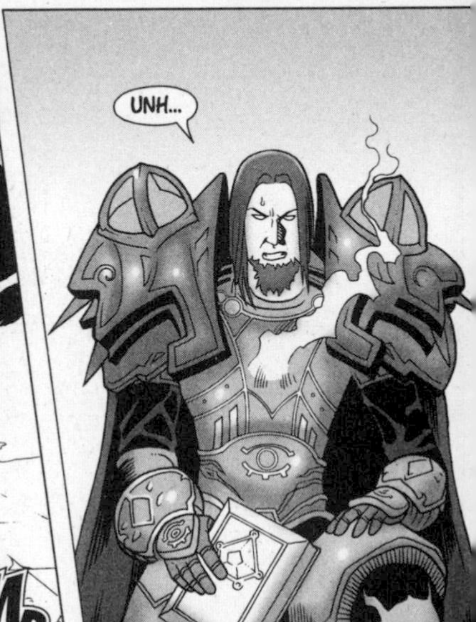
UNH...

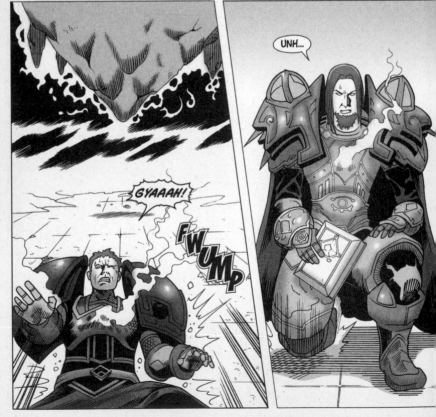

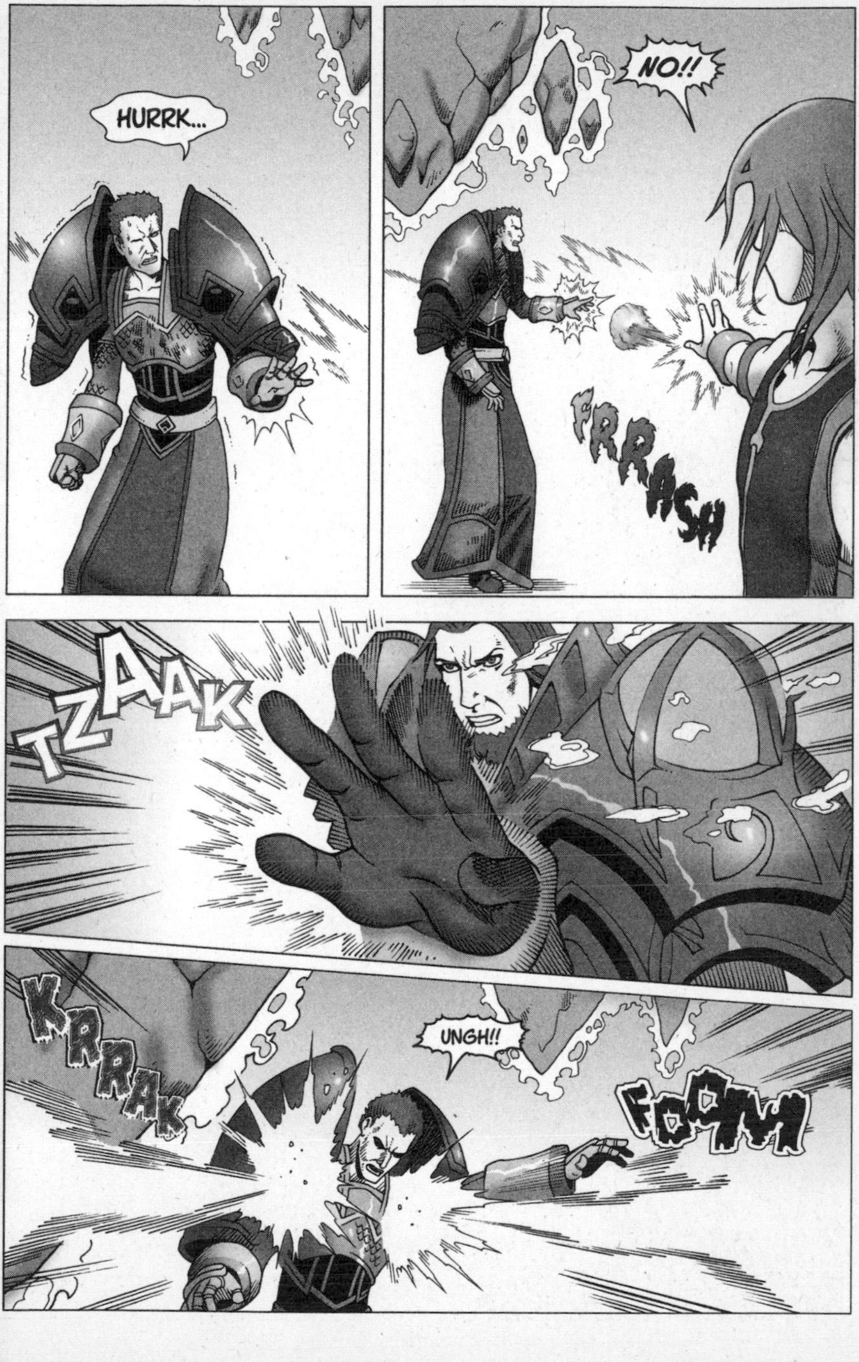
HURRK...
NO!!
FRRASH
TZAAK
KRRAK
UNGH!!
FOOM

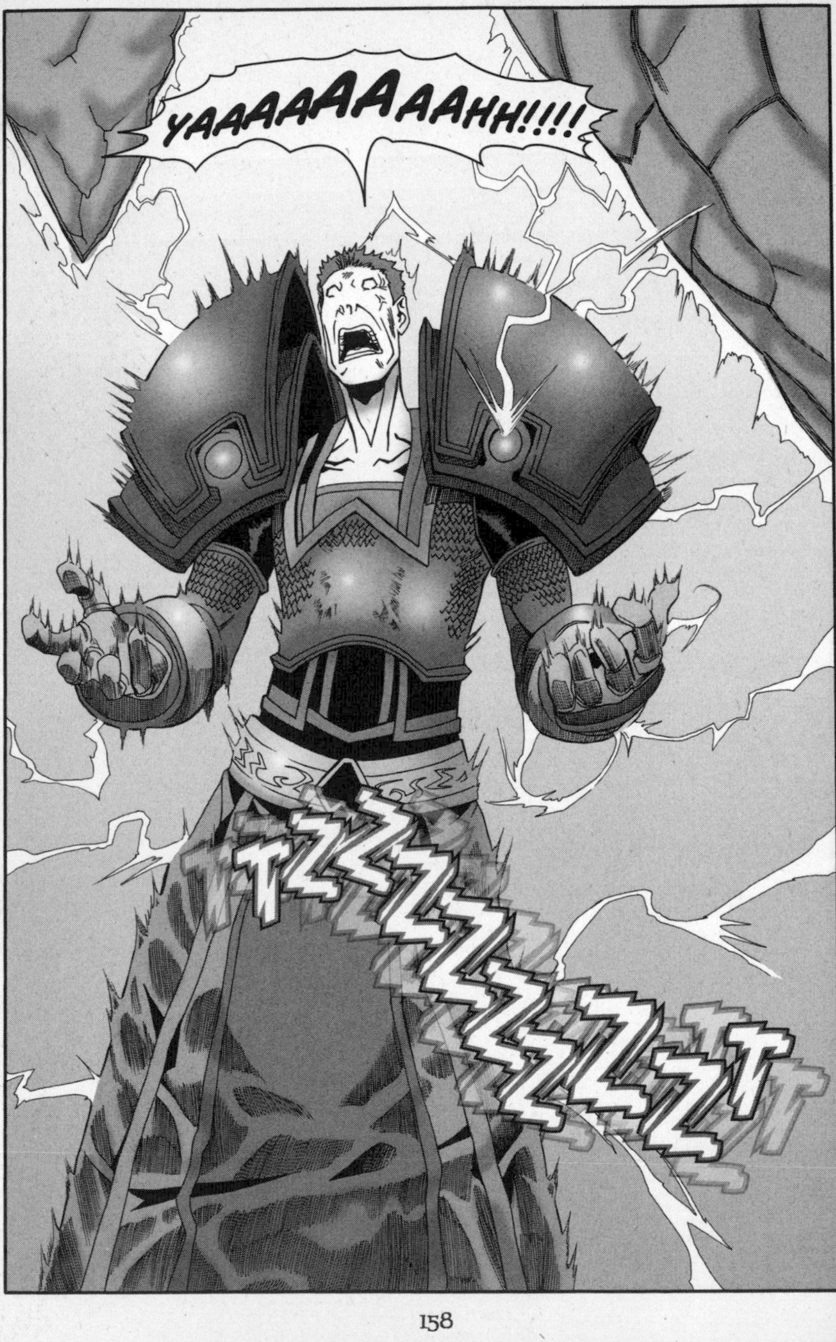
YAAAAAAAAAHH!!!!
TZZZZZZZZZT

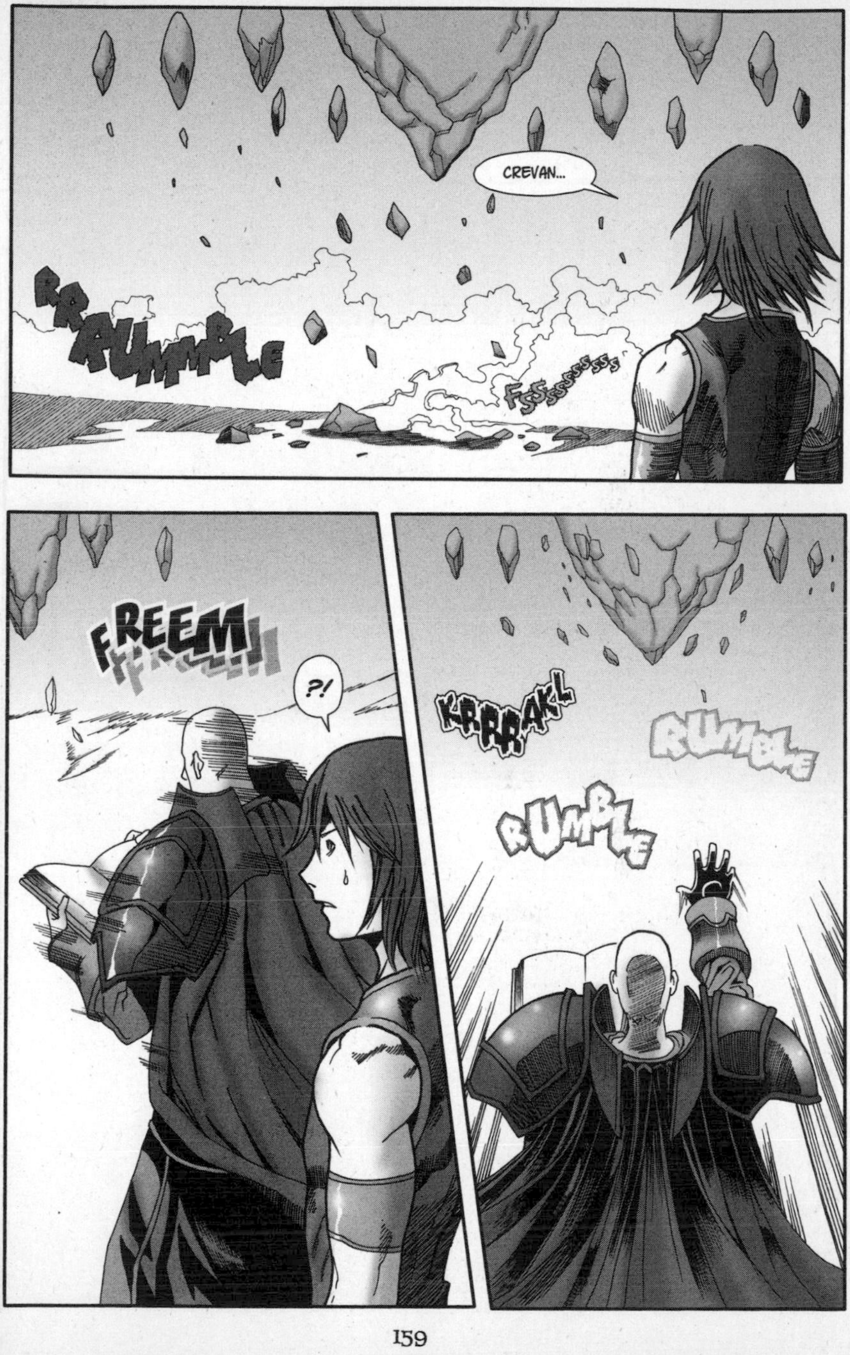
CREVAN...
RRRUMMBLE
FSSSSSSSSSS
FREEM
?!
KRRRAKL
RUMBLE
RUMBLE

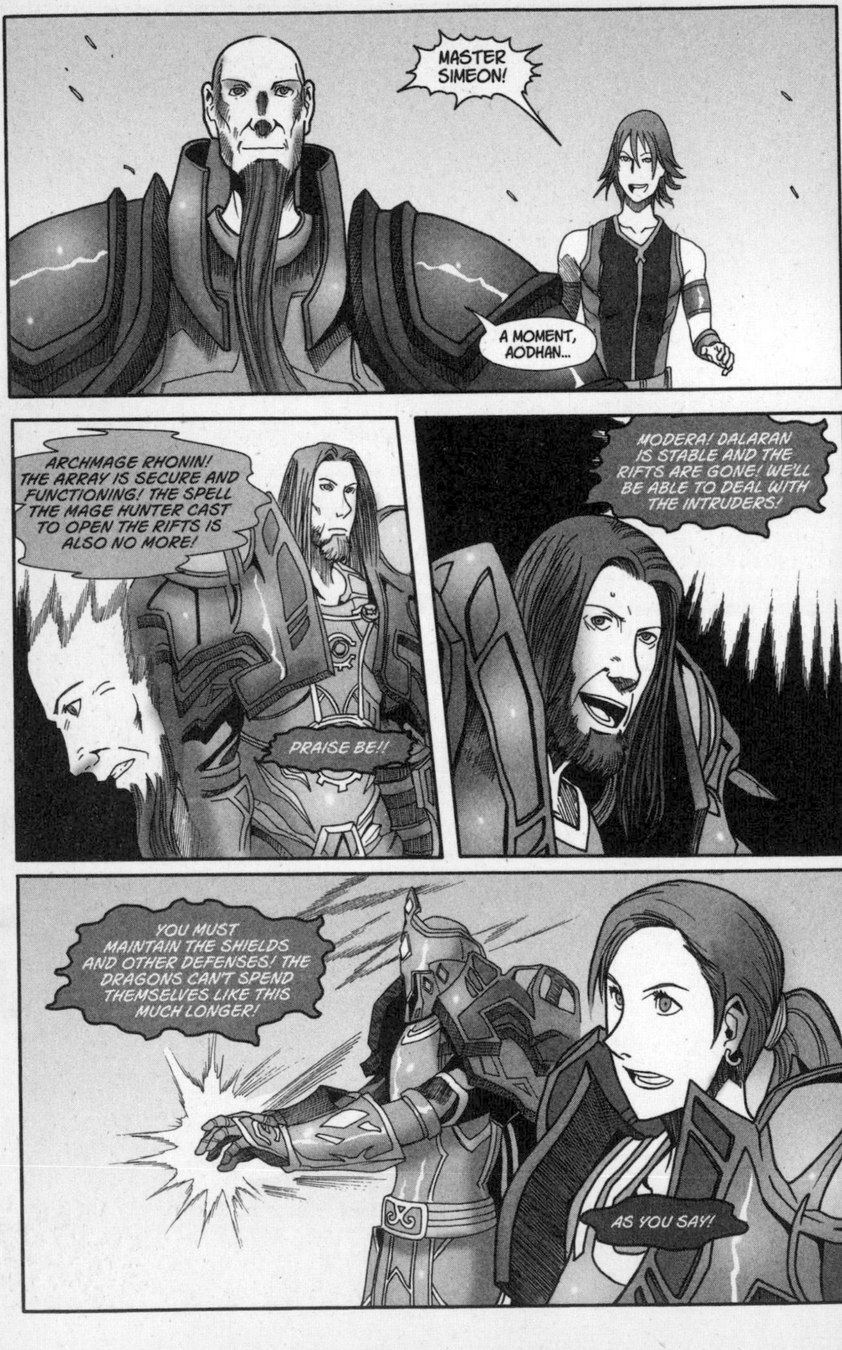
MASTER SIMEON!
A MOMENT, AODHAN...
ARCHMAGE RHONIN! THE ARRAY IS SECURE AND FUNCTIONING! THE SPELL THE MAGE HUNTER CAST TO OPEN THE RIFTS IS ALSO NO MORE!
PRAISE BE!!
MODERA! DALARAN IS STABLE AND THE RIFTS ARE GONE! WE'LL BE ABLE TO DEAL WITH THE INTRUDERS!
YOU MUST MAINTAIN THE SHIELDS AND OTHER DEFENSES! THE DRAGONS CAN'T SPEND THEMSELVES LIKE THIS MUCH LONGER!
AS YOU SAY!

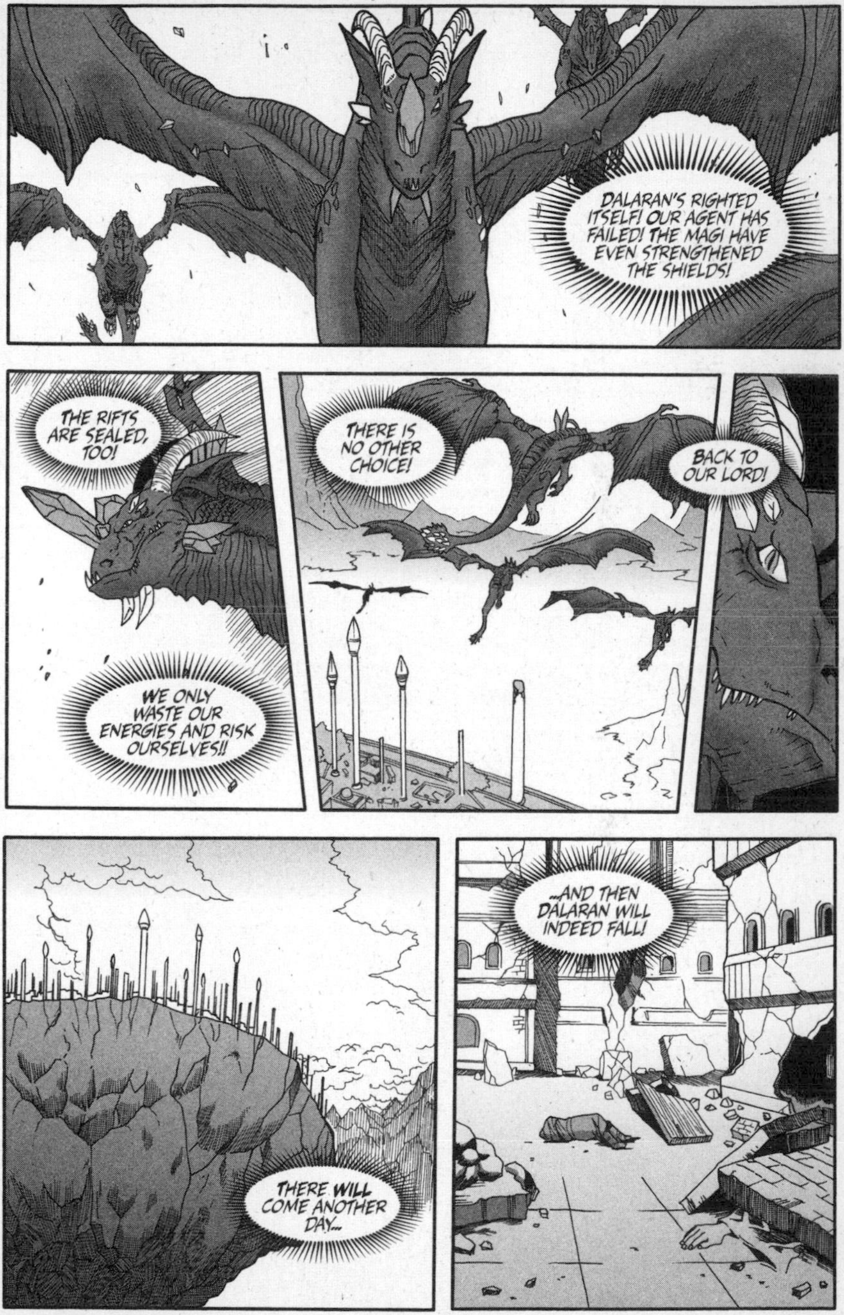
DALARAN'S RIGHTED ITSELF! OUR AGENT HAS FAILED! THE MAGI HAVE EVEN STRENGTHENED THE SHIELDS!
THE RIFTS ARE SEALED, TOO!
WE ONLY WASTE OUR ENERGIES AND RISK OURSELVES!!
THERE IS NO OTHER CHOICE!
BACK TO OUR LORD!
THERE WILL COME ANOTHER DAY...
...AND THEN DALARAN WILL INDEED FALL!

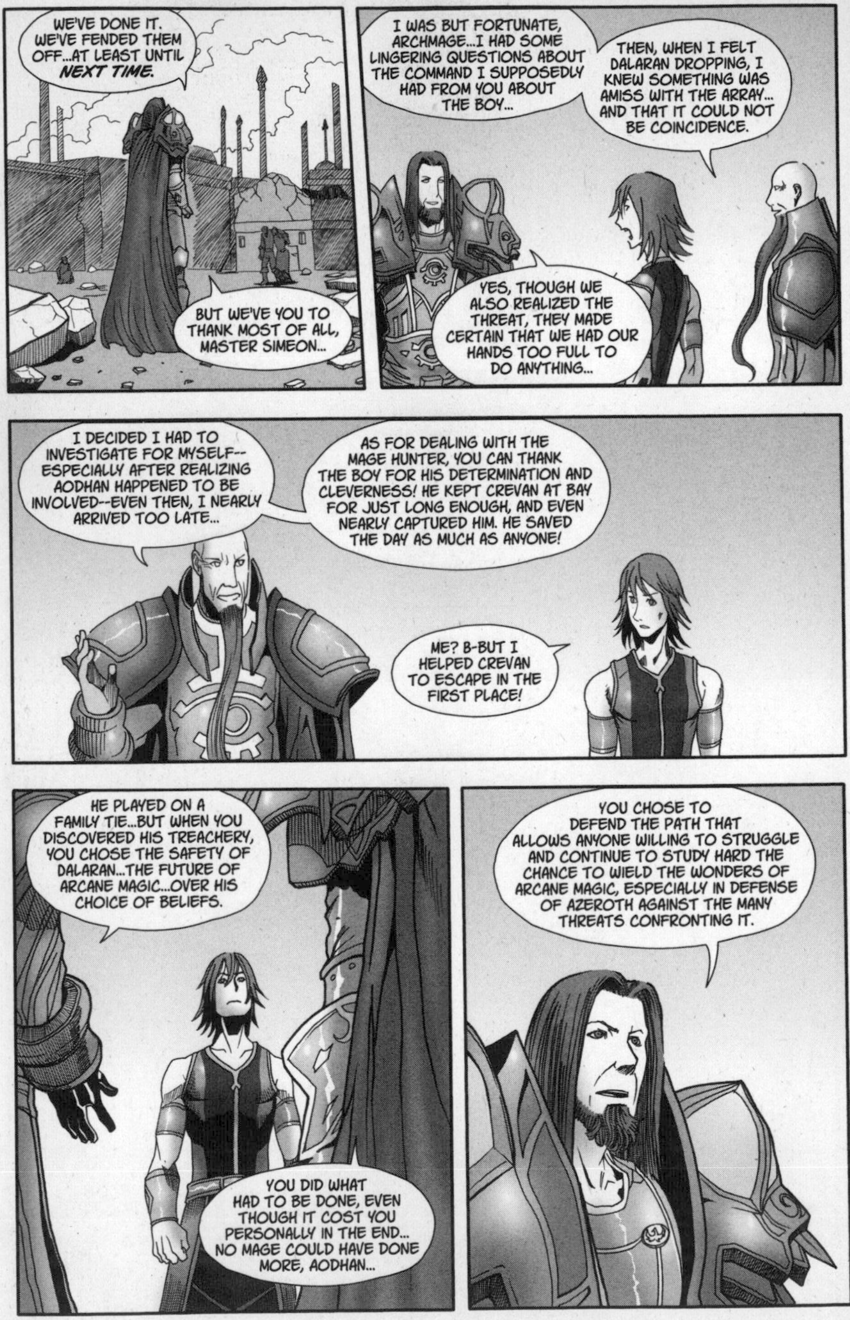
WE'VE DONE IT. WE'VE FENDED THEM OFF...AT LEAST UNTIL *NEXT TIME*.
BUT WE'VE YOU TO THANK MOST OF ALL, MASTER SIMEON...
I WAS BUT FORTUNATE, ARCHMAGE...I HAD SOME LINGERING QUESTIONS ABOUT THE COMMAND I SUPPOSEDLY HAD FROM YOU ABOUT THE BOY...
THEN, WHEN I FELT DALARAN DROPPING, I KNEW SOMETHING WAS AMISS WITH THE ARRAY... AND THAT IT COULD NOT BE COINCIDENCE.
YES, THOUGH WE ALSO REALIZED THE THREAT, THEY MADE CERTAIN THAT WE HAD OUR HANDS TOO FULL TO DO ANYTHING...
I DECIDED I HAD TO INVESTIGATE FOR MYSELF--ESPECIALLY AFTER REALIZING AODHAN HAPPENED TO BE INVOLVED--EVEN THEN, I NEARLY ARRIVED TOO LATE...
AS FOR DEALING WITH THE MAGE HUNTER, YOU CAN THANK THE BOY FOR HIS DETERMINATION AND CLEVERNESS! HE KEPT CREVAN AT BAY FOR JUST LONG ENOUGH, AND EVEN NEARLY CAPTURED HIM. HE SAVED THE DAY AS MUCH AS ANYONE!
ME? B-BUT I HELPED CREVAN TO ESCAPE IN THE FIRST PLACE!
HE PLAYED ON A FAMILY TIE...BUT WHEN YOU DISCOVERED HIS TREACHERY, YOU CHOSE THE SAFETY OF DALARAN...THE FUTURE OF ARCANE MAGIC...OVER HIS CHOICE OF BELIEFS.
YOU DID WHAT HAD TO BE DONE, EVEN THOUGH IT COST YOU PERSONALLY IN THE END... NO MAGE COULD HAVE DONE MORE, AODHAN...
YOU CHOSE TO DEFEND THE PATH THAT ALLOWS ANYONE WILLING TO STRUGGLE AND CONTINUE TO STUDY HARD THE CHANCE TO WIELD THE WONDERS OF ARCANE MAGIC, ESPECIALLY IN DEFENSE OF AZEROTH AGAINST THE MANY THREATS CONFRONTING IT.

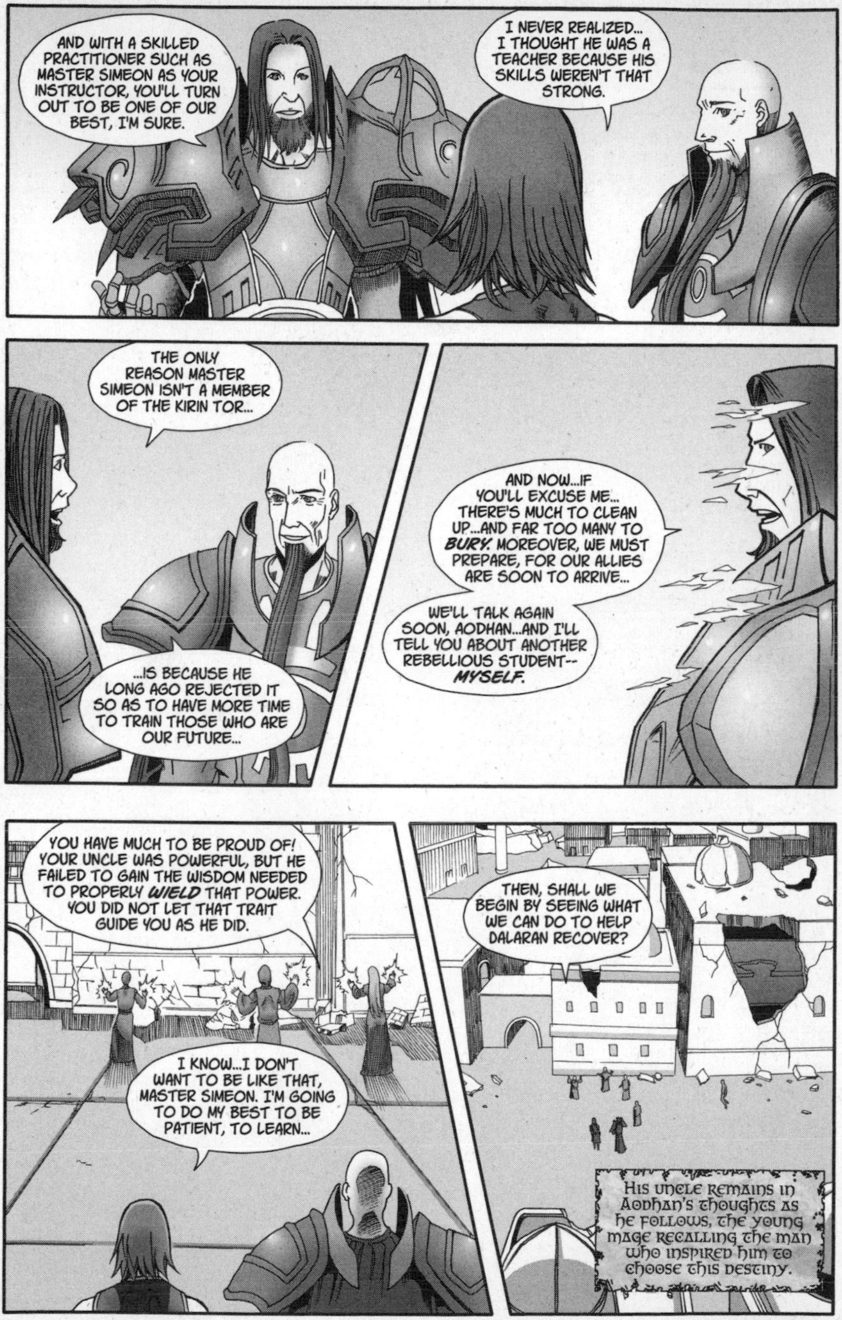
AND WITH A SKILLED PRACTITIONER SUCH AS MASTER SIMEON AS YOUR INSTRUCTOR, YOU'LL TURN OUT TO BE ONE OF OUR BEST, I'M SURE.
I NEVER REALIZED... I THOUGHT HE WAS A TEACHER BECAUSE HIS SKILLS WEREN'T THAT STRONG.
THE ONLY REASON MASTER SIMEON ISN'T A MEMBER OF THE KIRIN TOR...
...IS BECAUSE HE LONG AGO REJECTED IT SO AS TO HAVE MORE TIME TO TRAIN THOSE WHO ARE OUR FUTURE...
AND NOW...IF YOU'LL EXCUSE ME... THERE'S MUCH TO CLEAN UP...AND FAR TOO MANY TO *BURY.* MOREOVER, WE MUST PREPARE, FOR OUR ALLIES ARE SOON TO ARRIVE...
WE'LL TALK AGAIN SOON, AODHAN...AND I'LL TELL YOU ABOUT ANOTHER REBELLIOUS STUDENT-- *MYSELF*.
YOU HAVE MUCH TO BE PROUD OF! YOUR UNCLE WAS POWERFUL, BUT HE FAILED TO GAIN THE WISDOM NEEDED TO PROPERLY *WIELD* THAT POWER. YOU DID NOT LET THAT TRAIT GUIDE YOU AS HE DID.
I KNOW...I DON'T WANT TO BE LIKE THAT, MASTER SIMEON. I'M GOING TO DO MY BEST TO BE PATIENT, TO LEARN...
THEN, SHALL WE BEGIN BY SEEING WHAT WE CAN DO TO HELP DALARAN RECOVER?
His uncle remains in Aodhan's thoughts as he follows, the young mage recalling the man who inspired him to choose this destiny.

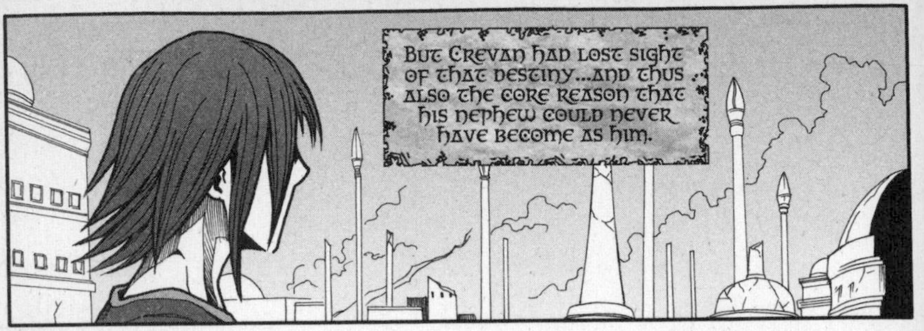
But Crevan had lost sight of that destiny...and thus also the core reason that his nephew could never have become as him.
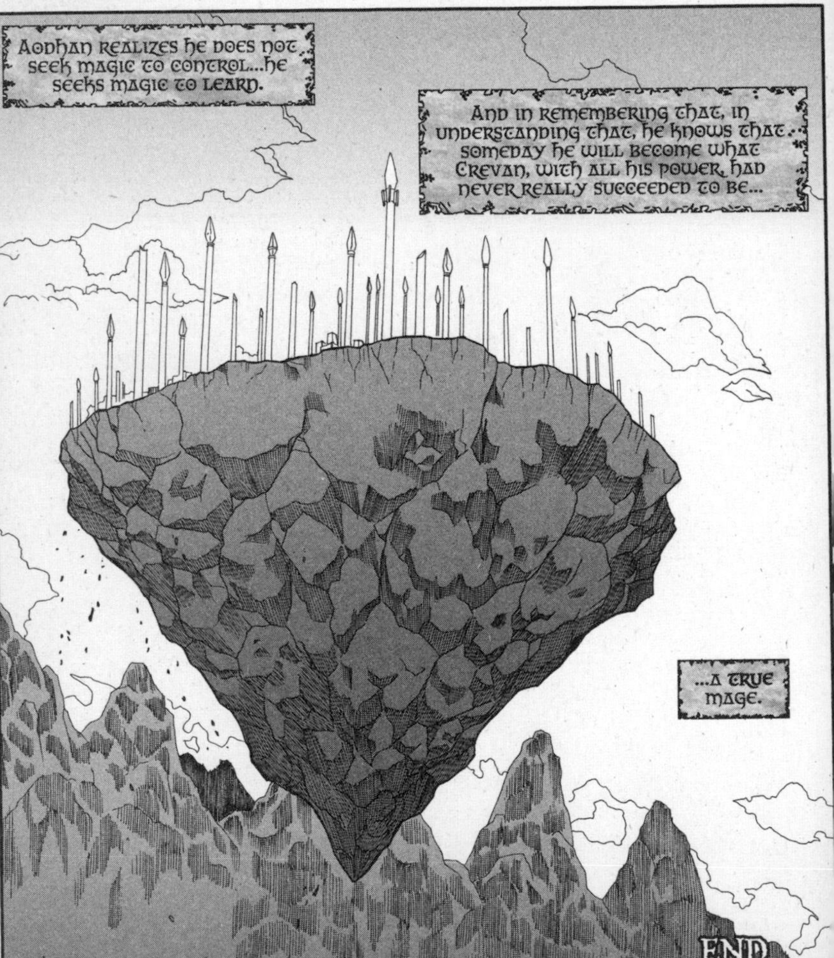
Aodhan realizes he does not seek magic to control...he seeks magic to learn.
And in remembering that, in understanding that, he knows that someday he will become what Crevan, with all his power, had never really succeeded to be...
...a true mage.
END

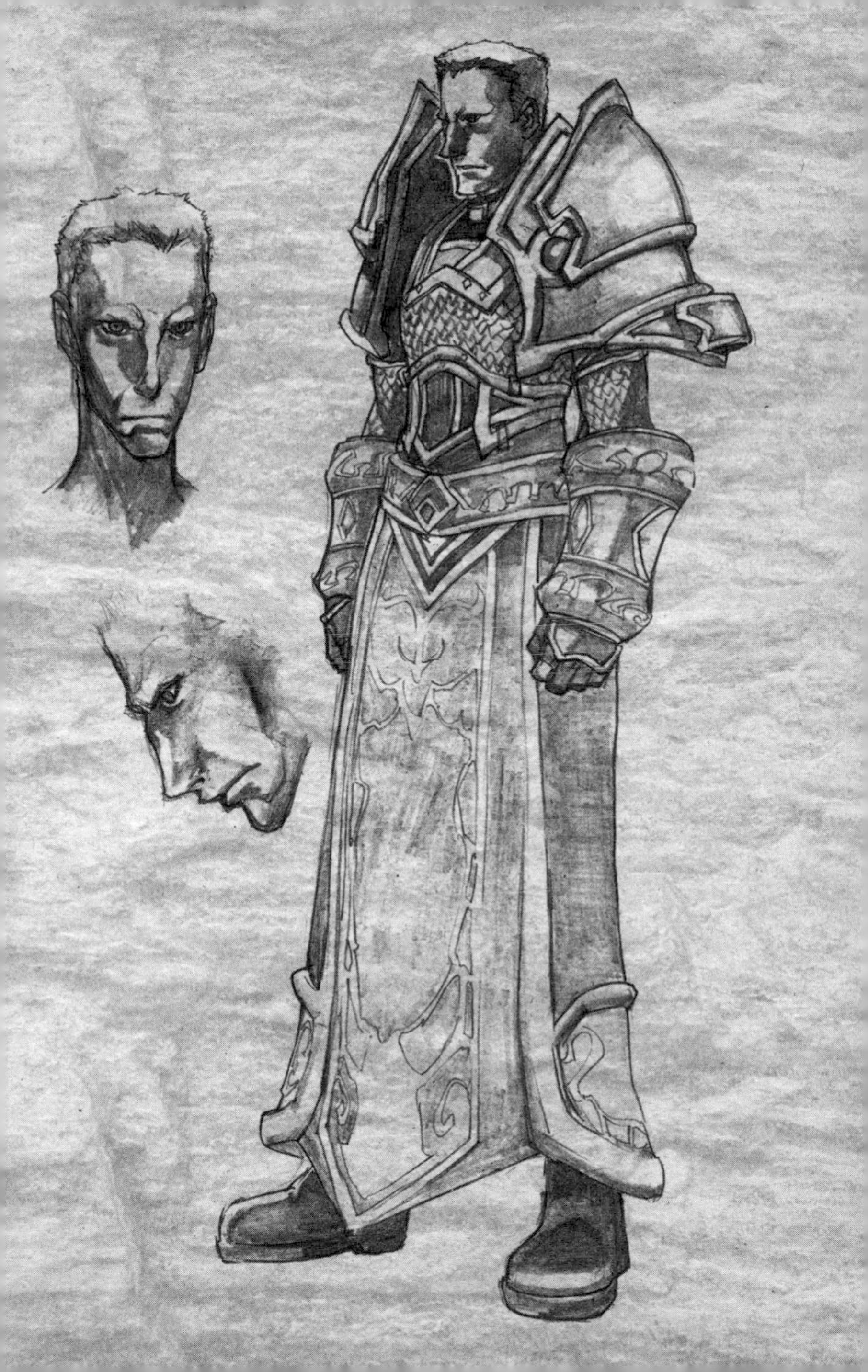

# SPECIAL THANKS

On behalf of TOKYOPOP and Blizzard, we hope you enjoyed the time you spent in Dalaran and with *World of Warcraft: Mage.* If you liked this class-based *Warcraft* manga, there's more on the horizon! *World of Warcraft: Shaman* will be throwing its totems down in October 2010! Keep your eyes peeled for a sneak peek at *World of Warcraft: Shaman* inside the pages of this very book!

Of course, we wouldn't be able to bring you all of this pulse-pounding, class-based action without the excellent publishing team at Blizzard. Their attention to detail and the amount of care they have for the *Warcraft* world never ceases to amaze. Many thanks to Jason Bischoff, Joshua Horst, James Waugh, Micky Neilson, Evelyn Fredericksen, Samwise Didier, Cameron Dayton, Tommy Newcomer and Chris Metzen!

In many ways, Ryo--our peerless Mage artist--reminds us of our book's protagonist, Aodhan. He's quiet and unassuming. But, like the bookish Aodhan, Ryo rose to the challenge and became a legendary hero! Ryo delivered page after page of pencils at a breathtaking speed, never sacrificing quality. He tackled a near-impossible deadline and saved the day!

As Ryo's pages were coming in hot, Matias Timarchi and the fine folks at Altercomics Studios added inks and tones to Ryo's line art. Like Ryo, they worked tirelessly against a loudly clicking tock...and emerged victorious! So, here's hearty thank you to inkers Roberto Viacava, Nahuel Sagarnaga Cozman, Ariel Iacci, Gaston Zubeldia, Perla Pilucki, Fernando Melek, Matias Montenegro, and toners Gabriel Peralta, Marcelo Blanco and Gonzalo Duarte. You guys all rock!

He's no stranger to the *World of Warcraft,* and by now, he should be no stranger to praise--the peerless Richard A. Knaak. As always, Richard enters Azeroth and emerges with a compelling story and fascinating characters. Thanks for the fantastic work, Richard!

We'd like to take a moment to thank TOKYOPOP's secret *World of Warcraft* weapon...and his name is Michael Paolilli. Michael is incredibly talented. He can letter a book, he can make art fixes and he has an encyclopedic knowledge of the *Warcraft* universe. Thanks for being not just the heart of production, but the spine, the ribs, the fingers, toes...

Lastly, we want to express our gratitude to all of the fans. Without you, these books wouldn't exist. So, do us a favor and buy a ton of copies so we can keep making awesome Warcraft stories. After all, we're doing it for you!

- Paul Morrissey and Troy Lewter
Editors

# CREATOR BIO'S
# RICHARD A. KNAAK

Richard A. Knaak is the New York Times and USA Today bestselling fantasy author of 40 novels and over a dozen short stories, including most recently the national bestseller, *World of Warcraft: Stormrage*. He is also well known for such favorites as *The Legend of Huma* & *The Minotaur Wars* for Dragonlance, the *War of the Ancients* trilogy for *Warcraft*, and his own *Dragonrealm* series. In addition to the TOKYOPOP series *Warcraft: The Sunwell Trilogy*, he is the author of its sequel series, *World of Warcraft: Shadow Wing*, a well as five short stories featured in *Warcraft: Legends* Volumes 1-5. He also recently released *The Gargoyle King*, the third in his *Ogre Titans* saga for Dragonlance and *Legends of the Dragonrealm*, which combines the first three novels of his world. A second volume will be released in October. To find out more about Richard's projects, visit his website at www.richardaknaak.com.

# RYO KAWAKAMI

Born in Miyako Island, Japan, Ryo lived in Okinawa Island until 1990, after which he and his family moved to the United States. Ryo currently resides in Greenville, N.C., where he studied Fine Art for two years at Coastal Community College. Ryo was runner-up artist in TOKYOPOP's *Rising Stars of Manga* Volume 6 for the short story "Little Miss Witch Hater," and his first full full-volume manga work, *Orange Crows*, was also published by TOKYOPOP (available in stores now). Ryo was the artist for the short manga stories "Blood Runs Thicker" and "A Cleansing Fire," two short manga stories featured in *Warcraft: Legends* Volumes 4 and 5.

# EXCLUSIVE INTERVIEW WITH PAUL BENJAMIN—WRITER OF *WORLD OF WARCRAFT: SHAMAN*

**You've worn many hats throughout your career. Tell us a little bit about your background.**

Fedora, baseball, fez, yarmulke... oh, you didn't mean hats I've *literally* worn? My business card says, "Writer, Editor, Supermodel" which comprises having been a development executive for film and television, an editor for comics and graphic novels, and a video game producer. As a writer I've worked on video games featuring characters like Wolverine, G.I. JOE, Hulk and Spider-Man. A few of my comic book writing highlights include MARVEL ADVENTURES HULK and SPIDER-MAN, MONSTERS, INC., STARCRAFT and now, I'm excited to say, SHAMAN. As a supermodel I've walked the runways of Paris and Milan as well as... oh, never mind. You've all seen the billboards...

**So, you are clearly an avid role-playing gamer. Is it safe to assume that you've played a fair amount of WARCRAFT? Do you have a favorite class to play?**

My main is a pally retadin. That's a paladin built to do lots of damage for any noobs reading this (Hi, Mom!). I tend to do a fair amount of solo play because if I play with a group I'm on for too long and wouldn't make any of my Warcraft writing deadlines! The pally is great for soloing because I can heal myself and do plenty of damage. That said, I do have a lot of fun playing with guildies or doing random heroics when I've got the time. And, of course, since writing SHAMAN I've really been digging my new shammy character as well.

**Give the fans the inside scoop on WORLD OF WARCRAFT: SHAMAN. What's the story about? Is it true that it will tie into the upcoming CATACLYSM expansion?**

SHAMAN is the tale of a group many players have seen around Azeroth and beyond: the Earthen Ring. The main characters are Muln, the tauren High Shaman of the Earthen Ring, and his orc apprentice, Kettara. The focus is on them and the elder council of the Earthen Ring, so I've gotten to write draenei and trolls as well as a few very important (and well known) orcs from Orgrimmar. The secrets of CATACLYSM are quite closely guarded at the time of this writing, but there's a lot of connection between this book and the upcoming expansion. I *can* tell you that the elements are in upheaval and that's wreaking chaos with the powers of Muln and the Earthen Ring. SHAMAN is a story about tradition versus change and choosing which one is more important. It's also full of shaman calling down lightning, summoning elementals and manifesting totems to help them smack down any monsters stupid enough to threaten the shaman way of life. And it's all beautifully illustrated by DEATH KNIGHT artist Rocio Zucchi, so I imagine fans will be as excited to read the book as I have been to see those pages coming in as she works!

**You've also written several STARCRAFT: FRONTLINE stories. Tell us a bit about those stories and how they came about.**

Those were a lot of fun. I co-wrote them with my game designer friend, Dave Shramek. It all started with a story in the first STARCRAFT: FRONTLINE book in which we introduced Colin Phash, the psionic son of a senator. The two of them were trapped in a mine with zerg and hilarity ensued. The folks at Blizzard dug the story and had us write a follow up in volume three. Then we wrote another story in volume four that was a lead in to STARCRAFT: GHOST ACADEMY where Colin and Senator Phash are important characters in their own subtle ways. It's been fantastic to work in the worlds of STARCRAFT and WARCRAFT. I'm hoping that I'll even get to see some of the characters I've written show up in the games!

# A SNEAK PEEK AT THE NEXT THRILLING CLASS-BASED MANGA FROM TOKYOPOP AND BLIZZARD...

# WORLD OF WARCRAFT: SHAMAN

Earthquakes. Fires. Floods. Tornados. The elements of Azeroth are out of control, unleashing devastating natural disasters that threaten to tear Azeroth asunder. All hope rests with the shaman, who are able to commune with the elements. Muln Earthfury, the shaman leader of the secretive Earthen Ring, attempts to pacify the elements--but his pleas fall on deaf ears. The elements are unresponsive, full of confusion and chaos. The Earthen Ring is riddled with doubt. Have the shaman lost their ability to corral and guide the elements?

Mysteriously, Shotoa arrives. This Tauren shaman doesn't just merely tend to the elements--he **forces** them to do his bidding. Shotoa promises to lead the Earthen Ring into a new era of Shamanism... As the world crumbles around them, Muln and the Earthen Ring must decide if Shotoa is a hero or a heretic...

Written by Paul Benjamin (***StarCraft: Frontline***) and drawn by Rocio Zucchi (***World of Warcraft: Death Knight***), ***WORLD OF WARCRAFT: SHAMAN*** ties into the upcoming ***World of Warcraft: Cataclysm*** expansion in stunning ways!

**Available October 2010!**

# COMMUNING WITH A COVER

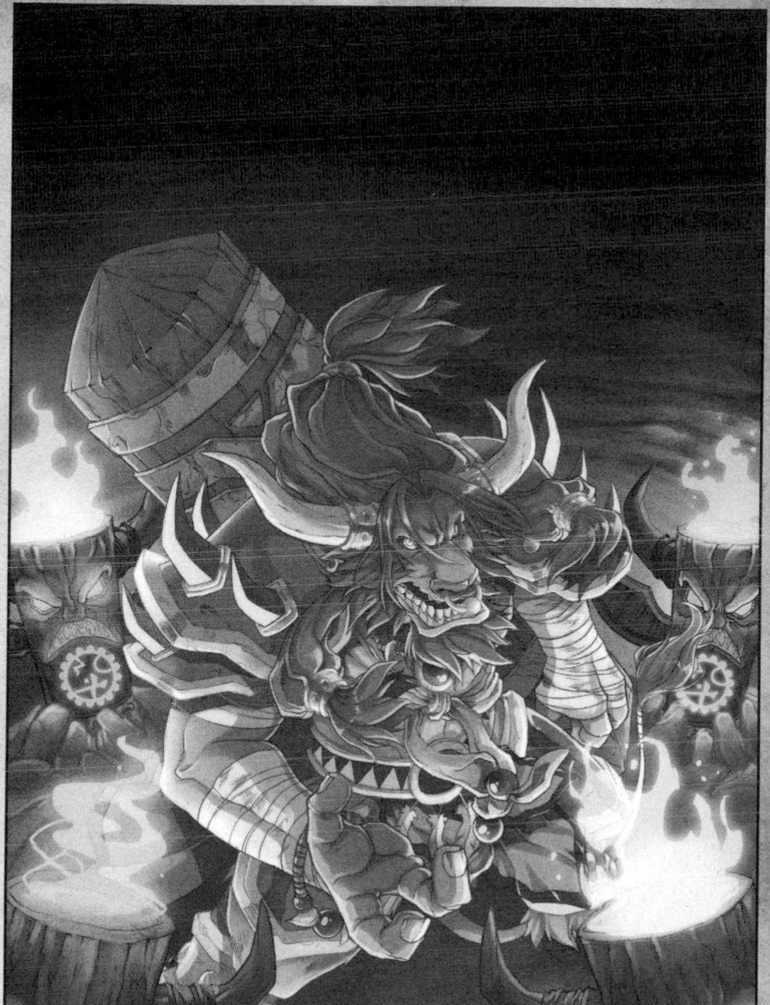

*World of Warcraft: Death Knight* artist Rocio Zucchi returns for another tour of duty in the realm of Azeroth! As you can tell by her latest draft of the spectacular *Shaman* cover, this story is going to be intense!

# -COMMUNING WITH A CAST-

## MULN EARTHFURY

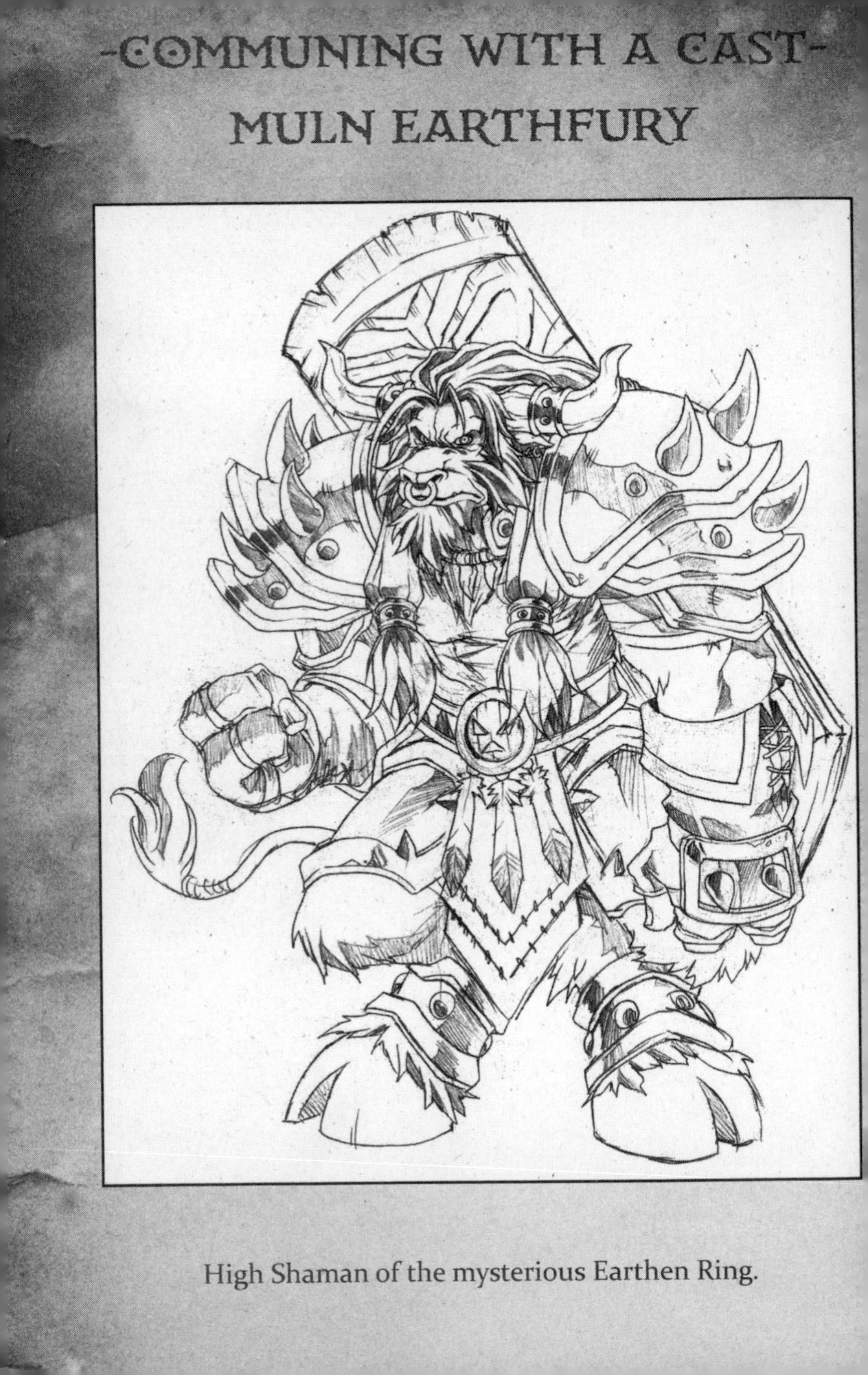

High Shaman of the mysterious Earthen Ring.

# KETTARA BLOODTHIRST

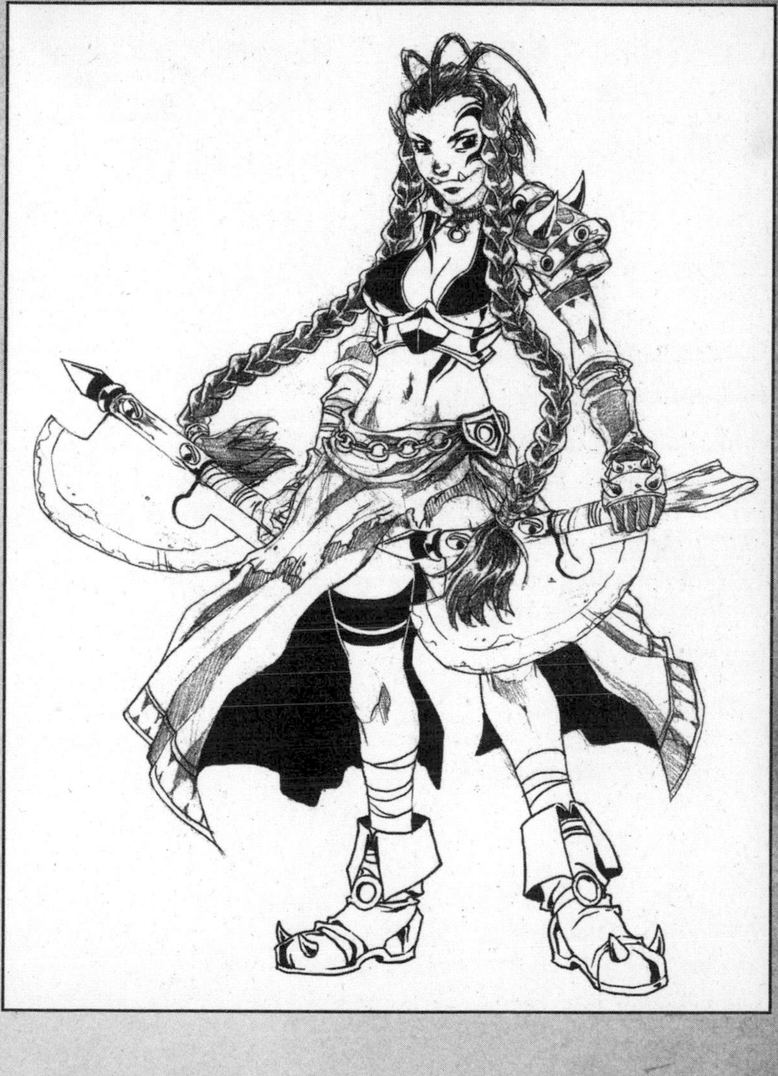

The most gorgeous orc you've ever seen, Kettara Bloodthirst is Muln's apprentice.

# PREVIEW

TOKYOPOP and BLIZZARD ENTERTAINMENT present *World of Warcraft: Shadow Wing,* the thrilling sequel to the international bestseller *Warcraft: The Sunwell Trilogy!*

In *Warcraft: The Sunwell Trilogy,* a good-natured but brash blue dragon, Tyrygosa, and the human Jorad Mace, a paladin struggling to reconnect with the Light, emerged victorious in the Ghostlands after ending the undead Scourge's quest to obtain the Sunwell's potent energies. Yet as arduous as that task was, Tyri and Jorad's journey is far from over. Both are drawn into the Dark Portal and transported to the shattered world of Outland, where they encounter a group of enigmatic creatures unlike any they have ever seen: the incorporeal nether dragons. But watching from the shadows is the ruthless Ragnok Bloodreaver, one of the original death knights. He has evil plans for the nether dragons that can change Outland and Azeroth forever...

Written by bestselling author Richard A. Knaak and drawn by international superstar Jae-Hwan Kim, *World of Warcraft: Shadow Wing* takes readers on an incredible journey through the mysterious regions of Outland. This epic manga also reveals details about the nether dragons' origins and connection to Deathwing, the corrupt Dragon Aspect responsible for the devastating events in the upcoming *World of Warcraft* expansion, *Cataclysm.*

*Available now!*

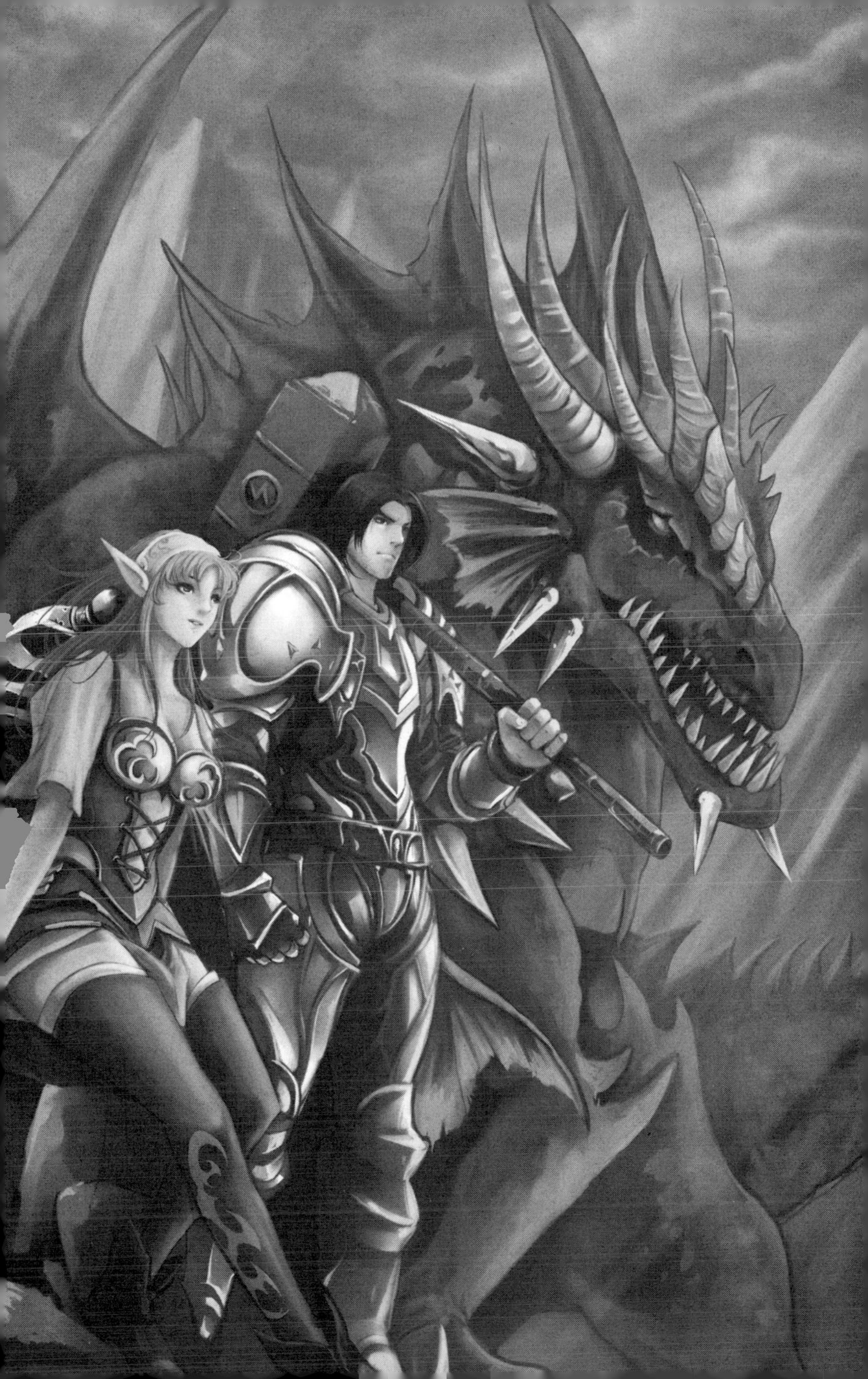

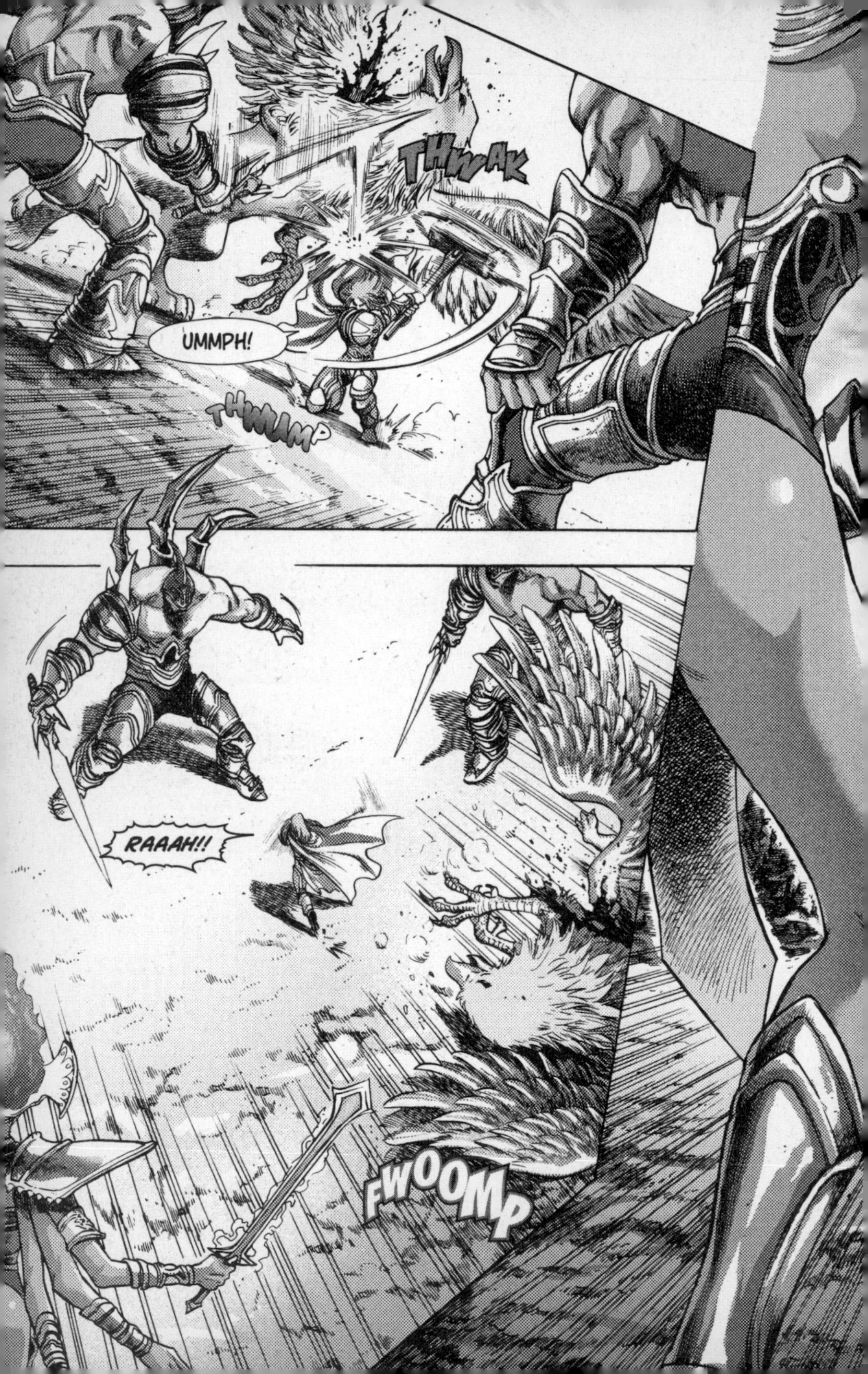
THWAK
UMMPH!
THWUMP
RAAAH!!
FWOOMP

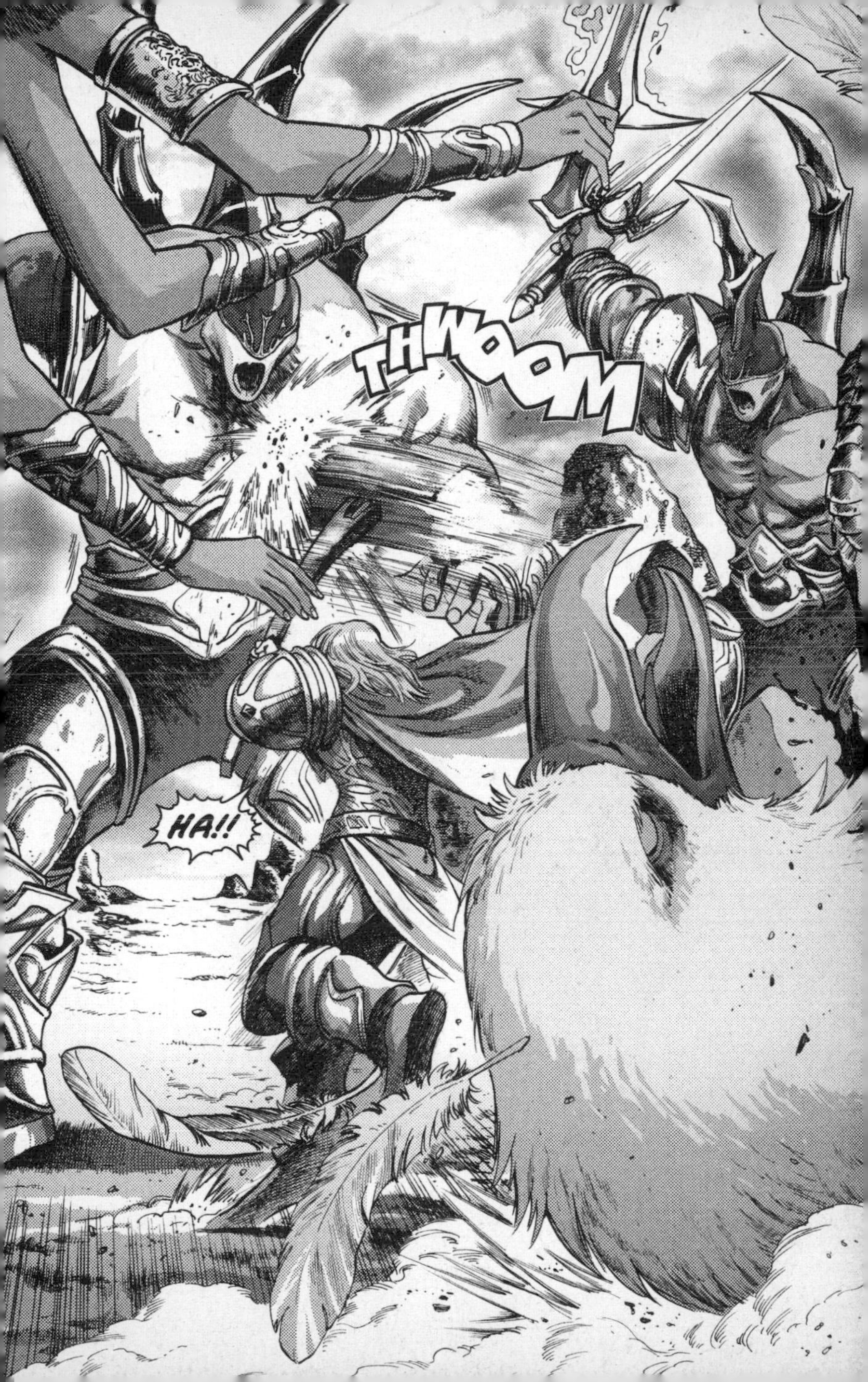
THWOOM
HA!!

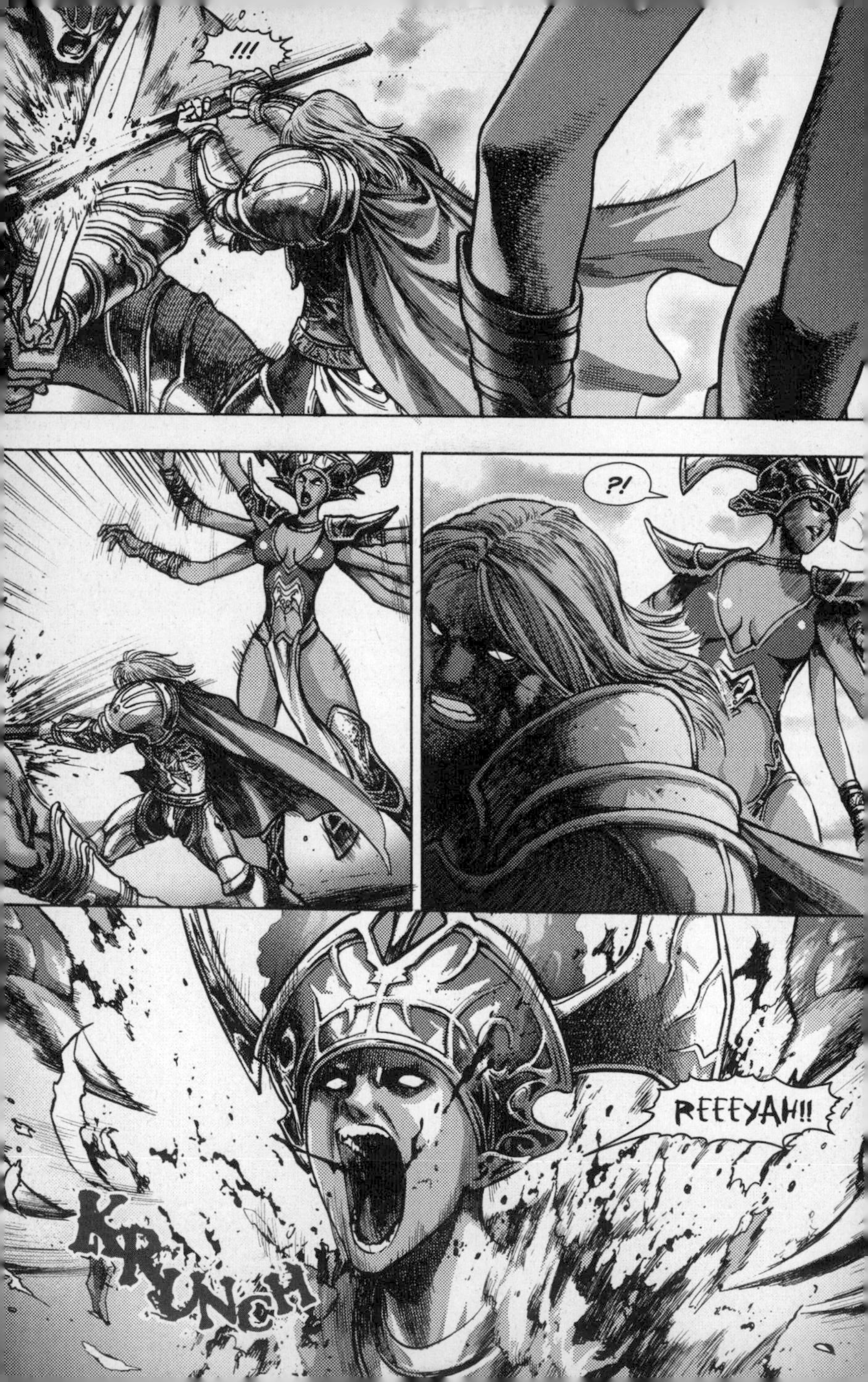
!!!
?!
REEEYAH!!
KRUNCH

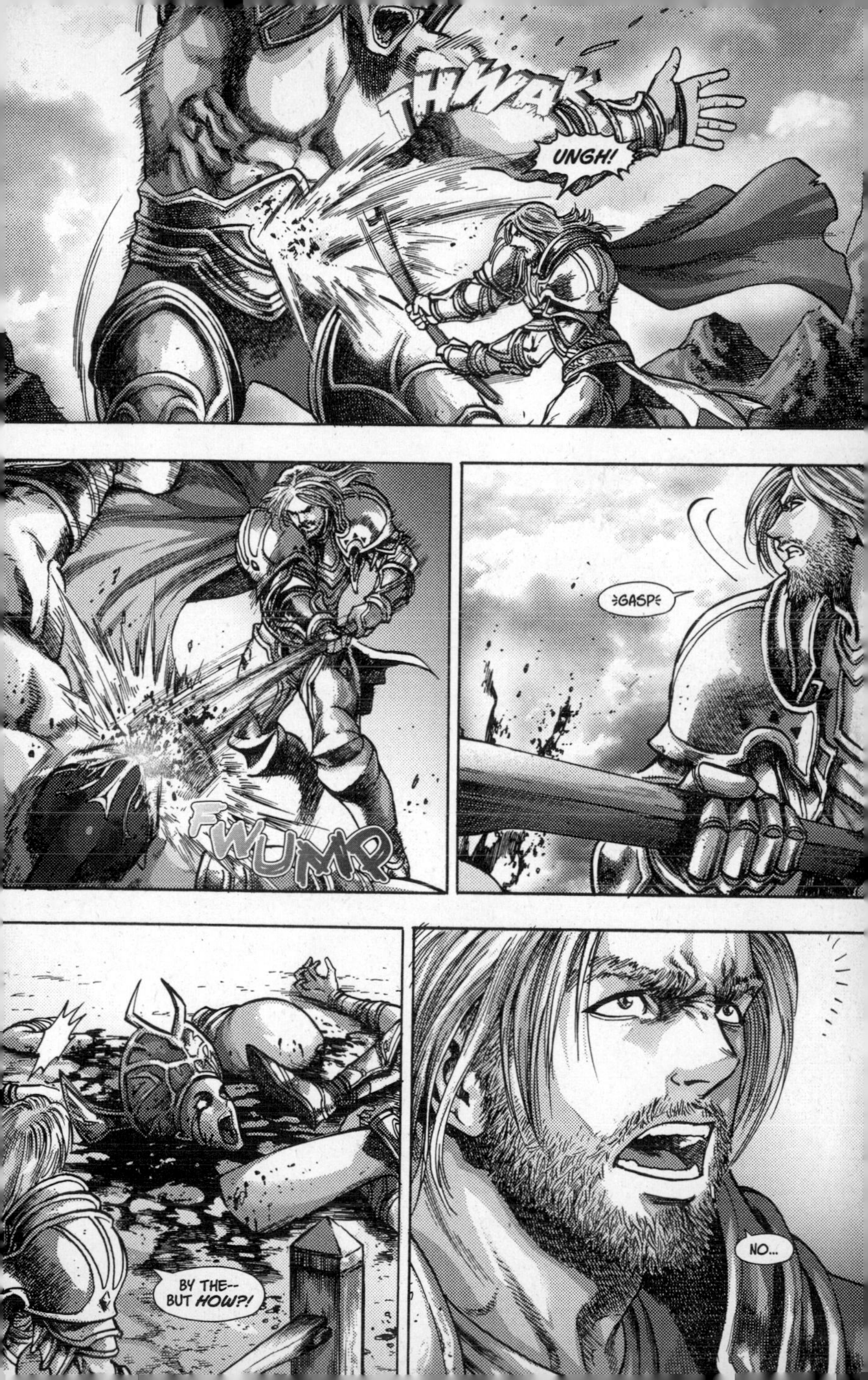
THWAK
UNGH!
FWUMP
GASP
BY THE-- BUT *HOW?!*
NO...

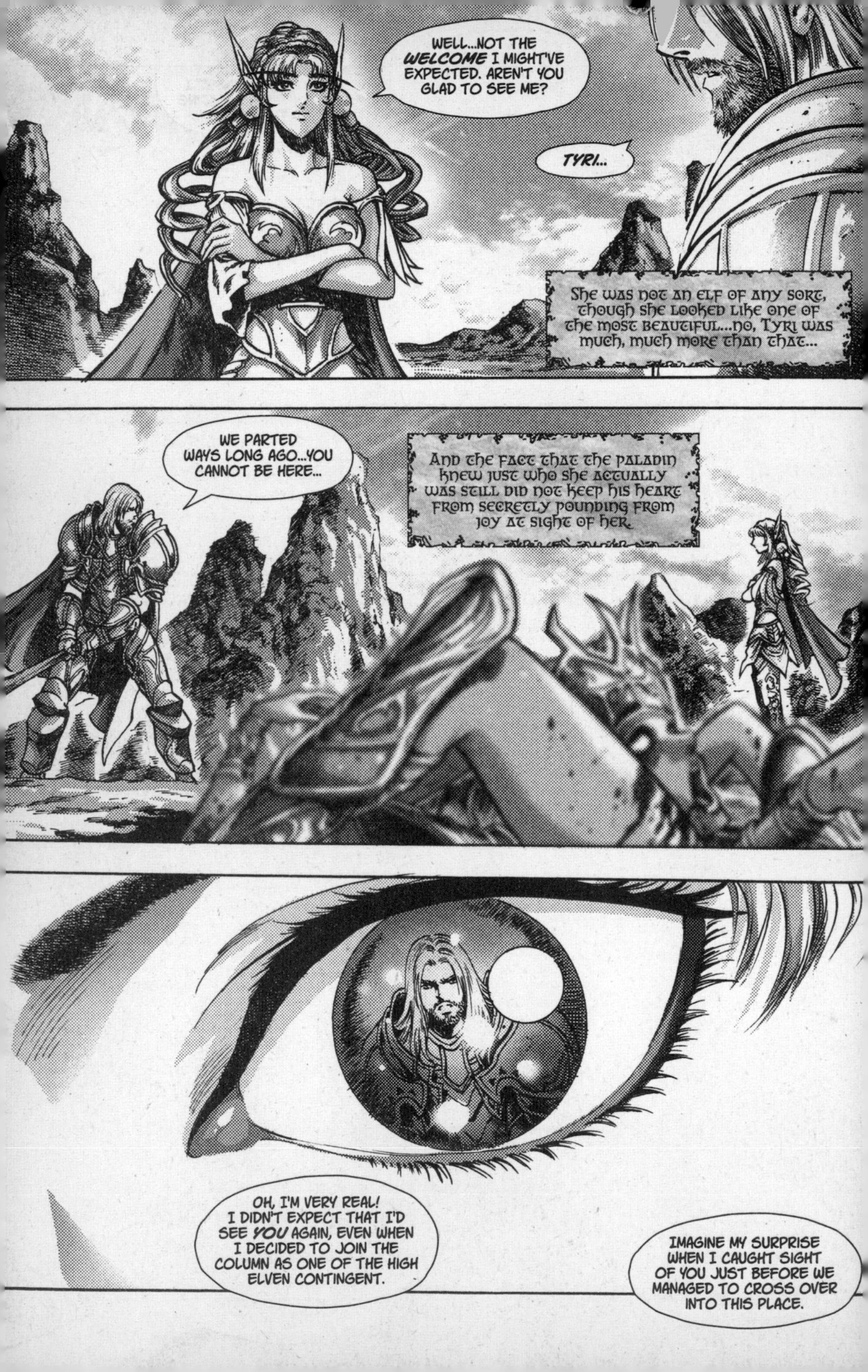
WELL...NOT THE WELCOME I MIGHT'VE EXPECTED. AREN'T YOU GLAD TO SEE ME?
TYRI...
She was not an elf of any sort, though she looked like one of the most beautiful...no, Tyri was much, much more than that...
WE PARTED WAYS LONG AGO...YOU CANNOT BE HERE...
And the fact that the paladin knew just who she actually was still did not keep his heart from secretly pounding from joy at sight of her.
OH, I'M VERY REAL! I DIDN'T EXPECT THAT I'D SEE YOU AGAIN, EVEN WHEN I DECIDED TO JOIN THE COLUMN AS ONE OF THE HIGH ELVEN CONTINGENT.
IMAGINE MY SURPRISE WHEN I CAUGHT SIGHT OF YOU JUST BEFORE WE MANAGED TO CROSS OVER INTO THIS PLACE.

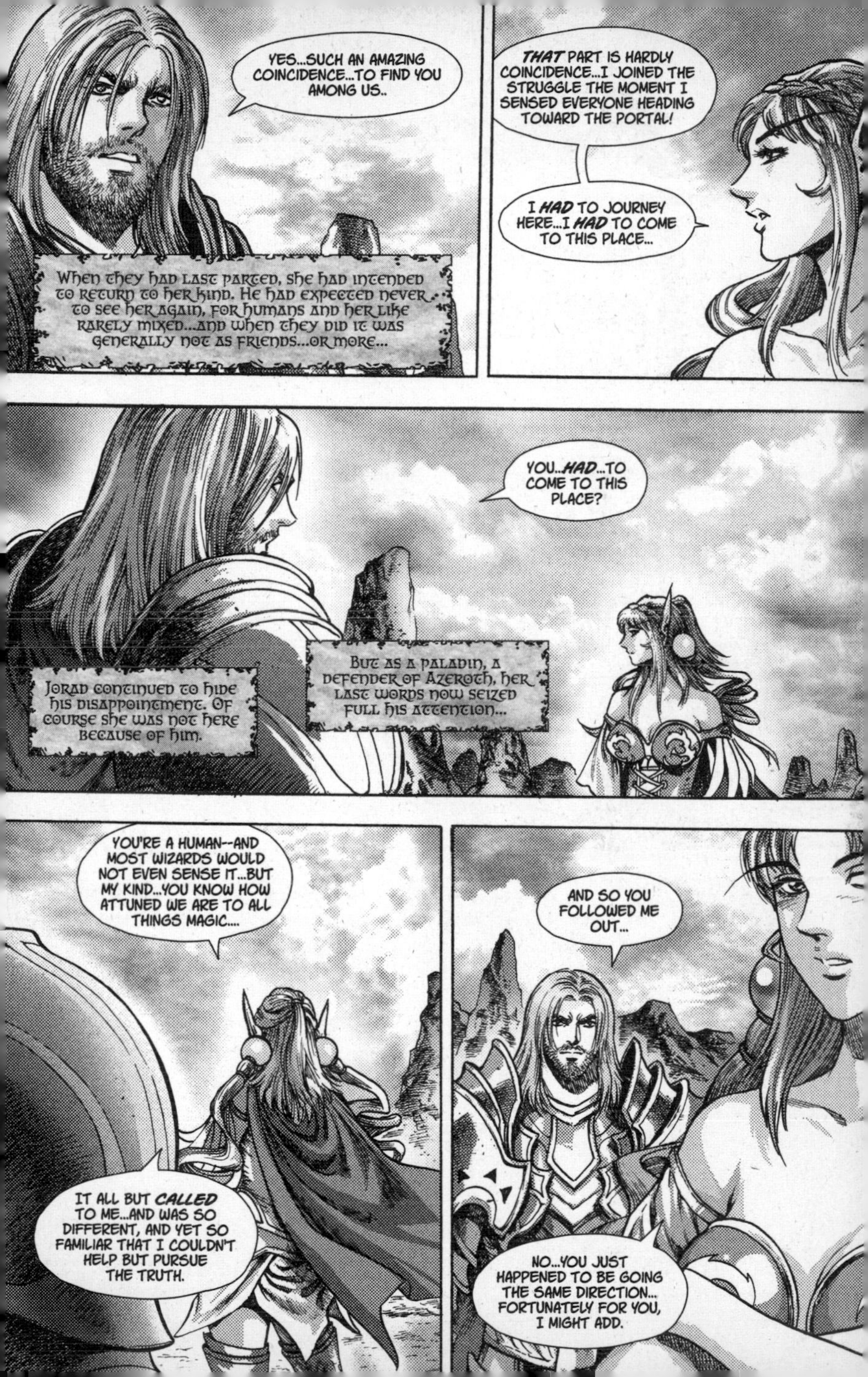
YES...SUCH AN AMAZING COINCIDENCE...TO FIND YOU AMONG US..
When they had last parted, she had intended to return to her kind. He had expected never to see her again, for humans and her like rarely mixed...and when they did it was generally not as friends...or more...
*THAT* PART IS HARDLY COINCIDENCE...I JOINED THE STRUGGLE THE MOMENT I SENSED EVERYONE HEADING TOWARD THE PORTAL!
I *HAD* TO JOURNEY HERE...I *HAD* TO COME TO THIS PLACE...
YOU...*HAD*...TO COME TO THIS PLACE?
Jorad continued to hide his disappointment. Of course she was not here because of him.
But as a paladin, a defender of Azeroth, her last words now seized full his attention...
YOU'RE A HUMAN--AND MOST WIZARDS WOULD NOT EVEN SENSE IT...BUT MY KIND...YOU KNOW HOW ATTUNED WE ARE TO ALL THINGS MAGIC....
IT ALL BUT *CALLED* TO ME...AND WAS SO DIFFERENT, AND YET SO FAMILIAR THAT I COULDN'T HELP BUT PURSUE THE TRUTH.
AND SO YOU FOLLOWED ME OUT...
NO...YOU JUST HAPPENED TO BE GOING THE SAME DIRECTION... FORTUNATELY FOR YOU, I MIGHT ADD.

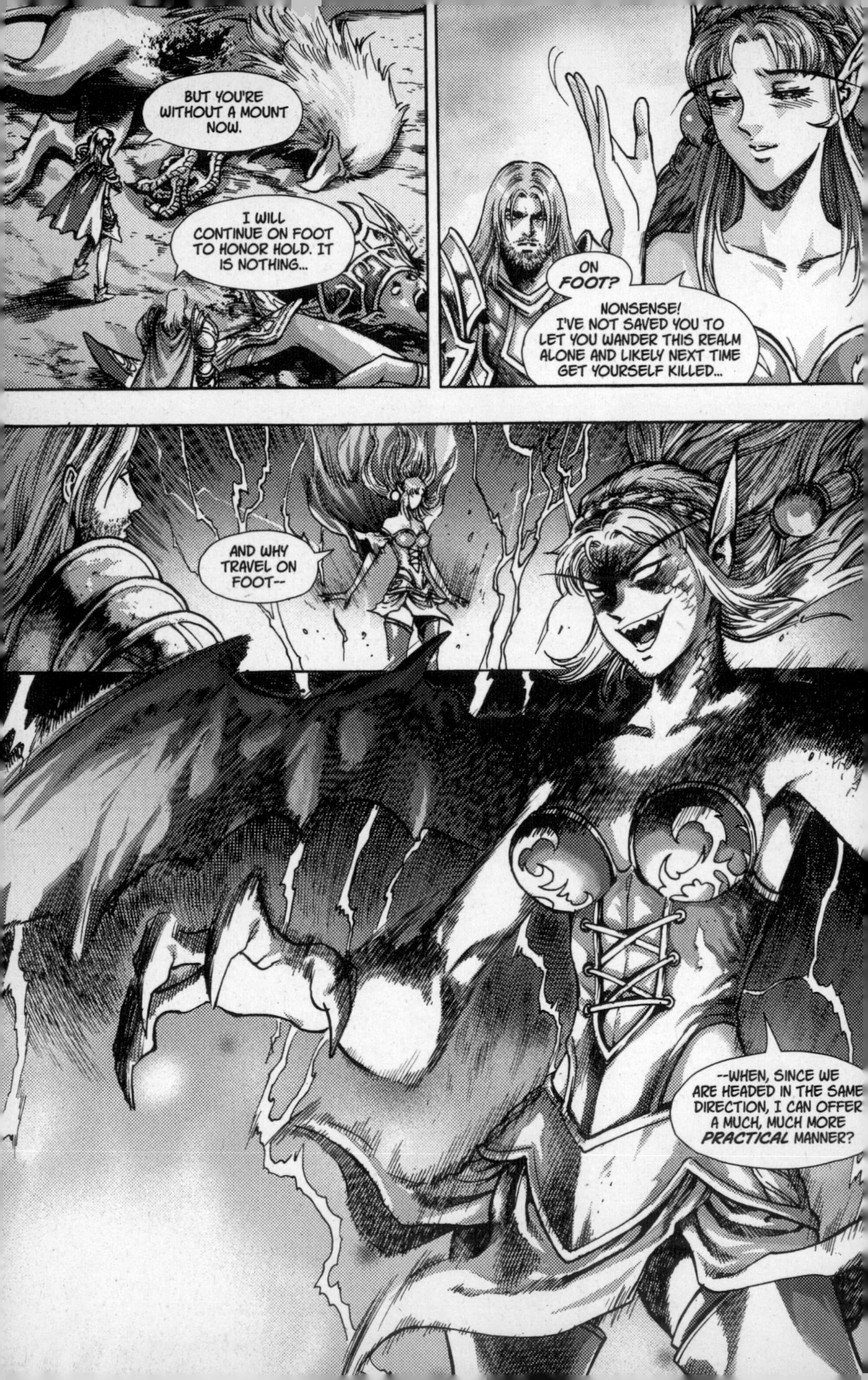
BUT YOU'RE WITHOUT A MOUNT NOW.
I WILL CONTINUE ON FOOT TO HONOR HOLD. IT IS NOTHING...
ON *FOOT?*
NONSENSE! I'VE NOT SAVED YOU TO LET YOU WANDER THIS REALM ALONE AND LIKELY NEXT TIME GET YOURSELF KILLED...
AND WHY TRAVEL ON FOOT--
--WHEN, SINCE WE ARE HEADED IN THE SAME DIRECTION, I CAN OFFER A MUCH, MUCH MORE *PRACTICAL* MANNER?

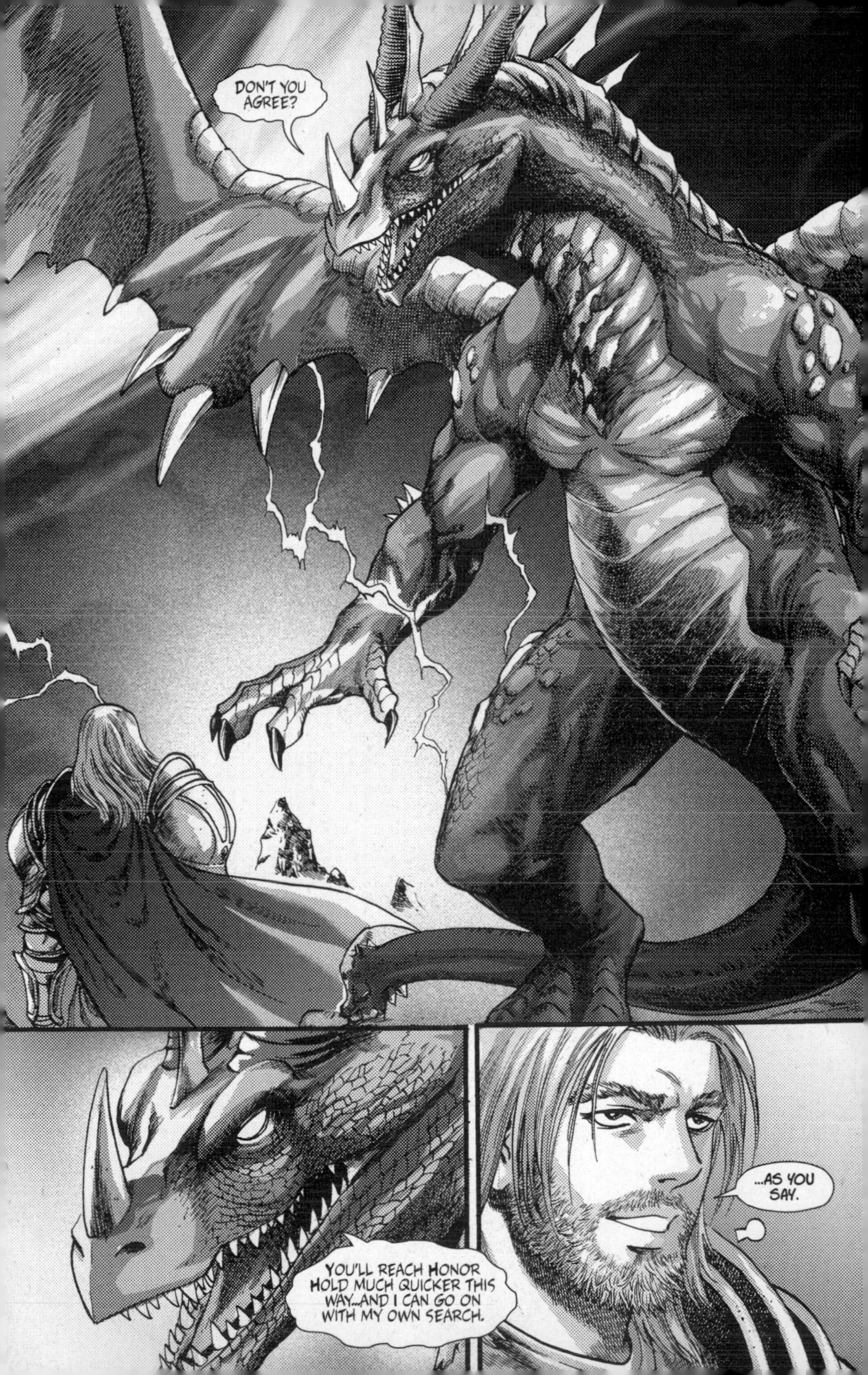
DON'T YOU AGREE?
YOU'LL REACH HONOR HOLD MUCH QUICKER THIS WAY...AND I CAN GO ON WITH MY OWN SEARCH.
...AS YOU SAY.

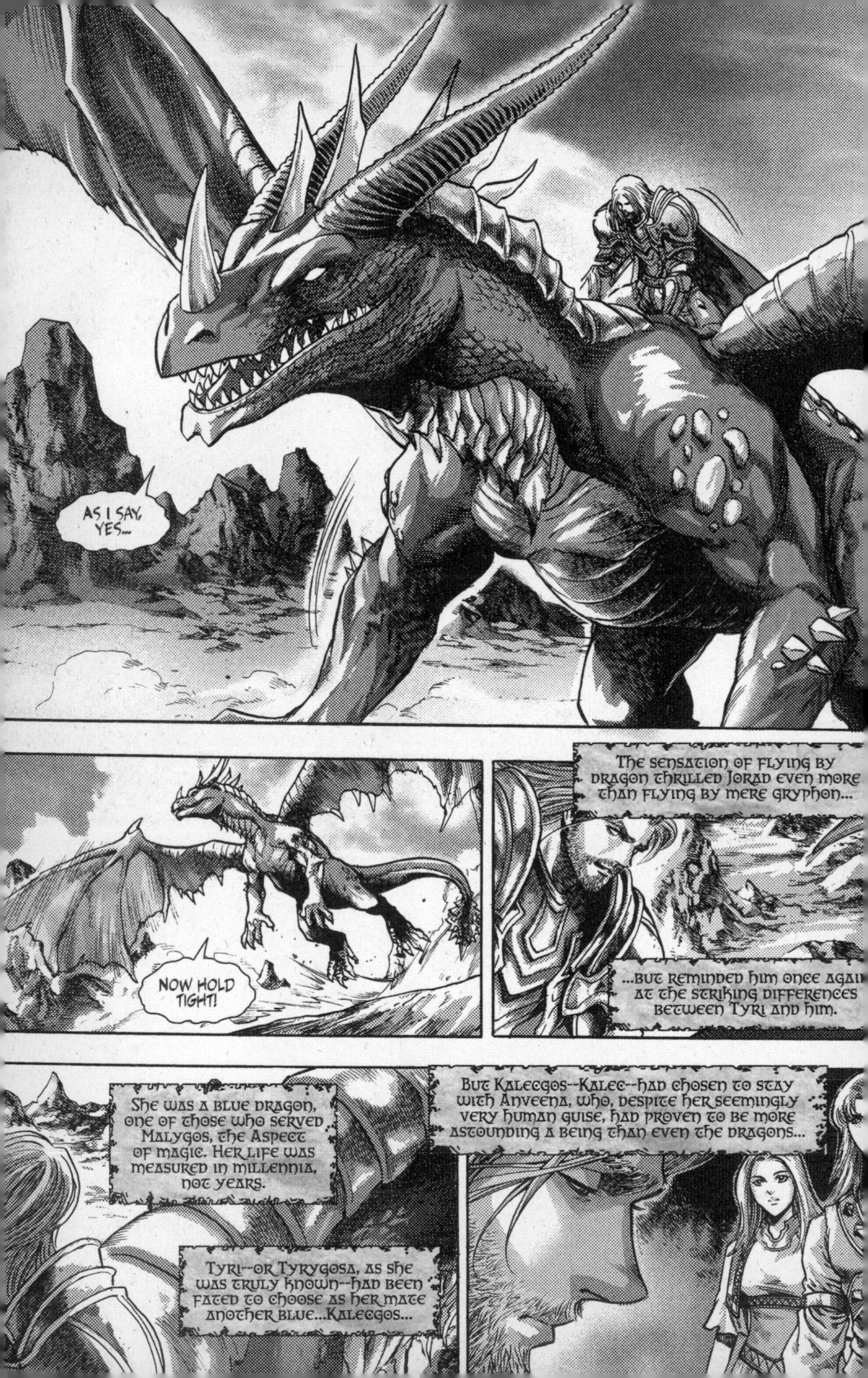
AS I SAY, YES...
NOW HOLD TIGHT!
The sensation of flying by dragon thrilled Jorad even more than flying by mere gryphon...
...but reminded him once agai at the striking differences between Tyri and him.
She was a blue dragon, one of those who served Malygos, the Aspect of magic. Her life was measured in millennia, not years.
Tyri--or Tyrygosa, as she was truly known--had been fated to choose as her mate another blue...Kalecgos...
But Kalecgos--Kalec--had chosen to stay with Anveena, who, despite her seemingly very human guise, had proven to be more astounding a being than even the dragons...

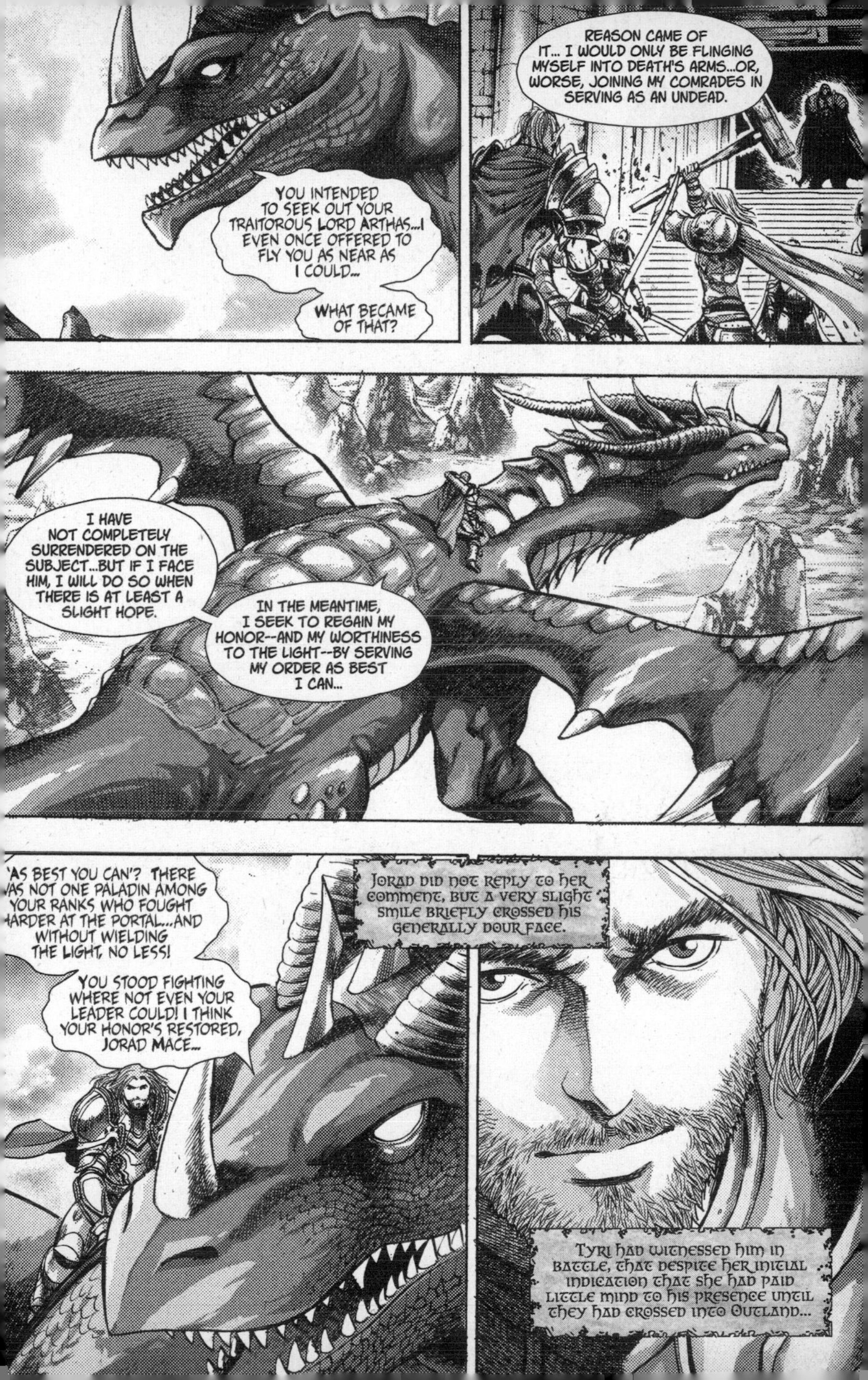
YOU INTENDED TO SEEK OUT YOUR TRAITOROUS LORD ARTHAS...I EVEN ONCE OFFERED TO FLY YOU AS NEAR AS I COULD...
WHAT BECAME OF THAT?
REASON CAME OF IT... I WOULD ONLY BE FLINGING MYSELF INTO DEATH'S ARMS...OR, WORSE, JOINING MY COMRADES IN SERVING AS AN UNDEAD.
I HAVE NOT COMPLETELY SURRENDERED ON THE SUBJECT...BUT IF I FACE HIM, I WILL DO SO WHEN THERE IS AT LEAST A SLIGHT HOPE.
IN THE MEANTIME, I SEEK TO REGAIN MY HONOR--AND MY WORTHINESS TO THE LIGHT--BY SERVING MY ORDER AS BEST I CAN...
'AS BEST YOU CAN'? THERE WAS NOT ONE PALADIN AMONG YOUR RANKS WHO FOUGHT HARDER AT THE PORTAL...AND WITHOUT WIELDING THE LIGHT, NO LESS!
YOU STOOD FIGHTING WHERE NOT EVEN YOUR LEADER COULD! I THINK YOUR HONOR'S RESTORED, JORAD MACE...
Jorad did not reply to her comment, but a very slight smile briefly crossed his generally dour face.
Tyri had witnessed him in battle, that despite her initial indication that she had paid little mind to his presence until they had crossed into Outland...

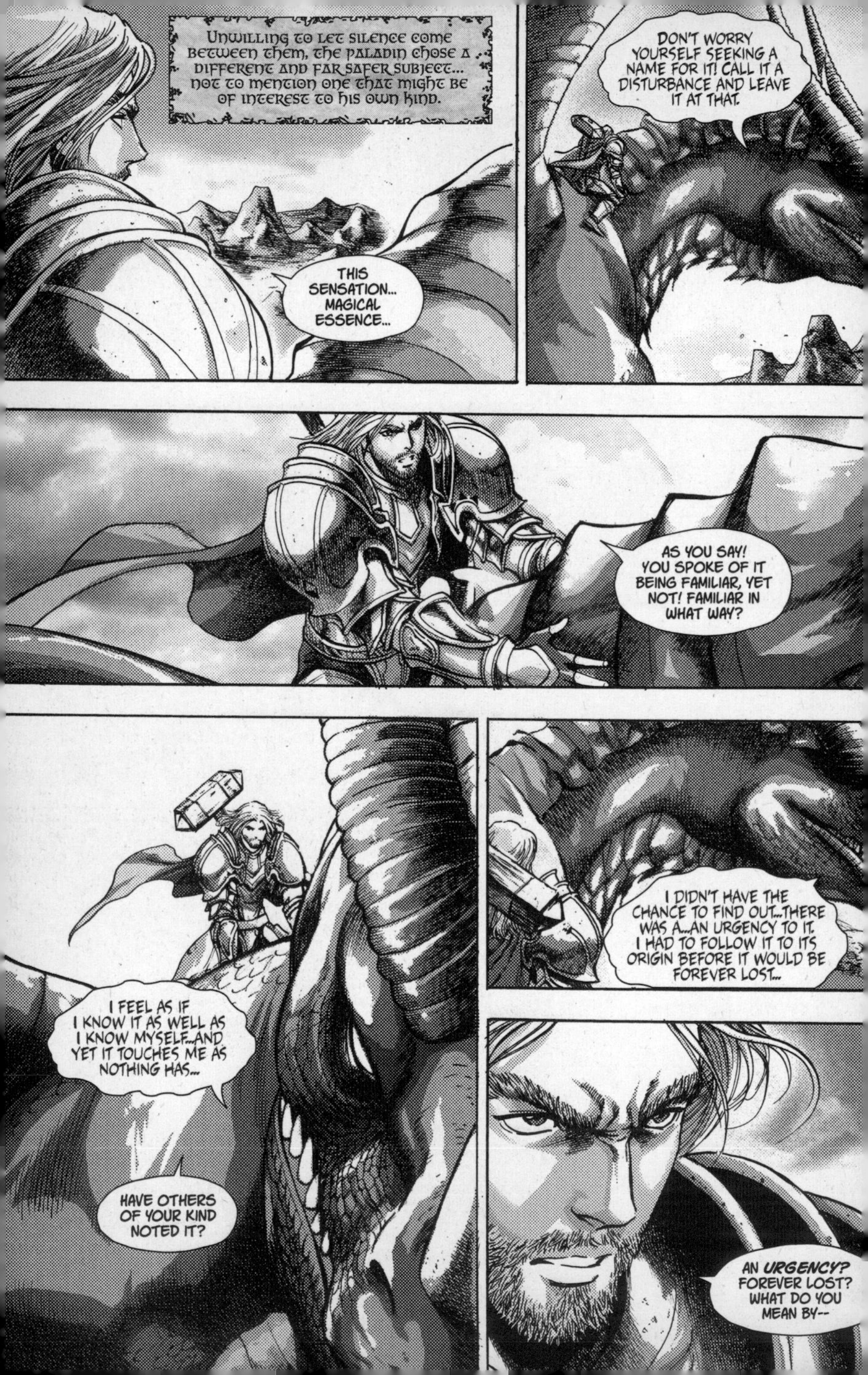
Unwilling to let silence come between them, the paladin chose a different and far safer subject... not to mention one that might be of interest to his own kind.
THIS SENSATION... MAGICAL ESSENCE...
DON'T WORRY YOURSELF SEEKING A NAME FOR IT! CALL IT A DISTURBANCE AND LEAVE IT AT THAT.
AS YOU SAY! YOU SPOKE OF IT BEING FAMILIAR, YET NOT! FAMILIAR IN WHAT WAY?
I FEEL AS IF I KNOW IT AS WELL AS I KNOW MYSELF...AND YET IT TOUCHES ME AS NOTHING HAS...
HAVE OTHERS OF YOUR KIND NOTED IT?
I DIDN'T HAVE THE CHANCE TO FIND OUT...THERE WAS A...AN URGENCY TO IT. I HAD TO FOLLOW IT TO ITS ORIGIN BEFORE IT WOULD BE FOREVER LOST...
AN *URGENCY*? FOREVER LOST? WHAT DO YOU MEAN BY--

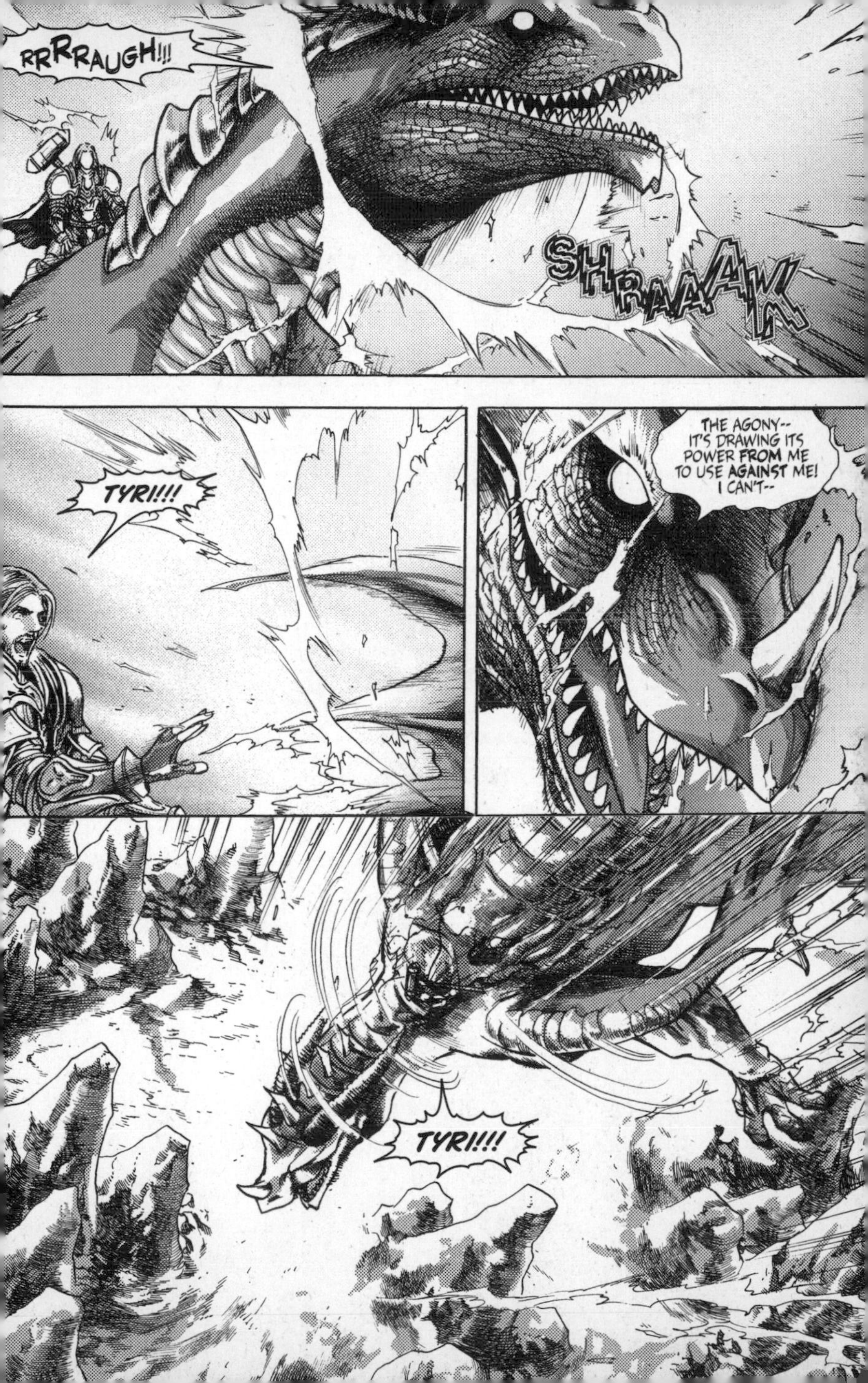
RRRRAUGH!!!
SHRAAAAK
TYRI!!!!
THE AGONY-- IT'S DRAWING ITS POWER FROM ME TO USE AGAINST ME! I CAN'T--
TYRI!!!

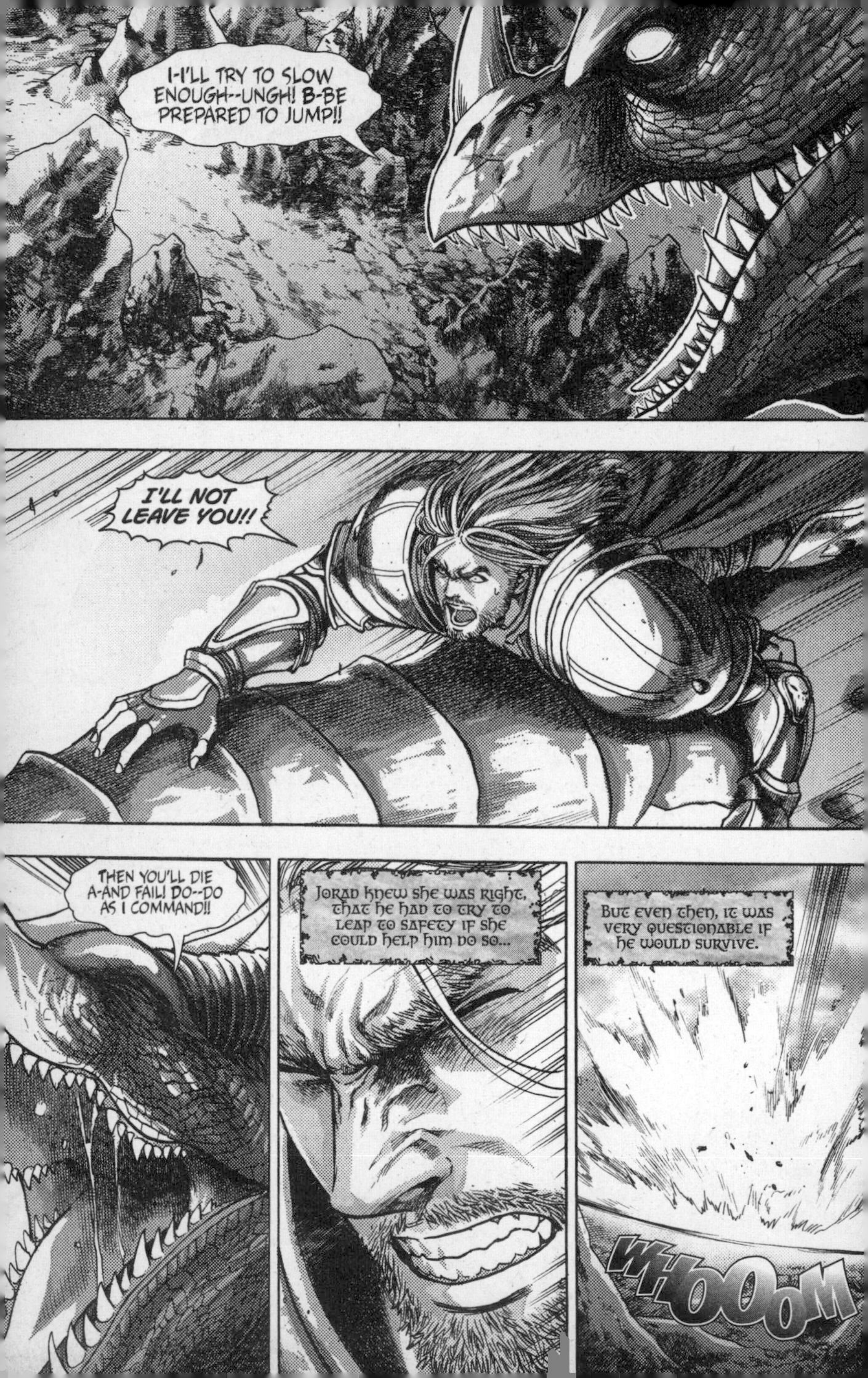
I-I'LL TRY TO SLOW ENOUGH--UNGH! B-BE PREPARED TO JUMP!!
I'LL NOT LEAVE YOU!!
THEN YOU'LL DIE A-AND FAIL! DO--DO AS I COMMAND!!
Jorad knew she was right, that he had to try to leap to safety if she could help him do so...
But even then, it was very questionable if he would survive.
WHOOOM

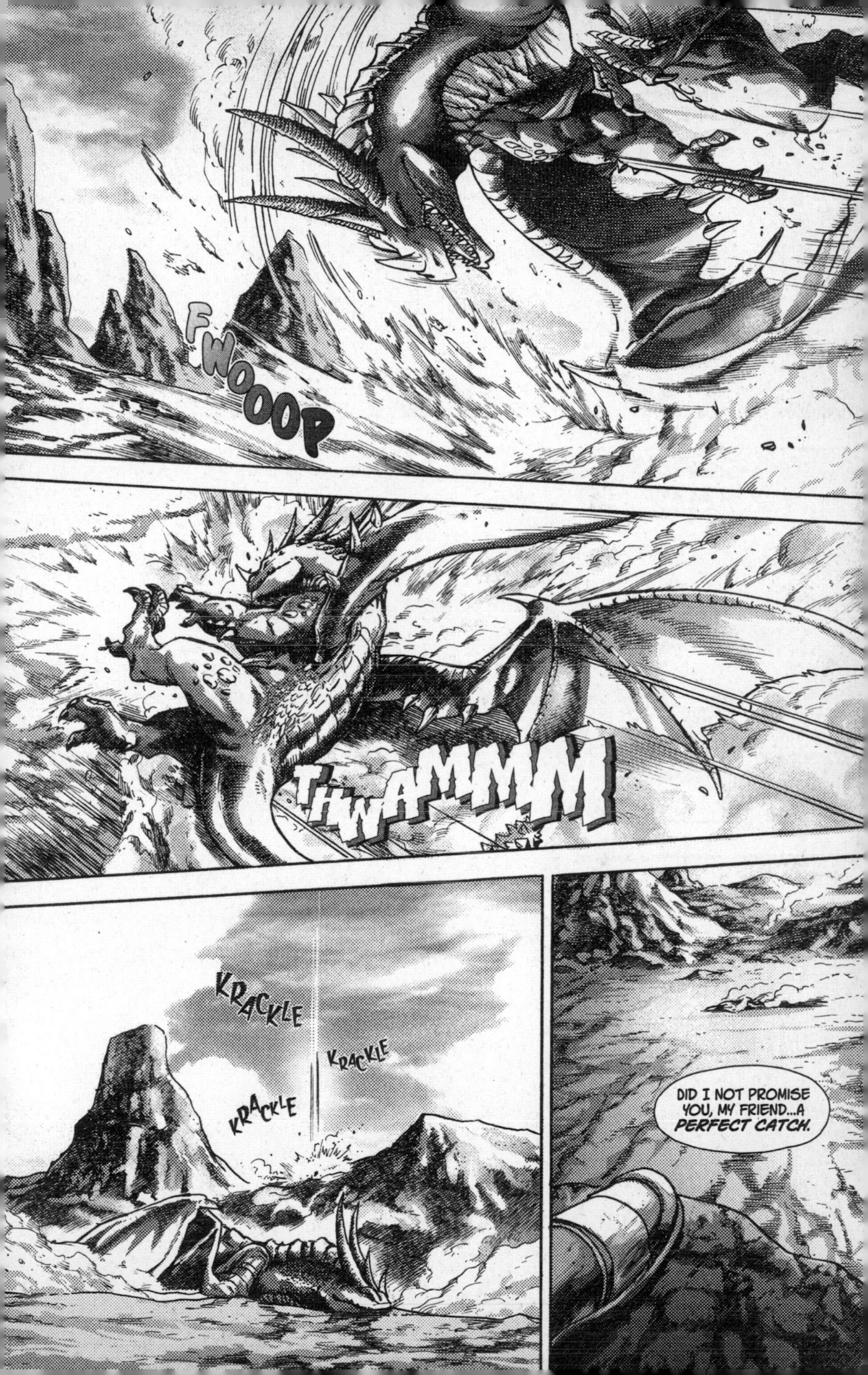
FWOOOP
THWAMMMM
KRACKLE
KRACKLE
KRACKLE
DID I NOT PROMISE YOU, MY FRIEND...A *PERFECT CATCH.*

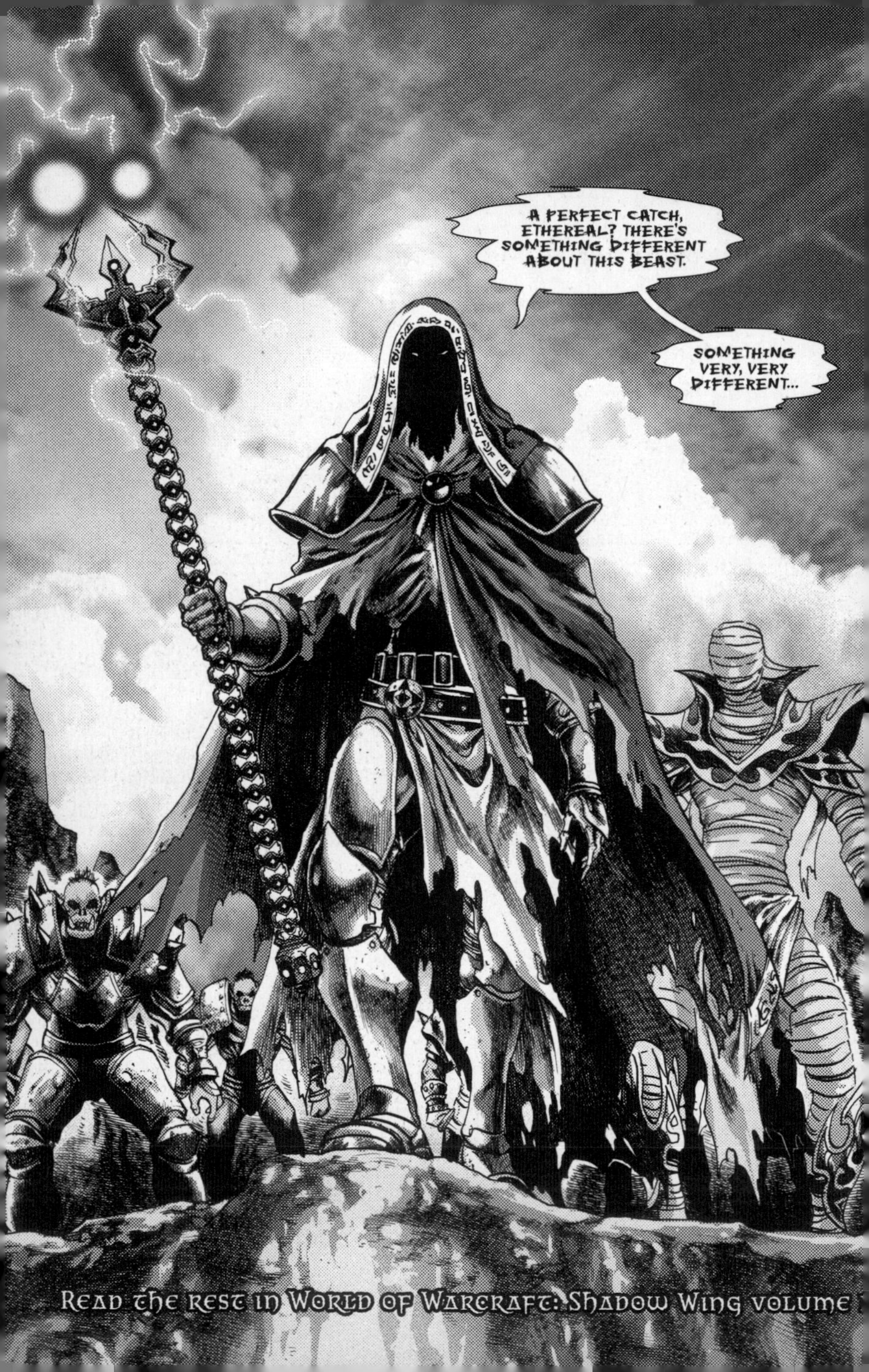
A PERFECT CATCH, ETHEREAL? THERE'S SOMETHING DIFFERENT ABOUT THIS BEAST.
SOMETHING VERY, VERY DIFFERENT...
Read the rest in World of Warcraft: Shadow Wing volume

TOKYOPOP MANGA SUPPLEMENT

# DISCOVER STARCRAFT GHOST ACADEMY

ENROLLMENT BEGINS JANUARY 2010
STARCRAFT
GHOST ACADEMY
DECANDIDO
FURUKAWA
1


*Ghosts* – The terrans' powerful assassins, capable of reading minds and calling nuclear strikes... These ultimate weapons of Emporer Mengsk's arsenal are crafted at a sinister instiution – the Ghost Academy.

In this never-before-seen chapter in ghost prodigy Nova's life, the doors of t Ghost Academy are flung wide open! Join Nova as she navigates the challenges of brutal training, both physical and psychological, along with fellow cadets whose unusual telepathic and telekinetic powers are being twistec to serve the Dominion. But the cadets have no choice other than to endure anc overcome, because at this school, failure is not an option.

THE MANGA REVOLUTION • LEADING THE MANGA REVOLUTION • LEADING

漫画革命

SCI-FI

T TEEN AGE 13+

LICENSED BLIZZARD ENTERTAINMENT PRODUCT



FOR MORE INFORMATION VISIT: WWW.TOKYOPOP.COM/STARCRAFT

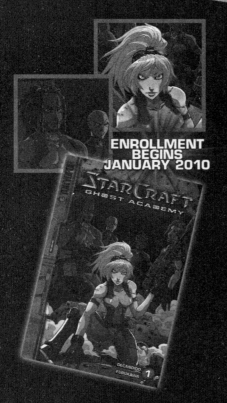

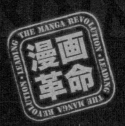